Approximation Theory and Related Applications

Approximation Theory and Related Applications

Editor

Yurii Kharkevych

MDPI • Basel • Beijing • Wuhan • Barcelona • Belgrade • Manchester • Tokyo • Cluj • Tianjin

Editor
Yurii Kharkevych
Theory of Functions
and Methods of
Teaching Mathematics
Lesya Ukrainka Volyn
National University
Lutsk
Ukraine

Editorial Office
MDPI
St. Alban-Anlage 66
4052 Basel, Switzerland

This is a reprint of articles from the Special Issue published online in the open access journal *Axioms* (ISSN 2075-1680) (available at: www.mdpi.com/journal/axioms/special_issues/approximation_theory_applications).

For citation purposes, cite each article independently as indicated on the article page online and as indicated below:

LastName, A.A.; LastName, B.B.; LastName, C.C. Article Title. *Journal Name* **Year**, *Volume Number*, Page Range.

ISBN 978-3-0365-6232-2 (Hbk)
ISBN 978-3-0365-6231-5 (PDF)

Contents

About the Editor

Yurii Kharkevych

Yurii Kharkevych graduated from Lesya Ukrainka Lutsk State Pedagogical Institute, Faculty of Mathematics, Ukraine, in 1987. He conducted his PhD research at the Institute of Mathematics of the National Academy of Sciences of Ukraine, Kyiv. He received a PhD degree in Mathematics and Physics in 1992. Now he is a Professor at the Department of the Theory of Functions and Methods of Teaching Mathematics of Lesya Ukrainka Volyn National University, Lutsk, Ukraine. Mathematical analysis with a special focus on the theory of approximation is the main field of his research. He is the author of more than a hundred scientific publications on approximation theory, including four monographs.

Preface to "Approximation Theory and Related Applications"

This book covers a wide range of issues, concepts and methods of modern approximation theory and its practical application. The book includes 14 articles published in the Special Issue "Approximation Theory and Related Applications" in the Mathematical Analysis section. This Special Issue contains new and important results of researchers from different countries of the world, in particular, from Ukraine, USA, China, Canada, Italy, Portugal, India, Ireland, Israel, Bulgaria, Czech Republic, Slovakia, Azerbaijan, Egypt, Taiwan and South Africa.

In the modern world, approximation theory is successfully used in various fields of science and technology, in particular in mathematical physics, in solving differential and integral equations, in chemistry, in control theory, in probability theory and statistics, in mathematical modeling, in neural networks, in transmission and reproduction of information and signals, etc. The articles in this Special Issue are very diverse and contain not only fundamental research in the field of approximation theory, but also important practical applications.

Taking this opportunity, I would like to express my immense gratitude to all the authors who responded to the invitation and submitted their articles to the Special Issue, to the reviewers who conducted detailed analyzes of the articles, gave valuable advice, recommendations and contributed to improving the content of our Special Issue. I would like to thank the editors of *Axioms*, especially Ms. Leila Zhang for her constant attention and support during the work on the Special Issue.

Yurii Kharkevych
Editor

axioms

MDPI

Editorial

Approximation Theory and Related Applications

Yurii Kharkevych

Faculty of Information Technologies and Mathematics, Lesya Ukrainka Volyn National University, 43025 Lutsk, Ukraine; kharkevich.juriy@gmail.com

The theory of approximation of functions is one of the central branches of mathematical analysis. It arose as a result of not only the internal development of mathematical science, but also the demands of practice. In terms of the concept of a function, it reflects a fundamental idea—the approximation (or replacement) of complex objects by ones that are simpler and more convenient to use. This idea is decisive regarding the relationship between mathematics and practice, which has always stimulated the development of approximation theory and which we hope will continue to garner interest in in the future.

This book is a collection of 14 papers included in the Special Issue "Approximation Theory and Related Applications" of the journal *Axioms*; it discusses contemporary problems in approximation theory, its applications in other areas of mathematics, and its practical uses. The main purpose of this Special Issue is to disseminate ideas and methods in approximation theory, to present new and significant results in this area, and to highlight related issues.

In [1], the authors discussed the well-known BMO class of functions of bounded mean oscillation by John–Nirenberg, which, long ago, became one of the most important concepts in harmonic analysis, partial differential equations, and related areas. Specifically, they investigated its applications to modern mapping theory. The authors established a series of criteria involving BMO to determine the existence of approximate solutions to the Beltrami equations in the whole complex plane, with asymptotic homogeneity at infinity. Note that such mappings inherit the main geometric properties of conformal mappings. These results can be applied to the fluid mechanics in strongly anisotropic and inhomogeneous media because the Beltrami equation is a complex form of the main equation of hydromechanics.

In [2], the authors considered abstract rings of multisets with components in a Banach algebra. These investigations are related to symmetric and supersymmetric polynomials and function calculus in algebras of analytic functions.

In [3], the authors showed that the Fréchet algebras of all entire bounded-type symmetric functions in the complex Banach space of all integrable essentially bounded functions in the arbitrary union of Lebesgue–Rohlin-measurable spaces are isomorphic to the Fréchet algebra of all entire bounded-type symmetric functions in the complex Banach space L_∞ of all Lebesgue-measurable essentially bounded functions in $[0,1]$.

The problems considered in paper [4] relate to rational approximations of the analytical functions of several variables—one of the main directions in the modern theory of continued and branched continued fractions. The authors constructed and investigated branched continued fraction expansions for ratios of the confluent hypergeometric function $\Phi_D^{(N)}$. Several numerical experiments are presented to indicate the power and efficiency of branched continued fractions as an approximation tool compared to multiple power series.

In [5], the authors solved one extremal problem of the theory of approximation of functional classes using linear methods. Namely, asymptotic equalities were obtained for the least upper bounds of the approximations of functions from the classes $W^r_{\beta,\infty}$ via generalized Abel–Poisson integrals in a uniform metric. These formulas provide a solution to the corresponding Kolmogorov–Nikol'skii problem.

Citation: Kharkevych, Y. Approximation Theory and Related Applications. *Axioms* **2022**, *11*, 736. https://doi.org/10.3390/axioms11120736

Received: 14 December 2022
Accepted: 14 December 2022
Published: 16 December 2022

In [6], the authors used the averaging method, which is one of the most effective tools for constructing approximate solutions, including optimal control problems for ODEs and PDEs. The Krasnoselski–Krein theorem and its various modifications play an essential role in all such considerations, since it guarantees a limit transition in perturbed problems with fast-oscillating coefficients. The authors used this approach for a nonlinear parabolic system with fast-oscillating (w.r.t. time variable) coefficients on an infinite time interval. They proved that control of the problem using averaging coefficients could be considered "approximately" optimal for the initial perturbed system.

In [7], the authors investigated the ideas of deferred weighted statistical Riemann integrability and statistical deferred weighted Riemann summability for sequences of functions. They prove the existence of an inclusion theorem connecting these two concepts and two Korovkin-type approximation theorems using algebraic test functions.

In [8], with the help of Fubini's theorem, as well as a straightforward outcome of Keller's chain rule on time scales, the authors demonstrated new dynamic Hardy-type inequalities, which are reverse inequalities on time scales. Moreover, they generalized a number of other inequalities to a general time scale and obtained the discrete and continuous inequalities as special cases of the main results.

In [9], the authors studied the pointwise estimations of an unknown function in a regression model with multiplicative and additive noise. The authors found a linear wavelet estimator using the wavelet method and studied the order of the pointwise convergence of this estimator in the local Hölder space. They also constructed a nonlinear wavelet estimator using the hard thresholding method.

In [10], the authors refined the notion of the partial modular metric defined by Hosseinzadeh and Parvaneh to eliminate the occurrence of discrepancies in the non-zero self-distance and triangular inequality. The common fixed-point theorem for four self-mappings was proven, and the authors applied their results to establishing the existence of a solution for a system of Volterra integral equations.

In [11], a fractional model of the Hopfield neural network was considered in the application of the generalized proportional Caputo fractional derivative. The authors studied the stability of the Hopfield neural network using the generalized proportional Caputo-type fractional derivative and defined the equilibrium of the studied model.

In [12], the authors studied the relationship between the intuitionistic fuzzy reasoning and interval-valued fuzzy reasoning algorithms, and proved that there is a bijection between the solutions of the intuitionistic fuzzy triple I algorithm and the interval-valued fuzzy triple I algorithm. They also showed that there is a bijection between the solutions of the intuitionistic fuzzy reverse triple I algorithm and the interval-valued fuzzy reverse triple I algorithm.

In [13], the authors developed symbolic regression models for waste gasification. When evaluating CEET models based on input data, two different statistical metrics are usually used to quantify their accuracy: the mean square error and the Pearson correlation coefficient. The authors also demonstrated a universal method based on dynamic system criteria that can detect suitable models with good properties following statistical metrics.

In [14], the authors defined the quasi-density of natural number subsets, and they determined the necessary conditions to ensure that the quasi-statistical convergence was equivalent to that of the matrix summability method for a special class of triangular matrices with real coefficients.

Funding: This research received no external funding.

Data Availability Statement: Not applicable.

Conflicts of Interest: The author declares no conflict of interest.

References

1. Gutlyanskii, V.; Ryazanov, V.; Sevost'yanov, E.; Yakubov, E. BMO and Asymptotic Homogeneity. *Axioms* **2022**, *11*, 171. [CrossRef]
2. Chernega, I.; Zagorodnyuk, A. Supersymmetric Polynomials and a Ring of Multisets of a Banach Algebra. *Axioms* **2022**, *11*, 511. [CrossRef]
3. Vasylyshyn, T.; Zhyhallo, K. Entire Symmetric Functions on the Space of Essentially Bounded Integrable Functions on the Union of Lebesgue-Rohlin Spaces. *Axioms* **2022**, *11*, 460. [CrossRef]
4. Antonova, T.; Dmytryshyn, R.; Kurka, R. Approximation for the Ratios of the Confluent Hypergeometric Function by the Branched Continued Fractions. *Axioms* **2022**, *11*, 426. [CrossRef]
5. Kal'chuk, I.; Kharkevych, Y. Approximation Properties of the Generalized Abel-Poisson Integrals on the Weyl-Nagy Classes. *Axioms* **2022**, *11*, 161. [CrossRef]
6. Kapustian, O.A.; Kapustyan, O.V.; Ryzhov, A.; Sobchuk, V. Approximate Optimal Control for a Parabolic System with Perturbations in the Coefficients on the Half-Axis. *Axioms* **2022**, *11*, 175. [CrossRef]
7. Srivastava, H.M.; Jena, B.B.; Paikray, S.K. Some Korovkin-Type Approximation Theorems Associated with a Certain Deferred Weighted Statistical Riemann-Integrable Sequence of Functions. *Axioms* **2022**, *11*, 128. [CrossRef]
8. El-Deeb, A.A.; Cesarano, C. On Some Generalizations of Reverse Dynamic Hardy Type Inequalities on Time Scales. *Axioms* **2022**, *11*, 336. [CrossRef]
9. Kou, J.; Huang, Q.; Guo, H. Pointwise Wavelet Estimations for a Regression Model in Local Hölder Space. *Axioms* **2022**, *11*, 466. [CrossRef]
10. Das, D.; Narzary, S.; Singh, Y.M.; Khan, M.S.; Sessa, S. Fixed Point Results on Partial Modular Metric Space. *Axioms* **2022**, *11*, 62. [CrossRef]
11. Almeida, R.; Agarwal, R.P.; Hristova, S.; O'Regan, D. Quadratic Lyapunov Functions for Stability of the Generalized Proportional Fractional Differential Equations with Applications to Neural Networks. *Axioms* **2021**, *10*, 322. [CrossRef]
12. Luo, M.; Li, W.; Shi, H. The Relationship between Fuzzy Reasoning Methods Based on Intuitionistic Fuzzy Sets and Interval-Valued Fuzzy Sets. *Axioms* **2022**, *11*, 419. [CrossRef]
13. Praks, P.; Lampart, M.; Praksová, R.; Brkić, D.; Kozubek, T.; Najser, J. Selection of Appropriate Symbolic Regression Models Using Statistical and Dynamic System Criteria: Example of Waste Gasification. *Axioms* **2022**, *11*, 463. [CrossRef]
14. Masarova, R.; Visnyai, T.; Vrabel, R. Quasi-Density of Sets, Quasi-Statistical Convergence and the Matrix Summability Method. *Axioms* **2022**, *11*, 88. [CrossRef]

axioms

Article

BMO and Asymptotic Homogeneity

Vladimir Gutlyanskii [1], Vladimir Ryazanov [1,2], Evgeny Sevost'yanov [1,3,*] and Eduard Yakubov [4]

[1] Institute of Applied Mathematics and Mechanics, National Academy of Sciences of Ukraine, 84100 Slavyansk, Ukraine; vgutlyanskii@gmail.com (V.G.); ryazanov@nas.gov.ua (V.R.)
[2] Laboratory of Mathematical Physics, Department of Physics, Bogdan Khmelnytsky National University of Cherkasy, 18031 Cherkasy, Ukraine
[3] Department of Mathematical Analysis, Business Analysis and Statistics, Zhytomyr Ivan Franko State University, 10008 Zhytomyr, Ukraine
[4] H.I.T. Holon Institute of Technology, Holon 5810201, Israel; yakubov@hit.ac.il
* Correspondence: esevostyanov2009@gmail.com

Abstract: First, we prove that the BMO condition by John–Nirenberg leads in the natural way to the asymptotic homogeneity at the origin of regular homeomorphic solutions of the degenerate Beltrami equations. Then, on this basis we establish a series of criteria for the existence of regular homeomorphic solutions of the degenerate Beltrami equations in the whole complex plane with asymptotic homogeneity at infinity. These results can be applied to the fluid mechanics in strongly anisotropic and inhomogeneous media because the Beltrami equation is a complex form of the main equation of hydromechanics.

Keywords: BMO; degenerate Beltrami equations; asymptotic homogeneity at infinity; conformality by Belinskii and by Lavrent'iev; hydromechanics; fluid mechanics

MSC: Primary 30C62; 30C65; 30H35; 35J70; Secondary 35Q35; 76B03

Citation: Gutlyanskii, V.; Ryazanov, V.; Sevost'yanov, E.; Yakubov, E. BMO and Asymptotic Homogeneity. *Axioms* **2022**, *11*, 171. https://doi.org/10.3390/axioms11040171

Academic Editor: Costanza Conti

Received: 1 March 2022
Accepted: 2 April 2022
Published: 12 April 2022

1. Introduction

A real-valued function u in a domain D in $\mathbb{C}$ is said to be of **bounded mean oscillation** in D, abbr. $u \in \mathrm{BMO}(D)$, if $u \in L^1_{\mathrm{loc}}(D)$ and

$$\|u\|_* := \sup_B \frac{1}{|B|} \int_B |u(z) - u_B|\, dm(z) < \infty\,, \tag{1}$$

where the supremum is taken over all discs B in D and

$$u_B = \frac{1}{|B|} \int_B u(z)\, dm(z)\,.$$

Recall that the class BMO was introduced by John and Nirenberg (1961) in the paper [1] and soon became an important concept in harmonic analysis, partial differential equations and related areas, see, e.g., [2,3].

A function φ in BMO is said to have **vanishing mean oscillation**, abbr. $\varphi \in \mathrm{VMO}$, if the supremum in (1) taken over all balls B in D with $|B| < \varepsilon$ converges to 0 as $\varepsilon \to 0$. Recall that VMO has been introduced by Sarason in [4]. There are a number of papers devoted to the study of partial differential equations with coefficients of the class VMO, see, e.g., [5–9]. Note, by the way, that $W^{1,2}(D) \subset VMO(D)$, see [10].

Let D be a domain in the complex plane $\mathbb{C}$, i.e., a connected open subset of $\mathbb{C}$, and let $\mu : D \to \mathbb{C}$ be a measurable function with $|\mu(z)| < 1$ a.e. (almost everywhere) in D. A **Beltrami equation** is an equation of the form

$$\overline{\partial} f(z) = \mu(z) \cdot \partial f(z) \tag{2}$$

with the formal complex derivatives $\overline{\partial} f = (f_x + if_y)/2$, $\partial f = (f_x - if_y)/2$, $z = x + iy$, where f_x and f_y are usual partial derivatives of f in x and y, correspondingly. The function μ is said to be the **complex coefficient** and

$$K_\mu(z) := \frac{1 + |\mu(z)|}{1 - |\mu(z)|} \tag{3}$$

the **dilatation quotient** of Equation (2). The Beltrami equation is called **degenerate** if $\operatorname{ess\,sup} K_\mu(z) = \infty$. Homeomorphic solutions of the Beltrami equations with $K_\mu \leq Q < \infty$ in the Sobolev class $W^{1,1}_{\text{loc}}$ are called **Q-quasiconformal mappings**.

It is known that if K_μ is bounded, then the Beltrami equation has homeomorphic solutions, see, e.g., [11–14]. Recently, a series of effective criteria for the existence of homeomorphic $W^{1,1}_{\text{loc}}$ solutions have been also established for degenerate Beltrami equations, see, e.g., historic comments with relevant references in monographs the [15–17].

These criteria were formulated both in terms of K_μ and the more refined quantity that takes into account not only the modulus of the complex coefficient μ but also its argument

$$K^T_\mu(z, z_0) := \frac{\left|1 - \frac{\overline{z - z_0}}{z - z_0}\mu(z)\right|^2}{1 - |\mu(z)|^2} \tag{4}$$

that is called the **tangent dilatation quotient** of the Beltrami equation with respect to a point $z_0 \in \mathbb{C}$, see, e.g., [18–23]. Note that

$$K^{-1}_\mu(z) \leqslant K^T_\mu(z, z_0) \leqslant K_\mu(z) \qquad \forall\, z \in D\,,\ z_0 \in \mathbb{C}\,. \tag{5}$$

The geometrical sense of K^T_μ can be found, e.g., in the monograph [16].

A function f in the Sobolev class $W^{1,1}_{\text{loc}}$ is called a **regular solution** of the Beltrami Equation (2) if f satisfies it a.e. and its Jacobian $J_f(z) = |\partial f(z)|^2 - |\overline{\partial} f(z)|^2 > 0$ a.e. in $\mathbb{C}$.

By the well-known Gehring–Lehto–Menchoff theorem, see [24,25], or see the monographs [11,13], each homeomorphic $W^{1,1}_{\text{loc}}$ solution f of the Beltrami equation is differentiable a.e. Recall that a function $f : D \to \mathbb{C}$ is **differentiable by Darboux Stolz at a point** $z_0 \in D$ if

$$f(z) - f(z_0) = \partial f(z_0) \cdot (z - z_0) + \overline{\partial} f(z_0) \cdot \overline{(z - z_0)} + o(|z - z_0|) \tag{6}$$

where $o(|z - z_0|)/|z - z_0| \to 0$ as $z \to z_0$. Moreover, f is called **conformal at the point** z_0 if in addition $f_{\overline{z}}(z_0) = 0$ but $f_z(z_0) \neq 0$.

The example $w = z(1 - \ln|z|)$ of B.V. Shabat, see [26], p. 40, shows that, for a continuous complex characteristic $\mu(z)$, the quasiconformal mapping $w = f(z)$ can be non-differentiable by Darboux Stolz at the origin. If the characteristic $\mu(z)$ is continuous at a point $z_0 \in D$, then, as was first established, apparently, by P.P. Belinskij in [26], p. 41, the mapping $w = f(z)$ is differentiable at z_0 in the following meaning:

$$\Delta w = A(\rho)\left[\Delta z + \mu_0 \overline{\Delta z} + o(\rho)\right], \tag{7}$$

where $\mu_0 = \mu(z_0)$, $\rho = |\Delta z + \mu_0 \overline{\Delta z}|$, $A(\rho)$ depends only on ρ and $o(\rho)/\rho \to 0$ as $\rho \to 0$. As it was clarified later in [27], see also [28], here $A(\rho)$ may not have a limit with $\rho \to 0$; however,

$$\lim_{\rho \to 0} \frac{A(t\rho)}{A(\rho)} = 1 \quad \forall t > 0\,. \tag{8}$$

Following [27], a mapping $f : D \to \mathbb{C}$ is called **differentiable by Belinskij at a point** $z_0 \in D$ if conditions (7) and (8) hold with some $\mu_0 \in \mathbb{D} := \{\mu \in \mathbb{C} : |\mu| < 1\}$. Note that here, in the case of discontinuous $\mu(z)$, it is not necessary $\mu_0 = \mu(z_0)$. If in addition $\mu_0 = 0$, then f is called **conformal by Belinskij at the point** z_0.

For quasiconformal mappings $f : D \to \mathbb{C}$ with $f(0) = 0 \in D$, it was shown in [27], see also [28], that the conformality by Belinskij of f at the origin is equivalent to each of its properties:

$$\boxed{\lim_{\tau\to 0} \frac{f(\tau\zeta)}{f(\tau)} = \zeta} \qquad \text{along the ray } \tau > 0 \quad \forall\, \zeta \in \mathbb{C}\,, \tag{9}$$

$$\boxed{\lim_{z\to 0} \left\{ \frac{f(z')}{f(z)} - \frac{z'}{z} \right\} = 0} \qquad \text{along } z, z' \in \mathbb{C},\ |z'| < \delta|z|, \quad \forall\, \delta > 0\,, \tag{10}$$

$$\boxed{\lim_{z\to 0} \frac{f(z\zeta)}{f(z)} = \zeta} \qquad \text{along } z \in \mathbb{C}^* := \mathbb{C} \setminus \{0\} \quad \forall\, \zeta \in \mathbb{C}\,, \tag{11}$$

and, finally, to the property of the limit in (11) to be locally uniform with respect to $\zeta \in \mathbb{C}$.

Following the article [28], the property (11) of a mapping $f : D \to \mathbb{C}$ with $f(0) = 0 \in D$ is called its **asymptotic homogeneity** at 0. In the sequel, we sometimes write (11) in the shorter form $f(\zeta z) \sim \zeta f(z)$.

In particular, we obtain from (10) under $|z'| = |z|$ that

$$\boxed{\lim_{r\to 0} \frac{\max\limits_{|z|=r} |f(z)|}{\min\limits_{|z|=r} |f(z)|} = 1} \tag{12}$$

i.e., that the Lavrent'iev characteristic is equal 1 at the origin. It is natural to say in the case of (12) that the mapping f is **conformal by Lavrent'iev** at 0. As we see, the usual conformality implies the conformality by Belinskij and the latter implies the conformality by Lavrent'iev at the origin meaning geometrically that the infinitesimal circle centered at zero is transformed into an infinitesimal circle also centered at zero.

However, condition (11) is much stronger than condition (12). We also obtain from (11) the asymptotic preserving angles

$$\boxed{\lim_{z\to 0} \arg \left[\frac{f(z\zeta)}{f(z)} \right] = \arg \zeta} \qquad \forall\, \zeta \in \mathbb{C}^* \tag{13}$$

and asymptotic preserving moduli of infinitesimal rings

$$\boxed{\lim_{z\to 0} \frac{|f(z\,\zeta)|}{|f(z)|} = |\zeta|} \qquad \forall\, \zeta \in \mathbb{C}^*\,. \tag{14}$$

The latter two geometric properties characterize asymptotic homogeneity and demonstrate that it is close to the usual conformality.

It should be noted that, despite (14), an asymptotically homogeneous map can send radial lines to infinitely winding spirals, as shown by the example $f(z) = ze^{i\sqrt{-\ln|z|}}$, see [26], p. 41. Moreover, the above Shabat example shows that the conformality by Belinskij admits infinitely great tensions and pressures at the corresponding points.

It was shown in [27] that a quasiconformal mapping $f : D \to \mathbb{C}$, whose complex characteristic $\mu(z)$ is approximately continuous at a point $z_0 \in D$, is differentiable by Belinskij at the point with $\mu_0 = \mu(z_0)$ and, in particular, is asymptotically homogeneous if $\mu(z_0) = 0$. Recall that $\mu(z)$ is called **approximately continuous at the point** z_0 if there is a measurable set E such that $\mu(z) \to \mu(z_0)$ as $z \to z_0$ in E and z_0 is a point of density for E, i.e.,

$$\lim_{\varepsilon\to 0} \frac{|E \cap D(z_0, \varepsilon)|}{|D(z_0, \varepsilon)|} = 1\,,$$

where $\mathbb{D}(z_0, \varepsilon) = \{z \in \mathbb{C} : |z - z_0| < \varepsilon\}$. Note also that, for functions μ in L^∞, the points of approximate continuity coincide with the Lebesgue points of μ, i.e., such z_0 for which

$$\lim_{r\to 0} \frac{1}{r^2} \int\limits_{|z-z_0|<r} |\mu(z) - \mu(z_0)| \, dm(z) = 0 ,$$

where $dm(z) := dxdy$, $z = x + iy$, stands to the Lebesgue measure (area) in $\mathbb{C}$.

The above results on the asymptotic homogeneity, i.e., on the conformality by Belinskij, are extended to the degenerate Beltrami equations with its dilatation K_μ in BMO. Just our approximate approach to the study of the degenerate Beltrami equations allowed us significantly to move forward.

As we saw, the asymptotic homogeneity inherits the main geometric properties of conformal mappings. Thus, our research is organically inserted into the stream of numerous works that were devoted to the study of conformality of mappings, see, e.g., [26,29–35].

2. FMO and the Main Lemma with Participation of BMO

Here and later on, we apply the notations

$$\mathbb{D}(z_0, r) := \{z \in \mathbb{C} : |z - z_0| < r\} , \quad \mathbb{D}(r) := \mathbb{D}(0, r) , \quad \mathbb{D} := \mathbb{D}(0, 1) ,$$

and of the mean value of integrable functions φ over the disks $\mathbb{D}(z_0, r)$

$$\fint_{\mathbb{D}(z_0,r)} \varphi(z) \, dm(z) := \frac{1}{|\mathbb{D}(z_0, r)|} \int\limits_{\mathbb{D}(z_0,r)} \varphi(z) \, dm(z) .$$

Following [36], we say that a function $\varphi : D \to \mathbb{R}$ has **finite mean oscillation** at a point $z_0 \in D$, abbr. $\varphi \in \mathrm{FMO}(z_0)$, if

$$\overline{\lim_{\varepsilon\to 0}} \fint_{\mathbb{D}(z_0,\varepsilon)} |\varphi(z) - \widetilde{\varphi}_\varepsilon(z_0)| \, dm(z) < \infty , \tag{15}$$

where

$$\widetilde{\varphi}_\varepsilon(z_0) = \fint_{\mathbb{D}(z_0,\varepsilon)} \varphi(z) \, dm(z) . \tag{16}$$

Note that the condition (15) includes the assumption that φ is integrable in some neighborhood of the point z_0. We say also that a function $\varphi : D \to \mathbb{R}$ is of **finite mean oscillation in D**, abbr. $\varphi \in \mathrm{FMO(D)}$ or simply $\varphi \in \mathrm{FMO}$, if $\varphi \in \mathrm{FMO}(z_0)$ for all points $z_0 \in D$.

Remark 1. *It is evident that* $\mathrm{BMO(D)} \subset \mathrm{BMO(D)}_{\mathrm{loc}} \subset \mathrm{FMO(D)}$ *and it is well-known by the John–Nirenberg lemma that* $\mathrm{BMO}_{\mathrm{loc}} \subset L^p_{\mathrm{loc}}$ *for all* $p \in [1, \infty)$*, see, e.g., [1] or [3]. However, FMO is not a subclass of* L^p_{loc} *for any* $p > 1$ *but only of* L^1_{loc}*, see, e.g., example 2.3.1 in [16]. Thus, the class FMO is much more wider than* $\mathrm{BMO}_{\mathrm{loc}}$.

The following statement is obvious by the triangle inequality.

Proposition 1. *If, for a collection of numbers* $\varphi_\varepsilon \in \mathbb{R}$, $\varepsilon \in (0, \varepsilon_0]$,

$$\overline{\lim_{\varepsilon\to 0}} \fint_{\mathbb{D}(z_0,\varepsilon)} |\varphi(z) - \varphi_\varepsilon| \, dm(z) < \infty , \tag{17}$$

then φ *is of finite mean oscillation at* z_0.

In particular, choosing here $\varphi_\varepsilon \equiv 0$, $\varepsilon \in (0, \varepsilon_0]$ in Proposition 1, we obtain the following.

Corollary 1. *If, for a point $z_0 \in D$,*

$$\overline{\lim_{\varepsilon\to 0}} \fint_{\mathbb{D}(z_0,\varepsilon)} |\varphi(z)|\, dm(z) < \infty\,, \tag{18}$$

then φ has finite mean oscillation at z_0.

Recall that a point $z_0 \in D$ is called a **Lebesgue point** of a function $\varphi : D \to \mathbb{R}$ if φ is integrable in a neighborhood of z_0 and

$$\lim_{\varepsilon\to 0} \fint_{\mathbb{D}(z_0,\varepsilon)} |\varphi(z) - \varphi(z_0)|\, dm(z) = 0\,. \tag{19}$$

It is known that, almost every point in D is a Lebesgue point for every function $\varphi \in L^1(D)$. Thus, we have by Proposition 1 the next corollary.

Corollary 2. *Every locally integrable function $\varphi : D \to \mathbb{R}$ has a finite mean oscillation at almost every point in D.*

Remark 2. *Note that the function $\varphi(z) = \log(1/|z|)$ belongs to BMO in the unit disk $\mathbb{D}$, see, e.g., [3], p. 5, and hence also to FMO. However, $\widetilde{\varphi}_\varepsilon(0) \to \infty$ as $\varepsilon \to 0$, showing that condition (18) is only sufficient but not necessary for a function φ to be of finite mean oscillation at z_0.*

Versions of the next statement has been first proved for the class BMO. For the FMO case, see the paper [36] and the monograph [16]. Here we prefer to use its following version, see Lemma 2.1 in [23], cf. also Lemma 5.3 in the monograph [16]:

Proposition 2. *Let $\varphi : D \to \mathbb{R}$ be a non-negative function with finite mean oscillation at $0 \in D$ and integrable in the disk $\mathbb{D}(1/2) \subset D$. Then*

$$\int\limits_{A(\varepsilon,1/2)} \frac{\varphi(z)\, dm(z)}{\left(|z| \log_2 \frac{1}{|z|}\right)^2} \le C \cdot \log_2 \log_2 \frac{1}{\varepsilon} \qquad \forall\, \varepsilon \in (0, 1/4)\,, \tag{20}$$

where

$$C = 4\pi\, (\varphi_0 + 6d_0)\,, \tag{21}$$

φ_0 is the average of φ over the disk $\mathbb{D}(1/2)$ and d_0 is the maximal dispersion of φ in $\mathbb{D}(1/2)$.

Recall that the **maximal dispersion** of the function φ in the disk $\mathbb{D}(z_0, r_0)$ is the quantity

$$\sup_{r\in(0,r_0]} \fint_{\mathbb{D}(z_0,r)} |\varphi(z) - \widetilde{\varphi}_r(z_0)|\, dm(z)\,. \tag{22}$$

Here and later on, we also use the following designations for the spherical rings in $\mathbb{C}$:

$$A(z_0, r_1, r_2) := \{z \in \mathbb{C} : r_1 < |z - z_0| < r_2\}, \quad A(r_1, r_2) := A(0, r_1, r_2). \tag{23}$$

Further, we denote by M the conformal modulus (or 2−modulus) of a family of paths in $\mathbb{C}$, see, e.g., [37]. Moreover, given sets E and F and a domain D in $\mathbb{C}$, we denote by $\Gamma(E, F, D)$ the family of all paths $\gamma : [0,1] \to \mathbb{C}$ joining E and F in D, that is, $\gamma(0) \in E$, $\gamma(1) \in F$ and $\gamma(t) \in D$ for all $t \in (0,1)$.

Let $Q : \mathbb{C} \to (0,\infty)$ be a Lebesgue measurable function. A mapping $f : D \to \mathbb{C}$ is called a **ring Q−mapping at a point** $z_0 \in D$, if

$$M(f(\Gamma(\mathbb{S}(z_0, r_1), \mathbb{S}(z_0, r_2), D))) \leqslant \int\limits_A Q(z) \cdot \eta^2(|z - z_0|)\, dm(z) \tag{24}$$

for each spherical ring $A = A(z_0, r_1, r_2)$ with arbitrary $0 < r_1 < r_2 < \delta_0 := \mathrm{dist}\,(z_0, \partial D)$ and all Lebesgue measurable functions $\eta : (r_1, r_2) \to [0, \infty]$ such that

$$\int_{r_1}^{r_2} \eta(r)\, dr \geqslant 1. \tag{25}$$

Here we use also the notations for the circles in $\mathbb{C}$ centered at a point z_0

$$\mathbb{S}(z_0, r_0) = \{ z \in \mathbb{C} : |z - z_0| = r_0 \}.$$

Remark 3. *Recall that regular homeomorphic solutions of the Beltrami Equation (2) are $Q_{z_0}-$mappings with $Q_{z_0}(z) = K^T_\mu(z, z_0)$ and, in particular, $Q-$mappings with $Q(z) = K_\mu(z)$ at each point $z_0 \in D$, see [38], see also Theorem 2.2 in [16].*

Later on, in the extended complex plane $\overline{\mathbb{C}} = \mathbb{C} \cup \{\infty\}$, we use the **spherical (chordal) metric** s defined by the equalities

$$s(z, \zeta) = \frac{|z - \zeta|}{\sqrt{1 + |z|^2}\sqrt{1 + |\zeta|^2}}, \quad z \neq \infty \neq \zeta, \quad s(z, \infty) = \frac{1}{\sqrt{1 + |z|^2}}, \tag{26}$$

see, e.g., [37] (Definition 12.1). For a given set E in $\overline{\mathbb{C}}$, we also use its **spherical diameter**

$$s(E) := \sup_{z, \zeta \in E} s(z, \zeta). \tag{27}$$

Given a domain D in $\mathbb{C}$, a prescribed point $z_0 \in D$ and a measurable $Q : D \to (0, \infty)$, later on $\mathfrak{R}^\Delta_Q$ denotes the class of all ring $Q-$homeomorphisms f at z_0 in D with

$$s(\overline{\mathbb{C}} \setminus f(D)) \geq \Delta > 0.$$

The following statement, see Theorem 4.3 in [23], provides us by the effective estimates of the distortion of the spherical distance under the ring $Q-$homeomorphisms, and it follows just on the basis of Proposition 2 on FMO functions above.

Proposition 3. *Let $f \in \mathfrak{R}^\Delta_Q(D)$ with $\Delta > 0$ and $Q : D \to \mathbb{R}$ be a non-negative function with finite mean oscillation at $\zeta_0 \in D$ and integrable in the disk $\mathbb{D}(\zeta_0, \varepsilon_0) \subset D$, $\varepsilon_0 > 0$. Then*

$$s(f(\zeta), f(\zeta_0)) \leq \frac{32}{\Delta} \cdot \left(\log \frac{2\varepsilon_0}{|\zeta - \zeta_0|} \right)^{-\frac{1}{\alpha_0}} \qquad \forall\, \zeta \in \mathbb{D}(\zeta_0, \varepsilon_0/2), \tag{28}$$

where

$$\alpha_0 = 2(q_0 + 6d_0), \tag{29}$$

q_0 is the average of Q over $\mathbb{D}(\zeta_0, \varepsilon_0)$ and d_0 is the maximal dispersion of Q in $\mathbb{D}(\zeta_0, \varepsilon_0)$.

Propositions 2 and 3 are key in establishing equicontinuity of classes of mappings associated with asymptotic homogeneity in the proof of the central lemma involving BMO.

Lemma 1. *Let D be a domain in $\mathbb{C}$, $0 \in D$, and let $f : D \to \mathbb{C}$ be a regular homeomorphic solution of the Beltrami Equation (2) with $f(0) = 0$. Suppose that its dilatation K_μ has a majorant $Q \in$ BMO(D). Then the family of mappings $f_z(\zeta) := f(\zeta z)/f(z)$ is equicontinuous with respect to the spherical metric at each point $\zeta_0 \in \mathbb{C}$ as $z \to 0$ along $z \in \mathbb{C}^* := \mathbb{C} \setminus \{0\}$.*

Proof. Indeed, for $\zeta_0 \in \mathbb{D}(\delta)$, $\delta > 1$, $0 < \delta_* < \mathrm{dist}\,(0, \partial D)$, $\tau_* := \delta_*/\delta < \delta_*$, we see that

$$\mathbb{D}(z\zeta_0, \rho_z) \subseteq \mathbb{D}(\delta_*) \subseteq D, \quad \text{where } \rho_z := \delta_* - |z\zeta_0| \geq \delta_*(1 - |\zeta_0|/\delta) > 0, z \in \overline{\mathbb{D}(\tau_*)} \setminus \{0\}.$$

Thus, by the construction the disks

$$\mathbb{D}(\zeta_0, R_z) \subseteq \mathbb{D}(\delta_*/|z|)\,, \quad \text{where } R_z := \delta_*/|z| - |\zeta_0| \geq \delta - |\zeta_0| > 0\,, z \in \overline{\mathbb{D}(\tau_*)} \setminus \{0\}\,,$$

belong to the domain of definition for the family of the functions $f_z(\zeta)$, $z \in \overline{\mathbb{D}(\tau_*)} \setminus \{0\}$.

It is clear, see, e.g., I.D(8) in [11], that $f_z(\zeta)$ is a regular homeomorphic solution of the Beltrami equation with the complex coefficient μ_z such that $|\mu_z(\zeta)| = |\mu(z\zeta)|$ and

$$K_{\mu_z}(\zeta) \leq Q_z(\zeta) := Q(z\zeta) \quad \forall\, \zeta_0 \in \mathbb{D}(\delta)\,,\ \zeta \in \mathbb{D}(\zeta_0, R_z)\,.$$

Note that the BMO norm of Q as well as its averages over disks are invariant under linear transformations of variables in $\mathbb{C}$. Moreover, the averages $\widetilde{Q}_z(\zeta_0)$ of the function Q over the disks $\mathbb{D}(z\zeta_0, \rho_z)$ forms a continuous function with respect to the parameter $z \in \overline{\mathbb{D}(\tau_*)} \setminus \{0\}$ in view of absolute continuity of its indefinite integrals and it can be extended by continuity to $z = 0$ as its (finite !) average over the disk $\mathbb{D}(\delta_*)$. Since the closed disk $\overline{\mathbb{D}(\tau_*)}$ is compact,

$$Q_0 := \max_{z \in \overline{\mathbb{D}(\tau_*)}} \widetilde{Q}_z(\zeta_0) < \infty\,.$$

Note also that by Remark 4 f_z, $z \in \overline{\mathbb{D}(\tau_*)}$, belongs to the class $\mathfrak{R}^{\Delta}_{Q_\tau}$ at ζ_0 in the punctured disk $\mathbb{D}(\zeta_0, \delta - |\zeta_0|) \setminus \{0\}$ with $\Delta = 1 > 0$ if $\zeta_0 \neq 0$, and in $D(\zeta_0, \delta - |\zeta_0|) \setminus \{1\}$ with $\Delta = 1/\sqrt{2} > 1/2$ if $\zeta_0 \neq 1$. Hence by Proposition 3 in any case we obtain the following estimate

$$s(f_\tau(\zeta), f_\tau(\zeta_0)) \leq 64 \left(\log \frac{2(\delta - |\zeta_0|)}{|\zeta - \zeta_0|} \right)^{-\frac{1}{\alpha_0}} \tag{30}$$

for all $z \in \overline{\mathbb{D}(\tau_*)}$ and $\zeta \in \mathbb{D}(\zeta_0, (\delta - |\zeta_0|)/2)$, where $\alpha_0 = 2(Q_0 + 6\|Q\|_*)$, i.e., the family of the mappings $f_z(\zeta)$, $z \in \overline{\mathbb{D}(\tau_*)}$, is equicontinuous at each point $\zeta_0 \in \mathbb{D}(\delta)$. In view of arbitrariness of $\delta > 1$, the latter is true for all $\zeta_0 \in \mathbb{C}$ at all. □

By the Ascoli theorem, see, e.g., 20.4 in [37], and Lemma 1 we obtain the next conclusion.

Corollary 3. *Let a mapping $f : D \to \mathbb{C}$ satisfy the hypotheses of Lemma 1. Then mappings $f_z(\zeta) := f(\zeta z)/f(z)$ form a normal family, i.e., every sequence $f_{z_n}(\zeta)$, $n = 1, 2, \ldots$ with $|z_n| \to +0$ as $n \to \infty$ contains a subsequence $f_{z_{n_k}}(\zeta)$, $k = 1, 2, \ldots$ that converges with respect to the spherical metric locally uniformly in $\mathbb{C}$ as $k \to \infty$ to a continuous mapping $f_0 : \mathbb{C} \to \overline{\mathbb{C}}$ with $f_0(0) = 0$ and $f_0(1) = 1$.*

Furthermore, we are dealing with the so-called approximate solutions of the Beltrami equations. Namely, given a domain D in $\mathbb{C}$, a homeomorphic ACL (absolutely continuous on lines) solution f of the Beltrami Equation (2) in D is called its **approximate solution** if f is a locally uniform limit in D as $n \to \infty$ of (quasiconformal) homeomorphic ACL solutions f_n of the Beltrami equations with the complex coefficients

$$\mu_n(z) := \begin{cases} \mu(z), & \text{if } \mu(z) \leqslant 1 - 1/n\,, \\ 0, & \text{otherwise}\,. \end{cases}$$

Let us give a proof of the following important fact.

Proposition 4. *Every approximate solution f of Beltrami Equation (2) with $K_\mu \in L^1_{\rm loc}$ is its regular homeomorphic solution and, moreover, $f^{-1} \in W^{1,2}_{\rm loc}$.*

Proof. Indeed, let f be an approximate solution of the Beltrami Equation (2) and let f_n be its approximating sequence. Then first of all $f \in W^{1,1}_{\rm loc}$ by Theorem 2.1 in [16].

Let us now prove that $f^{-1} \in W^{1,2}_{\rm loc}$. Indeed, by Lemma 2.16 in [16] $g_n := f_n^{-1} \to g := f^{-1}$ uniformly in $\overline{\mathbb{C}}$ as $n \to \infty$. Note that f_n and $g_n \in W^{1,2}_{\rm loc}$, $n = 1, 2, \ldots$, because they are quasiconformal mappings. Consequently, these homeomorphisms are locally absolutely continuous, see, e.g., Theorem III.6.1 in [13]. Observe also that $\mu_n := (g_n)_{\overline{w}}/(g_n)_w = -\mu_n \circ g_n$, see, e.g., Section I.C in [11]. Thus, replacing variables in the integrals, see, e.g., Lemma III.2.1 in [13]), we obtain that

$$\int\limits_{B} |\partial g_n(w)|^2 \, dm(w) \;=\; \int\limits_{g_n(B)} \frac{dm(z)}{1 - |\mu_n(z)|^2} \;\leqslant\; \int\limits_{B^*} K_\mu(z) \, dm(z) \;<\; \infty$$

for sufficiently large n, where B and B^* are arbitrary domains in $\mathbb{C}$ with compact closures in $f(D)$ and D, respectively, such that $g(\overline{B}) \subset B^*$. It follows from the latter that the sequence g_n is bounded in the space $W^{1,2}(B)$ in each such domain B. Hence $f^{-1} \in W^{1,2}_{\rm loc}$, see, e.g., Lemma III.3.5 in [39].

Finally, the latter brings in turn that g has $(N)-$property, see Theorem III.6.1 in [13]. Hence $J_f(z) \neq 0$ a.e., see Theorem 1 in [40]. Thus, f is really a regular solution of the Beltrami Equation (2). □

Note also that Lemma 2.12 in the monograph in [16] is extended from quasiconformal mappings to approximate solutions of the Beltrami Equation (2) immediately by the definition of such solutions.

Proposition 5. *Let $f : \mathbb{D} \to \overline{\mathbb{C}} \setminus \{a, b\}$, $a, b \in \overline{\mathbb{C}}$, $s(a, b) \geq \delta > 0$, be an approximate solution of the Beltrami Equation (2). Suppose that $s(f(z_1), f(0)) \geq \delta$ for $z_1 \in \mathbb{D}\setminus\{0\}$. Then, for every point z with $|z| < min(1 - |z_1|, |z_1|/2)$,*

$$s(f(z), f(0)) \geq \psi(|z|) \tag{31}$$

where ψ is a nonnegative strictly increasing function depending only on δ and $||K_\mu||_1$.

In turn, Propositions 4 and 5 make it possible to prove the following useful statement.

Proposition 6. *Let D be a domain in $\mathbb{C}$ and $f_n : D \to \overline{\mathbb{C}}$ be a sequence of approximate solutions of the Beltrami equations $\overline{\partial} f_n = \mu_n \partial f_n$. Suppose that $f_n \to f$ as $n \to \infty$ locally uniformly in D with respect to the spherical metric and the norms $||K_{\mu_n}||_1$, $n = 1, 2, \ldots$ are locally equipotentially bounded. Then either f is constant or it is a homeomorphism.*

Proof. Consider the case when f is not constant in D. Let us first show that then no point in D has a neighborhood of the constancy for f. Indeed, assume that there is at least one point $z_0 \in D$ such that $f(z) \equiv c$ for some $c \in \overline{\mathbb{C}}$ in a neighborhood of z_0. Note that the set Ω_0 of such points z_0 is open. The set $E_c = \{z \in D : s(f(z), c) > 0\}$ is also open by continuity of f and not empty if f is not constant. Thus, there is a point $z_0 \in \partial\Omega_0 \cap D$ because D is connected. By continuity of f we have that $f(z_0) = c$. However, by the construction there is a point $z_1 \in E_c = D \setminus \overline{\Omega_0}$ such that $|z_0 - z_1| < r_0 = \text{dist}\,(z_0, \partial D)$ and, thus, by the lower estimate of the distance $s(f(z_0), f(z))$ in Proposition 5 we obtain a contradiction for $z \in \Omega_0$. Then again by Proposition 5 we obtain that the mapping f is discrete. Hence f is a homeomorphism by Proposition 2.6 in the monograph [16]. □

Corollary 4. *Let a mapping $f : D \to \mathbb{C}$ satisfy the hypotheses of Lemma 1 and f be an approximate solution of the Beltrami Equation (2) and, moreover,*

$$\limsup_{r \to 0} \frac{1}{r^2} \int\limits_{|z|<r} |K_\mu(z)| \, dm(z) \;<\; \infty \,. \tag{32}$$

Then each limit mapping f_0 *of a sequence* $f_{z_n}(\zeta) := f(\zeta z_n)/f(z_n)$, $z_n \in \mathbb{C} \setminus \{0\}$, $n = 1, 2, \ldots$ *with* $z_n \to 0$ *as* $n \to \infty$ *is a homeomorphism of* $\mathbb{C}$ *into* $\mathbb{C}$.

Proof. Indeed, f_n are approximate solutions of the Beltrami equations $\overline{\partial} f_n = \mu_n \partial f_n$ with $|\mu_n(\zeta)| = |\mu(z_n\zeta)|$, see, e.g., Section I.C in [11], and by simple calculations, for all $R > 0$,

$$\overline{\lim_{n\to\infty}} \int\limits_{|\zeta|<R} |K_{\mu_n}(\zeta)|\, dm(\zeta) \;=\; R^2 \cdot \overline{\lim_{r\to 0}} \frac{1}{(R|z_n|)^2} \int\limits_{|z|<R|z_n|} |K_\mu(z)|\, dm(z) \;<\; \infty \tag{33}$$

and, thus, by Proposition 6 the mapping f_0 is a homeomorphism in $\mathbb{C}$.

Now, let us assume that $f_0(\zeta_0) = \infty$ for some $\zeta_0 \in \mathbb{C}$. Since f_n are homeomorphisms, there exist points $\zeta_n \in \mathbb{S}(\zeta_0, 1)$ such that $s(\zeta_n, \infty) > s(\zeta_0, \infty)$ for all large enough n. We may assume in addition, with no loss of generality, that $\zeta_n \to \zeta_* \in \mathbb{S}(\zeta_0, 1)$ because the circle $\mathbb{S}(\zeta_0, 1)$ is a compact set. Then $f_0(\zeta_*) = \lim_{n\to\infty} f_n(\zeta_n) = \infty$ because by Lemma 1 the sequence f_n is equicontinuous and, for such sequences, the pointwise convergence $f_n \to f_0$ is equivalent to its continuous convergence, see, e.g., Theorem 7.1 in [17]. However, the latter leads to a contradiction because $\zeta_* \neq \zeta_0$ and by the first part f_0 is a homeomorphism. The obtained contradiction disproves the above assumption and, thus, really $f_0(\zeta) \neq \infty$ for all $\zeta \in \mathbb{C}$, i.e., f_0 is a homeomorphism of $\mathbb{C}$ into $\mathbb{C}$. □

3. The Main Theorems and Consequences on Asymptotic Homogeneity at the Origin

The following theorem shows, in particular, that the Belinskij conformality still remains to be equivalent to the property of asymptotic homogeneity for regular homeomorphic solutions of the degenerate Beltrami Equations (2) if its dilatation K_μ has a majorant Q in BMO.

Theorem 1. *Let* D *be a domain in* $\mathbb{C}$, $0 \in D$, *and let* $f : D \to \mathbb{C}$ *be a regular homeomorphic solution of the Beltrami equation with* $f(0) = 0$ *and* K_μ *have a majorant* $Q \in$ BMO(D). *Then the following assertions are equivalent:*

(1) f *is conformal by Belinskij at the origin,*

(2) for all $\zeta \in \mathbb{C}$,

$$\lim_{\substack{\tau\to 0,\\ \tau>0}} \frac{f(\tau\zeta)}{f(\tau)} = \zeta\,, \tag{34}$$

(3) for all $\delta > 0$, *along* $z \in \mathbb{C}^* := \mathbb{C} \setminus \{0\}$ *and* $z' \in \mathbb{C}$ *with* $|z'| \leq \delta|z|$,

$$\lim_{z\to 0} \left\{ \frac{f(z')}{f(z)} - \frac{z'}{z} \right\} = 0\,, \tag{35}$$

(4) for all $\zeta \in \mathbb{C}$,

$$\lim_{\substack{z\to 0,\\ z\in\mathbb{C}^*}} \frac{f(z\zeta)}{f(z)} = \zeta\,, \tag{36}$$

(5) the limit in (36) is uniform in the parameter ζ *on each compact subset of* $\mathbb{C}$.

Proof. Let us follow the scheme (1) ⇒ (2) ⇒ (3) ⇒ (4) ⇒ (5) ⇒ (1) and set

$$f_0(\zeta) = \zeta\,, \quad f_z(\zeta) = f(\zeta z)/f(z) \qquad \forall\, z \in D \setminus \{0\}\,,\ \zeta \in \mathbb{C} : z\zeta \in D\,.$$

(1) ⇒ (2). Immediately the definition of the conformality by Belinskij yields the convergence $f_\tau(\zeta) \to f_0(\zeta)$ as $\tau \to 0$ along $\tau > 0$ for every fixed $\zeta \in \mathbb{C}$, i.e., just (34).

(2) $\Rightarrow$ (3). In view of Lemma 1, the pointwise convergence in (34) for each $\zeta \in \mathbb{C}$ implies the uniform convergence there on compact sets in $\mathbb{C}$, see, e.g., Theorem 7.1 in [17]. To obtain on this basis the implication (2) $\Rightarrow$ (3), let us note the identities

$$f_z(\zeta) \;=\; \frac{f_{|z|}(\zeta z/|z|)}{f_{|z|}(z/|z|)} \;=\; \frac{f(z')}{f(z)} \qquad \forall\, \zeta = \frac{z'}{z} \in \mathbb{C}\,,\; z \in \mathbb{C}^* := \mathbb{C} \setminus \{0\}\,.$$

Hence to prove (35) it is sufficient to show that $f_z(\zeta) - f_0(\zeta) \to 0$ as $z \to 0$, $z \in \mathbb{C}^*$ uniformly with respect to the parameter ζ in the closed disks $\mathbb{D}_\delta := \{\zeta \in \mathbb{C} : |\zeta| \le \delta\}$, $\delta > 0$.

Indeed, let us assume the inverse. Then there is a number $\varepsilon > 0$ and consequences $\zeta_n \in D_\delta$, $z_n \to 0$, $z_n \in \mathbb{C}^*$, such that $|g_n(\zeta_n) - \zeta_n| \ge \varepsilon$, where $g_n(\zeta) = f_{z_n}(\zeta)$, $\zeta \in \mathbb{C}$. Since the closed disk $\mathbb{D}_\delta$ and the unit circle $\partial\mathbb{D}_1$ are compact sets, then with no loss of generality we may in addition to assume that $\zeta_n \to \zeta_0 \in \mathbb{D}_\delta$ and $\eta_n = z_n/|z_n| \to \eta_0 \in \partial\mathbb{D}_1$ as $n \to \infty$.

Let us denote by $\varphi_n(\zeta)$ the mappings $f_{|z_n|}(\zeta)$, $\zeta \in \mathbb{C}$, $n = 1, 2, \ldots$. Then $\varphi_n(\zeta) \to \zeta$ as $n \to \infty$ uniformly on $\mathbb{D}_\delta \cup \partial\mathbb{D}_1$ and $g_n(\zeta) = \varphi_n(\eta_n\zeta)/\varphi_n(\eta_n)$. Consequently, $g_n(\zeta) \to \zeta$ as $n \to \infty$ uniformly on $\mathbb{D}_\delta$. Hence $g_n(\zeta_n) \to \zeta_0$ as $n \to \infty$ because the uniform convergence of continuous mappings on compact sets implies the so-called continuous convergence, see, e.g., Remark 7.1 in [17]. Thus, the obtained contradiction disproves the above assumption.

(3) $\Rightarrow$ (4). Setting in (35) $z' = z\zeta$ and $\delta = |\zeta|$, we immediately obtain (36).

(4) $\Rightarrow$ (5). The limit relation (36) means in the other words that $f_z(\zeta) \to f_0(\zeta)$ as $z \to 0$ along $z \in \mathbb{C}^*$ pointwise in $\mathbb{C}$. In view of Lemma 1, the latter implies the locally uniform convergence $f_z \to f_0$ as $z \to 0$ in $\mathbb{C}$, see again Theorem 7.1 in [17].

(5) $\Rightarrow$ (1). From (36) for $z = \rho > 0$, $\zeta = e^{i\vartheta}$, $\vartheta \in \mathbb{R}$, and $w = \zeta z = \rho\, e^{i\vartheta}$ we obtain that $f(w) = f(\rho)(\zeta + \alpha(\rho))$, where $\alpha(\rho) \to 0$ as $\rho \to 0$. Consequently,

$$f(w) = A(\rho)(w + o(\rho))\,,$$

where $A(\rho) = f(\rho)/\rho$ and $o(\rho)/\rho \to 0$ as $\rho \to 0$. Moreover, by (36) with $z = \rho > 0$ and $\zeta = t > 0$ we have that A satisfies the condition

$$\lim_{\rho \to 0} \frac{A(t\rho)}{A(\rho)} = 1 \quad \forall\, t > 0\,,$$

i.e., f is conformal by Belinskij at the origin. □

The following result is fundamental for further study of asymptotic homogeneity because it facilitates considerably the verification of (36) and at the same time reveals the nature of the notion. Let Z be an arbitrary set in the complex plane $\mathbb{C}$, $0 \notin Z$, with the origin as its accumulation point. Further, we use the following characteristic of its sparseness:

$$\mathbb{S}_Z(\rho) \;:=\; \frac{\inf_{z \in Z, |z| \ge \rho,} |z|}{\sup_{z \in Z, |z| \le \rho,} |z|} \qquad \forall\, \rho \;>\; 0\,. \tag{37}$$

Theorem 2. *Let f satisfy the hypotheses of Theorem 1. Suppose that*

$$\limsup_{\rho \to 0} \; \mathbb{S}_Z(\rho) \;<\; \infty \tag{38}$$

and

$$\lim_{\substack{z \to 0,\\ z \in Z}} \frac{f(z\zeta)}{f(z)} = \zeta \qquad \forall\, \zeta \in \mathbb{C}\,. \tag{39}$$

Then f is asymptotically homogeneous at the origin.

Remark 4. *For Theorem 2 to be true, the condition (38) on the extent of possible sparseness of Z is not only sufficient but also necessary as Proposition 2.1 in [28] in the case $Q \in L^\infty \subset BMO$ shows.*

In particular, any continuous path to the origin or a discrete set, say $1/n, n = 1, 2, \ldots$, can be taken as the set Z in Theorem 2. For instance, the conclusion of Theorem 2 is also true if Z has at least one point on each circle $|z| = \rho$ for all small enough $\rho > 0$.

Proof. Indeed, by (39) we have that, for functions $f_z(\zeta) := f(z\zeta)/f(z)$, pointwise

$$\lim_{\substack{z\to 0,\\ z\in Z}} f_z(\zeta) \;=\; \zeta \qquad \forall\, \zeta \in \mathbb{C} \tag{40}$$

and, by Theorem 7.1 in [17] and Lemma 1, the limit in (40) is locally uniform in $\zeta \in \mathbb{C}$.

Let us assume that (36) does not hold for f, in other words, there exist $\zeta \in \mathbb{C}$, $\varepsilon > 0$ and a sequence $z_n \in \mathbb{C}^*$, $n = 1, 2, \ldots$ such that $z_n \to 0$ as $n \to \infty$ and

$$|\, f_{z_n}(\zeta) \;-\; \zeta \,| \;>\; \varepsilon\,. \tag{41}$$

On the other hand, by (38) there is a sequence $z_n^* \in Z$ such that

$$0 \;<\; \delta \;\leq\; |\tau_n| \;\leq\; 1 \;<\; \infty$$

for all large enough $n = 1, 2, \ldots$, where

$$\tau_n \;=\; \frac{z_n}{z_n^*}\,, \qquad \delta \;=\; 1/2 \limsup_{\rho\to 0} \mathbb{S}_Z(\rho)\,.$$

With no loss of generality, we may assume in addition that $\tau_n \to \tau_0$ with $\delta \leq |\tau_0| \leq 1$ as $n \to \infty$ because the closed ring $R := \{z \in \mathbb{C} : \delta \leq |z| \leq 1\}$ is a compact set. Note also that

$$f_{z_n}(\zeta) \;=\; \frac{f_{z_n^*}(\zeta\tau_n)}{f_{z_n^*}(\tau_n)}\,.$$

Thus, $f_{z_n^*}(\zeta\tau_n) \sim \zeta\tau_0$ and $f_{z_n^*}(\tau_n) \sim \tau_0$ as $n \to \infty$ because the uniform convergence in (40) with respect to ζ over any compact set implies the so-called continuous convergence, see, e.g., Remark 7.1 in [17]. Consequently, $f_{z_n}(\zeta) \sim \zeta$ as $n \to \infty$ because $\tau_0 \neq 0$. However, the latter contradicts (41). The obtained contradiction disproves the above assumption and the conclusion of the theorem is true. □

Now, recall that the abstract spaces $\mathfrak{F}$ in which convergence is a primary notion were first considered by Frechet in his thesis in 1906. Later on, Uryson introduced the third axiom in these spaces: if a compact sequence $f_n \in \mathfrak{F}$ has its unique accumulation point $f \in \mathfrak{F}$, then $\lim\limits_{n\to\infty} f_n = f$, see, e.g., [41], Chapter 2, 20,1-II. Recall that $f_n \in \mathfrak{F}$, $n = 1, 2, \ldots$ is called a **compact sequence** if each its subsequence contains a converging subsequence and, moreover, $f \in \mathfrak{F}$ is said to be an **accumulation point** of the sequence $f_n \in \mathfrak{F}$ if f is a limit of some its subsequence. It is customary to call such spaces $\mathfrak{L}^*$**−spaces**.

Remark 5. *In particular, any convergence generated by a metric satisfies Uryson's axiom, see, e.g., [41], Chapter 2, 21, II. However, the well-known convergence almost everywhere of measurable functions yields a counter-example to Uryson's axiom: any sequence converging in measure is compact with respect to convergence almost everywhere, but not every such sequence converges almost everywhere. Later on, we apply the convergence generated by the uniform convergence of continuous functions, generated as known by the uniform norm.*

To prove the corresponding sufficient criteria for the asymptotic homogeneity at the origin for solutions of degenerate Beltrami equations, we need also the following general lemma.

Lemma 2. *Let D be a bounded domain in $\mathbb{C}$ and $f_n : D \to \mathbb{C}$, $n = 1, 2, \ldots$ be a sequence of $W^{1,1}$ solutions of the Beltrami equations $\overline{\partial} f_n = \mu_n \partial f_n$. Suppose that $f_n \to f$ as $n \to \infty$ in L^1 and the* *norms* $\|\bar{\partial} f_n\|_1$ *and* $\|\bar{\partial} f_n\|_1$ *are equipotentially bounded. Then* $f \in W^{1,1}$ *and* ∂f_n *and* $\bar{\partial} f_n$ *converge weakly in* L^1 *to* ∂f *and* $\bar{\partial} f$*, respectively. Moreover, if* $\mu_n \to \mu$ *a.e. or in measure as* $n \to \infty$*, then* $\bar{\partial} f = \mu \partial f$ *a.e.*

Proof. The first part of conclusions follow from Lemma III.3.5 in [39]. Let us prove the latter of these conclusions. Namely, assuming that $\mu_n(z) \to \mu(z)$ a.e. as $n \to \infty$ and, setting

$$\zeta(z) \;=\; \bar{\partial} f(z) - \mu(z) \cdot \partial f(z)\,,$$

let us show that $\zeta(z) = 0$. Indeed, since $\bar{\partial} f_n(z) - \mu_n(z) \partial f_n(z) = 0$, by the triangle inequality

$$\int\limits_D |\zeta(z)|\, dm(z) \;\leq\; I_1(n) \,+\, I_2(n) \,+\, I_3(n)\,,$$

where

$$I_1(n) \;:=\; \int\limits_D |\bar{\partial} f(z) - \bar{\partial} f_n(z)|\, dm(z)\,,$$

$$I_2(n) \;:=\; \int\limits_D |\mu(z)| \cdot |\partial f(z) - \partial f_n(z)|\, dm(z)\,,$$

$$I_3(n) \;:=\; \int\limits_D |\mu(z) - \mu_n(z)| \cdot |\partial f_n(z)|\, dm(z)\,.$$

By the first part of conclusions, with no loss of generality, assume that $|\bar{\partial} f(z) - \bar{\partial} f_n(z)| \to 0$ and $|\partial f(z) - \partial f_n(z)| \to 0$ as $n \to \infty$ weakly in L^1, see Corollary IV.8.10 in [42]. Thus, $I_1(n) \to 0$ and $I_2(n) \to 0$ as $n \to \infty$ because the dual space of L^1 is naturally isometric to L^∞, see, e.g., Theorem IV.8.5 in [42].

Moreover, by Corollary IV.8.11 in [42], for each $\varepsilon > 0$, there is $\delta > 0$ such that over every measurable set E in D with $|E| < \delta$

$$\int\limits_E |\,\partial f_n(z)|\, dm(z) < \varepsilon, \quad n = 1, 2, \ldots\,. \tag{42}$$

Further, by the Egoroff theorem, see, e.g., III.6.12 in [42], $\mu_n(z) \to \mu(z)$ as $n \to \infty$ uniformly on some set S in D with $|E| < \delta$ where $E = D \setminus S$. Hence $|\mu_n(z) - \mu(z)| < \varepsilon$ on S and

$$I_3(n) \leq \varepsilon \int\limits_S |\,\partial f_n(z)|\; dm(z) + 2\int\limits_E |\,\partial f_n(z)|\; dm(z) \;\leq\; \varepsilon(\|\partial f_n(z)\|_1 \,+\, 2)$$

for large enough n, i.e., $I_3(n) \to 0$ because $\varepsilon > 0$ is arbitrary. Thus, really $\zeta = 0$ a.e. □

Theorem 3. *Let* D *be a domain in* $\mathbb{C}$, $0 \in D$, $f : D \to \mathbb{C}$, $f(0) = 0$, *be an approximate solution of the Beltrami Equation (2) and* K_μ *have a majorant* $Q \in$ BMO(D). *Suppose that*

$$\limsup_{r \to 0} \frac{1}{\pi r^2} \int\limits_{|z|<r} K_\mu(z)\, dm(z) \;<\; \infty\,, \tag{43}$$

and

$$\lim_{r \to 0} \frac{1}{\pi r^2} \int\limits_{|z|<r} |\mu(z)|\, dm(z) \;=\; 0\,. \tag{44}$$

Then f *is asymptotically homogeneous at the origin.*

Proof. By Theorem 2 with $Z := \{2^{-n}\}_{n=N}^{\infty}$, where $2^{-N} < \mathrm{dist}(0, \partial D)$, it is sufficient to show that

$$\lim_{n\to\infty} f_{2^{-n}}(\zeta) = \zeta \quad \forall\, \zeta \in \mathbb{C}\,, \quad f_{2^{-n}}(\zeta) := \frac{f(2^{-n}\zeta)}{f(2^{-n})}\,.$$

By Corollary 3 the sequence $f_{2^{-n}}(\zeta)$ is compact with respect to locally uniform convergence in $\mathbb{C}$ and by Remark 5 it remains to prove that each its converging subsequence $f_k^* = f_{n_k}$ with $n_k \to \infty$ as $k \to \infty$ has the identity mapping of the complex plane $\mathbb{C}$ as its limit f_0.

Indeed, the mappings f_k^* are approximate solutions of Beltrami equations $\overline{\partial} f_k^* = \mu_k^* \cdot \partial f_k^*$ with $|\mu_k^*(\zeta)| = |\mu(2^{-n_k}\zeta)|$, see, e.g., calculations of Section I.C in [11]. Since such solutions are regular by Proposition 4, we have by the calculations that

$$|\,\overline{\partial} f_k^*| \le |\,\partial f_k^*| \le |\,\partial f_k^*| + |\,\overline{\partial} f_k^*| \le K_{\mu_k^*}^{1/2} J_{f_k^*}^{1/2} \qquad \text{a.e.}\,, \quad k = 1, 2, \ldots$$

where

$$K_{\mu_k^*}(\zeta) = K_{\mu}(2^{-n_k}\zeta)\,,\; J_{f_k^*}(\zeta) = |\partial f_k^*(\zeta)|^2 - |\overline{\partial} f_k^*(\zeta)|^2 = J_{f_{n_k}}(\zeta) = J_f(2^{-n_k}\zeta)/|f(2^{-n_k})|^2.$$

Consequently, by the Hölder inequality for integrals, see, e.g., Theorem 189 in [43], and Lemma III.3.3 in [13], we obtain that

$$\|\partial f_k^*\|_1(\mathbb{D}_l) \;\le\; \|K_{\mu_k^*}\|_1^{\frac{1}{2}}(\mathbb{D}_l) \cdot |f_k^*(\mathbb{D}_l)|^{\frac{1}{2}} \qquad \forall\, l = 1, 2, \ldots\,,\; \mathbb{D}_l := \mathbb{D}(2^l)\,.$$

Now, by the condition (43) and simple calculations, for each fixed $l = 1, 2, \ldots$,

$$\overline{\lim_{k\to\infty}}\, \|K_{\mu_k^*}\|_1(\mathbb{D}_l) \;=\; 2^{2l} \cdot \overline{\lim_{k\to\infty}}\, \frac{1}{(2^l 2^{-n_k})^2} \int\limits_{|z|<2^l 2^{-n_k}} |K_\mu(z)|\, dm(z) \;<\; \infty\,.$$

Next, choosing ζ_k in $\mathbb{S}_l := \{\zeta \in \mathbb{C} : |\zeta| = 2^l\}$ with $|f(2^{-n_k}\zeta_k)| = \max\limits_{\zeta\in\mathbb{S}_l} |f(2^{-n_k}\zeta)|$, we see that

$$|f_k^*(\mathbb{D}_l)| = |f_{n_k}(\mathbb{D}_l)| = \frac{\left|f(\mathbb{D}(2^{l-n_k}))\right|}{|f(2^{-n_k}\zeta_k)|^2} \cdot \frac{|f(2^{-n_k}\zeta_k)|^2}{|f(2^{-n_k})|^2} \;\le\; \pi |f_{2^{-n_k}}(\zeta_k)|^2\,.$$

With no loss of generality, we may assume that $\zeta_k \to \zeta_0 \in \mathbb{S}_l$ as $k \to \infty$ because the circle $\mathbb{S}_l$ is a compact set. Then $f_{2^{-n_k}}(\zeta_k) \to f_0(\zeta_0)$ because the uniform convergence implies the so-called continuous convergence, see, e.g., Remark 7.1 in [17]. However, $f_0(\zeta_0) \neq \infty$, see Corollary 4.

Thus, the norms of ∂f_k^* and $\overline{\partial} f_k^*$ are locally equipotentially bounded in L^1. Then f_0 is $W^{1,1}_{\mathrm{loc}}$ solution of the Beltrami equation with $\mu \equiv 0$ in $\mathbb{C}$ by Lemma 2 in view of (44). Moreover, f_0 is a homeomorphism of $\mathbb{C}$ into $\mathbb{C}$ by Corollary 4. Hence f_0 is a conformal mapping of $\mathbb{C}$ into $\mathbb{C}$, see, e.g., Corollary II.B.1 in [11]. Hence $f_0(\zeta)$ is a linear function $a + b\zeta$, see, e.g., Theorem 2.31.1 in [44]. In addition, by the construction $f_0(0) = 0$ and $f_0(1) = 1$. Thus, $f_0(\zeta) \equiv \zeta$ in the whole complex plane $\mathbb{C}$ and the proof is thereby complete. □

Remark 6. *Note that, in particular, both conditions (43) and (44) follow from the only one stronger condition*

$$\lim_{r\to 0} \frac{1}{\pi r^2} \int\limits_{|z|<r} K_\mu(z)\, dm(z) \;=\; 1 \tag{45}$$

because

$$|\mu(z)| \;\le\; \frac{|\mu(z)|}{1 - |\mu(z)|} \;=\; \frac{K_\mu(z) - 1}{2}\,. \tag{46}$$

Combinig Theorems 1 and 3, see also Proposition 4, we obtain the following conclusions.

Corollary 5. *Under hypotheses of Theorem 3, f is conformal by Lavrent'iev at the origin, i.e., f preserves infinitesimal circles centered at the origin:*

$$\lim_{r\to 0} \frac{\max\limits_{|z|=r} |f(z)|}{\min\limits_{|z|=r} |f(z)|} = 1 \,, \tag{47}$$

asymptotically preserves angles, i.e.,

$$\lim_{z\to 0} \arg \left[\frac{f(z\zeta)}{f(z)} \right] = \arg \zeta \quad \forall\, \zeta \in \mathbb{C}\,,\ |\zeta| = 1\,, \tag{48}$$

and asymptotically preserves the moduli of infinitesimal rings, i.e.,

$$\lim_{z\to 0} \frac{|f(z\zeta)|}{|f(z)|} = |\zeta| \quad \forall\, \zeta \in \mathbb{C}^* := \mathbb{C} \setminus \{0\}\,. \tag{49}$$

Corollary 6. *Under hypotheses of Theorem 3, for all $\delta > 0$, along $z \in \mathbb{C}^* := \mathbb{C} \setminus \{0\}$ and $z' \in \mathbb{C}$ with $|z'| \le \delta |z|$,*

$$\lim_{z\to 0} \left\{ \frac{|f(z')|}{|f(z)|} - \frac{|z'|}{|z|} \right\} = 0\,. \tag{50}$$

Moreover, by the theorem of Stolz (1885) and Cesaro (1888), see, e.g., Problem 70 in [45], we derive from Corollary 6 the next assertion on logarithms.

Corollary 7. *Under hypotheses of Theorem 3,*

$$\lim_{\substack{z\to 0\\ z\in\mathbb{C}^*}} \frac{\ln |f(z)|}{\ln |z|} = 1\,. \tag{51}$$

Proof. For brevity, let us introduce designations $t_n = -\ln |z_n|$, $\tau_n = -\ln |f(z_n)|$ and assume that (51) does not hold, i.e., there exist $\varepsilon > 0$ and a sequence $z_n \to 0$ such that

$$\left| \frac{\tau_n}{t_n} - 1 \right| \ge \varepsilon \quad \forall\, n = 1, 2, \ldots\,. \tag{52}$$

Passing, if necessary, to a subsequence, we can consider that $t_n - t_{n-1} \ge 1$ for all $n = 1, 2, \ldots$. Then, we can achieve that $t_n - t_{n-1} < 2$, by inserting, if necessary, the mean arithmetic values between neighboring terms of the subsequence t_n, $n = 1, 2, \ldots$. In this case, inequality (52) holds for the infinite number of terms of the subsequence.

Thus, the sequence $\rho_n = |z_n| = e^{-t_n}$ satisfies the inequalities $e^{-2} < \rho_n/\rho_{n-1} \le e^{-1}$. Relations (50) implies that $\exp(\tau_{n-1} - \tau_n) = \exp(t_{n-1} - t_n) + \alpha_n$, where $\alpha_n \to 0$ as $n \to \infty$, or, in the other form, $\exp(\tau_{n-1} - \tau_n) = (1 + \beta_n) \exp(t_{n-1} - t_n)$ with $\beta_n \to 0$ as $n \to \infty$. The latter gives that $(\tau_n - \tau_{n-1}) = (t_n - t_{n-1}) + \gamma_n$ with $\gamma_n \to 0$ as $n \to \infty$ and, since $t_n - t_{n-1} \ge 1$, we have that $(\tau_n - \tau_{n-1})/(t_n - t_{n-1}) = 1 + \delta_n$, where $\delta_n \to 0$ as $n \to \infty$. By the Stolz theorem, then we conclude that $\tau_n/t_n \to 1$ in contradiction with (52). This contradiction disproves the above assumption, i.e., (51) is true. □

Theorem 4. *Let D be a domain in $\mathbb{C}$ and let $f : D \to \mathbb{C}$ be an approximate solution of the Beltrami Equation (2), K_μ have a majorant $Q \in$ BMO(D) and at a point $z_0 \in D$*

$$\limsup_{r\to 0} \frac{1}{\pi r^2} \int\limits_{|z-z_0|<r} K_\mu(z)\, dm(z) < \infty\,. \tag{53}$$

Suppose that $\mu(z)$ is approximately continuous at z_0. Then the mapping f is differentiable by Belinskij at this point with $\mu_0 = \mu(z_0)$.

Proof. First of all, $|\mu(z_0)| < 1$ because by the hypotheses $K_\mu \in L^1_{\rm loc}$ and $\mu(z)$ is approximately continuous at z_0. Note also that f is differentiable by Belinskij with $\mu_0 = \mu(z_0)$ at z_0 if and only if $g := h \circ \varphi^{-1}$ is conformal by Belinskij at zero, where $h(z) = f(z_0 + z) - f(z_0)$ and $\varphi(z) = z + \mu_0 \bar{z}$. It is evident that $\mu_h(z) = \mu(z + z_0)$ and $K_{\mu_h} = K_\mu(z + z_0)$ and by elementary calculations, see, e.g., Section I.C(6) in [11], $\mu_g \circ \varphi = (\mu_h - \mu_0)/(1 - \overline{\mu_0}\mu_h)$ and $K_{\mu_g} \le K_0 \cdot K_{\mu_h} \circ \varphi^{-1} \le K_0 Q_0$, where $K_0 = (1 + |\mu_0|)/(1 - |\mu_0|)$ and $Q_0(w) = Q(z_0 + \varphi^{-1}(w))$ belongs to BMO in $D_0 := \varphi(D)$ because φ and φ^{-1} are K_0-quasiconformal mappings, see the paper [46] and the monograph [3]. Thus, Theorem 4 follows from Theorem 3. □

4. On Homeomorphic Solutions in Extended Complex Plane

Here we start from establishing a series of criteria for existence of approximate solutions $f : \mathbb{C} \to \mathbb{C}$ to the degenerate Beltrami equations in the whole complex plane $\mathbb{C}$ with the normalization $f(0) = 0$, $f(1) = 1$ and $f(\infty) = \infty$.

It is easy to give examples of locally quasiconformal mappings of $\mathbb{C}$ onto the unit disk $\mathbb{D}$, consequently, there exist locally uniform elliptic Beltrami equations with no such solutions. Hence, compared with our previous articles, the main goal here is to find the corresponding additional conditions on dilatation quotients of the Beltrami equations at infinity.

Lemma 3. *Let a function $\mu : \mathbb{C} \to \mathbb{C}$ be measurable with $|\mu(z)| < 1$ a.e., $K_\mu \in L^1_{\rm loc}(\mathbb{C})$. Suppose that, for every $z_0 \in \overline{\mathbb{C}}$, there exist $\varepsilon_0 = \varepsilon(z_0) > 0$ and a family of measurable functions $\psi_{z_0,\varepsilon} : (0,\infty) \to (0,\infty)$ such that*

$$I_{z_0}(\varepsilon) \, : = \int\limits_{\varepsilon}^{\varepsilon_0} \psi_{z_0,\varepsilon}(t)\, dt \, < \, \infty \qquad \forall\, \varepsilon \in (0, \varepsilon_0) \tag{54}$$

and

$$\int\limits_{\varepsilon<|z-z_0|<\varepsilon_0} K^T_\mu(z,z_0) \cdot \psi^2_{z_0,\varepsilon}(|z-z_0|)\, dm(z) \;=\; o(I^2_{z_0}(\varepsilon)) \qquad as\ \varepsilon \to 0 \ \ \forall\ z_0 \in \mathbb{C} \tag{55}$$

and, moreover,

$$\int\limits_{\varepsilon<|\zeta|<\varepsilon_\infty} K^T_\mu(\zeta,\infty) \cdot \psi^2_{\infty,\varepsilon}(|\zeta|)\, \frac{dm(\zeta)}{|\zeta|^4} \;=\; o(I^2_\infty(\varepsilon)) \qquad as\ \varepsilon \to 0\,, \tag{56}$$

where $K^T_\mu(\zeta,\infty) := K^T_\mu(1/\zeta, 0)$.

Then the Beltrami Equation (2) has an approximate homeomorphic solution f in $\mathbb{C}$ with the normalization $f(0) = 0$, $f(1) = 1$ and $f(\infty) = \infty$.

Remark 7. *After the replacements of variables $\zeta \longmapsto z := 1/\zeta$, $\varepsilon \longmapsto R := 1/\varepsilon$, $\varepsilon_\infty \longmapsto R_0 := 1/\varepsilon_\infty$ and functions $\psi_{\infty,\varepsilon}(t) \longmapsto \psi_R(t) := \psi_{\infty,1/R}(1/t)$, the condition (56) can be rewritten in the more convenient form:*

$$\int\limits_{R_0<|z|<R} K^T_\mu(z,0)\ \psi^2_R(|z|)\, \frac{dm(z)}{|z|^4} \;=\; o(I^2(R)) \qquad as\ R \to \infty\,, \tag{57}$$

with the family of measurable functions $\psi_R : (0,\infty) \to (0,\infty)$ such that

$$I(R) \, : = \int\limits_{R_0}^{R} \psi_R(t)\, \frac{dt}{t^2} \, < \, \infty \qquad \forall\, R \in (R_0, \infty)\,. \tag{58}$$

Before arriving at the proof of Lemma 3, let us recall that a **condenser** in $\mathbb{C}$ is a domain $\mathcal{R}$ in $\mathbb{C}$ whose complement in $\overline{\mathbb{C}}$ is the union of two distinguished disjoint compact sets C_1 and C_2. For convenience, it is written $\mathcal{R} = \mathcal{R}(C_1, C_2)$. A **ring** in $\mathbb{C}$ is a condenser $\mathcal{R} = \mathcal{R}(C_1, C_2)$ with connected C_1 and C_2 that are called the **complementary components** of $\mathcal{R}$. It is known that the (conformal) capacity of a ring $\mathcal{R} = \mathcal{R}(C_1, C_2)$ in $\mathbb{C}$ is equal to the (conformal) modulus of all paths in $\mathcal{R}$ connecting C_1 and C_2, see, e.g., Theorem A.8 in [17].

Proof. By the first item of the proof of Lemma 3 in [21] the Beltrami Equation (2) has under the conditions (55) an approximate homeomorphic solution f in $\mathbb{C}$ with $f(0) = 0$ and $f(1) = 1$. Moreover, by Lemma 3 in [21] we may also assume that f is a ring $Q-$homeomorphism with $Q(z) = K^T_\mu(z, 0)$ at the origin, i.e., for every ring $A = A(r_1, r_2) := \{z \in \mathbb{C} : r_1 < |z| < r_2\}$, we have the estimate of the capacity $C_f(r_1, r_2)$ of its image under the mapping f:

$$C_f(r_1, r_2) \leq \int\limits_{A(r_1,r_2)} K^T_\mu(z, 0)\, dm(z) \qquad \forall\, r_1, r_2 :\ 0 < r_1 < r_2 < \infty\,.$$

Let us consider the mapping $F(z) := 1/f(1/z)$ in $\mathbb{C}_* := \overline{\mathbb{C}} \setminus \{0\}$. Note that $F(\infty) = \infty$ because $f(0) = 0$. Since the capacity is invariant under conformal mappings, we have by the change of variables $z \longmapsto \zeta := 1/z$ as well as $r_1 \longmapsto \varepsilon_2 := 1/r_1$ and $r_2 \longmapsto \varepsilon_1 := 1/r_2$ that

$$C_F(\varepsilon_1, \varepsilon_2) \leq \int\limits_{A(\varepsilon_1,\varepsilon_2)} K^T_\mu(1/\zeta, 0)\, \frac{dm(\zeta)}{|\zeta|^4} \qquad \forall\, \varepsilon_1, \varepsilon_2 :\ 0 < \varepsilon_1 < \varepsilon_2 < \infty\,,$$

i.e., F is a ring $\tilde{Q}-$homeomorphism at the origin with $\tilde{Q}(\zeta) := K^T_\mu(1/\zeta, 0)/|\zeta|^4$. Thus, in view of the condition (56), we obtain by Lemma 6.5 in [16] that F has a continuous extension to the origin. Let us assume that $c := \lim\limits_{\zeta \to 0} F(\zeta) \neq 0$.

However, $\overline{\mathbb{C}}$ is homeomorphic to the sphere $\mathbb{S}^2$ by stereographic projection and hence by the Brouwer theorem in $\mathbb{S}^2$ on the invariance of domain the set $C_* := F(\mathbb{C}_*)$ is open in $\overline{\mathbb{C}}$, see, e.g., Theorem 4.8.16 in [47]. Consequently, $c \notin C_*$ because F is a homeomorphism. Then the extended mapping $\tilde{F}$ is a homeomorphism of $\overline{\mathbb{C}}$ into $\mathbb{C}_*$ because $f \neq \infty$ in $\mathbb{C}$. Thus, again by the Brouwer theorem, the set $C := \tilde{F}(\overline{\mathbb{C}})$ is open in $\overline{\mathbb{C}}$ and $0 \in \overline{\mathbb{C}} \setminus C \neq \emptyset$. On the other hand, the set C is compact as a continuous image of the compact space $\overline{\mathbb{C}}$. Hence the set $\overline{\mathbb{C}} \setminus C \neq \emptyset$ is also open in $\overline{\mathbb{C}}$. The latter contradicts the connectivity of $\overline{\mathbb{C}}$, see, e.g., Proposition I.1.1 in [48].

The obtained contradiction disproves the assumption that $c \neq 0$. Thus, we have proved that f is extended to a homeomorphism of $\overline{\mathbb{C}}$ onto itself with $f(\infty) = \infty$. □

Choosing $\psi_{z_0,\varepsilon}(t) \equiv 1/(t \log(1/t))$ in Lemma 3, we obtain by Proposition 2 the following.

Theorem 5. *Let $\mu : \mathbb{C} \to \mathbb{C}$ be measurable with $|\mu(z)| < 1$ a.e., $K_\mu \in L^1_{\mathrm{loc}}(\mathbb{C})$ and*

$$\int\limits_{R_0<|z|<R} K_\mu(z)\, \psi^2(|z|)\, \frac{dm(z)}{|z|^4} = o(I^2(R)) \qquad \text{as } R \to \infty \tag{59}$$

for some $R_0 > 0$ and a measurable function $\psi : (0, \infty) \to (0, \infty)$ such that

$$I(R) : = \int\limits_{R_0}^{R} \psi(t)\, \frac{dt}{t^2} < \infty \qquad \forall\, R \in (R_0, \infty)\,. \tag{60}$$

Suppose also that $K^T_\mu(z, z_0) \leqslant Q_{z_0}(z)$ a.e. in U_{z_0} for every point $z_0 \in \mathbb{C}$, a neighborhood U_{z_0} of z_0 and a function $Q_{z_0} : U_{z_0} \to [0, \infty]$ in the class $\mathrm{FMO}(z_0)$.

Then the Beltrami Equation (2) has a regular homeomorphic solution f in $\mathbb{C}$ with the normalization $f(0) = 0$, $f(1) = 1$ and $f(\infty) = \infty$.

In particular, by Proposition 1 the conclusion of Theorem 5 holds if every point $z_0 \in \mathbb{C}$ is the Lebesgue point of the function Q_{z_0}.

By Corollary 1 we obtain the next nice consequence of Theorem 5, too.

Corollary 8. *Let $\mu : \mathbb{C} \to \mathbb{C}$ be measurable with $|\mu(z)| < 1$ a.e., $K_\mu \in L^1_{\rm loc}(\mathbb{C})$, (59) and*

$$\overline{\lim_{\varepsilon \to 0}} \fint_{\mathbb{D}(z_0,\varepsilon)} K^T_\mu(z, z_0)\, dm(z) < \infty \qquad \forall\, z_0 \in \mathbb{C}\,. \tag{61}$$

Then the Beltrami Equation (2) has a regular homeomorphic solution f in $\mathbb{C}$ with the normalization $f(0) = 0$, $f(1) = 1$ and $f(\infty) = \infty$.

By (5), we also obtain the following consequences of Theorem 5.

Corollary 9. *Let $\mu : \mathbb{C} \to \mathbb{C}$ be measurable with $|\mu(z)| < 1$ a.e., (59) and K_μ have a dominant $Q : \mathbb{C} \to [1, \infty)$ in the class* BMO$_{\rm loc}$. *Then the Beltrami Equation (2) has a regular homeomorphic solution f in $\mathbb{C}$ with the normalization $f(0) = 0$, $f(1) = 1$ and $f(\infty) = \infty$.*

Remark 8. *In particular, the conclusion of Corollary 7 holds if $Q \in W^{1,2}_{\rm loc}$ because $W^{1,2}_{\rm loc} \subset$ VMO$_{\rm loc}$, see, e.g., [10].*

Corollary 10. *Let $\mu : \mathbb{C} \to \mathbb{C}$ be measurable with $|\mu(z)| < 1$ a.e., (59) and $K_\mu(z) \leqslant Q(z)$ a.e. in $\mathbb{C}$ with a function Q in the class* FMO$(\mathbb{C})$. *Then the Beltrami Equation (2) has a regular homeomorphic solution f in $\mathbb{C}$ with the normalization $f(0) = 0$, $f(1) = 1$ and $f(\infty) = \infty$.*

Similarly, choosing $\psi_{z_0,\varepsilon}(t) \equiv 1/t$ in Lemma 3, we come to the next statement.

Theorem 6. *Let $\mu : \mathbb{C} \to \mathbb{C}$ be measurable with $|\mu(z)| < 1$ a.e., $K_\mu \in L^1_{\rm loc}(\mathbb{C})$, (59) and*

$$\int\limits_{\varepsilon<|z-z_0|<\varepsilon_0} K^T_\mu(z, z_0)\, \frac{dm(z)}{|z - z_0|^2} = o\left(\left[\log \frac{1}{\varepsilon}\right]^2\right) \qquad as\ \varepsilon \to 0 \qquad \forall\, z_0 \in \mathbb{C} \tag{62}$$

for some $\varepsilon_0 = \varepsilon(z_0) > 0$. Then the Beltrami Equation (2) has a regular homeomorphic solution f in $\mathbb{C}$ with the normalization $f(0) = 0$, $f(1) = 1$ and $f(\infty) = \infty$.

Remark 9. *Choosing $\psi_{z_0,\varepsilon}(t) \equiv 1/(t \log 1/t)$ instead of $\psi(t) = 1/t$ in Lemma 2, we are able to replace (62) by*

$$\int\limits_{\varepsilon<|z-z_0|<\varepsilon_0} \frac{K^T_\mu(z, z_0)\, dm(z)}{\left(|z - z_0| \log \frac{1}{|z-z_0|}\right)^2} = o\left(\left[\log\log \frac{1}{\varepsilon}\right]^2\right) \tag{63}$$

In general, we are able to give here the whole scale of the corresponding conditions in log *using functions $\psi(t)$ of the form $1/(t \log 1/t \cdot \log\log 1/t \cdot \ldots \cdot \log \ldots \log 1/t)$.*

Now, choosing in Lemma 3 the functional parameter $\psi_{z_0,\varepsilon}(t) \equiv \psi_{z_0}(t) := 1/[t k^T_\mu(z_0, t)]$, where $k^T_\mu(z_0, r)$ is the integral mean value of $K^T_\mu(z, z_0)$ over the circle $S(z_0, r) := \{z \in \mathbb{C} : |z - z_0| = r\}$, we obtain one more important conclusion.

Theorem 7. *Let $\mu : \mathbb{C} \to \mathbb{C}$ be measurable with $|\mu(z)| < 1$ a.e., $K_\mu \in L^1_{\rm loc}(\mathbb{C})$, (59) and*

$$\int\limits_0^{\varepsilon_0} \frac{dr}{r k^T_\mu(z_0, r)} = \infty \qquad \forall\, z_0 \in \mathbb{C} \tag{64}$$

for some $\varepsilon_0 = \varepsilon(z_0) > 0$. Then the Beltrami Equation (2) has a regular homeomorphic solution f in $\mathbb{C}$ with the normalization $f(0) = 0$, $f(1) = 1$ and $f(\infty) = \infty$.

Corollary 11. *Let $\mu : \mathbb{C} \to \mathbb{C}$ be measurable with $|\mu(z)| < 1$ a.e., $K_\mu \in L^1_{\mathrm{loc}}(\mathbb{C})$, (59) and*

$$k_\mu^T(z_0, \varepsilon) = O\left(\log\frac{1}{\varepsilon}\right) \qquad \text{as } \varepsilon \to 0 \qquad \forall\, z_0 \in \mathbb{C}\,. \tag{65}$$

Then the Beltrami Equation (2) has a regular homeomorphic solution f in $\mathbb{C}$ with the normalization $f(0) = 0$, $f(1) = 1$ and $f(\infty) = \infty$.

Remark 10. *In particular, the conclusion of Corollary 10 holds if*

$$K_\mu^T(z, z_0) = O\left(\log\frac{1}{|z - z_0|}\right) \qquad \text{as} \quad z \to z_0 \quad \forall\, z_0 \in \overline{D}\,. \tag{66}$$

Moreover, the condition (65) can be replaced by the whole series of more weak conditions

$$k_\mu^T(z_0, \varepsilon) = O\left(\left[\log\frac{1}{\varepsilon}\cdot\log\log\frac{1}{\varepsilon}\cdot\ldots\cdot\log\ldots\log\frac{1}{\varepsilon}\right]\right) \qquad \forall\, z_0 \in \overline{D}\,. \tag{67}$$

For further consequences, the following statement is useful, see e.g., Theorem 3.2 in [22].

Proposition 7. *Let $Q : \mathbb{D} \to [0, \infty]$ be a measurable function such that*

$$\int\limits_{\mathbb{D}} \Phi(Q(z))\, dm(z) < \infty \tag{68}$$

where $\Phi : [0, \infty] \to [0, \infty]$ is a non-decreasing convex function such that

$$\int\limits_{\delta}^{\infty} \frac{d\tau}{\tau\Phi^{-1}(\tau)} = \infty \tag{69}$$

for some $\delta > \Phi(+0)$. Then

$$\int\limits_{0}^{1} \frac{dr}{rq(r)} = \infty \tag{70}$$

where $q(r)$ is the average of the function $Q(z)$ over the circle $|z| = r$.

Here we use the following notions of the inverse function for monotone functions. Namely, for every non-decreasing function $\Phi : [0, \infty] \to [0, \infty]$ the inverse function $\Phi^{-1} : [0, \infty] \to [0, \infty]$ can be well-defined by setting

$$\Phi^{-1}(\tau) := \inf_{\Phi(t) \geqslant \tau} t\,. \tag{71}$$

Here inf is equal to ∞ if the set of $t \in [0, \infty]$ such that $\Phi(t) \geqslant \tau$ is empty. Note that the function Φ^{-1} is non-decreasing, too. It is evident immediately by the definition that $\Phi^{-1}(\Phi(t)) \leqslant t$ for all $t \in [0, \infty]$ with the equality except intervals of constancy of the function $\Phi(t)$.

Let us recall the connection of condition (69) with other integral conditions, see, e.g., Theorem 2.5 in [22].

Remark 11. *Let $\Phi : [0, \infty] \to [0, \infty]$ be a non-decreasing function and set*

$$H(t) = \log\Phi(t)\,. \tag{72}$$

Then the equality

$$\int_{\Delta}^{\infty} H'(t)\,\frac{dt}{t} = \infty, \tag{73}$$

implies the equality

$$\int_{\Delta}^{\infty} \frac{dH(t)}{t} = \infty\,, \tag{74}$$

and (74) is equivalent to

$$\int_{\Delta}^{\infty} H(t)\,\frac{dt}{t^2} = \infty \tag{75}$$

for some $\Delta > 0$*, and (75) is equivalent to each of the equalities*

$$\int_{0}^{\delta_*} H\left(\frac{1}{t}\right) dt = \infty \tag{76}$$

for some $\delta_* > 0$*,*

$$\int_{\Delta_*}^{\infty} \frac{d\eta}{H^{-1}(\eta)} = \infty \tag{77}$$

for some $\Delta_* > H(+0)$ *and to (69) for some* $\delta > \Phi(+0)$.

Moreover, (73) is equivalent to (74) and hence to (75)–(77) as well as to (69) are equivalent to each other if Φ is in addition absolutely continuous. In particular, all the given conditions are equivalent if Φ is convex and non-decreasing.

Note that the integral in (74) is understood as the Lebesgue–Stieltjes integral and the integrals in (73) and (75)–(77) as the ordinary Lebesgue integrals. It is necessary to give one more explanation. From the right hand sides in the conditions (73)–(77) we have in mind $+\infty$. If $\Phi(t) = 0$ for $t \in [0, t_*]$, then $H(t) = -\infty$ for $t \in [0, t_*]$ and we complete the definition $H'(t) = 0$ for $t \in [0, t_*]$. Note, the conditions (74) and (75) exclude that t_* belongs to the interval of integrability because in the contrary case the left hand sides in (74) and (75) are either equal to $-\infty$ or indeterminate. Hence we may assume in (73)–(76) that $\delta > t_0$, correspondingly, $\Delta < 1/t_0$ where $t_0 := \sup\limits_{\Phi(t)=0} t$, and set $t_0 = 0$ if $\Phi(0) > 0$.

The most interesting of the above conditions is (75) that can be rewritten in the form:

$$\int_{\Delta}^{\infty} \log\,\Phi(t)\,\frac{dt}{t^2} \;=\; +\infty \qquad \text{for some } \Delta > 0\,. \tag{78}$$

Combining Theorems 7, Proposition 7 and Remark 11, we obtain the following result.

Theorem 8. *Let* $\mu : \mathbb{C} \to \mathbb{C}$ *be measurable with* $|\mu(z)| < 1$ *a.e.,* $K_\mu \in L^1_{\rm loc}(\mathbb{C})$*, (59) and*

$$\int_{U_{z_0}} \Phi_{z_0}\left(K^T_\mu(z, z_0)\right) dm(z) < \infty \qquad \forall\; z_0 \in \mathbb{C} \tag{79}$$

for a neighborhood U_{z_0} *of* z_0 *and a convex non-decreasing function* $\Phi_{z_0} : [0, \infty] \to [0, \infty]$ *with*

$$\int_{\Delta(z_0)}^{\infty} \log\,\Phi_{z_0}(t)\,\frac{dt}{t^2} \;=\; +\infty \tag{80}$$

for some $\Delta(z_0) > 0$. *Then the Beltrami Equation (2) has a regular homeomorphic solution* f *in* $\mathbb{C}$ *with the normalization* $f(0) = 0$, $f(1) = 1$ *and* $f(\infty) = \infty$.

Corollary 12. *Let* $\mu : \mathbb{C} \to \mathbb{C}$ *be measurable with* $|\mu(z)| < 1$ *a.e.,* $K_\mu \in L^1_{\text{loc}}(\mathbb{C})$, *(59) and*

$$\int\limits_{U_{z_0}} e^{\alpha(z_0) K^T_\mu(z,z_0)}\, dm(z) < \infty \qquad \forall\, z_0 \in \mathbb{C} \tag{81}$$

for some $\alpha(z_0) > 0$ *and a neighborhood* U_{z_0} *of the point* z_0. *Then the Beltrami Equation (2) has a regular homeomorphic solution* f *in* $\mathbb{C}$ *with the normalization* $f(0) = 0$, $f(1) = 1$ *and* $f(\infty) = \infty$.

Since $K^T_\mu(z, z_0) \leqslant K_\mu(z)$ for z and $z_0 \in \mathbb{C}$, we also obtain the following consequences of Theorem 8.

Corollary 13. *Let* $\mu : \mathbb{C} \to \mathbb{C}$ *be measurable with* $|\mu(z)| < 1$ *a.e., (59) and*

$$\int\limits_{C} \Phi(K_\mu(z))\, dm(z) < \infty \tag{82}$$

over each compact C *in* $\mathbb{C}$ *for a convex non-decreasing function* $\Phi : [0, \infty] \to [0, \infty]$ *with*

$$\int\limits_{\delta}^{\infty} \log\, \Phi(t)\, \frac{dt}{t^2} \;=\; +\infty \tag{83}$$

for some $\delta > 0$. *Then the Beltrami Equation (2) has a regular homeomorphic solution* f *in* $\mathbb{C}$ *with the normalization* $f(0) = 0$, $f(1) = 1$ *and* $f(\infty) = \infty$.

Corollary 14. *Let* $\mu : \mathbb{C} \to \mathbb{C}$ *be measurable with* $|\mu(z)| < 1$ *a.e., (59) and, for some* $\alpha > 0$, *over each compact* C *in* $\mathbb{C}$,

$$\int\limits_{C} e^{\alpha K_\mu(z)}\, dm(z) \;<\; \infty\,. \tag{84}$$

Then the Beltrami Equation (2) has a regular homeomorphic solution f *in* $\mathbb{C}$ *with the normalization* $f(0) = 0$, $f(1) = 1$ *and* $f(\infty) = \infty$.

5. On Existence of Solutions with Asymptotics at Infinity

In the extended complex plane $\overline{\mathbb{C}} = \mathbb{C} \cup \{\infty\}$, we will use the so-called **spherical area** whose element can be given through the element $dm(z)$ of the Lebesgue measure (usual area)

$$dS(z) \;:=\; \frac{4\, d\, m(z)}{(1 + |z|^2)^2} \;=\; \frac{4\, dx\, dy}{(1 + |z|^2)^2}\,, \qquad z = x + iy\,. \tag{85}$$

Let us start from the following general lemma on the existence of regular homeomorhic solutions for the Beltrami equations in $\mathbb{C}$ with asymptotic homogeneity at infinity.

Lemma 4. *Let a function* $\mu : \mathbb{C} \to \mathbb{C}$ *be measurable with* $|\mu(z)| < 1$ *a.e.,* K_μ *have a majorant* Q *of the class BMO in a connected open (punctured at* ∞*) neighborhood* U *of infinity,*

$$\int\limits_{|z|>R} |\mu(z)|\, dS(z) \;=\; o\left(\frac{1}{R^2}\right) \tag{86}$$

and, moreover,

$$\int\limits_{|z|>R} K_\mu(z)\, dS(z) \;=\; O\left(\frac{1}{R^2}\right)\,. \tag{87}$$

Suppose also that, for every $z_0 \in \mathbb{C} \setminus U$, there exist $\varepsilon_0 = \varepsilon(z_0) > 0$ and a family of measurable functions $\psi_{z_0,\varepsilon} : (0,\infty) \to (0,\infty)$ such that

$$I_{z_0}(\varepsilon) \, := \, \int\limits_{\varepsilon}^{\varepsilon_0} \psi_{z_0,\varepsilon}(t)\, dt \, < \, \infty \qquad \forall\, \varepsilon \in (0, \varepsilon_0) \tag{88}$$

and

$$\int\limits_{\varepsilon<|z-z_0|<\varepsilon_0} K^T_\mu(z, z_0) \cdot \psi^2_{z_0,\varepsilon}(|z - z_0|)\, dm(z) \, = \, o(I^2_{z_0}(\varepsilon)) \qquad \text{as } \varepsilon \to 0 \;\; \forall\, z_0 \in \mathbb{C}\,. \tag{89}$$

Then the Beltrami Equation (2) has an approximate homeomorphic solution f in $\mathbb{C}$ with $f(0) = 0$, $f(1) = 1$ and $f(\infty) = \infty$ that is asymptotically homogeneous at infinity, $f(\zeta z) \sim \zeta f(z)$ as $z \to \infty$ for all $\zeta \in \mathbb{C}$, i.e.,

$$\boxed{\lim_{\substack{z\to\infty,\\ z\in\mathbb{C}}} \frac{f(z\zeta)}{f(z)} = \zeta} \qquad \forall\, \zeta \in \mathbb{C} \tag{90}$$

and the limit (90) is locally uniform with respect to the parameter ζ in $\mathbb{C}$.

Remark 12. *(86) and (87) can be replaced by only one (stronger) condition*

$$\lim_{r\to\infty} \frac{R^2}{\pi} \int\limits_{|z|>R} K_\mu(z)\, dS(z) \, = \, 1\,. \tag{91}$$

Note also that, arguing similarly to the proofs of Theorem 1 and Corollary 7, we see that the locally uniform property of the asymptotic homogeneity of f at infinity (90) implies its **conformality by Belinskij at infinity**, i.e.,

$$\boxed{f(z) \, = \, A(\rho) \cdot [\, z \, + \, o(\rho)\,]} \qquad \text{as } z \to \infty\,, \tag{92}$$

where $A(\rho)$ depends only on $\rho = |z|$, $o(\rho)/\rho \to 0$ as $\rho \to \infty$ and, moreover,

$$\boxed{\lim_{\rho\to\infty} \frac{A(t\rho)}{A(\rho)} = 1} \qquad \forall\, t > 0\,, \tag{93}$$

its **conformality by Lavrent'iev at infinity**, i.e.,

$$\boxed{\lim_{R\to\infty} \frac{\max\limits_{|z|=R} |f(z)|}{\min\limits_{|z|=R} |f(z)|} \, = \, 1}\,, \tag{94}$$

the logarithmic property at infinity

$$\boxed{\lim_{z\to\infty} \frac{\ln |f(z)|}{\ln |z|} \, = \, 1}\,, \tag{95}$$

asymptotic preserving angles at infinity, i.e.,

$$\boxed{\lim_{z\to\infty} \arg \left[\frac{f(z\zeta)}{f(z)}\right] = \arg \zeta} \qquad \forall\, \zeta \in \mathbb{C}^* \tag{96}$$

and asymptotic preserving moduli of rings at infinity, i.e.,

$$\boxed{\lim_{z\to\infty}\frac{|f(z\zeta)|}{|f(z)|} = |\zeta|} \qquad \forall\,\zeta\in\mathbb{C}^*\,. \tag{97}$$

The latter two geometric properties characterize asymptotic homogeneity at infinity and demonstrate that it is very close to the usual conformality at infinity.

Proof. The extended complex plane $\overline{\mathbb{C}} = \mathbb{C}\cup\{\infty\}$ is a metric space with a measure with respect to the spherical (chordal) metric s, see (26), and the spherical area S, see (85). This space is regular by Ahlfors that is evident from the geometric interpretation of $\overline{\mathbb{C}}$ as the so-called stereographic projection of a sphere in $\mathbb{R}^3$, see details, e.g., in Section 13 and Supplement B in the monograph [17].

Let us recall only here that, if the function Q belongs to the class BMO in U with respect to the Euclidean distance and the usual area in $\mathbb{C}$, then Q is in BMO with respect to the spherical distance and the spherical area not only in U but also in $U\cup\{\infty\}$, see Lemma B.3 and Proposition B.1 in [17]. Moreover, we have an analog of Proposition 2 in terms of spherical metric and area, see Lemma 13.2 and Remark 13.3 in [17], that in turn can be rewritten in terms of the Euclidean distance and area at infinity in the following form:

$$\int\limits_{R_0<|z|<R} \frac{Q(z)}{\log^2|z|}\,\frac{dm(z)}{|z|^2} = O(\log\log R) \qquad \text{as } R\to\infty \tag{98}$$

for large enough R_0 with $\{z\in\mathbb{C} : |z| > R_0\}\subseteq U$. Consequently, we have the condition (57) with $\psi_R(t) \equiv \psi(t) := t^{-1}log\,t$ and by Lemma 3, see also Remark 7, the Beltrami Equation (2) has an approximate solution f in $\mathbb{C}$ with the normalization $f(0)=0$, $f(1)=1$ and $f(\infty)=\infty$. Recall that f is its regular homeomorphic solution by Proposition 4.

Setting $f^*(\xi) := 1/f(1/\xi)$ in $\overline{\mathbb{C}}$, we see that $f^*(0)=0$, $f^*(1)=1$, $f^*(\infty)=\infty$ and that f^* is an approximate solution in $\mathbb{C}^* = \mathbb{C}\setminus\{0\}$ of the Beltrami equation with

$$\mu^*(\xi) := \mu\left(\frac{1}{\xi}\right)\cdot\frac{\xi^2}{\bar{\xi}^2}\,, \qquad K_{\mu^*}(\xi) = K_\mu\left(\frac{1}{\xi}\right), \tag{99}$$

because

$$f^*_{\bar\xi}(\xi) = \frac{1}{\bar{\xi}^2}\cdot\frac{f_{\bar z}(\frac{1}{\xi})}{f^2(\frac{1}{\xi})}\,, \qquad f^*_{\xi}(\xi) = \frac{1}{\xi^2}\cdot\frac{f_{z}(\frac{1}{\xi})}{f^2(\frac{1}{\xi})} \qquad \text{a.e. in } \mathbb{C}\,, \tag{100}$$

see, e.g., Section I.C and the proof of Theorem 3 of Section V.B in [11].

Note that f^* belongs to the class $W^{1,1}_{\text{loc}}(\mathbb{C}^*)$ and, consequently, f^* is ACL (absolutely continuous on lines) in $\mathbb{C}$, see, e.g., Theorems 1 and 2 of Section 1.1.3 and Theorem of Section 1.1.7 in [49]. However, it is not clear directly from (100) whether the derivatives $f^*_{\bar\xi}$ and f^*_{ξ} are integrable in a neighborhood of the origin, because of the first factors in (100). Thus, to prove that f^* is a regular homeomorphic solution of the Beltrami equation in $\mathbb{C}$, it remains to establish the latter fact in another way.

Namely, after the replacements of variables $z \longmapsto \xi := 1/z$ and $R\longmapsto r := 1/R$, in view of (99), the condition (87) can be rewritten in the form

$$\limsup_{r\to 0}\frac{1}{r^2}\int\limits_{|\xi|<r} K_{\mu^*}(\xi)\,dm(\xi) < \infty\,, \tag{101}$$

and the latter implies, in particular, that, for some $r_0\in(0,1]$,

$$\frac{1}{r_0^2}\int\limits_{|\xi|<r_0} K_{\mu^*}(\xi)\,dm(\xi) < \infty\,, \tag{102}$$

i.e., the dilatation quotient K_{μ^*} of the given Beltrami equation is integrable in the disk $\mathbb{D}(r_0)$.

Now, since f^* is a regular homeomorphism in $\mathbb{C}^*$, in particular, its Jacobian $J(\xi) = |f^*_\xi|^2 - |f^*_{\bar\xi}|^2 \neq 0$ a.e. and hence $|f^*_\xi| - |f^*_{\bar\xi}| \neq 0$ a.e. as well as $f^*_\xi \neq 0$ a.e., the following identities are also correct a.e.

$$|f^*_\xi(\xi)| + |f^*_{\bar\xi}(\xi)| = \left[\frac{|f^*_\xi(\xi)| + |f^*_{\bar\xi}(\xi)|}{|f^*_\xi(\xi)| - |f^*_{\bar\xi}(\xi)|}\right]^{\frac{1}{2}} \cdot J^{\frac{1}{2}}(\xi) = K^{\frac{1}{2}}_{\mu^*}(\xi) \cdot J^{\frac{1}{2}}(\xi)\,. \tag{103}$$

Hence by the Hölder inequality for integrals, see, e.g., Theorem 189 in [43], we have that

$$\int\limits_{|\xi|<r_0} \left(|f^*_\xi(\xi)| + |f^*_{\bar\xi}(\xi)|\right) dm(\xi) \leq \left(\int\limits_{|\xi|<r_0} K_{\mu^*}(\xi)\, dm(\xi)\right)^{\frac{1}{2}} \cdot \left(\int\limits_{|\xi|<r_0} J(\xi)\, dm(\xi)\right)^{\frac{1}{2}} \tag{104}$$

and, since the latter factor in (104) is estimated by the area of $f^*(\mathbb{D}(r_0))$, see, e.g., the Lebesgue theorem in Section III.2.3 of the monograph [13], we conclude that both partial derivatives f^*_ξ and $f^*_{\bar\xi}$ are integrable in the disk $\mathbb{D}(r_0)$.

Next, note that the function $Q_*(\xi) := Q(1/\xi)$ is of the class BMO in a neighborhood of the origin with respect to the spherical area as well as with respect to the usual area, see, e.g., again Lemma B.3 in [17], because also the spherical area is invariant under rotations of the sphere $\mathbb{S}^2$ in the stereographic projection. Moreover, by (86) and (99), we obtain that

$$\lim_{r\to 0} \frac{1}{r^2} \int\limits_{|\xi|<r} |\mu^*(\xi)|\, dm(\xi) = 0\,. \tag{105}$$

Thus, by Theorems 3 we conclude that f^* is asymptotically homogeneous at the origin, i.e.,

$$\lim_{\substack{\xi\to 0,\\ \xi\in\mathbb{C}^*}} \frac{f^*(\xi\zeta)}{f^*(\xi)} = \zeta \quad \forall\, \zeta \in \mathbb{C} \tag{106}$$

and, furthermore, the limit in (106) is locally uniform in the parameter ζ.

After the inverse replacements of the variables $\xi \longmapsto w := 1/\xi$ and the functions $f^*(\xi) \longmapsto f(w) = 1/f^*(1/w)$ the relation (106) can be rewritten in the form

$$\lim_{\substack{w\to\infty,\\ w\in\mathbb{C}}} \frac{f(w)}{f(w\zeta^{-1})} = \zeta \quad \forall\, \zeta \in \mathbb{C}\,. \tag{107}$$

Finally, after one more change of variables $w \longmapsto z := w\zeta^{-1}$, the latter is transformed into (90), where the limit is locally uniform with respect to the parameter $\zeta \in \mathbb{C}$. □

Choosing $\psi_{z_0,\varepsilon}(t) \equiv 1/(t\log(1/t))$ in Lemma 4, we obtain by Proposition 2 the following.

Theorem 9. *Let a function $\mu : \mathbb{C} \to \mathbb{C}$ be measurable with $|\mu(z)| < 1$ a.e., K_μ have a majorant Q of the class BMO in a neighborhood U of ∞ and satisfy (91). Suppose also that $K^T_\mu(z, z_0) \leqslant Q_{z_0}(z)$ a.e. in U_{z_0} for every point $z_0 \in \mathbb{C} \setminus U$, a neighborhood U_{z_0} of z_0 and a function $Q_{z_0} : U_{z_0} \to [0,\infty]$ in the class $\mathrm{FMO}(z_0)$. Then the Beltrami Equation (2) has a regular homeomorphic solution f in $\mathbb{C}$ with $f(0) = 0$, $f(1) = 1$ and $f(\infty) = \infty$ that is asymptotically homogeneous at infinity.*

As a particular case of Theorem 9, we obtain the following central theorem in terms of BMO.

Theorem 10. *Let a function $\mu : \mathbb{C} \to \mathbb{C}$ be measurable with $|\mu(z)| < 1$ a.e., K_μ have a majorant Q of the class* BMO($\mathbb{C}$) *and satisfy (91). Then the Beltrami Equation (2) has a regular homeomorphic solution f in $\mathbb{C}$ with $f(0) = 0$, $f(1) = 1$ and $f(\infty) = \infty$ that is asymptotically homogeneous at infinity.*

Note also that, in particular, by Proposition 1 the conclusion of Theorem 9 holds if every point $z_0 \in \mathbb{C} \setminus U$ is the Lebesgue point of the function Q_{z_0}.

By Corollary 1 we obtain the next fine consequence of Theorem 9, too.

Corollary 15. *Let $\mu : \mathbb{C} \to \mathbb{C}$ be a measurable function with $|\mu(z)| < 1$ a.e., K_μ have a majorant Q of the class BMO in a neighborhood U of ∞, satisfy (91) and*

$$\overline{\lim_{\varepsilon\to 0}} \fint_{\mathbb{D}(z_0,\varepsilon)} K_\mu^T(z,z_0)\, dm(z) < \infty \qquad \forall\, z_0 \in \mathbb{C} \setminus U . \tag{108}$$

Then the Beltrami Equation (2) has a regular homeomorphic solution f in $\mathbb{C}$ with $f(0) = 0$, $f(1) = 1$ and $f(\infty) = \infty$ that is asymptotically homogeneous at infinity.

By (5), we also obtain the following consequences of Theorem 9.

Corollary 16. *Let $\mu : \mathbb{C} \to \mathbb{C}$ be a measurable function with $|\mu(z)| < 1$ a.e., K_μ have a majorant Q of the class BMO in $\mathbb{C}$ and satisfy (91). Then the Beltrami Equation (2) has a regular homeomorphic solution f in $\mathbb{C}$ with $f(0) = 0$, $f(1) = 1$ and $f(\infty) = \infty$ that is asymptotically homogeneous at infinity.*

Corollary 17. *Let $\mu : \mathbb{C} \to \mathbb{C}$ be a measurable function with $|\mu(z)| < 1$ a.e., K_μ have a majorant Q of the class BMO in a neighborhood U of ∞, satisfy (91) and $K_\mu(z) \leqslant Q_*(z)$ a.e. in $\mathbb{C} \setminus U$ with a function $Q : \mathbb{C} \to \mathbb{R}^+$ of the class* FMO$(\mathbb{C} \setminus U)$*. Then the Beltrami Equation (2) has a regular homeomorphic solution f in $\mathbb{C}$ with $f(0) = 0$, $f(1) = 1$ and $f(\infty) = \infty$ that is asymptotically homogeneous at infinity.*

Remark 13. *In particular, the conclusion of Corollary 17 holds if $Q_* \in$* $W^{1,2}_{\text{loc}}$ *because* $W^{1,2}_{\text{loc}} \subset$ VMO_{loc}, *see, e.g., [10].*

Similarly, choosing $\psi_{z_0,\varepsilon}(t) \equiv 1/t$ in Lemma 4, we come also to the next statement.

Theorem 11. *Let $\mu : \mathbb{C} \to \mathbb{C}$ be a measurable function with $|\mu(z)| < 1$ a.e., K_μ have a majorant Q of the class BMO in a neighborhood U of ∞, satisfy (91) and, for some $\varepsilon_0 = \varepsilon(z_0) > 0$,*

$$\int\limits_{\varepsilon<|z-z_0|<\varepsilon_0} K_\mu^T(z,z_0)\,\frac{dm(z)}{|z-z_0|^2} = o\left(\left[\log\frac{1}{\varepsilon}\right]^2\right) \qquad \text{as } \varepsilon \to 0 \qquad \forall\, z_0 \in \mathbb{C} \setminus U . \tag{109}$$

Then the Beltrami Equation (2) has a regular homeomorphic solution f in $\mathbb{C}$ with $f(0) = 0$, $f(1) = 1$ and $f(\infty) = \infty$ that is asymptotically homogeneous at infinity.

Remark 14. *Choosing $\psi_{z_0,\varepsilon}(t) \equiv 1/(t \log 1/t)$ instead of $\psi(t) = 1/t$ in Lemma 4, we are able to replace (109) by*

$$\int\limits_{\varepsilon<|z-z_0|<\varepsilon_0} \frac{K_\mu^T(z,z_0)\, dm(z)}{\left(|z-z_0| \log \frac{1}{|z-z_0|}\right)^2} = o\left(\left[\log\log\frac{1}{\varepsilon}\right]^2\right) \tag{110}$$

In general, we are able to give here the whole scale of the corresponding conditions in log *using functions $\psi(t)$ of the form $1/(t \log 1/t \cdot \log\log 1/t \cdot \ldots \cdot \log\ldots\log 1/t)$.*

Now, choosing in Lemma 4 the functional parameter $\psi_{z_0,\varepsilon}(t) \equiv \psi_{z_0}(t) := 1/[tk_\mu^T(z_0,t)]$, where $k_\mu^T(z_0,r)$ is the average of $K_\mu^T(z,z_0)$ over the circle $S(z_0,r) := \{z \in \mathbb{C} : |z-z_0| = r\}$, we obtain one more important conclusion.

Theorem 12. *Let $\mu : \mathbb{C} \to \mathbb{C}$ be a measurable function with $|\mu(z)| < 1$ a.e., K_μ have a majorant Q of the class BMO in a neighborhood U of ∞, satisfy (91) and, for some $\varepsilon_0 = \varepsilon(z_0) > 0$,*

$$\int\limits_0^{\varepsilon_0} \frac{dr}{rk_\mu^T(z_0,r)} = \infty \qquad \forall\, z_0 \in \mathbb{C} \setminus U\,. \tag{111}$$

Then the Beltrami Equation (2) has a regular homeomorphic solution f in $\mathbb{C}$ with $f(0) = 0$, $f(1) = 1$ and $f(\infty) = \infty$ that is asymptotically homogeneous at infinity.

Corollary 18. *Let $\mu : \mathbb{C} \to \mathbb{C}$ be a measurable function with $|\mu(z)| < 1$ a.e., K_μ have a majorant Q of the class BMO in a neighborhood U of ∞, satisfy (91) and*

$$k_\mu^T(z_0,\varepsilon) = O\left(\log\frac{1}{\varepsilon}\right) \qquad as\ \varepsilon \to 0 \qquad \forall\, z_0 \in \mathbb{C} \setminus U\,. \tag{112}$$

Then the Beltrami Equation (2) has a regular homeomorphic solution f in $\mathbb{C}$ with $f(0) = 0$, $f(1) = 1$ and $f(\infty) = \infty$ that is asymptotically homogeneous at infinity.

Remark 15. *In particular, the conclusion of Corollary 18 holds if*

$$K_\mu^T(z,z_0) = O\left(\log\frac{1}{|z-z_0|}\right) \qquad \text{as} \quad z \to z_0 \quad \forall\, z_0 \in \mathbb{C} \setminus U\,. \tag{113}$$

Moreover, the condition (112) can be replaced by the whole series of more weak conditions

$$k_\mu^T(z_0,\varepsilon) = O\left(\left[\log\frac{1}{\varepsilon} \cdot \log\log\frac{1}{\varepsilon} \cdot \ldots \cdot \log\ldots\log\frac{1}{\varepsilon}\right]\right) \qquad \forall\, z_0 \in \mathbb{C} \setminus U\,. \tag{114}$$

Combining Theorems 12, Proposition 4 and Remark 1, we obtain the following result.

Theorem 13. *Let $\mu : \mathbb{C} \to \mathbb{C}$ be a measurable function with $|\mu(z)| < 1$ a.e., K_μ have a majorant Q of the class BMO in a neighborhood U of ∞, satisfy (91) and*

$$\int\limits_{U_{z_0}} \Phi_{z_0}\left(K_\mu^T(z,z_0)\right) dm(z) < \infty \qquad \forall\, z_0 \in \mathbb{C} \setminus U \tag{115}$$

for a neighborhood U_{z_0} of z_0 and a convex non-decreasing function $\Phi_{z_0} : [0,\infty] \to [0,\infty]$ with

$$\int\limits_{\Delta(z_0)}^{\infty} \log\,\Phi_{z_0}(t)\,\frac{dt}{t^2} = +\infty \quad for\ some\ \Delta(z_0) > 0\,. \tag{116}$$

Then the Beltrami Equation (2) has a regular homeomorphic solution f in $\mathbb{C}$ with $f(0) = 0$, $f(1) = 1$ and $f(\infty) = \infty$ that is asymptotically homogeneous at infinity.

Corollary 19. *Let $\mu : \mathbb{C} \to \mathbb{C}$ be a measurable function with $|\mu(z)| < 1$ a.e., K_μ have a majorant Q of the class BMO in a neighborhood U of ∞, satisfy (91) and, for some $\alpha(z_0) > 0$ and a neighborhood U_{z_0} of the point z_0,*

$$\int\limits_{U_{z_0}} e^{\alpha(z_0)K_\mu^T(z,z_0)}\, dm(z) < \infty \qquad \forall\, z_0 \in \mathbb{C} \setminus U\,. \tag{117}$$

Then the Beltrami Equation (2) has a regular homeomorphic solution f in $\mathbb{C}$ with $f(0) = 0$, $f(1) = 1$ and $f(\infty) = \infty$ that is asymptotically homogeneous at infinity.

Since $K^T_\mu(z, z_0) \leqslant K_\mu(z)$ for z and $z_0 \in \mathbb{C}$, we also obtain the following consequences of Theorem 13.

Corollary 20. *Let $\mu : \mathbb{C} \to \mathbb{C}$ be a measurable function with $|\mu(z)| < 1$ a.e., K_μ have a majorant Q of the class BMO in a neighborhood U of ∞, satisfy (91) and*

$$\int\limits_{\mathbb{C}\setminus U} \Phi(K_\mu(z))\, dm(z) < \infty \tag{118}$$

for a convex non-decreasing function $\Phi : [0, \infty] \to [0, \infty]$ such that, for some $\delta > 0$,

$$\int\limits_{\delta}^{\infty} \log \Phi(t) \frac{dt}{t^2} = +\infty\,. \tag{119}$$

Then the Beltrami Equation (2) has a regular homeomorphic solution f in $\mathbb{C}$ with $f(0) = 0$, $f(1) = 1$ and $f(\infty) = \infty$ that is asymptotically homogeneous at infinity.

Corollary 21. *Let $\mu : \mathbb{C} \to \mathbb{C}$ be a measurable function with $|\mu(z)| < 1$ a.e., K_μ have a majorant Q of the class BMO in a neighborhood U of ∞, satisfy (91) and, for some $\alpha > 0$,*

$$\int\limits_{\mathbb{C}\setminus U} e^{\alpha K_\mu(z)}\, dm(z) < \infty\,. \tag{120}$$

Then the Beltrami Equation (2) has a regular homeomorphic solution f in $\mathbb{C}$ with $f(0) = 0$, $f(1) = 1$ and $f(\infty) = \infty$ that is asymptotically homogeneous at infinity.

Corollary 22. *Recall that by Theorem 5.1 in [22] the condition (119) is not only sufficient but also necessary for the existence of regular homeomorphic solutions for all Beltrami Equation (2) with the integral constraints (118), see also Remark 11.*

6. Conclusions

Thus, this paper contains a number of effective criteria for the existence of regular homeomorphic solutions for the Beltrami equations with asymptotic homogeneity at infinity where the BMO condition in a neighborhood of infinity plays a key role.

Finally, these results can be applied to the fluid mechanics in strongly anisotropic and inhomogeneous media because the Beltrami equation is a complex form of the main equation of hydromechanics, see, e.g., Theorem 16.1.6 in [15]; these results will be published elsewhere.

Author Contributions: Conceptualization, V.G., V.R., E.S. and E.Y.; methodology, V.G., V.R.; formal analysis V.G. and V.R.; investigation, E.S. and E.Y.; writing—original draft preparation, V.R., E.S.; writing—review and editing, V.G. and E.S.; supervision, V.R.; project administration, E.S. All authors have read and agreed to the published version of the manuscript.

Funding: This research received no external funding.

Acknowledgments: Dedicated to the memory of mathematicians Fritz John and Louis Nirenberg.

Conflicts of Interest: The authors declare no conflict of interest.

References

1. John, F.; Nirenberg, L. On functions of bounded mean oscillation. *Comm. Pure Appl. Math.* **1961**, *14*, 415–426. [CrossRef]
2. Heinonen, J.; Kilpelainen, T.; Martio, O. *Nonlinear Potential Theory of Degenerate Elliptic Equations*; Oxford Mathematical Monographs, Clarendon Press: Oxford, UK, 1993.

3. Reimann, H.M.; Rychener, T. *Funktionen Beschränkter Mittlerer Oscillation*; Lecture Notes in Math.; Springer: Berlin/Heidelberg, Germany, 1975; Volume 487.
4. Sarason, D. Functions of vanishing mean oscillation. *Trans. Am. Math. Soc.* **1975**, *207*, 391–405. [CrossRef]
5. Chiarenza, F.; Frasca, M.; Longo, P. $W^{2,p}$-solvability of the Dirichlet problem for nondivergence elliptic equations with VMO coefficients. *Trans. Am. Math. Soc.* **1993**, *336*, 841–853.
6. Iwaniec, T.; Sbordone, C. Riesz transforms and elliptic PDEs with VMO coefficients. *J. d'Anal. Math.* **1998**, *74*, 183–212. [CrossRef]
7. Palagachev, D.K. Quasilinear elliptic equations with VMO coefficients. *Trans. Am. Math. Soc.* **1995**, *347*, 2481–2493. [CrossRef]
8. Ragusa, M.A. Elliptic boundary value problem in vanishing mean oscillation hypothesis. *Comment. Math. Univ. Carol.* **1999**, *40*, 651–663.
9. Ragusa, M.A.; Tachikawa, A. Partial regularity of the minimizers of quadratic functionals with VMO coefficients. *J. Lond. Math. Soc. II. Ser.* **2005**, *72*, 609–620. [CrossRef]
10. Brezis, H.; Nirenberg, L. Degree theory and BMO. I. Compact manifolds without boundaries. *Selecta Math.* **1995**, *1*, 197–263. [CrossRef]
11. Ahlfors, L. *Lectures on Quasiconformal Mappings*; Van Nostrand: New York, NY, USA, 1966.
12. Bojarski, B. Generalized solutions of a system of differential equations of the first order of the elliptic type with discontinuous coefficients. *Mat. Sb. N. Ser.* **1958**, *43*, 451–503.
13. Lehto, O.; Virtanen, K.I. *Quasiconformal Mappings in the Plane*; Die Grundlehren der Mathematischen Wissenschaften 126; Springer: Berlin/Heidelberg, Germany, 1973.
14. Vekua, I.N. *Generalized Analytic Functions*; Pergamon Press: London, UK, 1962.
15. Astala, K.; Iwaniec, T.; Martin, G. *Elliptic Partial Differential Equations and Quasiconformal Mappings in the Plane*; Princeton Mathematical Series 48; Princeton University Press: Princeton, NJ, USA, 2009.
16. Gutlyanskii, V.; Ryazanov, V.; Srebro, U., Yakubov, E. *The Beltrami Equation: A Geometric Approach*; Developments in Mathematics 26; Springer: Berlin/Heidelberg, Germany, 2012.
17. Martio, O.; Ryazanov, V.; Srebro, U.; Yakubov, E. *Moduli in Modern Mapping Theory*; Springer Monographs in Mathematics; Springer: New York, NY, USA, 2009.
18. Andreian Cazacu, C. On the length-area dilatation. *Complex Var. Theory Appl. Int. J.* **2005**, *50*, 765–776. [CrossRef]
19. Gutlyanskii, V.; Martio, O.; Sugawa, T.; Vuorinen, M. On the degenerate Beltrami equation. *Trans. Am. Math. Soc.* **2005**, *357*, 875–900. [CrossRef]
20. Lehto, O. Homeomorphisms with a prescribed dilatation. *Lect. Notes Math.* **1968**, *118*, 58–73.
21. Ryazanov, V.; Srebro, U; Yakubov, E. On the theory of the Beltrami equation. *Ukr. Math. J.* **2006**, *58*, 1786–1798. [CrossRef]
22. Ryazanov, V.; Srebro, U; Yakubov, E. Integral conditions in the theory of the Beltrami equations. *Complex Var. Elliptic Equ.* **2012**, *57*, 1247–1270. [CrossRef]
23. Ryazanov, V.; Srebro, U; Yakubov, E. The Beltrami equation and ring homeomorphisms. *Ukrainian Math. Bull.* **2007**, *4*, 79–115.
24. Gehring, F.W.; Lehto, O. On the total differentiability of functions of a complex variable. *Ann. Acad. Sci. Fenn. A I Math.* **1959**, *272*, 1–9.
25. Menchoff, D. Sur les differentielles totales des fonctions univalentes. *Math. Ann.* **1931**, *105*, 75–85. [CrossRef]
26. Belinskii, P.P. *General Properties of Quasiconformal Mappings*; Nauka: Novosibirsk, Russia, 1974. (In Russian)
27. Ryazanov, V.I. A criterion for differentiability in the sense of Belinskii and its consequences. *Ukr. Math. J.* **1992**, *44*, 254–258. [CrossRef]
28. Gutlyanskii, V.Ya.; Ryazanov, V.I. On the local behaviour of quasi-conformal mappings. *Izv. Math.* **1995**, *59*, 471–498. [CrossRef]
29. Brakalova, M. Suffcient and necessary conditions for conformality at a point. I. Geometric viewpoint. *Complex Var. Elliptic Equ.* **2010**, *55*, 137–155. [CrossRef]
30. Brakalova, M. Suffcient and necessary conditions for conformality. II. Analytic viewpoint. *Ann. Acad. Sci. Fenn. Math.* **2010**, *35*, 235–254. [CrossRef]
31. Brakalova, M.; Jenkins, J.A. On the local behavior of certain homeomorphisms. *Kodai Math. J.* **1994**, *17*, 201–213. [CrossRef]
32. Brakalova, M.; Jenkins, J.A. On the local behavior of certain homeomorphisms. II. *J. Math. Sci.* **1999**, *95*, 2178–2184; *Zap. Nauchn. Semin. POMI.* **1997**, *236*, 11–20. [CrossRef]
33. Gutlyanskii, V.; Martio, O. Conformality of a quasiconformal mapping at a point. *J. Anal. Math.* **2003**, *91*, 179–192. [CrossRef]
34. Lehto, O. On the differentiability of quasi-conformal mappings with prescribed complex dilatation. *Ann. Acad. Sci. Fenn. Ser. A I* **1960**, *275*, 28.
35. Teichmüller, O. Untersuchungen über konforme und quasikonforme Abbildung. *Dtsch. Math.* **1938**, *3*, 621–678.
36. Ignat'ev, A.A.; Ryazanov, V.I. Finite mean oscillation in the mapping theory. *Ukrainian Math. Bull.* **2005**, *2*, 403–424.
37. Väisälä, J. *Lectures on n-Dimensional Quasiconformal Mappings*; Lecture Notes in Mathematics 229; Springer: Berlin/Heidelberg, Germany, 1971.
38. Salimov, R. On regular homeomorphisms in the plane. *Ann. Acad. Sci. Fenn. Math.* **2010**, *35*, 285–289. [CrossRef]
39. Reshetnyak, Y.G. *Space Mappings with Bounded Distortion*; Translations of Mathematical Monographs 73; American Mathematical Society (AMS): Providence, RI, USA, 1989.
40. Ponomarev, S.P. The $N^{-1}-$property of mappings, and Lusin s $(N)-$condition. *Mat. Zametki.* **1995**, *58*, 411–418; *Math. Notes.* **1995**, *58*, 960–965.

41. Kuratowski, K. *Topology*; New Edition, Revised and Augmented. (English); Academic Press: London, UK; PWN-Polish Scientific Publishers: Warszawa, Poland, 1966; Volume I.
42. Dunford, N.; Schwartz Jacob, T. *Linear Operators. I. General Theory*; Pure and Applied Mathematics; Interscience Publishers: New York, NY, USA; London, UK, 1958; Volume 7.
43. Hardy, G.H.; Littlewood, J.E.; Polya, G. *Inequalities*; Cambridge University Press: Cambridge, UK, 1988.
44. Lawrentjew, M.A.; Schabat, B.W. *Methoden der Komplexen Funktionentheorie. (German) Mathematik für Naturwissenschaft und Technik 13*; VEB Deutscher Verlag der Wissenschaften: Berlin, Germany, 1967.
45. Polya, G.; Szego, G. *Aufgaben und Lehrsätze aus der Analysis. Bd. I: Reihen, Integralrechnung, Funktionentheorie*; (German)-Die Grundlehren der Mathematischen Wissenschaften in Einzeldarstellungen 19; Springer: Berlin/Heidelberg, Germany, 1925.
46. Reimann, H.M. Functions of bounded mean oscillation and quasiconformal mappings. *Comment. Math. Helv.* **1974**, *49*, 260–276. [CrossRef]
47. Spanier, E.H. *Algebraic Topology*; Springer: Berlin/Heidelberg, Germany, 1995.
48. Fischer, W.; Lieb, I. *A Course in Complex Analysis. From Basic Results to Advanced Topics*; Vieweg + Teubner: Wiesbaden, Germany, 2012.
49. Mazya, V.G. *Sobolev Spaces*; Springer: Berlin/Heidelberg, Germany, 1985.

axioms

MDPI

Article

Supersymmetric Polynomials and a Ring of Multisets of a Banach Algebra

Iryna Chernega [1] and Andriy Zagorodnyuk [2,*]

1 Institute for Applied Problems of Mechanics and Mathematics, Ukrainian Academy of Sciences, 3b, Naukova Str., 79060 Lviv, Ukraine
2 Faculty of Mathematics and Computer Science, Vasyl Stefanyk Precarpathian National University, 57 Shevchenka Str., 76018 Ivano-Frankivsk, Ukraine
* Correspondence: andriy.zagorodnyuk@pnu.edu.ua

Abstract: In this paper, we consider rings of multisets consisting of elements of a Banach algebra. We investigate the algebraic and topological structures of such rings and the properties of their homomorphisms. The rings of multisets arise as natural domains of supersymmetric functions. We introduce a complete metrizable topology on a given ring of multisets and extend some known results about structures of the rings to the general case. In addition, we consider supersymmetric polynomials and other supersymmetric functions related to these rings. This paper contains a number of examples and some discussions.

Keywords: set of multisets; topological rings; supersymmetric polynomials; symmetric bases

MSC: 46H15; 46G20; 46G25

Citation: Chernega, I.; Zagorodnyuk, A. Supersymmetric Polynomials and a Ring of Multisets of a Banach Algebra. *Axioms* **2022**, *11*, 511. https://doi.org/10.3390/axioms11100511

Academic Editor: Hans J. Haubold

Received: 31 July 2022
Accepted: 25 September 2022
Published: 27 September 2022

1. Introduction

In recent years, symmetric structures and mappings in infinite-dimensional spaces have been studied by numerous authors [1–11]. In many problems of algebra and analysis [1,6], as well as in applications in symmetric neural networks (see, e.g., [12–15]), it is crucial to know the invariants of a given (semi)-group $\mathcal{S}$ acting on a Banach space X. The invariants can be described as elements of algebras of $\mathcal{S}$-symmetric functions on X. The Classical Invariant Theory, which was developed in the middle of the last century, investigated polynomial invariants of a group acting on a finite-dimensional linear space. The famous Nagata counterexample to the general case of Hilbert's fourteenth problem shows that polynomial algebras on $\mathbb{C}^n$ may be not finitely generated.

Symmetric polynomials and analytic functions on infinite-dimensional Banach spaces were investigated first by [16–19]. In particular, in [16,17], algebraic bases were described in algebras of symmetric polynomials on various Banach spaces with symmetric structures. These investigations were continued in [19–26] and others. To describe the spectrum of a uniform algebra of $\mathcal{S}$-symmetric functions on X, it is important to have more information about the quotient set $X/\sim$, where "$\sim$" is the relation of equivalence "up to the action of $\mathcal{S}$" on X. Such a quotient set may be interesting in itself and has applications in informatics and neural networks. If X is a sequence space and $\mathcal{S}$ is the group of permutations of elements of the sequences, then $X/\sim$ can be considered as a set of nonzero multisets—completed in a metrizable topology—induced from X. The set $X/\sim$ has a semiring structure with respect to natural algebraic operations. The commutative semiring can be extended to a ring by using a standard procedure from K-theory (see, e.g., [27]). Such a ring $\mathcal{M}$ of multisets for the case $X = \ell_1$ was investigated in [7,28]. In particular, homomorphisms and ideals of $\mathcal{M}$ were considered, and it was shown that each supersymmetric polynomial on $\ell_1 \times \ell_1$ can be extended to the ring $\mathcal{M}$. In [29], the properties of the ring of multisets of integer numbers were studied, and some applications to cryptography were found.

In this paper, we consider possible generalizations of the results obtained in [7] for more general cases. Instead of the sequence space ℓ_1, we consider the space of sequences $(x_1, x_2, \ldots, x_n, \ldots)$, where x_n are elements of a Banach algebra $\mathcal{A}$ and each sequence of norms, $(\|x_1\|_{\mathcal{A}}, \|x_2\|_{\mathcal{A}}, \ldots, \|x_n\|_{\mathcal{A}}, \ldots)$, is a vector in a Banach space X with a norm $\|\cdot\|_X$ and a symmetric basis $\{e_n\}$. Let us recall (see [30] for details) that a sequence $\{e_n\}$ is a *topological* (or *Schauder*) basis in a Banach space X if every element $x \in X$ can be uniquely expressed by

$$x = \sum_{n=1}^{\infty} x_n e_n = \lim_{m\to\infty} \sum_{n=1}^{m} x_n e_n,$$

where the limit is taken in $(X, \|\cdot\|_X)$. From here, in particular, we have that $x_n \to 0$ as $n \to \infty$.

A topological basis is called *symmetric* if it is equivalent to the basis $\{e_{\sigma(n)}\}$ for every permutation σ on the set of natural numbers $\mathbb{N}$. This means that for every σ, a series $\sum_{n=1}^{\infty} x_n e_n$ converges if and only if $\sum_{n=1}^{\infty} x_n e_{\sigma(n)}$ converges. It is known [30] (p. 114) that every Banach space X with a symmetric basis has an equivalent so-called *symmetric* norm such that

$$\left\| \sum_{n=1}^{\infty} x_n \theta_n e_{\sigma(n)} \right\|_X = \left\| \sum_{n=1}^{\infty} x_n e_n \right\|_X$$

for every permutation σ and sequence of numbers $\{\theta_n\}$ such that $|\theta_n| = 1$. Throughout this paper, we assume that X is endowed with a symmetric norm. In this case, we know that for every $x \in X$, $|x_n| \le 2\|x\|$.

In Section 2, we construct a ring of multisets $\mathcal{M}_X(\mathcal{D})$ of sets from a multiplicative semigroup $\mathcal{D}$ of $\mathcal{A}$ and investigate the basic properties. In particular, we show that $\mathcal{M}_X(\mathcal{D})$ is complete in a metrizable topology induced from X. In Section 3, we investigate homomorphisms of $\mathcal{M}_X(\mathcal{D})$ and related supersymmetric polynomials. In addition, we consider some examples and make discussions. We refer the reader to [31] for more information about polynomials on Banach spaces and to [32] for details on the classical theory of symmetric functions.

2. Group Rings of Multisets

Let X be a Banach space with a normalized symmetric basis $\{e_n\}$ and a symmetric norm $\|\cdot\|_X$, let $\mathcal{A}$ be a Banach algebra with an identity $\mathfrak{e}$, and let $\mathcal{D}$ be a closed multiplicative subgroup in $\mathcal{A}$ containing $\mathfrak{e}$. We denote by $X(\mathcal{D})$ the set of sequences $u = (x_1, \ldots, x_n, \ldots)$, $x_i \in \mathcal{D}$, and

$$\|u\| = \left\| \sum_{i=1}^{\infty} e_n \|x_n\|_{\mathcal{A}} \right\|_X.$$

In addition, let us denote by $\Lambda_X(\mathcal{D}) = X(\mathcal{D}) \times X(\mathcal{D})$, and we represent each element $v \in \Lambda_X(\mathcal{D})$ as

$$v = (y|x) = (\ldots, y_n, \ldots, y_2, y_1 | x_1, x_2, \ldots, x_n, \ldots),$$

$x, y \in X(\mathcal{D})$. Clearly, $\Lambda_X(\mathcal{A})$ is a Banach space with respect to the norm

$$\|v\| = \|x\| + \|y\|,$$

and $\Lambda_X(\mathcal{D})$ is its closed subset.

For a given $x \in \Lambda_X(\mathcal{D})$, we denote by $\operatorname{supp} x$ the subset of all natural numbers $n \in \mathbb{N}$ such that $x_n \ne 0$.

Let σ, μ be permutations on $\mathbb{N}$ and $(y|x) \in X(\mathcal{D})$. We define

$$(\sigma, \mu)(y|x) = (\ldots, y_{\sigma(n)}, \ldots, y_{\sigma(1)} | x_{\mu(1)}, \ldots, x_{\mu(n)}, \ldots).$$

Let $u = (y|x)$ and $w = (d|b)$ be in $\Lambda_X(\mathcal{D})$. Then,

$$u \bullet w = (y \bullet d|x \bullet b) = (\dots, d_n, y_n, \dots, d_1, y_1|x_1, b_1, \dots, x_n, b_n, \dots).$$

Note that if $x, b \in X(\mathcal{D})$, then $\|x \bullet b\| \leq \|x\| + \|b\|$. Hence, $u \bullet w \in \Lambda_X(\mathcal{D})$ for all $u, w \in \Lambda_X(\mathcal{D})$.

Let us consider an equivalence defined as $(y|x) \sim (y'|x')$ if and only if there are vectors $(a|a), (c|c) \in \Lambda_X(\mathcal{D})$, and bijections σ and μ such that σ maps $\operatorname{supp} x \bullet c$ onto $\operatorname{supp} x' \bullet a$ and μ maps $\operatorname{supp} y \bullet c$ onto $\operatorname{supp} y' \bullet a$; in addition,

$$(\sigma, \mu)\big((y'|x') \bullet (a|a)\big) = (y|x) \bullet (c|c). \tag{1}$$

Let us denote by $\mathcal{M}(\mathcal{D}) = \mathcal{M}_X(\mathcal{D})$ the quotient set $\Lambda_X(\mathcal{D})/\sim$ with respect to the equivalence "$\sim$". We denote by $[(y|x)] \in \mathcal{M}(\mathcal{D})$ the class of equivalence containing element $(y|x)$. Clearly, for every $a \in X(\mathcal{D})$, $(a|a) \sim (0|0)$, and so $[(y|x) \bullet (x|y)] = [(0|0)]$. In addition, we denote $\mathcal{M}^+(\mathcal{D}) = \{[(0|x)] : x \in \Lambda_X(\mathcal{D})\}$.

Let us explain the definition of the equivalence in a more detailed form. The requirement that σ and μ act bijectively between supports of corresponding vectors means that zero coordinates "do not matter", that is, for example,

$$(\dots, y_n, \dots, y_2, y_1|x_1, x_2, \dots, x_n, \dots) \sim (\dots, y_n, 0, \dots, 0, y_2, 0, y_1|x_1, 0, x_2, 0, \dots, 0, x_n, \dots).$$

In addition, for example,

$$(\dots, y_n, \dots, y_2, y_1|x_1, x_2, \dots, x_n, \dots) \sim (\dots, y_n, \dots, y_2, y_1, \lambda|\lambda, x_1, x_2, \dots, x_n, \dots)$$

for any $\lambda \in \mathbb{C}$. In addition, the classes of equivalence are invariant with respect to permutations of coordinates of x and of y separately. This approach allows us to consider $\mathcal{M}^+(\mathcal{D})$ as a set of multisets of $\mathcal{D}$. More exactly, the subset $\mathcal{M}^+_{00}(\mathcal{D})$ consisting of all elements in $\mathcal{M}^+(\mathcal{D})$ with finite supports can be naturally identified with the set of all finite multisets of *nonzero* elements in $\mathcal{D}$, and the operation "$\bullet$" is actually the union of multisets.

We say that $(y'|x')$ is an *irreducible* representative of $[u] \in \mathcal{M}(\mathcal{D})$ if $[(y'|x')] = [u]$, and $(y'|x') \sim (y|x)$ implies that

$$(y|x) = (\sigma, \mu)\big((y'|x') \bullet (a|a)\big)$$

for some permutations σ, μ on $\mathbb{N}$ and $(a|a) \in \Lambda_X(\mathcal{D})$. In other words, for every nonzero coordinate x'_i of x', we have $x'_i \neq y'_j$ for all coordinates y'_j of y'.

Proposition 1. *For every $[u] \in \mathcal{M}(\mathcal{D})$, there exists an irreducible representative.*

Proof. Let $(y|x)$ be a representative of $[u]$. Since elements $\sum_n e_n \|x_n\|_{\mathcal{A}}$ and $\sum_n e_n \|y_n\|_{\mathcal{A}}$ belong to the Banach space X with the Schauder basis e_n, it follows that $\|x_n\|_{\mathcal{A}} \to 0$, and $\|y_n\|_{\mathcal{A}} \to 0$ as $n \to \infty$. Without loss of generality, we may assume that the coordinates of x are ordered so that $\|x_1\|_{\mathcal{A}} \geq \|x_2\|_{\mathcal{A}} \geq \dots \geq \|x_n\|_{\mathcal{A}} \geq \cdots$. If there is j such that $x_1 = y_j$, then let us remove the coordinate x_1 in x and y_j in y, and we denote by $x^{(1)}$ and $y^{(1)}$ the resulting vectors. If such a number j does not exist, we denote $x^{(1)} = x$ and $y^{(1)} = y$. Suppose that $x^{(n)}$ and $y^{(n)}$ are already constructed. If there is j such that $x_{n+1} = y_j$, then we remove the coordinate x_{n+1} in $x^{(n)}$ and y_j in $y^{(n)}$ and denote by $x^{(n+1)}$ and $y^{(n+1)}$ the resulting vectors. Otherwise, we set $x^{(n+1)} = x^{(n)}$ and $y^{(n+1)} = y^{(n)}$. Thus, we obtain the sequence $(y^{(n)}|x^{(n)})$ in $\Lambda_X(\mathcal{D})$, which is obviously fundamental. By the completeness of $\Lambda_X(\mathcal{D})$, there exists a limit

$$(y'|x') = \lim_{n \to \infty} (y^{(n)}|x^{(n)}).$$

Let a be a vector in $X(\mathcal{D})$ such that its coordinates a_n are exactly removed coordinates from x. Then, $(y|x) = (y' \bullet a|x' \bullet a)$, and so $(y'|x')$ is a representative of $[u]$. By the construction, $(y'|x')$ is irreducible. □

Now, we can introduce a commutative operation "+" on $\mathcal{M}(\mathcal{D})$.

Definition 1. *For a given* $\mathbf{u} = [u] = [(y|x)]$ *and* $\mathbf{w} = [w] = [(d|b)]$ *in* $\mathcal{M}(\mathcal{D})$, *we define*

$$\mathbf{u} + \mathbf{w} := [u \bullet w] = [(y \bullet d|x \bullet b)].$$

In addition, we set $-\mathbf{u} = -[(y|x)] := [(x|y)]$.

Proposition 2. *The operation "+" is well defined on* $\mathcal{M}(\mathcal{D})$, *and* $(\mathcal{M}(\mathcal{D}), +)$ *is a commutative group with zero (the neutral element),* $0 = [(0|0)] = [(\ldots, 0|0, \ldots)]$.

Proof. From definition of the operation, it follows that $\mathbf{u} + 0 = \mathbf{u}$ and $\mathbf{u} - \mathbf{u} = 0$. If $\mathbf{u} = [(y'|x')]$ and $\mathbf{w} = [(d'|b')]$ are the irreducible representatives $\mathbf{u}$ and $\mathbf{w}$, then, according to (1) and Proposition 1, $(y|x) = (y' \bullet a|x' \bullet a)$ and $(d|b) = (d' \bullet c|b' \bullet c)$ for some a and c. Hence,

$$[(y|x)] + [(d|b)] = [(y'|x') \bullet (a|a)] + [(d'|b') \bullet (c|c)]$$
$$= [(y'|x')] + [(d'|b')] + [(a|a)] + [(c|c)] = [(y'|x')] + [(d'|b')].$$

So, the result does not depend of representatives. □

Let $x, y \in X(\mathcal{D})$. By $x \diamond y$, we denote the resulting sequence of ordering the set $\{x_i y_j : i, j \in \mathbb{N}\}$ with one single index in some fixed order.

Proposition 3. *Let* $x, y \in X(\mathcal{D})$. *Then,* $x \diamond y \in X(\mathcal{D})$ *and* $\|x \diamond y\| \leq 2\|x\|\|y\|$. *Moreover, if* $\mathcal{D}$ *is such that* $\|ab\| = \|a\|\|b\|$ *for every* $a, b \in \mathcal{D}$, *and* $X = c_0$ *or* ℓ_p *for some* $1 \leq p < \infty$, *then* $\|x \diamond y\| = \|x\|\|y\|$.

Proof. Let $k(i,j)$ be a bijection from $\mathbb{N} \times \mathbb{N}$ to $\mathbb{N}$. According to the straightforward calculations,

$$\|x \diamond y\| = \Big\| \sum_{i,j=1}^{\infty} \|x_i y_j\|_{\mathcal{A}} e_{k(i,j)} \Big\|_X \leq \sup_i \|x_i\|_{\mathcal{A}} \Big\| \sum_{i,j=1}^{\infty} \|y_j\|_{\mathcal{A}} e_j \Big\|_X \leq 2\|x\|\|y\|.$$

Let $\mathcal{D}$ be such that $\|ab\| = \|a\|\|b\|$ for every $a, b \in \mathcal{D}$. If $X = \ell_p(\mathcal{D})$, then

$$\|x \diamond y\|^p = \sum_{i,j=1}^{\infty} \|x_i y_j\|_{\mathcal{A}}^p = \sum_{i,j=1}^{\infty} \|x_i\|_{\mathcal{A}}^p \|y_j\|_{\mathcal{A}}^p = \|x\|^p \|y\|^p.$$

If $X = c_0$, then

$$\|x \diamond y\| = \sup_{i,j} \|x_i y_j\|_{\mathcal{A}} = \sup_{i,j} \|x_i\|_{\mathcal{A}} \|y_j\|_{\mathcal{A}} = \|x\|\|y\|.$$

□

Next, let us define a multiplication on $\mathcal{M}(\mathcal{D})$.

Definition 2. *If* $\mathbf{u} = [(0|x)]$ *and* $\mathbf{v} = [(0|y)]$, *we define* $\mathbf{uv} = [(0|x \diamond y)]$. *Finally, if* $\mathbf{u} = [(y|x)]$ *and* $\mathbf{v} = [(d|b)]$ *are in* $\mathcal{M}(\mathcal{D})$, *then we define*

$$\mathbf{uv} = [((y \diamond b) \bullet (x \diamond d)|(y \diamond d) \bullet (x \diamond b))].$$

Using routine calculations, it is easy to check (cf. [7,29]) that the multiplication is well defined and associative and that the distributive low with the addition holds on $\mathcal{M}(\mathcal{D})$. If $\mathcal{A}$ is a commutative Banach algebra, then the introduced multiplication is commutative. So, we have the following proposition.

Proposition 4. *$(\mathcal{M}(\mathcal{D}), +, \cdot)$ is a ring with zero, $0 = [(0|0)]$, and unity, $\mathbb{I} = [(0|\mathfrak{e}, 0, \ldots)]$. If $\mathcal{A}$ is commutative, then $(\mathcal{M}(\mathcal{D}), +, \cdot)$ is commutative.*

Note that $\mathcal{M}(\mathcal{D})$ is not an algebra, even if $\mathcal{D} = \mathbb{C}$, because it is not a linear space (see, e.g., [7]). However, it is possible to introduce a norm on a given ring that has natural properties and induces a metrizable topology. Let us recall the following definition (cf. [33]).

Definition 3. *If R is any ring, then a real-valued function $\|z\|$ defined on R is called a norm for R if it satisfies the following conditions for all $z, r \in R$:*

1. $\|z\| \geq 0$ *and* $\|z\| = 0$ *if and only if* $z = 0$,
2. $\|z + r\| \leq \|z\| + \|r\|$,
3. $\|-z\| = \|z\|$,
4. $\|zr\| \leq C\|z\|\|r\|$ *for some constant* $C > 0$.

Definition 4. *Let us define a norm on $\mathcal{M}(\mathcal{D})$ in the following way:*

$$\|\mathbf{u}\| = \|[(y|x)]\| := \|(y'|x')\| = \|x'\| + \|y'\|,$$

where $(y'|x')$ is an irreducible representative of $\mathbf{u}$.

Proposition 5. *The norm in Definition 4 is well defined on $\mathcal{M}(\mathcal{D})$ and satisfies the conditions of Definition 3. In addition,*

$$\|\mathbf{u}\| = \min_{(y|x)\in\mathbf{u}} (\|x\| + \|y\|).$$

Proof. Note that an irreducible representative of $\mathbf{u}$ is not unique in general. However, if $(y'|x')$ and $(y''|x'')$ are irreducible representatives of $\mathbf{u}$, then they consist of the same coordinates (up to a permutation (σ, μ) of nonzero coordinates), and so, $\|(y'|x')\| = \|(y''|x'')\|$. Thus, the norm is well-defined.

Clearly, if $\mathbf{u} = 0$, then $[(0|0)]$ is its irreducible representative, and so, $\|\mathbf{u}\| = 0$. Otherwise, $\|\mathbf{u}\| \geq 0$. The second property of the norm evidently follows from the corresponding triangle property of the norm on a linear space. In addition, $\|-\mathbf{u}\| = \|(x'|y')\| = \|(y'|x')\| = \|\mathbf{u}\|$.

For any representative $(y|x)$ of $\mathbf{u}$, we have that $\|(y|x)\| \geq \|(y'|x')\|$, where $\|(y'|x')\|$ is an irreducible representative of $\mathbf{u}$. So,

$$\|\mathbf{u}\| = \min_{(y|x)\in\mathbf{u}} (\|x\| + \|y\|).$$

Let $\mathbf{u} = [(y|x)] and \mathbf{w} = [(d|b)] \in \mathcal{M}(\mathcal{D})$, and let $(y'|x')$ and $(b'|d')$ be corresponding irreducible representatives. Then, by Proposition 3,

$$\begin{aligned}\|\mathbf{uw}\| &= \|[(y'|x')(b'|d')]\| = \|[((y' \diamond b') \bullet (x' \diamond d')|(y' \diamond d') \bullet (x' \diamond b'))]\| \\ &\leq \|((y' \diamond b') \bullet (x' \diamond d'))\| + \|((y' \diamond d') \bullet (x' \diamond b'))\| \\ &\leq 2\|y'\|\|b'\| + 2\|x'\|\|d'\| + 2\|y'\|\|b'\| + 2\|x'\|\|b'\| = 2\|\mathbf{u}\|\|\mathbf{w}\|.\end{aligned}$$

Thus, $\|\cdot\|$ satisfies Condition 4 in Definition 3 for $C = 2$. In addition, by Proposition 3, we can put $C = 1$ if $X = c_0$ or ℓ_p, $1 \leq p < \infty$. □

We define a metric ρ on $\mathcal{M}(\mathcal{D})$, associated with the norm in the natural way. Let $\mathbf{u}, \mathbf{w}$ be in $\mathcal{M}(\mathcal{D})$. We set

$$\rho(\mathbf{u}, \mathbf{w}) = \|\mathbf{u} - \mathbf{w}\|.$$

It is well known and easy to check that ρ is a metric.

Example 1. *Let $\mathbf{u}^{(n)} = [(0|h_n, 0, \ldots)]$, $h_n \in \mathcal{D}$ be a sequence in $\mathcal{M}(\mathcal{D})$ such that $h_n \to h$ as $n \to \infty$. If $h \neq 0$, then $\mathbf{u}^{(n)} \to [(0|h, 0, \ldots)]$ if and only if $h_n = h$ for all values of n that are big enough. Indeed, if $h_n \neq h$, then*

$$\|[(0|h_n, 0, \ldots)] - [(0|h, 0, \ldots)]\| = \|[(\ldots, 0, h_n|h, 0, \ldots)]\| = \|h_n\|_{\mathcal{A}} + \|h\|_{\mathcal{A}} \geq \|h\|_{\mathcal{A}}.$$

On the other hand, if $h = 0$, then $\|\mathbf{u}^{(n)} - 0\| = \|h_n\|_{\mathcal{A}} \to 0$ as $n \to \infty$.

Proposition 6. *The quotient map $(y|x) \mapsto [(y|x)]$ is discontinuous as a map from the Banach space $\Lambda_X(\mathcal{D})$ to the metric space $(\mathcal{M}(\mathcal{D}), \rho)$ at each point of $\Lambda_X(\mathcal{D})$, except for zero.*

Proof. Example 1 can be easily modified to show the discontinuity of the quotient map at any nonzero point. Indeed, let $v = (y|x) \neq 0$; then, without loss of generality, we can assume that $x_1 \neq 0$. Consider $u^{(n)} = (y|(1 - 1/n)x_1, x_2, \ldots, x_m, \ldots) \in \Lambda_X(\mathcal{D})$. Then, $u^{(n)} \to v$ in $\Lambda_X(\mathcal{D})$ as $n \to \infty$, but

$$\|[u^{(n)}] - [v]\| = \|[\ldots, 0, x_1|(1 - 1/n)x_1, 0, \ldots\| = 2\|x_1\|_{\mathcal{A}} - \frac{\|x_1\|_{\mathcal{A}}}{n} > \|x_1\|_{\mathcal{A}} > 0,$$

and so the quotient map is discontinuous at v. On the other hand, if a sequence $u^{(n)}$ tends to zero, then $\|[u^{(n)}]\| \to 0$ as $n \to \infty$, and thus, the quotient map is continuous at zero. □

Theorem 1. *The metric space $(\mathcal{M}(\mathcal{D}), \rho)$ is complete.*

Proof. Let $\mathbf{u}$ and $\mathbf{v}$ be in $\mathcal{M}(\mathcal{D})$ and let $(y|x)$ be an irreducible representative of $\mathbf{u}$. We claim that there exists an irreducible representative $(d'|b') \in \mathbf{v}$ such that in $\Lambda_X(\mathcal{D})$, $\|(y|x) - (d'|b')\| < \varepsilon$. Indeed, let $(d|b)$ be any irreducible representative of $\mathbf{v}$. The inequality

$$\|\mathbf{u} - \mathbf{v}\| = \|[(y \bullet b|x \bullet d)]\| < \varepsilon$$

implies that there is an irreducible representative $(c|a)$ of $(y \bullet b|x \bullet d)$ such that $\|c\| + \|a\| < \varepsilon$. Note that $(y \bullet b|x \bullet d)$ is not necessary irreducible. However, since both $(y|x)$ and $(d|b)$ are irreducible, it may happen that some coordinates of y are the same as some coordinates of d and that some coordinates of x are the same as some coordinates of b. Let us construct $(d'|b')$ such that d' is obtained by permutating the coordinates of d, and b' is obtained by permutating the coordinates of b, so the coordinates of d that are equal to some coordinates of y have the same positions in d' as the corresponding coordinates in y, and the coordinates of b that are equal to some coordinates of x have the same positions in b' as the corresponding coordinates in x. Then, $(d'|b') \sim (b|d)$ and

$$\|(y|x) - (d'|b')\| = \|[(y \bullet b'|x \bullet d')]\| = \|c\| + \|a\| < \varepsilon.$$

Let $\mathbf{u}^{(m)}$, $m \in \mathbb{N}$ be a Cauchy sequence in $(\mathcal{M}(\mathcal{D}), \rho)$. Taking a subsequence, if necessary, we can assume that if $n \geq N$ and $m \geq N$, then $\rho(\mathbf{u}^{(m)}, \mathbf{u}^{(n)}) < \frac{1}{2^{N+1}}$. Let us choose irreducible representatives $(y^{(m)}|x^{(m)})$ of $u^{(m)}$ with

$$\|(y^{(m+1)}|x^{(m+1)}) - (y^{(m)}|x^{(m)})\| = \rho(\mathbf{u}^{(m+1)}, \mathbf{u}^{(m)}) < \frac{1}{2^{m+1}}.$$

Thus, if $n \geq N$ and $m \geq N$, then

$$\|(y^{(m)}|x^{(m)}) - (y^{(n)}|x^{(n)})\| < \frac{1}{2^N}.$$

Hence, $(y^{(m)}|x^{(m)})$, $m \in \mathbb{N}$ is a Cauchy sequence in $X(\mathcal{D})$, so it has a limit $z^{(0)} = (y^{(0)}|x^{(0)})$. Let $z_i^{(m)}$ be the ith coordinate of $z^{(m)} = (y^{(m)}|x^{(m)})$, $i \in \mathbb{Z} \setminus \{0\}$, that is, $z_i^{(m)} = x_i^{(m)}$ if $i > 0$ and $z_i^{(m)} = y_{-i}^{(m)}$ if $i < 0$. Clearly, $z_i^{(m)} \to z_i^{(0)}$ as $m \to \infty$. We claim that if $z_i^{(0)} = c \neq 0$, then there is a number N such that for every $m > N$, $z_i^{(m)} = c$. Indeed, if it is not so, then for every $n, m \in \mathbb{N}$, that is big enough, $\rho(\mathbf{u}^{(m)}, \mathbf{u}^{(n)}) > c$, and we have a contradiction.

For a given $\varepsilon > 0$, we denote by z^ε a vector in $X(\mathcal{D})$ such that z^ε has a finite support, $z_i^\varepsilon = z_i^{(0)}$ or $z_i^\varepsilon = 0$, and

$$\rho\Big(\big[z^\varepsilon\big], \big[z^{(0)}\big]\Big) < \frac{\varepsilon}{3}.$$

Note that for this case, $\rho\Big(\big[z^\varepsilon\big], \big[z^{(0)}\big]\Big) = \|z^\varepsilon - z^{(0)}\|$. Let N be a number such that for every $n > N$, $z_i^\varepsilon = z_i^{(n)}$ for all $i \in \operatorname{supp} z^\varepsilon$ and $\|z^{(n)} - z^{(0)}\| < \frac{\varepsilon}{3}$. So,

$$\rho\Big(\big[z^{(n)}\big], \big[z^\varepsilon\big]\Big) = \|z^\varepsilon - z^{(n)}\| \leq \|z^\varepsilon - z^{(0)}\| + \|z^{(n)} - z^{(0)}\| < \frac{2}{3}\varepsilon.$$

Thus,

$$\rho\Big(\big[z^{(n)}\big], \big[z^{(0)}\big]\Big) \leq \rho\Big(\big[z^{(n)}, z^\varepsilon\big]\Big) + \rho\Big(\big[z^\varepsilon, z^{(0)}\big]\Big) < \varepsilon.$$

Therefore, $\mathbf{u} = \big[z^{(0)}\big]$ is the limit of $\mathbf{u}^{(m)}$, and thus, $(\mathcal{M}(\mathcal{D}), \rho)$ is complete. □

From the triangle and multiplicative triangle inequalities of the norm, we have that the algebraic operations are jointly continuous in $(\mathcal{M}(\mathcal{D}), \rho)$. Indeed, let $\rho(\mathbf{u}, \mathbf{u}') < \varepsilon_1$ and $\rho(\mathbf{v}, \mathbf{v}') < \varepsilon_2$; then,

$$\rho(\mathbf{u} + \mathbf{v}, \mathbf{u}' + \mathbf{v}') < \|(\mathbf{u} + \mathbf{v}) - (\mathbf{u}' + \mathbf{v}')\| < \varepsilon_1 + \varepsilon_2$$

and

$$\rho(\mathbf{u}\mathbf{v}, \mathbf{u}'\mathbf{v}') < 2\varepsilon_2\|\mathbf{u}\| + 2\varepsilon_1\|\mathbf{v}\| + 4\varepsilon_1\varepsilon_2.$$

The continuity of the addition implies that if Φ is an additive map from $\mathcal{M}(\mathcal{D})$ to an additive topological group and Φ is continuous at zero, then it is continuous at any point.

3. Homomorphisms and Supersymmetric Polynomials

Let $\mathcal{U}$ be a closed multiplicative semigroup of another Banach algebra $\mathcal{B}$ and let Y be a Banach space with a symmetric basis.

Theorem 2. *Let γ be a multiplicative map from $\mathcal{D}$ to $\mathcal{U}$. If there is a constant C_γ, such that $\|\gamma(z)\|_{\mathcal{B}} \leq C_\gamma\|z\|_{\mathcal{A}}$, $z \in \mathcal{D}$, then there exists a continuous ring homomorphism*

$$\Phi_\gamma\colon \mathcal{M}_X(\mathcal{D}) \to \mathcal{M}_Y(\mathcal{U})$$

defined by

$$\Phi_\gamma(\mathbf{u}) = \Phi_\gamma([(y|x)]) = [(\ldots, \gamma(y_n), \ldots, \gamma(y_2), \gamma(y_1)|\gamma(x_1), \gamma(x_2), \ldots, \gamma(x_n), \ldots)].$$

Proof. It is clear that $\Phi_\gamma([(y|x)])$ is additive and does not depend on the representative. In addition,

$$\|\Phi_\gamma([(y|x)])\| = \|[(\ldots, \gamma(y_n), \ldots, \gamma(y_2), \gamma(y_1)|\gamma(x_1), \gamma(x_2), \ldots, \gamma(x_n) \ldots)]\| \leq C_\gamma\|\mathbf{u}\|.$$

Let $\mathbf{u} \in \mathcal{M}_X(\mathcal{D})$ and let $(y|x)$ be its irreducible representative. Then,

$$\|\Phi_\gamma(\mathbf{u})\| = \|\gamma(x)\| + \|\gamma(y)\| \leq C_\gamma(\|x\| + \|y\|) = C_\gamma\|\mathbf{u}\|.$$

Hence, Φ_γ is continuous at zero, and according to the additivity, it is continuous at each point of $\mathcal{M}_X(\mathcal{D})$.

By the multiplicativity of γ,

$$\Phi_\gamma([(0|x)][(0|x')]) = [(0|\gamma(x_1)\gamma(x_1'),\ldots,\gamma(x_n)\gamma(x_j')\ldots)] = \Phi_\gamma([(0|x)])\Phi_\gamma([(0|x')]).$$

Thus,

$$\begin{gathered}\Phi_\gamma([(y|x)][(y'|x')]) \\ = \Phi_\gamma([(y|0)][(y'|0)]) + \Phi_\gamma([(0|x)][(0|x')]) - \Phi_\gamma([(0|x)][(0|y')]) - \Phi_\gamma([(0|0)][(0|x')]) \\ = \Phi_\gamma([(y|x)])\Phi_\gamma([(y'|x')]).\end{gathered}$$

□

Note that in Theorem 2, we do not need the continuity of γ.

Example 2. *Let $\mathcal{D} = B$ be an open unit ball centered at the origin of a Banach algebra $\mathcal{A}$ and $\mathcal{U} = B_\varepsilon \cup \{\mathfrak{e}\}$, where $\mathfrak{e}$ is the unity of $\mathcal{A}$, and B_ε is an open ball of radius $0 < \varepsilon < 1$, which is centered at the origin of $\mathcal{A}$. In addition, let $X = Y$. We define $\gamma\colon \mathcal{D} \to \mathcal{U}$ by*

$$\gamma(z) = \begin{cases} z & \text{if } z \in \mathcal{U}, \\ 0 & \text{otherwise.} \end{cases}$$

Then, Φ_γ satisfies the conditions of Theorem 2 and, thus, is continuous.

Corollary 1. *Any continuous homomorphism φ from a Banach algebra $\mathcal{A}$ to a Banach algebra $\mathcal{B}$ can be extended to a continuous homomorphism from $\mathcal{M}_X(\mathcal{A})$ to $\mathcal{M}_Y(\mathcal{B})$ for any infinite-dimensional Banach space Y with a symmetric basis.*

Proof. Since φ is a continuous linear and multiplicative operator from $\mathcal{A}$ to $\mathcal{B}$, it follows that

$$\|\varphi\|_{\mathcal{B}} \leq \|\varphi\|\|z\|_{\mathcal{A}}, \quad z \in \mathcal{A}.$$

Hence, Φ_γ satisfies the conditions of Theorem 2 for $\gamma = \varphi$; thus, Φ_φ is a continuous homomorphism from $\mathcal{M}_X(\mathcal{A})$ to $\mathcal{M}_Y(\mathcal{B})$. The map $z \mapsto [(0|z,0,\ldots)]$ is an embedding of $\mathcal{A}$ to $\mathcal{M}_X(\mathcal{A})$ and

$$\Phi_\varphi[(0|z,0,\ldots)] = [(0|\varphi(z),0,\ldots)].$$

Thus, we can consider Φ_φ as an extension of φ. Note that $z \mapsto [(0|z,0,\ldots)]$ is not a homomorphism of rings because it is not additive. □

The following example shows that for some cases, the condition $\|\gamma(z)\|_{\mathcal{B}} \leq C_\gamma\|z\|_{\mathcal{A}}$ is not necessary for the continuity of Φ_γ.

Example 3. *Let $X = \ell_p$ for $1 \leq p < \infty$, let $Y = \ell_1$, and let n be a natural number, $n \geq p$. We set $\gamma(z) = z^n$, $z \in \mathcal{A}$. Then, for every Banach algebra $\mathcal{A}$, the mapping Φ_γ from $\mathcal{M}_{\ell_p}(\mathcal{A})$ to $\mathcal{M}_{\ell_1}(\mathcal{A})$ is a continuous homomorphism. Indeed, since $n \geq p$, $\Phi_\gamma(\mathbf{u}) \in \mathcal{M}_{\ell_1}(\mathcal{A})$ for every $\mathbf{u} \in \mathcal{M}_{\ell_p}(\mathcal{A})$ and*

$$\|\Phi_\gamma(\mathbf{u})\| \leq \|\mathbf{u}\|^n.$$

Thus, Φ_γ is continuous at zero and, thus, continuous.

Example 4. *Let $\gamma(z) = \|z\|_{\mathcal{A}}$. Then, Φ_γ maps $\mathcal{M}_X(\mathcal{D})$ to $\mathcal{M}_X(\mathbb{C})$, and it is continuous and additive. If the norm $\mathcal{A}$ is multiplicative, then Φ_γ is multiplicative.*

Note that if Φ is a homomorphism from $\mathcal{M}_X(\mathcal{D})$ to $\mathcal{M}_Y(\mathcal{U})$ and for every $z \in \mathcal{D}$,

$$\Phi([0|z,0,\ldots]) = ([0|w,0,\ldots])$$

for some $w \in \mathcal{U}$, then the map $\gamma\colon z \mapsto w$ is multiplicative. However, we do not know if every homomorphism from $\mathcal{M}_X(\mathcal{D})$ to $\mathcal{M}_Y(\mathcal{U})$ is of the form in Theorem 2.

Let us consider vector-valued mappings on $\mathcal{M}(\mathcal{D})$. Let E be a linear normed space. We say that a mapping $f\colon \Lambda_X(\mathcal{D}) \to E$ is *supersymmetric* if $f(y|x) = f(y'|x')$ whenever $(y|x) \sim (y'|x')$. In fact, every supersymmetric function can be defined on $\mathcal{M}(\mathcal{D})$ by $\widetilde{f}([(y|x)]) = f(y|x)$. It is easy to check that if f is of the form

$$f(y|x) = \sum_{i=1}^{\infty} \gamma(x_i) - \sum_{j=1}^{\infty} \gamma(y_j), \tag{2}$$

where γ is a map from $\mathcal{M}(\mathcal{D})$ to E, then $\widetilde{f}$ is supersymmetric and additive. If γ is multiplicative, then $\widetilde{f}$ is so.

Example 5. *Let $(y|x)$ be an irreducible representative of $u \in \Lambda_X(\mathcal{D})$. We set*

$$f(u) = \|x\| - \|y\|.$$

Then, f is a supersymmetric complex-valued function.

If $\mathcal{D} = \mathcal{A}$ is a Banach algebra, then $\Lambda_X(\mathcal{A})$ is a Banach space, and we can consider *supersymmetric polynomials* on $\Lambda_X(\mathcal{A})$, that is, polynomial mappings to a normed space E that are supersymmetric. Let us recall that a mapping P_n from a normed space Z to E is an n-homogeneous polynomial if there exists a multi-linear mapping $\overline{P}_n$ on the nth Cartesian degree Z^n of Z such that $P_n(x) = \overline{P}_n(x,\ldots,x)$. A finite sum of homogeneous polynomials is a polynomial. Continuous polynomials on Banach spaces were studied by many authors (see, e.g., [31]). The following example gives us supersymmetric polynomials on $\Lambda_{\ell_p}(\mathcal{A})$ for $1 \le p \le \infty$.

Example 6. *Let $X = \ell_p$ for some $1 \le p < \infty$, and $E = \mathcal{A}$. For any integer $n \ge p$, we define*

$$T_m(y|x) = \sum_{i=1}^{\infty} x_i^m - \sum_{i=1}^{\infty} y_i^m.$$

Clearly, polynomials T_m are supersymmetric. Since the mapping $x_i \mapsto x_i^m$ is multiplicative and $\|T_m(y|x)\| \le (\|x\| + \|y\|)^m$, mappings $\widetilde{T}_m$ are continuous ring homomorphisms from $\mathcal{M}(\mathcal{A})$ to $\mathcal{A}$.

A polynomial P on $\Lambda_{\ell_p}(\mathbb{C})$ is *separately symmetric* if P is invariant with respect to all permutations (σ,μ) acting by

$$\sigma\colon (x_1,\ldots,x_n,\ldots) \mapsto (x_{\sigma(1)},\ldots,x_{\sigma(n)},\ldots)$$

and

$$\mu\colon (y_1,\ldots,y_n,\ldots) \mapsto (y_{\mu(1)},\ldots,y_{\mu(n)},\ldots).$$

Clearly, if P is supersymmetric, then it is separately symmetric, but the inverse statement is not true.

Example 7. *Let*

$$P(y|x) = \sum_{i<j} x_i x_j - \sum_{i<j} y_i y_j.$$

Evidently, P is separately symmetric. Moreover, $P(x|y) = -P(y|x)$. However, P is not supersymmetric. Indeed, $P(\ldots,0,-1|1,0,\ldots) = 0$ while $P(\ldots,0,1,-1|1,1,0,\ldots) = 2$. However, $(\ldots,0,-1|1,0,\ldots) \sim (\ldots,0,1,-1|1,1,0,\ldots)$. Thus, P has different values on equivalent vectors, and thus, it cannot be supersymmetric.

The minimal algebra generated by polynomials T_m, $m \in \mathbb{N}$ was studied in [7,29] for the case of $X = \ell_1$ and $\mathcal{D} = \mathcal{A} = \mathbb{C}$. The next theorem shows that every supersymmetric polynomial can be represented as a finite algebraic combination of polynomials T_m.

Theorem 3. *Let P be a supersymmetric polynomial on $\Lambda_{\ell_1}(\mathbb{C})$. Then, P is an algebraic combination (that is, a linear combination of finite products) of polynomials T_m, $m \in \mathbb{N}$.*

Proof. Let P be a supersymmetric polynomial on $\Lambda_{\ell_1}(\mathbb{C})$; then, $P(y|x)$ is separately symmetric. According to [34], P is an algebraic combination of polynomials F_m^+ and F_m^-, $m \in \mathbb{N}$, where

$$F_m^+(y|x) = \sum_{k=1}^{\infty} x_k^m \quad \text{and} \quad F_m^-(y|x) = \sum_{k=1}^{\infty} y_k^m.$$

Thus, we have

$$P(y|x) = \sum_{\substack{k_1+2k_2+\cdots+ik_i+\\ n_1+2n_2+\cdots jn_j=0}}^{m} c_{k_1\ldots k_i n_1\ldots n_j} F_1^+(x)^{k_1}\cdots F_i^+(x)^{k_i} F_1^-(y)^{n_1}\cdots F_j^-(y)^{n_j}$$

for some constants $c_{k_1\ldots k_i n_1\ldots n_j}$.

Clearly, $T_k = F_k^+ - F_k^-$. Denote $Q_k = F_k^+ + F_k^-$. Then, there is a polynomial $q\colon \mathbb{C}^n \to \mathbb{C}$ such that

$$P(y|x) = q(T_1(y|x),\ldots,T_m(y|x),Q_1(y|x),\ldots,Q_m(y|x)).$$

According to our assumption, $P(y \bullet a|x \bullet a) = P(y|x)$, $a \in \ell_1$. We can see that

$$T_k(y \bullet a|x \bullet a) = T_k(y|x) \quad \text{and} \quad Q_k(y \bullet a|x \bullet a) = Q_k(y|x) + 2F_k(a)$$

for every $k \in \mathbb{N}$. It is known that for every $(\lambda_1,\ldots,\lambda_m) \in \mathbb{C}^m$, there exists a vector $a \in \ell_1$ such that $F_n(a) = \lambda_n$, $1 \le n \le m$ (see, e.g., [19]). Thus, for every $(\lambda_1,\ldots,\lambda_m) \in \mathbb{C}^m$,

$$q(T_1(y|x),\ldots,T_m(y|x),Q_1(y|x),\ldots,Q_m(y|x))$$
$$= q(T_1(y|x),\ldots,T_m(y|x),Q_1(y|x)+\lambda_1,\ldots,Q_m(y|x)+\lambda_m).$$

However, this means that q does not depend on $Q_1,\ldots,Q_m$. Hence, P is an algebraic combination of polynomials T_m, $m \in \mathbb{N}$. □

In particular, in [29], it was proved that $[(y|x)] = [(y'|x')]$ in $\mathcal{M}_{\ell_1}(\mathbb{C})$ if and only if $T_m(y|x) = T_m(y'|x')$ for all $m \in \mathbb{N}$. The next example shows that in a more general case, supersymmetric polynomials do not separate points of $\mathcal{M}(\mathcal{D})$.

Example 8. *Let $X = \ell_1$ and $\mathcal{A} = \mathbb{C}^2$ be the algebra with respect to the coordinate-wise multiplication. Then, the vector*

$$(y|x) = \left(\ldots,0,\begin{pmatrix}1\\2\end{pmatrix},\begin{pmatrix}3\\4\end{pmatrix}\middle|\begin{pmatrix}3\\2\end{pmatrix},\begin{pmatrix}1\\4\end{pmatrix},0,\ldots\right)$$

is not equivalent to $(0|0)$, but

$$T_m(y|x) = \begin{pmatrix}3^m + 1^m - 1^m - 3^m\\ 4^m + 2^m - 2^m - 4^m\end{pmatrix} = \begin{pmatrix}0\\0\end{pmatrix}.$$

Let φ be a complex homomorphism of $\mathcal{A}$ and let Φ be a ring homomorphism from $\mathcal{M}(\mathcal{D})$ to $\mathcal{A}$; then, $\varphi \circ \Phi$ is a ring complex homomorphism of $\mathcal{M}(\mathcal{D})$. From the following example, we can see that there are complex homomorphisms of $\mathcal{M}(\mathcal{D})$ constructed in a different way.

Example 9. *Consider the case $\mathcal{M}_{\ell_1}(\mathbb{C}^2)$, as in Example 8. For arbitrary $k, n \in \mathbb{N}$, we set*

$$P_{kn}(y|x) = \sum_{i=1}^{\infty} x_i^k x_i'^n - \sum_{i=1}^{\infty} y_i^k y_i'^n,$$

where

$$(y|x) = \left(\cdots, \begin{pmatrix} y_2 \\ y_2' \end{pmatrix}, \begin{pmatrix} y_1 \\ y_1' \end{pmatrix} \middle| \begin{pmatrix} x_1 \\ x_1' \end{pmatrix}, \begin{pmatrix} x_2 \\ x_2' \end{pmatrix}, \cdots \right).$$

Note that $\|P_{kn}(y|x)\| \le (\|x\| + \|y\|)^{k+n}$. Polynomials P_{kn} are of the form (2) for $\gamma(x) = x_i^k x_i'^n$, and the map γ is multiplicative. So, $\widetilde{P}_{kn}$ are continuous complex homomorphisms.

Polynomials P_{kn} in Example 9, which are restricted to elements $(0|x)$, are called *block-symmetric* polynomials on $\ell_1(\mathbb{C}^2)$ (see, e.g., [4,23,26]) or *MacMahon* polynomials in the literature [35].

Example 10. *Let $X = \ell_1$, and let $\mathcal{A} = M_m$ be the algebra of all square matrices $m \times m$ for some fixed $m \in \mathbb{N}$. Then, $\mathcal{M}_{\ell_1}(M_m)$ is a noncommutative ring of matrix multisets. Let D be the following map from $\mathcal{M}_{\ell_1}(M_m)$ to $\mathcal{M}_{\ell_1}(\mathbb{C})$:*

$$D([(y|x)]) = [(\ldots, \det(y_n), \ldots, \det(y_2), \det(y_1) | \det(x_1), \det(x_2), \ldots, \det(x_n), \ldots)].$$

Since the determinant $\det(x_i)$ ia a multiplicative mapping, D is a homomorphism. The continuity of D follows from the fact that $\|D(y|x)\| \le (\|x\| + \|y\|)^m$.

4. Discussions and Conclusions

We considered the ring of multisets $\mathcal{M}_X(\mathcal{D})$ consisting of elements in a given multiplicative semigroup $\mathcal{D}$ of a Banach algebra $\mathcal{A}$ and endowed with some natural "supersymmetric" operations of addition and multiplication. We constructed a complete metrizable topology of $\mathcal{M}_X(\mathcal{D})$ generated by a ring norm. In addition, we investigated homomorphisms of $\mathcal{M}_X(\mathcal{D})$ and their relations with supersymmetric polynomials. Note that $\mathcal{M}_X(\mathcal{D})$ is not a linear space over $\mathbb{C}$ or $\mathbb{R}$ because there is no natural multiplication by scalars (see, e.g., [7]).

Rings of multisets may have wide applications in neural networks and machine learning. Computer algorithms are often invariant with respect to permutations of input data instances. This observation suggests the use of permutation-invariant sets instead of vectors of a fixed dimension for the organization of input data (see, e.g., [12]). For this purpose, multisets (sets with possible repetitions of elements) are actually more suitable. However, classical multisets have a poor algebraic structure. For example, a very important operation of the union of two multisets has no inverse. On the other hand, we can consider a set of multisets as a natural domain of symmetric functions (with respect to permutations of variables) that are defined on a linear space. Since the union of multisets does not preserve cardinality, it is convenient to use infinite-dimensional linear spaces of sequences, such as Banach spaces with symmetric bases. All symmetric functions on X can be extended to the set of multisets, and if $X = \ell_1$, then symmetric polynomials separate different points of the multisets. To get an operation that is inverse to the union, we have to use Grothendieck's well-known idea, which is widely used in K-theory. It leads to the construction of classes of equivalences of pairs $(y|x)$, where y plays the role of a "negative part" (while components of both vectors x and y are complex numbers or, in the general case, elements of an abstract

Banach algebra $\mathcal{A}$). If we consider x as vector coding information, then y consists of "negative" information in the sense that if both x and y contain the same piece of information (the same coordinate), then this piece of information will be annulated. Therefore, the union can be extended to a commutative group operation on the classes of equivalence, and together with a natural symmetric multiplication, they form a ring structure on the set of classes. Such a ring of multisets of complex numbers was considered in [7] for the case of $X = \ell_1$. In this paper, we investigated the situation when the "coordinates" of x and y were in a Banach algebra $\mathcal{A}$ and sequences of their norms belonged to a Banach space X with a symmetric basis. It is interesting that the basic results in [7] can be extended to the general case. In particular, the ring $\mathcal{M}_X(\mathcal{D})$ that was obtained is a complete metric space in a metrizable topology, and it is naturally induced by norms of $\mathcal{A}$ and X. The main difference is that supersymmetric polynomials separate points of $\mathcal{M}_{\ell_1}(\mathbb{C})$, while in the general case, they do not.

One can compare the rings of multisets and fuzzy sets. In a fuzzy set, each element may have a partial membership (between 0 and 1) [36]. In a ring of multisets, elements may have multiple memberships, and even negatively multiple memberships. Note that the ring $\mathcal{M}_X(\mathcal{D})$ is never algebra, even if $\mathcal{D} = \mathbb{C}$ (see [7]). However, it is known [33] that under some natural conditions, any metric ring R can be embedded into a normed algebra over the field of fractions over R. It would be interesting to construct such an algebra for the ring $\mathcal{M}_X(\mathcal{D})$ and compare it with fuzzy sets and other algebraic structures.

Author Contributions: Conceptualization and supervision of the study, A.Z.; investigation and preparation of the original draft of the manuscript, I.C. and A.Z. All authors have read and agreed to the published version of the manuscript.

Funding: This research received no external funding.

Institutional Review Board Statement: Not applicable.

Informed Consent Statement: Not applicable.

Data Availability Statement: Not applicable.

Acknowledgments: The authors were partially supported by the Ministry of Education and Science of Ukraine, project registration number: 0122U000857.

Conflicts of Interest: The authors declare no conflict of interest.

References

1. Aron, R.M.; Falcó, J.; García, D.; Maestre, M. Algebras of symmetric holomorphic functions of several complex variables. *Rev. Mat. Complut.* **2018**, *31*, 651–672. [CrossRef]
2. Aron, R.M.; Falcó, J.; Maestre, M. Separation theorems for group invariant polynomials. *J. Geom. Anal.* **2018**, *28*, 393–404. [CrossRef]
3. Aron, R.; Galindo, P.; Pinasco, D.; Zalduendo, I. Group-symmetric holomorphic functions on a Banach space. *Bull. Lond. Math. Soc.* **2016**, *48*, 779–796. [CrossRef]
4. Bandura, A.; Kravtsiv, V.; Vasylyshyn, T. Algebraic Basis of the Algebra of All Symmetric Continuous Polynomials on the Cartesian Product of ℓ_p-Spaces. *Axioms* **2022**, *11*, 41. [CrossRef]
5. Chernega, I.; Galindo, P.; Zagorodnyuk, A. Some algebras of symmetric analytic functions and their spectra. *Proc. Edinb. Math. Soc.* **2012**, *55*, 125–142. [CrossRef]
6. Falcó, J.; García, D.; Jung, M.; Maestre, M. Group-invariant separating polynomials on a Banach space. *Publ. Mat.* **2022**, *66*, 207–233. [CrossRef]
7. Jawad, F.; Zagorodnyuk, A. Supersymmetric polynomials on the space of absolutely convergent series. *Symmetry* **2019**, *11*, 1111. [CrossRef]
8. Halushchak, S. Spectra of Some Algebras of Entire Functions of Bounded Type, Generated by a Sequence of Polynomials. *Carpathian Math. Publ.* **2019**, *11*, 311–320. [CrossRef]
9. Vasylyshyn, T. Symmetric analytic functions on the Cartesian power of the complex Banach space of Lebesgue measurable essentially bounded functions on $[0,1]$. *J. Math. Anal. Appl.* **2022**, *509*, 125977. [CrossRef]
10. Vasylyshyn, T.V. The algebra of symmetric polynomials on $(L_\infty)^n$. *Mat. Stud.* **2019**, *52*, 71–85. [CrossRef]
11. Vasylyshyn, T. Algebras of symmetric analytic functions on Cartesian powers of Lebesgue integrable in a power $p \in [1, +\infty)$ functions. *Carpathian Math. Publ.* **2021**, *13*, 340–351. [CrossRef]

12. Zaheer, M.; Kottur, S.; Ravanbakhsh, S.; Poczos, B.; Salakhutdinov, R.R.; Smola, A.J. Deep sets. In *Advances in Neural Information Processing Systems*; Guyon, I., Luxburg, U.V., Bengio, S., Wallach, H., Fergus, R., Vishwanathan, S., Garnett, R., Eds.; Neural Info Process Sys F: La Jolla, CA, USA, 2017; pp. 3391–3401. Available online: https://papers.nips.cc/paper/2017 (accessed on 31 July 2021).
13. Yarotsky, D. Universal Approximations of Invariant Maps by Neural Networks. *Constr. Approx.* **2022**, *55*, 407–474. [CrossRef]
14. Wagstaff, E.; Fuchs, F.B.; Engelcke, M.; Osborne, M.A.; Posner, I. Universal Approximation of Functions on Sets. *J. Mach. Learn. Res.* **2022**, *23*, 1–56. Available online: https://www.jmlr.org/papers/volume23/21-0730/21-0730.pdf (accessed on 31 July 2021).
15. Balan, R.; Haghani, N.; Singh, M. Permutation Invariant Representations with Applications to Graph Deep Learning. *arXiv* **2022**. [CrossRef]
16. Nemirovskii, A.; Semenov, S. On polynomial approximation of functions on Hilbert space. *Mat. USSR-Sbornik* **1973**, *21*, 255–277. [CrossRef]
17. González, M.; Gonzalo, R.; Jaramillo, J.A. Symmetric polynomials on rearrangement-invariant function spaces. *J. Lond. Math. Soc.* **1999**, *59*, 681–697. [CrossRef]
18. Hájek, P. Polynomial algebras on classical Banach Spaces. *Israel J. Math.* **1998**, *106*, 209–220. [CrossRef]
19. Alencar, R.; Aron, R.; Galindo, P.; Zagorodnyuk, A. Algebra of symmetric holomorphic functions on ℓ_p. *Bull. Lond. Math. Soc.* **2003**, *35*, 55–64. [CrossRef]
20. Chernega, I.; Galindo, P.; Zagorodnyuk, A. A multiplicative convolution on the spectra of algebras of symmetric analytic functions. *Rev. Mat. Complut.* **2014**, *27*, 575–585. [CrossRef]
21. Vasylyshyn, T. Symmetric polynomials on $(L_p)^n$. *Eur. J. Math.* **2020**, *6*, 164–178. [CrossRef]
22. Galindo, P.; Vasylyshyn, T.; Zagorodnyuk, A. Analytic structure on the spectrum of the algebra of symmetric analytic functions on L_∞. *RACSAM* **2020**, *114*, 56. [CrossRef]
23. Kravtsiv, V. Algebraic basis of the algebra of block-symmetric polynomials on $\ell_1 \oplus \ell_\infty$. *Carpathian Math. Publ.* **2019**, *11*, 89–95. [CrossRef]
24. Kravtsiv, V. Analogues of the Newton formulas for the block-symmetric polynomials. *Carpathian Math. Publ.* **2020**, *12*, 17–22. [CrossRef]
25. Kravtsiv, V. Zeros of block-symmetric polynomials on Banach spaces. *Mat. Stud.* **2020**, *53*, 206–211. [CrossRef]
26. Vasylyshyn, T. Symmetric functions on spaces $\ell_p(\mathbb{R}^n)$ and $\ell_p(\mathbb{C}^n)$. *Carpathian Math. Publ.* **2020**, *12*, 5–16. [CrossRef]
27. Karoubi, M. K-theory, an elementary introduction. In *Cohomology of Groups and Algebraic K-Theory*; Advanced Lectures in Mathematics (ALM); International Press: Somerville, MA, USA, 2010; Volume 12, pp. 197–215.
28. Chernega, I.; Fushtei, V.; Zagorodnyuk, A. Power Operations and Differentiations Associated With Supersymmetric Polynomials on a Banach Space. *Carpathian Math. Publ.* **2020**, *12*, 360–367. [CrossRef]
29. Chopyuk, Y.; Vasylyshyn, T.; Zagorodnyuk, A. Rings of Multisets and Integer Multinumbers. *Mathematics* **2022**, *10*, 778. [CrossRef]
30. Lindestrauss, J.; Tzafriri, L. *Classical Banach Spaces i. Sequence Spaces*; Springer: New York, NY, USA, 1977.
31. Mujica, J. *Complex Analysis in Banach Spaces*; North-Holland: Amsterdam, The Netherlands; New York, NY, USA; Oxford, UK, 1986.
32. Macdonald, I.G. *Symmetric Functions and Orthogonal Polynomials*; University Lecture Serie; AMS: Providence, RI, USA, 1997; Volume 12.
33. Aurora, S. Multiplicative norms for metric rings. *Pacific J. Math.* **1957**, *7*, 1279–1304. [CrossRef]
34. Jawad, F. Note on separately symmetric polynomials on the Cartesian product of ℓ_p. *Mat. Stud.* **2018**, *50*, 204–210. [CrossRef]
35. Rosas, M. MacMahon symmetric functions, the partition lattice, and Young subgroups. *J. Combin. Theory Ser. A* **2001**, *96*, 326–340. [CrossRef]
36. Zadeh, L.A. Fuzzy sets, fuzzy logic, and fuzzy systems: selected papers by Lotfi A. In *Advances in Fuzzy Systems River Edge: NJ World Scientific. Applications and Theory*; World Scientific: Singapore, 1996; pp. 394–432. [CrossRef]

axioms

MDPI

Article

Entire Symmetric Functions on the Space of Essentially Bounded Integrable Functions on the Union of Lebesgue-Rohlin Spaces

Taras Vasylyshyn [1] and Kostiantyn Zhyhallo [2,*]

[1] Faculty of Mathematics and Computer Sciences, Vasyl Stefanyk Precarpathian National University, 76018 Ivano-Frankivsk, Ukraine
[2] Department of Theory of Functions and Methods of Teaching Mathematics, Lesya Ukrainka Volyn National University, 43025 Lutsk, Ukraine
* Correspondence: zhyhallo.kostia@gmail.com or konstantin.zhyhallo@modulsoft.eu

Abstract: The class of measure spaces which can be represented as unions of Lebesgue-Rohlin spaces with continuous measures contains a lot of important examples, such as $\mathbb{R}^n$ for any $n \in \mathbb{N}$ with the Lebesgue measure. In this work we consider symmetric functions on Banach spaces of all complex-valued integrable essentially bounded functions on such unions. We construct countable algebraic bases of algebras of continuous symmetric polynomials on these Banach spaces. The completions of such algebras of polynomials are Fréchet algebras of all complex-valued entire symmetric functions of bounded type on the abovementioned Banach spaces. We show that each such Fréchet algebra is isomorphic to the Fréchet algebra of all complex-valued entire symmetric functions of bounded type on the complex Banach space of all complex-valued essentially bounded functions on $[0,1]$.

Keywords: symmetric polynomial on a Banach space; continuous polynomial on a Banach space; algebraic basis; Lebesgue-Rohlin space

MSC: 46G25; 47H60; 46G20

Citation: Vasylyshyn, T.; Zhyhallo, K. Entire Symmetric Functions on the Space of Essentially Bounded Integrable Functions on the Union of Lebesgue-Rohlin Spaces. *Axioms* **2022**, *11*, 460. https://doi.org/10.3390/axioms11090460

Academic Editor: Mircea Merca

Received: 31 July 2022
Accepted: 2 September 2022
Published: 7 September 2022

1. Introduction

The study of symmetric polynomials on infinite dimensional spaces started with the work [1] (for classical results in the finite dimensional case, see, e.g., [2–4]). In [1], the authors considered symmetric continuous polynomials on real Banach spaces ℓ_p and $L_p[0,1]$, where $p \in [1,+\infty)$. In particular, in [1] the authors constructed algebraic bases of algebras of the abovementioned polynomials. In [5], the authors considered symmetric continuous polynomials on separable sequence real Banach spaces with a symmetric basis (see [6] (Def. 3.a.1, p. 113)) and on a separable rearrangement invariant function the real Banach spaces (see [7] (Definition 2.a.1, p. 117)). Topological algebras of symmetric holomorphic functions on ℓ_p were studied first in [8]. Symmetric polynomials and symmetric holomorphic functions of bounded type on sequence Banach spaces were studied in [9–34] (see also the survey [35]). Symmetric holomorphic functions of unbounded type on sequence Banach spaces were studied in [36–39]. Symmetric polynomials and symmetric holomorphic functions on Banach spaces of Lebesgue measurable functions and on Cartesian powers of such spaces were studied in [40–49]. In [50–54], the authors used the most general approach to the study of symmetric functions.

In [41], the authors constructed an algebraic basis of the algebra of symmetric continuous complex-valued polynomials on the complex Banach space $L_\infty[0,1]$ of complex-valued Lebesgue measurable essentially bounded functions on $[0,1]$ and described the spectrum of the Fréchet algebra $H_{bs}(L_\infty[0,1])$ of symmetric analytic entire functions, which are bounded on bounded sets, on $L_\infty[0,1]$. In [42], the authors showed that the algebra $H_{bs}(L_\infty[0,1])$

is isomorphic to the algebra of all analytic functions on the strong dual of the topological vector space of entire functions on the complex plane $\mathbb{C}$. In addition in [42], it was shown that the algebra $H_{bs}(L_\infty[0,1])$ is a test algebra for the famous Michael problem (see [55]). In [49], the authors showed that the algebra $H_{bs}(L_\infty[0,1])$ is isomorphic to the algebra of symmetric entire functions on the complex Banach space of complex-valued Lebesgue integrable essentially bounded functions on the semi-axis.

In this work, we generalize the results of the work [49], replacing the semi-axis with the arbitrary union of Lebesgue-Rohlin spaces (which are also known as standard probability spaces) with continuous measures. Note that there are a lot of important measure spaces which can be represented as the abovementioned union. For example, $\mathbb{R}^n$ for any $n \in \mathbb{N}$ with the Lebesgue measure is one such space. We consider symmetric functions on Banach spaces of all complex-valued integrable essentially bounded functions on the unions of Lebesgue-Rohlin spaces with continuous measures. We construct countable algebraic bases of algebras of continuous symmetric polynomials on these Banach spaces. The completions of such algebras of polynomials are Fréchet algebras of all complex-valued entire symmetric functions of bounded type on the abovementioned Banach spaces. We show that every such Fréchet algebra is isomorphic to the Fréchet algebra $H_{bs}(L_\infty[0,1])$.

2. Preliminaries

Let us denote by $\mathbb{N}$ and $\mathbb{Z}_+$ the set of all positive integers and the set of all nonnegative integers, respectively.

2.1. Polynomials

Let X be a complex Banach space.

Let $N \in \mathbb{N}$. A mapping $P : X \to \mathbb{C}$, which is the restriction to the diagonal of some N-linear mapping $A_P : X^N \to \mathbb{C}$, i.e.,

$$P(x) = A_P(\underbrace{x, \ldots, x}_{N})$$

for every $x \in X$, is called an N-homogeneous polynomial.

A mapping $P : X \to \mathbb{C}$, which can be represented in the form

$$P = P_0 + P_1 + \ldots + P_N,$$

where $N \in \mathbb{N}$, P_0 is a constant mapping, and $P_n : X \to \mathbb{C}$ is an n-homogeneous polynomial for every $n \in \{1, \ldots, N\}$, is called a polynomial of a degree at most N.

It is known that a polynomial $P : X \to \mathbb{C}$ is continuous if and only if its norm

$$\|P\| = \sup_{\|x\| \le 1} |P(x)|$$

is finite. Consequently, for every continuous N-homogeneous polynomial $P : X \to \mathbb{C}$ and for every $x \in X$ we have the following inequality:

$$|P(x)| \le \|P\| \|x\|^N. \tag{1}$$

2.2. Holomorphic Functions

Definition 1. ([56] (Def. 2.1, p. 53)) *A subset U of a vector space E is said to be* finitely open *if $U \cap F$ is an open subset of the Euclidean space F for each finite dimensional subspace F of E.*

(See [56] (p. 53)). The finitely open subsets of E define a translation invariant topology τ_f. The balanced τ_f-neighborhoods of zero form a basis for the τ_f-neighborhoods of zero. On a topological vector space (E, τ), the topology τ_f is finer than τ, i.e., $\tau_f \ge \tau$.

Definition 2. (See [56] (Def. 2.2, p. 54)) *The complex-valued function f, defined on a finitely open subset U of a complex vector space E is said to be* G-holomorphic *if for each $a \in U, b \in E$ the complex-valued function of one complex variable*

$$\lambda \mapsto f(a + \lambda b)$$

is holomorphic in some neighborhood of zero. We let $H_G(U)$ denote the set of all G-holomorphic mappings from U into $\mathbb{C}$.

The following proposition is a partial result of [56] (Prop. 2.4, p. 55).

Proposition 1. *If U is a finitely open subset of a complex vector space E and $f \in H_G(U)$, then for each $a \in U$ there exists a unique sequence of homogeneous polynomials from E into $\mathbb{C}$, $\{f_m^{(a)}\}_{m=0}^{\infty}$, such that*

$$f(a + y) = \sum_{m=0}^{\infty} f_m^{(a)}(y)$$

for all y in some τ_f-neighborhood of zero. This series is called the Taylor series of f at a.

Definition 3. (See [56] (Def. 2.6, p. 57)) *Let (E, τ) be a complex locally convex space, and let U be a finitely open subset of E. A function $f : U \to \mathbb{C}$ is called* holomorphic *or* analytic *if it is G-holomorphic and for each $a \in U$ the function*

$$y \mapsto \sum_{m=0}^{\infty} f_m^{(a)}(y)$$

converges and defines a continuous function on some τ-neighborhood of zero. We let $H(U)$ denote the algebra of all holomorphic functions from U into $\mathbb{C}$ endowed with the compact open topology (the topology of uniform convergence on the compact subsets of U). A function, which is holomorphic on E, is called entire.

The following proposition is a partial result of [56] (Lemma 2.8, p. 58).

Proposition 2. *If U is an open subset of a complex locally convex space E and $f : U \to \mathbb{C}$ is G-holomorphic, then $f \in H(U)$ if and only if f is locally bounded.*

The following proposition is a partial result of [56] (Cor. 2.9, p. 59).

Proposition 3. *Let E be a complex locally convex space. Let U be an open subset of E, and suppose $f \in H(U)$. Then for every a in U and every $m \in \mathbb{N}$, the m-homogeneous polynomial $f_m^{(a)}$ is continuous.*

(See [56] (p. 166)). Let U be an open subset of a complex locally convex space E, and let B be a balanced closed subset of E. We let

$$d_B(a, U) = \sup\{|\lambda| : \lambda \in \mathbb{C}, a + \lambda B \subset U\}$$

for every $a \in U$. If E is a complex normed linear space and B is the unit ball of E, then $d_B(a, U)$ is the usual distance of a to the complement of U in E.

Let $f \in H(U)$. The B-radius of boundedness of f at $a \in U$, is defined as

$$r_f(a, B) = \sup\Big\{|\lambda| : \lambda \in \mathbb{C}, a + \lambda B \subset U, \sup_{y \in a + \lambda B} |f(y)| < \infty\Big\}.$$

The B-radius of uniform convergence of f at $a \in U$ is defined as

$$R_f(a,B) = \sup\Big\{|\lambda| : \lambda \in \mathbb{C}, a + \lambda B \subset U, \text{and the Taylor series of } f \text{ at } a \\ \text{converges to } f \text{ uniformly on } a + \lambda B\Big\}.$$

The following proposition is a partial result of [56] (Prop. 4.7, p. 166).

Proposition 4. *Let U be an open subset of a complex locally convex space E. Suppose $f \in H(U)$. If $a \in U$, B is a closed balanced subset of E and $r_f(a,B) > 0$, then*

$$r_f(a,B) = R_f(a,B) = \min\left\{ d_B(a,U), \left(\limsup_{n\to\infty} \sup_{y\in B} \left| f_n^{(a)}(y) \right|^{1/n} \right)^{-1} \right\}.$$

Let E be a complex normed space. An entire function $f : X \to \mathbb{C}$, for which $r_f(0,B) = +\infty$, where B is a closed unit ball in E, is called a function of *bounded type*. In other words, f is called a function of bounded type if it is bounded on every bounded subset of E. By Proposition 4, for every such a function f, its Taylor series at zero, $\sum_{m=0}^{\infty} f_m$, converges uniformly to f on every bounded subset of E (we denote $f_m^{(0)}$ by f_m).

By [57] (Cor. 7.3, p. 47),

$$f_m(y) = \frac{1}{2\pi i} \int_{|\xi|=r} \frac{f(\xi y)}{\xi^{m+1}}\, d\xi, \qquad (2)$$

where $m \in \mathbb{Z}_+$, $y \in E$ and $r > 0$. Equation (2) is called the Cauchy Integral Formula.

Let E be a complex Banach space. Let $H_b(E)$ be the Fréchet algebra of all entire functions of bounded type $f : E \to \mathbb{C}$ endowed with the topology of the uniform convergence on bounded subsets. Let

$$\|f\|_r = \sup_{\|x\| \le r} |f(x)|$$

for $f \in H_b(E)$ and $r \in (0, +\infty)$. The topology of the Fréchet algebra $H_b(E)$ is generated by any set of norms

$$\{\|\cdot\|_r : r \in I\},$$

where I is an arbitrary unbounded subset of $(0, +\infty)$.

For details on holomorphic functions on Banach spaces, we refer the reader to [57] or [56,58] .

2.3. Measure Spaces

A measure space is a triple $(\Omega, \mathcal{F}, \nu)$, where Ω is a set, $\mathcal{F}$ is a σ algebra of its subsets, and $\nu : \mathcal{F} \to [0, +\infty]$ is a measure. In addition, we assume ν to be a complete measure, i.e., every subset of a measurable set with null measure (so called null set) is measurable too. An isomorphism between two measure spaces $(\Omega_1, \mathcal{F}_1, \nu_1)$ and $(\Omega_2, \mathcal{F}_2, \nu_2)$ is an invertible map $f : \Omega_1 \to \Omega_2$ such that f and f^{-1} are both measurable and measure-preserving maps. In the case $(\Omega_1, \mathcal{F}_1, \nu_1) = (\Omega_2, \mathcal{F}_2, \nu_2)$, the mapping f is called a measurable automorphism. Two measure spaces $(\Omega_1, \mathcal{F}_1, \nu_1)$ and $(\Omega_2, \mathcal{F}_2, \nu_2)$ are called isomorphic modulo zero if there exist null sets $M \subset \Omega_1$ and $N \subset \Omega_2$ such that measure spaces $\Omega_1 \setminus M$ and $\Omega_2 \setminus N$ are isomorphic [59] (§1, No. 5).

Let a measure space $(\Omega, \mathcal{F}, \nu)$ be such that $\nu(\Omega) = 1$. The measure space $(\Omega, \mathcal{F}, \nu)$ is called separable ([59] (§2, No. 1)), if there exists a countable system $\mathcal{G}$ of measurable sets having the following two properties:

1. For every measurable set $A \subset \Omega$, there exists a set B such that $A \subset B \subset \Omega$, B is identical with A modulo zero, and B is an element of the σ algebra generated by $\mathcal{G}$.
2. For every pair of points $x, y \in \Omega$, there exists a set $G \subset \mathcal{G}$ such that either $x \in G, y \notin G$, or $x \notin G, y \in G$.

Every countable system $\mathcal{G}$ of measurable sets satisfying conditions (1) and (2) is called a basis of the space $(\Omega, \mathcal{F}, \nu)$.

Let $(\Omega, \mathcal{F}, \nu)$ be a separable measure space, and let $B = \{B_n\}_{n=1}^{\infty}$ be an arbitrary basis in $(\Omega, \mathcal{F}, \nu)$. If all intersections of the form $\cap_{n=1}^{\infty} A_n$, where A_n is one of the two sets B_n and $\Omega \setminus B_n$, are nonempty, then the space $(\Omega, \mathcal{F}, \nu)$ is called complete with respect to the basis B. By [59] (§2, No. 2), if the space $(\Omega, \mathcal{F}, \nu)$ is complete modulo zero (i.e., isomorphic modulo zero to some complete measure space) with respect to some basis, then it is complete modulo zero with respect to every other basis. Separable measure spaces which are complete modulo zero with respect to their bases are called Lebesgue-Rohlin spaces or standard probability spaces. By [59] (§2, No. 4), every Lebesgue-Rohlin space with continuous measure (i.e., there are no points of positive measure) is isomorphic modulo zero to $[0,1]$ with Lebesgue measure. The following simple lemma shows that every such space is isomorphic to $[0,1]$ with Lebesgue measure.

Lemma 1. *Every Lebesgue-Rohlin measure space with continuous measure is isomorphic to $[0,1]$ with Lebesgue measure.*

Proof. Let $(\Omega, \mathcal{F}, \nu)$ be a Lebesgue-Rohlin measure space with continuous measure. By [59] (§2, No. 4), $(\Omega, \mathcal{F}, \nu)$ is isomorphic modulo zero to $[0,1]$ with Lebesgue measure, i.e., there exist null sets $M \subset \Omega$ and $N \subset [0,1]$ such that $\Omega \setminus M$ is isomorphic to $[0,1] \setminus N$. Let $f : \Omega \setminus M \to [0,1] \setminus N$ be the isomorphism. Let K be an arbitrary null subset of $[0,1] \setminus N$ with the cardinality of the continuum. Then $f^{-1}(K)$ is a null subset of $\Omega \setminus M$ with the cardinality of the continuum. Consequently, both sets $C_1 = M \cup f^{-1}(K)$ and $C_2 = N \cup K$ are null sets of the cardinality of the continuum. Let $h : C_1 \to C_2$ be a bijection. Let $g : \Omega \to [0,1]$ be defined by

$$g(t) = \begin{cases} h(t), & \text{if } t \in C_1, \\ f(t), & \text{if } t \in [0,1] \setminus C_1. \end{cases}$$

Evidently, g is an isomorphism between $(\Omega, \mathcal{F}, \nu)$ and $[0,1]$ with Lebesgue measure. □

2.4. Symmetric Functions

In general, symmetric functions are defined in the following way.

Definition 4. *Let A be an arbitrary nonempty set, and let S be a nonempty set of mappings acting from A to itself. A function f, defined on A, is called symmetric with respect to the set S if $f(s(a)) = f(a)$ for every $s \in S$ and $a \in A$.*

Let us describe the partial case of Definition 4, which we will use in this work. The set of all measurable automorphisms of some measure space $(\Omega, \mathcal{F}, \nu)$ we will denote by Ξ_Ω. A complex Banach space X of measurable functions $x : \Omega \to \mathbb{C}$ such that $x \circ \sigma$ belongs to X for every $x \in X$ and $\sigma \in \Xi_\Omega$ will be in the role of the set A from Definition 4. The set of operators

$$\{x \in X \mapsto x \circ \sigma \in X : \ \sigma \in \Xi_\Omega\}$$

will be in the role of the set S from Definition 4. So, a function f, defined on X, is called *symmetric* if

$$f(x \circ \sigma) = f(x)$$

for every $x \in X$ and $\sigma \in \Xi_\Omega$.

2.5. Algebraic Combinations

A mapping

$$t \in T \mapsto Q(f_1(t), \ldots, f_k(t)) \in \mathbb{C},$$

where T is a nonempty set, $k \in \mathbb{N}$, $f_1, \ldots, f_k$ are mappings acting from T to $\mathbb{C}$ and Q is a polynomial acting from $\mathbb{C}^k$ to $\mathbb{C}$, is called an algebraic combination of mappings $f_1, \ldots, f_k$.

Let $\mathcal{A}$ be some algebra of complex-valued mappings. Let $\mathcal{B} \subset \mathcal{A}$ be such that every element of $\mathcal{A}$ can be uniquely represented as an algebraic combination of some elements of $\mathcal{B}$. Then $\mathcal{B}$ is called an *algebraic basis* of $\mathcal{A}$.

2.6. Entire Symmetric Functions on $L_\infty[0,1]$

Let $L_\infty[0,1]$ be the complex Banach space of all Lebesgue measurable essentially bounded complex-valued functions x on $[0,1]$ with norm

$$\|x\|_\infty = \operatorname{ess\,sup}_{t\in[0,1]} |x(t)|.$$

For every $n \in \mathbb{N}$, let $R_n : L_\infty[0,1] \to \mathbb{C}$ be defined by

$$R_n(x) = \int_{[0,1]} (x(t))^n \, dt.$$

Note that R_n is a symmetric continuous n-homogeneous polynomial such that $\|R_n\| = 1$ for every $n \in \mathbb{N}$.

Theorem 1. ([41] (Theorem 4.3)) *Every symmetric continuous n-homogeneous polynomial $P : L_\infty[0,1] \to \mathbb{C}$ can be uniquely represented as*

$$P(x) = \sum_{k_1+2k_2+\ldots+nk_n=n} \alpha_{k_1,\ldots,k_n} R_1^{k_1}(x) \cdots R_n^{k_n}(x),$$

where $k_1, \ldots, k_n \in \mathbb{Z}_+$ and $\alpha_{k_1,\ldots,k_n} \in \mathbb{C}$. In other words, $\{R_n\}$ forms an algebraic basis in the algebra of symmetric continuous polynomials on $L_\infty[0,1]$.

Theorem 2. ([41] (Theorem 3.1)) *For every sequence $\xi = \{\xi_n\}_{n=1}^\infty \subset \mathbb{C}$ such that the sequence $\{\sqrt[n]{|\xi_n|}\}_{n=1}^\infty$ is bounded, there exists $x_\xi \in L_\infty[0,1]$ such that $R_n(x_\xi) = \xi_n$ for every $n \in \mathbb{N}$ and*

$$\|x_\xi\|_\infty \le \frac{2}{M} \sup_{n\in\mathbb{N}} \sqrt[n]{|\xi_n|},$$

where

$$M = \prod_{k=1}^\infty \cos\left(\frac{\pi}{2} \cdot \frac{1}{k+1}\right). \tag{3}$$

Let $H_{bs}(L_\infty[0,1])$ be the subalgebra of the Fréchet algebra $H_b(L_\infty[0,1])$, which consists of all symmetric elements of $H_b(L_\infty[0,1])$. It can be checked that $H_{bs}(L_\infty[0,1])$ is closed in $H_b(L_\infty[0,1])$.

For every function $f \in H_{bs}(L_\infty[0,1])$, its Taylor series converges uniformly to f on every bounded set. The nth term, where $n \in \mathbb{N}$, of the Taylor series is a continuous n-homogeneous polynomial, which is symmetric by the symmetry of f and by the Cauchy Integral Equation (2). Therefore, by Theorem 1, every $f \in H_{bs}(L_\infty[0,1])$ can be represented as

$$f(x) = \alpha_0 + \sum_{n=1}^\infty \sum_{\substack{k_1+2k_2+\ldots+nk_n=n \\ k_1,\ldots,k_n\in\mathbb{Z}_+}} \alpha_{k_1,\ldots,k_n} R_1^{k_1}(x) \cdots R_n^{k_n}(x) \tag{4}$$

where $\alpha_{k_1,\ldots,k_n} \in \mathbb{C}$, $x \in L_\infty[0,1]$, and the series converges uniformly on every bounded subset of $L_\infty[0,1]$.

for $t \in \Omega_{\gamma_k}$, $k \in \mathbb{N}$. Note that the mapping $v_{\{\gamma_n\}_{n=1}^\infty}$ is an isomorphism between $\bigsqcup_{n=1}^{\infty} \Omega_{\gamma_n}$ and $[0, +\infty)$.

Let us define the mapping $V_{\{\gamma_n\}_{n=1}^\infty} : (L_1 \cap L_\infty)[0, +\infty) \to (L_1 \cap L_\infty)\left(\bigsqcup_{n=1}^{\infty} \Omega_{\gamma_n}\right)$ by

$$V_{\{\gamma_n\}_{n=1}^\infty}(x) = x \circ v_{\{\gamma_n\}_{n=1}^\infty},$$

where $x \in (L_1 \cap L_\infty)[0, +\infty)$. Since the mapping $v_{\{\gamma_n\}_{n=1}^\infty}$ is an isomorphism, it follows that the mapping $V_{\{\gamma_n\}_{n=1}^\infty}$ is a linear isometric bijection.

Let us define the mapping $I_{\{\gamma_n\}_{n=1}^\infty} : (L_1 \cap L_\infty)\left(\bigsqcup_{n=1}^{\infty} \Omega_{\gamma_n}\right) \to (L_1 \cap L_\infty)(\Omega)$ by

$$I_{\{\gamma_n\}_{n=1}^\infty}(x)(t) = \begin{cases} x(t), & \text{if } t \in \bigsqcup_{n=1}^{\infty} \Omega_{\gamma_n}, \\ 0, & \text{if } t \in \Omega \setminus \bigsqcup_{n=1}^{\infty} \Omega_{\gamma_n}, \end{cases}$$

where $x \in (L_1 \cap L_\infty)\left(\bigsqcup_{n=1}^{\infty} \Omega_{\gamma_n}\right)$. It can be checked that the mapping $I_{\{\gamma_n\}_{n=1}^\infty}$ is linear, isometric and injective.

Since mappings $V_{\{\gamma_n\}_{n=1}^\infty}$ and $I_{\{\gamma_n\}_{n=1}^\infty}$ are linear and continuous, and the mapping P is a continuous n-homogeneous polynomial, it follows that the mapping $P \circ I_{\{\gamma_n\}_{n=1}^\infty} \circ V_{\{\gamma_n\}_{n=1}^\infty}$ is a continuous n-homogeneous polynomial. It can be checked that $P \circ I_{\{\gamma_n\}_{n=1}^\infty} \circ V_{\{\gamma_n\}_{n=1}^\infty}$ is symmetric. Therefore, by Theorem 3, $P \circ I_{\{\gamma_n\}_{n=1}^\infty} \circ V_{\{\gamma_n\}_{n=1}^\infty}$ can be uniquely represented in the form

$$(P \circ I_{\{\gamma_n\}_{n=1}^\infty} \circ V_{\{\gamma_n\}_{n=1}^\infty})(x) = \sum_{\substack{k_1+2k_2+\ldots+nk_n=n \\ k_1,\ldots,k_n \in \mathbb{Z}_+}} \beta_{k_1,\ldots,k_n} \hat{R}_1^{k_1}(x) \cdots \hat{R}_n^{k_n}(x),$$

where $x \in (L_1 \cap L_\infty)[0, +\infty)$ and $\beta_{k_1,\ldots,k_n} \in \mathbb{C}$. Since the mapping $V_{\{\gamma_n\}_{n=1}^\infty}$ is an isomorphism, it follows that

$$(P \circ I_{\{\gamma_n\}_{n=1}^\infty})(y) = \sum_{\substack{k_1+2k_2+\ldots+nk_n=n \\ k_1,\ldots,k_n \in \mathbb{Z}_+}} \beta_{k_1,\ldots,k_n} \times \left((\hat{R}_1 \circ V^{-1}_{\{\gamma_n\}_{n=1}^\infty})(y)\right)^{k_1} \cdots \left((\hat{R}_n \circ V^{-1}_{\{\gamma_n\}_{n=1}^\infty})(y)\right)^{k_n} \quad (12)$$

for every $y \in (L_1 \cap L_\infty)\left(\bigsqcup_{n=1}^{\infty} \Omega_{\gamma_n}\right)$. Let us show that coefficients $\beta_{k_1,\ldots,k_n}$ coincide with respective coefficients $\alpha_{k_1,\ldots,k_n}$, obtained in (11). Let us define the mapping $T : L_\infty(\Omega_{\gamma_1}) \to (L_1 \cap L_\infty)\left(\bigsqcup_{n=1}^{\infty} \Omega_{\gamma_n}\right)$ by

$$T(x)(t) = \begin{cases} x(t), & \text{if } t \in \Omega_{\gamma_1} \\ 0, & \text{if } t \in \bigsqcup_{n=2}^{\infty} \Omega_{\gamma_n}, \end{cases}$$

where $x \in L_\infty(\Omega_{\gamma_1})$. It can be verified that the mapping T is linear, isometric and injective. We have the following diagram:

$$L_\infty[0,1] \xrightarrow{W_{\gamma_1}} L_\infty(\Omega_{\gamma_1}) \xrightarrow{T} (L_1 \cap L_\infty)\left(\bigsqcup_{n=1}^{\infty} \Omega_{\gamma_n}\right) \xrightarrow{I_{\{\gamma_n\}_{n=1}^\infty}} (L_1 \cap L_\infty)(\Omega) \xrightarrow{P} \mathbb{C}.$$

By (12),

$$(P \circ I_{\{\gamma_n\}_{n=1}^{\infty}} \circ T \circ W_{\gamma_1})(x) = \sum_{\substack{k_1+2k_2+\ldots+nk_n=n \\ k_1,\ldots,k_n \in \mathbb{Z}_+}} \beta_{k_1,\ldots,k_n} \times$$

$$\Big((\hat{R}_1 \circ V^{-1}_{\{\gamma_n\}_{n=1}^{\infty}} \circ T \circ W_{\gamma_1})(x)\Big)^{k_1} \cdots \Big((\hat{R}_n \circ V^{-1}_{\{\gamma_n\}_{n=1}^{\infty}} \circ T \circ W_{\gamma_1})(x)\Big)^{k_n} \quad (13)$$

for every $x \in L_\infty[0,1]$. Taking into account that $P \circ I_{\{\gamma_n\}_{n=1}^{\infty}} \circ T \circ W_{\gamma_1} = Q_{\gamma_1}$ and $\tilde{R}_j \circ V^{-1}_{\{\gamma_n\}_{n=1}^{\infty}} \circ T \circ W_{\gamma_1} = R_j$ for every $j \in \mathbb{N}$, by (13),

$$Q_\gamma(x) = \sum_{\substack{k_1+2k_2+\ldots+nk_n=n \\ k_1,\ldots,k_n \in \mathbb{Z}_+}} \beta_{k_1,\ldots,k_n} R_1^{k_1}(x) \cdots R_n^{k_n}(x)$$

for every $x \in L_\infty[0,1]$. By the uniqueness of the representation (11), we obtain the equality $\beta_{k_1,\ldots,k_n} = \alpha_{k_1,\ldots,k_n}$ for every $k_1,\ldots,k_n \in \mathbb{Z}_+$ such that $k_1 + 2k_2 + \ldots + nk_n = n$. Therefore, by (12),

$$(P \circ I_{\{\gamma_n\}_{n=1}^{\infty}})(y) = \sum_{\substack{k_1+2k_2+\ldots+nk_n=n \\ k_1,\ldots,k_n \in \mathbb{Z}_+}} \alpha_{k_1,\ldots,k_n} \times$$

$$\Big((\hat{R}_1 \circ V^{-1}_{\{\gamma_n\}_{n=1}^{\infty}})(y)\Big)^{k_1} \cdots \Big((\hat{R}_n \circ V^{-1}_{\{\gamma_n\}_{n=1}^{\infty}})(y)\Big)^{k_n},$$

for every $y \in (L_1 \cap L_\infty)\Big(\bigsqcup_{n=1}^{\infty} \Omega_{\gamma_n}\Big)$. Consequently, for every $z \in (L_1 \cap L_\infty)(\Omega)$, which belongs to $I_{\{\gamma_n\}_{n=1}^{\infty}}\Big((L_1 \cap L_\infty)\Big(\bigsqcup_{n=1}^{\infty} \Omega_{\gamma_n}\Big)\Big)$,

$$P(z) = \sum_{\substack{k_1+2k_2+\ldots+nk_n=n \\ k_1,\ldots,k_n \in \mathbb{Z}_+}} \alpha_{k_1,\ldots,k_n} \times$$

$$\Big((\hat{R}_1 \circ V^{-1}_{\{\gamma_n\}_{n=1}^{\infty}} \circ I^{-1}_{\{\gamma_n\}_{n=1}^{\infty}})(z)\Big)^{k_1} \cdots \Big((\hat{R}_n \circ V^{-1}_{\{\gamma_n\}_{n=1}^{\infty}} \circ I^{-1}_{\{\gamma_n\}_{n=1}^{\infty}})(z)\Big)^{k_n}.$$

Taking into account that

$$(\hat{R}_j \circ V^{-1}_{\{\gamma_n\}_{n=1}^{\infty}} \circ I^{-1}_{\{\gamma_n\}_{n=1}^{\infty}})(z) = \tilde{R}_j(z)$$

for every $j \in \mathbb{N}$,

$$P(z) = \sum_{\substack{k_1+2k_2+\ldots+nk_n=n \\ k_1,\ldots,k_n \in \mathbb{Z}_+}} \alpha_{k_1,\ldots,k_n} \big(\tilde{R}_1(z)\big)^{k_1} \cdots \big(\tilde{R}_n(z)\big)^{k_1} \quad (14)$$

for every $z \in (L_1 \cap L_\infty)(\Omega)$, which belongs to $I_{\{\gamma_n\}_{n=1}^{\infty}}\Big((L_1 \cap L_\infty)\Big(\bigsqcup_{n=1}^{\infty} \Omega_{\gamma_n}\Big)\Big)$. As we can see, coefficients in this equality do not depend on the choice of the sequence of indexes $\{\gamma_n\}_{n=1}^{\infty}$.

Let us show that the equality (14) holds for every $z \in (L_1 \cap L_\infty)(\Omega)$. Let z be an arbitrary element of the space $(L_1 \cap L_\infty)(\Omega)$. Since

$$\|z\|_1 = \int_\Omega |z(t)|\,dt = \sum_{\gamma \in \Gamma} \int_{\Omega_\gamma} |z(t)|\,dt$$

is finite, there exists not more than a countable set of indexes $\gamma \in \Gamma$ such that $\int_{\Omega_\gamma} |z(t)|\, dt > 0$. So, there exists a sequence of pairwise distinct indexes $\{\gamma_n\}_{n=1}^{\infty} \subset \Gamma$ such that $z = 0$ a. e. on the set Ω_γ for every index $\gamma \in \Gamma \setminus \{\gamma_n\}_{n=1}^{\infty}$. Therefore, $z \in I_{\{\gamma_n\}_{n=1}^{\infty}}\left((L_1 \cap L_\infty)\left(\bigsqcup_{n=1}^{\infty} \Omega_{\gamma_n}\right)\right)$. Consequently, for the element z the equality (14) holds. This completes the proof. □

Theorem 4 and the Cauchy Integral Equation (2) imply the following corollary.

Corollary 1. *Every function $f \in H_{bs}((L_1 \cap L_\infty)(\Omega))$ can be uniquely represented in the form*

$$f = \alpha_0 + \sum_{n=1}^{\infty} \sum_{\substack{k_1+2k_2+\ldots+nk_n=n \\ k_1,\ldots,k_n \in \mathbb{Z}_+}} \alpha_{k_1,\ldots,k_n} \tilde{R}_1^{k_1} \cdots \tilde{R}_n^{k_n},$$

where $\alpha_{k_1 k_2 \ldots k_n} \in \mathbb{C}$, and the series converges uniformly on bounded sets.

Lemma 4. *For every $y \in (L_1 \cap L_\infty)(\Omega)$, there exists $x_y \in L_\infty[0,1]$ such that $\tilde{R}_n(y) = R_n(x_y)$ for every $n \in \mathbb{N}$ and the following estimate holds:*

$$\|x_y\|_\infty \le \frac{2}{M}\|y\|, \tag{15}$$

where M is defined by (3).

Proof. Consider the sequence $c = \{c_n\}_{n=1}^{\infty}$, where $c_n = \tilde{R}_n(y)$ for $n \in \mathbb{N}$. Since $\tilde{R}_n$ is an n-homogeneous polynomial and $\|\tilde{R}_n\| = 1$, by (1),

$$|\tilde{R}_n(y)| \le \|y\|^n$$

for every $n \in \mathbb{N}$. Consequently,

$$\sup_{n \in \mathbb{N}} \sqrt[n]{|c_n|} \le \|y\| < \infty.$$

Therefore, by Theorem 2, there exists $x_c \in L_\infty[0,1]$ such that $R_n(x_c) = c_n$ for every $n \in \mathbb{N}$ and

$$\|x_c\|_\infty \le \frac{2}{M} \sup_{n \in \mathbb{N}} \sqrt[n]{|c_n|} \le \frac{2}{M}\|y\|,$$

where M is defined by (3). We set $x_y := x_c$. This completes the proof. □

Let us define the mapping $J : H_{bs}(L_\infty[0,1]) \to H_{bs}((L_1 \cap L_\infty)(\Omega))$ in the following way. Let $f \in H_{bs}(L_\infty[0,1])$. Then f can be uniquely represented in the form (4), that is,

$$f = \alpha_0 + \sum_{n=1}^{\infty} \sum_{\substack{k_1+2k_2+\ldots+nk_n=n \\ k_1,\ldots,k_n \in \mathbb{Z}_+}} \alpha_{k_1,\ldots,k_n} R_1^{k_1} \cdots R_n^{k_n}. \tag{16}$$

Let

$$J(f) = \alpha_0 + \sum_{n=1}^{\infty} \sum_{\substack{k_1+2k_2+\ldots+nk_n=n \\ k_1,\ldots,k_n \in \mathbb{Z}_+}} \alpha_{k_1,\ldots,k_n} \tilde{R}_1^{k_1} \cdots \tilde{R}_n^{k_n}. \tag{17}$$

Let us show that $J(f) \in H_{bs}((L_1 \cap L_\infty)(\Omega))$.

Proposition 5. *$J(f) \in H_{bs}((L_1 \cap L_\infty)(\Omega))$ for every $f \in H_{bs}(L_\infty[0,1])$ and*

$$\|J(f)\|_r \le \|f\|_{\frac{2}{M}r} \tag{18}$$

for every $r > 0$, where M is defined by (3).

Proof. By Lemma 4, for every $y \in (L_1 \cap L_\infty)(\Omega)$ there exists $x_y \in L_\infty[0,1]$ such that

$$\tilde{R}_n(y) = R_n(x_y) \tag{19}$$

for every $n \in \mathbb{N}$ and the inequality (15) holds. By (16), (17) and (19),

$$J(f)(y) = f(x_y) \tag{20}$$

for every $f \in H_{bs}(L_\infty[0,1])$ and $y \in (L_1 \cap L_\infty)(\Omega)$. By (15) and (20),

$$\begin{aligned} \|J(f)\|_r &= \sup\{|J(f)(y)| : \ y \in (L_1 \cap L_\infty)(\Omega) \text{ such that } \|y\| \le r\} \\ &= \sup\{|f(x_y)| : \ y \in (L_1 \cap L_\infty)(\Omega) \text{ such that } \|y\| \le r\} \\ &\le \sup\Big\{|f(x)| : \ x \in L_\infty[0,1] \text{ such that } \|x\|_\infty \le \frac{2}{M} r\Big\} \\ &\le \|f\|_{\frac{2}{M}r} \end{aligned} \tag{21}$$

for every $f \in H_{bs}(L_\infty[0,1])$ and $r > 0$. Thus, we have proved (18).

Let $f \in H_{bs}(L_\infty[0,1])$. Let us show that $J(f) \in H_{bs}((L_1 \cap L_\infty)(\Omega))$. The inequality (21) and the fact that f is the function of bounded type imply the fact that $J(f)$ is the function of bounded type. By (17) and by the symmetry of $\tilde{R}_n$, the function $J(f)$ is symmetric. Let us show that $J(f)$ is entire. By Proposition 4,

$$\limsup_{n\to\infty} \|P_n\|_1^{1/n} = 0, \tag{22}$$

where $P_0 = \alpha_0$ and

$$P_n = \sum_{\substack{k_1+2k_2+\ldots+nk_n=n \\ k_1,\ldots,k_n \in \mathbb{Z}_+}} \alpha_{k_1,\ldots,k_n} R_1^{k_1} \cdots R_n^{k_n}$$

for $n \in \mathbb{N}$. Consider the series

$$\sum_{n=0}^{\infty} \tilde{P}_n, \tag{23}$$

where $\tilde{P}_0 = \alpha_0$ and

$$\tilde{P}_n = \sum_{\substack{k_1+2k_2+\ldots+nk_n=n \\ k_1,\ldots,k_n \in \mathbb{Z}_+}} \alpha_{k_1,\ldots,k_n} \tilde{R}_1^{k_1} \cdots \tilde{R}_n^{k_n}$$

for $n \in \mathbb{N}$. Note that $\tilde{P}_n = J(P_n)$; therefore, by (21),

$$\|\tilde{P}_n\|_1 \le \|P_n\|_{\frac{2}{M}}$$

for every $n \in \mathbb{N}$. By the n-homogeneity of the polynomial P_n,

$$\|P_n\|_{\frac{2}{M}} = \sup_{\|x\| \le \frac{2}{M}} |P_n(x)| = \sup_{\|x\| \le 1} \Big|P_n\Big(\frac{2}{M}x\Big)\Big| = \Big(\frac{2}{M}\Big)^n \sup_{\|x\| \le 1} |P_n(x)| = \Big(\frac{2}{M}\Big)^n \|P_n\|_1.$$

Therefore,

$$\|\tilde{P}_n\|_1 \le \Big(\frac{2}{M}\Big)^n \|P_n\|_1. \tag{24}$$

By (22) and (24),

$$0 \le \limsup_{n\to\infty} \|\tilde{P}_n\|_1^{1/n} \le \frac{2}{M} \limsup_{n\to\infty} \|P_n\|_1^{1/n} = 0.$$

Therefore,

$$\limsup_{n\to\infty} \|\tilde{P}_n\|_1^{1/n} = 0$$

and, consequently, by Proposition 4, the series (23) converges to some entire function on the space $(L_1 \cap L_\infty)(\Omega)$ with the infinite radius of boundedness. By (17), this function is $J(f)$. Consequently, $J(f)$ is an entire function of bounded type. Thus, $J(f) \in H_{bs}((L_1 \cap L_\infty)(\Omega))$. □

Theorem 5. *The mapping J, defined by* (17), *is an isomorphism of Fréchet algebras $H_{bs}(L_\infty[0,1])$ and $H_{bs}((L_1 \cap L_\infty)(\Omega))$.*

Proof. Let us show that J is linear. Let $f, g \in H_{bs}(L_\infty[0,1])$. Then functions f and g can be uniquely represented as

$$f = \alpha_0 + \sum_{n=1}^{\infty} \sum_{\substack{k_1+2k_2+\ldots+nk_n=n \\ k_1,\ldots,k_n \in \mathbb{Z}_+}} \alpha_{k_1,\ldots,k_n} R_1^{k_1} \cdots R_n^{k_n},$$

$$g = \beta_0 + \sum_{n=1}^{\infty} \sum_{\substack{k_1+2k_2+\ldots+nk_n=n \\ k_1,\ldots,k_n \in \mathbb{Z}_+}} \beta_{k_1,\ldots,k_n} R_1^{k_1} \cdots R_n^{k_n}$$

respectively. Let $\lambda \in \mathbb{C}$. Note that

$$\lambda f = \lambda\alpha_0 + \sum_{n=1}^{\infty} \sum_{\substack{k_1+2k_2+\ldots+nk_n=n \\ k_1,\ldots,k_n \in \mathbb{Z}_+}} \lambda\alpha_{k_1,\ldots,k_n} R_1^{k_1} \cdots R_n^{k_n}$$

and

$$f + g = \alpha_0 + \beta_0 + \sum_{n=1}^{\infty} \sum_{\substack{k_1+2k_2+\ldots+nk_n=n \\ k_1,\ldots,k_n \in \mathbb{Z}_+}} (\alpha_{k_1,\ldots,k_n} + \beta_{k_1,\ldots,k_n}) R_1^{k_1} \cdots R_n^{k_n}.$$

Therefore,

$$J(\lambda f) = \lambda\alpha_0 + \sum_{n=1}^{\infty} \sum_{\substack{k_1+2k_2+\ldots+nk_n=n \\ k_1,\ldots,k_n \in \mathbb{Z}_+}} \lambda\alpha_{k_1,\ldots,k_n} \tilde{R}_1^{k_1} \cdots \tilde{R}_n^{k_n} = \lambda J(f)$$

and

$$J(f+g) = \alpha_0 + \beta_0 + \sum_{n=1}^{\infty} \sum_{\substack{k_1+2k_2+\ldots+nk_n=n \\ k_1,\ldots,k_n \in \mathbb{Z}_+}} (\alpha_{k_1,\ldots,k_n} + \beta_{k_1,\ldots,k_n}) \tilde{R}_1^{k_1} \cdots \tilde{R}_n^{k_n} = J(f) + J(g).$$

Thus, J is linear.

Let us show that J is continuous. Since J is a linear mapping between Fréchet algebras, it follows that for J the continuity and the boundedness are equivalent. In turn, the boundedness of J follows from (18). Thus, J is continuous.

Let us show that J is multiplicative. By (17),

$$J(R_1^{k_1} \cdots R_n^{k_n}) = \tilde{R}_1^{k_1} \cdots \tilde{R}_n^{k_n} \tag{25}$$

for every $n \in \mathbb{N}$ and $k_1, \ldots, k_n \in \mathbb{Z}_+$. As a consequence of Theorem 1, every symmetric continuous polynomial $P : L_\infty[0,1] \to \mathbb{C}$ can be uniquely represented as

$$P = \alpha_0 + \sum_{n=1}^{N} \sum_{k_1+2k_2+\ldots+nk_n=n} \alpha_{k_1,\ldots,k_n} R_1^{k_1} \cdots R_n^{k_n},$$

where $N \in \mathbb{N}$, $k_1, \ldots, k_n \in \mathbb{Z}_+$ and $\alpha_{k_1,\ldots,k_n} \in \mathbb{C}$. Therefore, since J is linear, taking into account (25),

$$J(P) = \alpha_0 + \sum_{n=1}^{N} \sum_{k_1+2k_2+\ldots+nk_n=n} \alpha_{k_1,\ldots,k_n} \tilde{R}_1^{k_1} \cdots \tilde{R}_n^{k_n}. \tag{26}$$

By using (26), it can be verified the equality

$$J(P_1P_2) = J(P_1)J(P_2) \tag{27}$$

for arbitrary symmetric continuous polynomials $P_1, P_2 : L_\infty[0,1] \to \mathbb{C}$. Let $f, g \in H_{bs}(L_\infty[0,1])$. Let us show that $J(fg) = J(f)J(g)$. Let $f = \sum_{n=0}^{\infty} f_n$ and $g = \sum_{n=0}^{\infty} g_n$ be the Taylor series expansions of f and g respectively. Then

$$fg = \sum_{k=0}^{\infty} \sum_{s=0}^{k} f_s g_{k-s}.$$

Consequently, since J is linear and continuous, taking into account (26),

$$J(fg) = \sum_{k=0}^{\infty} \sum_{s=0}^{k} J(f_s g_{k-s}) = \sum_{k=0}^{\infty} \sum_{s=0}^{k} J(f_s)J(g_{k-s}) = \left(\sum_{n=0}^{\infty} J(f_n) \right) \left(\sum_{n=0}^{\infty} J(g_n) \right) = J(f)J(g).$$

Thus, J is multiplicative.

Let us show that J is a bijection. Let γ_0 be an arbitrary element of Γ. Let $v : L_\infty[0,1] \to (L_1 \cap L_\infty)(\Omega)$ be defined by

$$v = J_{\gamma_0} \circ W_{\gamma_0}, \tag{28}$$

where W_{γ_0} is defined by (5), and J_{γ_0} is defined by (6). Since W_{γ_0} is a linear isometrical bijection and J_{γ_0} is a linear isometrical injective mapping (by Lemma 2), it follows that v is a linear isometrical injective mapping. Therefore, for every $r > 0$, the image of the closed ball with the center at 0 and the radius r of the space $L_\infty[0,1]$ under v is a subset of the closed ball with the center at 0 and the radius r of the space $(L_1 \cap L_\infty)(\Omega)$. Therefore,

$$\begin{aligned} &\sup\{|g(v(x))| : x \in L_\infty[0,1], \ \|x\|_\infty \le r\} \\ &\qquad \le \sup\{|g(y)| : y \in (L_1 \cap L_\infty)(\Omega), \ \|y\| \le r\}. \end{aligned} \tag{29}$$

for every function of bounded type $g : (L_1 \cap L_\infty)(\Omega) \to \mathbb{C}$ and for every $r > 0$. Let us prove the following auxiliary statement.

Lemma 5. *For every function $f \in H_{bs}((L_1 \cap L_\infty)(\Omega))$, the function $f \circ v$ belongs to the Fréchet algebra $H_{bs}(L_\infty[0,1])$.*

Proof of Lemma 5. Let $f \in H_{bs}((L_1 \cap L_\infty)(\Omega))$. Since f is a function of bounded type, it follows that the value $\|f\|_r$ is finite for every $r > 0$. Therefore, by (29), the value $\|f \circ v\|_r$ is finite for every $r > 0$. Thus, the function $f \circ v$ is of bounded type.

Let us show that $f \circ v$ is symmetric. For every $\sigma \in \Xi_{[0,1]}$, let us define the function $\hat{\sigma} : \Omega \to \Omega$ by

$$\hat{\sigma}(t) = \begin{cases} (w_{\gamma_0}^{-1} \circ \sigma \circ w_{\gamma_0})(t), & \text{if } t \in \Omega_{\gamma_0} \\ t, & \text{if } t \in \Omega \setminus \Omega_{\gamma_0}. \end{cases}$$

It can be checked that $\hat{\sigma} \in \Xi_\Omega$ and $v(x \circ \sigma) = v(x) \circ \hat{\sigma}$ for every $x \in L_\infty[0,1]$. Therefore, taking into account the symmetry of f,

$$(f \circ v)(x \circ \sigma) = f(v(x) \circ \hat{\sigma}) = f(v(x)) = (f \circ v)(x)$$

for every $\sigma \in \Xi_{[0,1]}$ and $x \in L_\infty[0,1]$. Thus, $f \circ v$ is symmetric.

Let us show that $f \circ v$ is an entire function. Since the function f is an entire function of bounded type, its Taylor series, terms of which we denote by $f_0, f_1, \ldots, f_n, \ldots$, is uniformly convergent to f on every bounded subset of the space $(L_1 \cap L_\infty)(\Omega)$. By Proposition 4,

$$\limsup_{n\to\infty} \|f_n\|_1^{1/n} = 0.$$

Consider the series

$$\sum_{n=0}^{\infty} f_n \circ v. \tag{30}$$

By (29), $\|f_n \circ v\|_1 \le \|f_n\|_1$ for every $n \in \mathbb{N}$. Consequently,

$$\limsup_{n\to\infty} \|f_n \circ v\|_1^{1/n} = 0,$$

that is, the series (30) converges uniformly to some entire function of bounded type on every bounded subset of the space $L_\infty[0,1]$. Let us show that this function is equal to $f \circ v$. Since $\sum_{n=0}^{\infty} f_n$ converges uniformly to f on every bounded subset of $(L_1 \cap L_\infty)(\Omega)$, it follows that for every $\varepsilon > 0$ and $r > 0$ there exists $N \in \mathbb{N}$ such that

$$\left\| f - \sum_{n=0}^{m} f_n \right\|_r < \varepsilon$$

for every $m > N$. Therefore, by (29),

$$\left\| f \circ v - \sum_{n=0}^{m} f_n \circ v \right\|_r \le \left\| f - \sum_{n=0}^{m} f_n \right\|_r < \varepsilon,$$

where $m > N$. Thus, the series (30) converges uniformly to $f \circ v$ on every bounded subset of the space $L_\infty[0,1]$. Consequently, the function $f \circ v$ is entire. This completes the proof of Lemma 5. □

We now continue with the proof of Theorem 5. Let us show that J is surjective. Let g be an arbitrary element of $H_{bs}((L_1 \cap L_\infty)(\Omega))$. Then g can be represented in the form

$$g = \alpha_0 + \sum_{n=1}^{\infty} \sum_{\substack{k_1+2k_2+\ldots+nk_n=n \\ k_1,\ldots,k_n \in \mathbb{Z}_+}} \alpha_{k_1,\ldots,k_n} \tilde{R}_1^{k_1} \cdots \tilde{R}_n^{k_n}. \tag{31}$$

Let $f = g \circ v$. By Lemma 5, $f \in H_{bs}(L_\infty[0,1])$. By (31),

$$f = \alpha_0 + \sum_{n=1}^{\infty} \sum_{\substack{k_1+2k_2+\ldots+nk_n=n \\ k_1,\ldots,k_n \in \mathbb{Z}_+}} \alpha_{k_1,\ldots,k_n} (\tilde{R}_1 \circ v)^{k_1} \cdots (\tilde{R}_n \circ v)^{k_n}.$$

Taking into account the equality $\tilde{R}_n \circ v = R_n$,

$$f = \alpha_0 + \sum_{n=1}^{\infty} \sum_{\substack{k_1+2k_2+\ldots+nk_n=n \\ k_1,\ldots,k_n \in \mathbb{Z}_+}} \alpha_{k_1,\ldots,k_n} R_1^{k_1} \cdots R_n^{k_n}.$$

By (17), $J(f) = g$. Thus, the mapping J is surjective and

$$J(f) \circ v = f \tag{32}$$

for every $f \in H_{bs}(L_\infty[0,1])$.

Let us prove that J is injective. Recall that J is linear. For a linear mapping, the injectivity is equivalent to the fact that the image of every nonzero element is nonzero. Let

f be a nonzero element of $H_{bs}(L_\infty[0,1])$. Let us show that $J(f) \neq 0$. Suppose $J(f) = 0$. Then $J(f) \circ v = 0$. Therefore, by (32), $f = 0.$, which is a contradiction. Thus, $J(f) \neq 0$. Consequently, J is injective. So, J is bijective.

By (18) and (29),

$$\|f\|_r \leq \|J(f)\|_r \leq \|f\|_{\frac{2}{M}r}$$

for every $f \in H_{bs}(L_\infty[0,1])$ and for every $r > 0$. This inequality implies the continuity of J and J^{-1}. This completes the proof of Theorem 5. □

4. Conclusions

This work is a significant generalization of the work [49]. We consider symmetric functions on Banach spaces of all complex-valued integrable essentially bounded functions on the unions of Lebesgue-Rohlin spaces with continuous measures. Note that there are a lot of important measure spaces which can be represented as the abovementioned union. For example, $\mathbb{R}^n$ for any $n \in \mathbb{N}$ with the Lebesgue measure is one such space. We investigate algebras of symmetric polynomials and entire symmetric functions on the abovementioned spaces. In particular, we show that Fréchet algebras of all complex-valued entire symmetric functions of bounded type on these Banach spaces are isomorphic to the Fréchet algebra of all complex-valued entire symmetric functions of bounded type on the complex Banach space $L_\infty[0,1]$.

The next step in this investigation is to consider the case of unions of arbitrary Lebesgue-Rohlin spaces.

Author Contributions: Conceptualization, T.V.; methodology, T.V.; writing—original draft preparation, T.V. and K.Z.; writing—review and editing, T.V. and K.Z. All authors have read and agreed to the published version of the manuscript.

Funding: This research received no external funding.

Institutional Review Board Statement: Not applicable.

Acknowledgments: The authors were partially supported by the Ministry of Education and Science of Ukraine, project registration number 0122U000857.

Conflicts of Interest: The authors declare no conflict of interest.

References

1. Nemirovskii, A.S.; Semenov, S.M. On polynomial approximation of functions on Hilbert space. *Mat. USSR Sbornik* **1973**, *21*, 255–277. [CrossRef]
2. Weyl, H. *The classical Groups: Their Invariants and Representations*; Princeton university Press: Princenton, NJ, USA, 1973.
3. van der Waerden, B.L. *Modern Algebra*; Ungar Publishing: New York, NY, USA, 1953; Volume 1.
4. Macdonald, I.G. *Symmetric Functions and Orthogonal Polynomials*; University Lecture Series, 12; AMS: Providence, RI, USA, 1998.
5. González, M.; Gonzalo, R.; Jaramillo, J.A. Symmetric polynomials on rearrangement invariant function spaces. *J. Lond. Math. Soc.* **1999**, *59*, 681–697. [CrossRef]
6. Lindenstrauss, J.; Tzafriri L. *Classical Banach Spaces, Vol. I, Sequence Spaces*; Springer: Berlin, Germany, 1977.
7. Lindenstrauss, J.; Tzafriri L. *Classical Banach Spaces, Vol. II, Function Spaces*; Springer: Berlin, Germany, 1979.
8. Alencar, R.; Aron, R.; Galindo, P.; Zagorodnyuk, A. Algebras of symmetric holomorphic functions on ℓ_p. *Bull. Lond. Math. Soc.* **2003**, *35*, 55–64. [CrossRef]
9. Chernega, I.; Holubchak, O.; Novosad, Z.; Zagorodnyuk, A. Continuity and hypercyclicity of composition operators on algebras of symmetric analytic functions on Banach spaces. *Eur. J. Math.* **2020**, *6*, 153–163. [CrossRef]
10. Halushchak, S.I. Spectra of some algebras of entire functions of bounded type, generated by a sequence of polynomials. *Carpatian Math. Publ.* **2019**, *11*, 311–320. [CrossRef]
11. Halushchak, S.I. Isomorphisms of some algebras of analytic functions of bounded type on Banach spaces. *Mat. Stud.* **2021**, *56*, 106–112. [CrossRef]
12. Burtnyak, I.; Chernega, I.; Hladkyi, V.; Labachuk, O.; Novosad, Z. Application of symmetric analytic functions to spectra of linear operators. *Carpathian Math. Publ.* **2021**, *13*, 701–710. [CrossRef]
13. Chernega, I.V. A semiring in the spectrum of the algebra of symmetric analytic functions in the space ℓ_1. *J. Math. Sci.* **2016**, *212*, 38–45. [CrossRef]

14. Chernega, I.V.; Fushtei, V.I.; Zagorodnyuk, A.V. Power operations and differentiations associated with supersymmetric polynomials on a Banach space. *Carpathian Math. Publ.* **2020**, *12*, 360–367. [CrossRef]
15. Chernega, I.; Galindo, P.; Zagorodnyuk, A. Some algebras of symmetric analytic functions and their spectra. *Proc. Edinb. Math. Soc.* **2012**, *55*, 125–142. [CrossRef]
16. Chernega, I.; Galindo, P.; Zagorodnyuk, A. The convolution operation on the spectra of algebras of symmetric analytic functions. *J. Math. Anal. Appl.*, **2012**, *395*, 569–577. [CrossRef]
17. Chernega, I.; Galindo, P.; Zagorodnyuk, A. A multiplicative convolution on the spectra of algebras of symmetric analytic functions, *Rev. Mat. Complut.* **2014**, *27*, 575–585. [CrossRef]
18. Chernega, I.V.; Zagorodnyuk, A.V. Note on bases in algebras of analytic functions on Banach spaces. *Carpathian Math. Publ.* **2019**, *11*, 42–47. [CrossRef]
19. Jawad, F.; Karpenko, H.; Zagorodnyuk, A. Algebras generated by special symmetric polynomials on ℓ_1. *Carpathian Math. Publ.* **2019**, *11*, 335–344. [CrossRef]
20. Jawad, F.; Zagorodnyuk, A. Supersymmetric polynomials on the space of absolutely convergent series. *Symmetry* **2019**, *11*, 1111. [CrossRef]
21. Holubchak, O.M.; Zagorodnyuk, A.V. Topological and algebraic structures on a set of multisets. *J. Math. Sci.* **2021**, *258*, 446–454. [CrossRef]
22. Novosad, Z.; Zagorodnyuk, A. Analytic automorphisms and transitivity of analytic mappings. *Mathematics* **2020**, *8*, 2179. [CrossRef]
23. Holubchak, O.M. Hilbert space of symmetric functions on ℓ_1. *J. Math. Sci.* **2012**, *185*, 809–814. [CrossRef]
24. Novosad, Z.; Zagorodnyuk, A. Polynomial automorphisms and hypercyclic operators on spaces of analytic functions. *Archiv. Math.* **2007**, *89*, 157–166. [CrossRef]
25. Martsinkiv, M.; Zagorodnyuk, A. Approximations of symmetric functions on Banach spaces with symmetric bases. *Symmetry* **2021**, *13*, 2318. [CrossRef]
26. Aron, R.; Gonzalo, R.; Zagorodnyuk, A. Zeros of real polynomials. *Linearand Multilinear Algebra* **2000**, *48*, 107–115. [CrossRef]
27. Jawad, F. Note on separately symmetric polynomials on the Cartesian product of ℓ_1. *Mat. Stud.* **2018**, *50*, 204–210. [CrossRef]
28. Kravtsiv, V. The analogue of Newton's formula for block-symmetric polynomials. *Int. J. Math. Anal.* **2016**, *10*, 323–327. [CrossRef]
29. Kravtsiv, V.V. Algebraic basis of the algebra of block-symmetric polynomials on $\ell_1 \otimes \ell_\infty$. *Carpathian Math. Publ.* **2019**, *11*, 89–95. [CrossRef]
30. Kravtsiv, V.V. Analogues of the Newton formulas for the block-symmetric polynomials. *Carpathian Math. Publ.* **2020**, *12*, 17–22. [CrossRef]
31. Kravtsiv, V.V. Zeros of block-symmetric polynomials on Banach spaces. *Mat. Stud.* **2020**, *53*, 206–211. doi: 10.30970/ms.53.2.206-211. [CrossRef]
32. Kravtsiv, V.V.; Zagorodnyuk, A.V. Multiplicative convolution on the algebra of block-symmetric analytic functions. *J. Math. Sci.* **2020**, *246*, 245–255. [CrossRef]
33. Kravtsiv, V.; Vasylyshyn, T.; Zagorodnyuk, A. On algebraic basis of the algebra of symmetric polynomials on $\ell_p(\mathbb{C}^n)$. *J. Funct. Spaces* **2017**, *2017*, 4947925. [CrossRef]
34. Vasylyshyn, T. Symmetric functions on spaces $\ell_p(\mathbb{R}^n)$ and $\ell_p(\mathbb{C}^n)$. *Carpathian Math. Publ.* **2020**, *12*, 5–16. [CrossRef]
35. Chernega, I. Symmetric polynomials and holomorphic functions on infinite dimensional spaces. *J. Vasyl Stefanyk Precarpathian Natl. Univ.* **2015**, *2*, 23–49. [CrossRef]
36. Chernega, I.; Zagorodnyuk, A. Unbounded symmetric analytic functions on ℓ_1. *Math. Scand.* **2018**, *122*, 84–90. [CrossRef]
37. Hihliuk, A.; Zagorodnyuk, A. Entire analytic functions of unbounded type on Banach spaces and their lineability. *Axioms* **2021**, *10*, 150. [CrossRef]
38. Hihliuk, A; Zagorodnyuk, A. Algebras of entire functions containing functions of unbounded type on a Banach space. *Carpathian Math. Publ.* **2021**, *13*, 426–432. [CrossRef]
39. Hihliuk, A.; Zagorodnyuk, A. Classes of entire analytic functions of unbounded type on Banach spaces. *Axioms* **2020**, *9*, 133. [CrossRef]
40. Galindo, P.; Vasylyshyn, T.; Zagorodnyuk, A. Symmetric and finitely symmetric polynomials on the spaces ℓ_∞ and $L_\infty[0, +\infty)$. *Math. Nachr.* **2018**, *291*, 1712–1726. [CrossRef]
41. Galindo, P.; Vasylyshyn, T.; Zagorodnyuk, A. The algebra of symmetric analytic functions on L_∞. *Proc. Roy. Soc. Edinburgh Sect. A* **2017**, *147*, 743–761. [CrossRef]
42. Galindo, P.; Vasylyshyn, T.; Zagorodnyuk, A. Analytic structure on the spectrum of the algebra of symmetric analytic functions on L_∞. *Rev. R. Acad. Cienc. Exactas Fís. Nat. Ser. A Mat.* **2020**, *114*, 56. [CrossRef]
43. Vasylyshyn, T. Symmetric polynomials on $(L_p)^n$. *Eur. J. Math.* **2020**, *6*, 164–178. [CrossRef]
44. Vasylyshyn, T.V. Symmetric polynomials on the Cartesian power of L_p on the semi-axis. *Mat. Stud.* **2018**, *50*, 93–104. [CrossRef]
45. Vasylyshyn, T. Algebras of symmetric analytic functions on Cartesian powers of Lebesgue integrable in a power $p \in [1, +\infty)$ functions. *Carpathian Math. Publ.* **2021**, *13*, 340–351. [CrossRef]
46. Vasylyshyn, T.V. The algebra of symmetric polynomials on $(L_\infty)^n$. *Mat. Stud.* **2019**, *52*, 71–85. [CrossRef]
47. Vasylyshyn, T. Symmetric analytic functions on the Cartesian power of the complex Banach space of Lebesgue measurable essentially bounded functions on $[0, 1]$. *J. Math. Anal. Appl.* **2022**, *509*, 125977. [CrossRef]

48. Vasylyshyn, T. Symmetric polynomials on the space of bounded integrable functions on the semi-axis. *Int. J. Pure Appl. Math.* **2017**, *117*, 425–430. [CrossRef]
49. Vasylyshyn, T. Algebras of entire symmetric functions on spaces of Lebesgue measurable essentially bounded functions. *J. Math. Sci.* **2020**, *246*, 264–276. [CrossRef]
50. Aron, R.M.; Falcó, J.; García, D.; Maestre, M. Algebras of symmetric holomorphic functions of several complex variables. *Rev. Mat. Complut.*, **2018**, *31*, 651–672. [CrossRef]
51. Aron, R.M.; Falcó, J.; Maestre, M. Separation theorems for group invariant polynomials. *J. Geom. Anal.* **2018**, *28*, 393–404. [CrossRef]
52. Choi, Y.S.; Falcó, J.; García, D.; Jung, M.; Maestre, M. Group invariant separating polynomials on a Banach space. *Publ. Mat.* **2022**, *66*, 207–233.
53. Aron, R.; Galindo, P.; Pinasco, D.; Zalduendo, I. Group-symmetric holomorphic functions on a Banach space. *Bull. Lond. Math. Soc.* **2016**, *48*, 779–796. [CrossRef]
54. García, D.; Maestre, M.; Zalduendo, I. The spectra of algebras of group-symmetric functions. *Proc. Edinb. Math. Soc.* **2019**, *62*, 609–623. [CrossRef]
55. Michael, E. *Locally multiplicatively convex topological algebras. Mem. Amer. Math. Soc.* **1952**, *11*, Providence. [CrossRef]
56. Dineen, S. *Complex Analysis in Locally Convex Spaces*; North-Holland: Amsterdam, The Netherlands; New York, NY, USA; Oxford, UK, 1981.
57. Mujica, J. *Complex Analysis in Banach Spaces*, North Holland: Amsterdam, The Netherlands, 1986.
58. Dineen, S. *Complex Analysis on Infinite Dimensional Spaces, Monographs in Mathematics*; Springer: New York, NY, USA, 1999.
59. Rohlin, V.A. On the fundamental ideas of measure theory. *Am. Math. Soc. Transl.* **1952**, *71*, 1–54.
60. Bennett, C.; Sharpley, R. *Interpolation of Operators*; Academic Press: Boston, MA, USA, 1981.

axioms

MDPI

Article

Approximation for the Ratios of the Confluent Hypergeometric Function $\Phi_D^{(N)}$ by the Branched Continued Fractions

Tamara Antonova [1], Roman Dmytryshyn [2,*] and Roman Kurka [1]

[1] Institute of Applied Mathematics and Fundamental Sciences, Lviv Polytechnic National University, 12 Stepana Bandera Str., 79013 Lviv, Ukraine

[2] Faculty of Mathematics and Computer Science, Vasyl Stefanyk Precarpathian National University, 57 Shevchenko Str., 76018 Ivano-Frankivsk, Ukraine

* Correspondence: roman.dmytryshyn@pnu.edu.ua

Abstract: The paper deals with the problem of expansion of the ratios of the confluent hypergeometric function of N variables $\Phi_D^{(N)}(a,\bar{b};c;\bar{z})$ into the branched continued fractions (BCF) of the general form with N branches of branching and investigates the convergence of these BCF. The algorithms of construction for BCF expansions of confluent hypergeometric function $\Phi_D^{(N)}$ ratios are based on some given recurrence relations for this function. The case of nonnegative parameters $a, b_1, \ldots, b_{N-1}$ and positive c is considered. Some convergence criteria for obtained BCF with elements in $\mathbb{R}^N$ and $\mathbb{C}^N$ are established. It is proven that these BCF converge to the functions which are an analytic continuation of the above-mentioned ratios of function $\Phi_D^{(N)}(a,\bar{b};c;\bar{z})$ in some domain of $\mathbb{C}^N$.

Keywords: confluent hypergeometric function of several variables; recurrence relations; branched continued fraction; approximant; uniform convergence

MSC: 33C65; 11J70; 30B70; 40A15

Citation: Antonova, T.; Dmytryshyn, R.; Kurka, R. Approximation for the Ratios of the Confluent Hypergeometric Function $\Phi_D^{(N)}$ by the Branched Continued Fractions. *Axioms* **2022**, *11*, 426. https://doi.org/10.3390/axioms11090426

Academic Editor: Natália Martins

Received: 31 July 2022

Accepted: 23 August 2022

Published: 24 August 2022

1. Introduction

In the course of the last three centuries the necessity of solving the problems arising in the fields of hydrodynamics, control theory, classical and quantum mechanics stimulated the development of the theory of special functions of one and several variables [1–5]. Functions of hypergeometric type constitute an important class of special functions.

For hypergeometric functions of one variables there exists a well-developed theory with numerous applications. All advanced computer algebra systems support calculations involving hypergeometric functions. In the multivariate case there exist several approaches to the notion of a hypergeometric functions. Such a function can be defined as a sum of a power series of a certain kind (the so-called Γ-series), as a solution to a system of partial differential equations, as the Euler-type integral or as the Mellin–Barnes integral [1,3].

It is known that continued fractions have numerous applications in the theory of approximation of hypergeometric functions of one variable [6–9]. Multidimensional generalizations of continued fractions can be considered as a tool of rational approximation of functions of several variables [10–20]. In particular, branched continued fractions (BCF) of the form

$$d_0(\bar{z}) + \mathop{\mathrm{D}}_{k=1}^{\infty} \sum_{i_k=1}^{N} \frac{c_{i(k)}(\bar{z})}{d_{i(k)}(\bar{z})} = d_0(\bar{z}) + \sum_{i_1=1}^{N} \cfrac{c_{i(1)}(\bar{z})}{d_{i(1)}(\bar{z}) + \sum\limits_{i_2=1}^{N} \cfrac{c_{i(2)}(\bar{z})}{d_{i(2)}(\bar{z}) + \sum\limits_{i_3=1}^{N} \cfrac{c_{i(3)}(\bar{z})}{d_{i(3)}(\bar{z}) + \ddots}}}, \quad (1)$$

where $N \in \mathbb{N}$, $i(k) = (i_1, i_2, \ldots, i_k)$ be a multi-index,

$$\mathcal{I} = \{i(k) : 1 \le i_r \le N,\ 1 \le r \le k,\ k \ge 1\}$$

be a set of multi-indices, the $d_0(\bar{z})$ and the elements $c_{i(k)}(\bar{z})$ and $d_{i(k)}(\bar{z})$, $i(k) \in \mathcal{I}$ are certain polynomials, $\bar{z} = (z_1, z_2, \ldots, z_N) \in \mathbb{C}^N$ are used to approximate the ratios of some hypergeometric functions of one or several variables [21–29]. Note that the symbol D, proposed by I. Sleshynsky in 1888 [30], is used here to denote BCF.

In this paper, we construct the branched continued fraction expansions for confluent hypergeometric functions of N variables $\Phi_D^{(N)}$ ratios and investigate their convergence. The confluent hypergeometric function $\Phi_D^{(N)}$ is defined by the multiply power series [3]

$$\Phi_D^{(N)}(a, \bar{b}; c; \bar{z}) = \sum_{k_1, k_2, \ldots, k_N = 0}^{\infty} \frac{(a)_{k_1+k_2+\ldots+k_N}(b_1)_{k_1}(b_2)_{k_2}\cdots(b_{N-1})_{k_{N-1}}}{(c)_{k_1+k_2+\ldots+k_N}} \frac{z_1^{k_1}}{k_1!}\frac{z_2^{k_2}}{k_2!}\cdots\frac{z_N^{k_N}}{k_N!}, \quad (2)$$

where $a, b_1, \ldots, b_{N-1}, c$ are complex constants (parameters of function), $c \ne 0, -1, -2, \ldots$, $\bar{b} = (b_1, \ldots, b_{N-1})$, $(\alpha)_k$ is the Pochhammer symbol: $(\alpha)_0 = 1$, $(\alpha)_k = \alpha(\alpha+1)_{k-1}$, $k \ge 1$. Series (2) converges for $|z_i| < 1$, $1 \le i \le N-1$, $z_N \in \mathbb{C}$. Function $\Phi_D^{(N)}$ was originated by H. Exton and H. Srivastava. This function is a generalization of the Humbert function $\Phi_D^{(2)} = \Phi_1$. At $z_N = 0$ value of the function, $\Phi_D^{(N)}$ coincides with the value of the Lauricella function $F_D^{(N-1)}$.

The algorithms of construction for branched continued fraction expansions of confluent hypergeometric function $\Phi_D^{(N)}$ ratios are based on some recurrence relations for this function (Section 2). We stated and proved some convergence properties for the obtained BCF (Section 3).

Let us recall some basic concepts and notations (we refer the reader to the books [31,32] to learn more). The finite BCF

$$f_n(\bar{z}) = d_0(\bar{z}) + \mathop{\mathrm{D}}_{k=1}^{n} \sum_{i_k=1}^{N} \frac{c_{i(k)}(\bar{z})}{d_{i(k)}(\bar{z})}$$

is called the nth approximant of the BCF (1). Note that for each $n \in \mathbb{N}$ the approximant $f_n(\bar{z})$ can also be written as

$$f_n(\bar{z}) = d_0(\bar{z}) + \sum_{i_1=1}^{N} \frac{c_{i(1)}(\bar{z})}{Q_{i(1)}^{(n)}(\bar{z})},$$

where the tails, $Q_{i(k)}^{(n)}(\bar{z})$, $i(k) \in \mathcal{I}$, $1 \le k \le n$, are defined as follows

$$Q_{i(n)}^{(n)}(\bar{z}) = d_{i(n)}(\bar{z}), \quad n \ge 1, \quad (3)$$

$$Q_{i(k)}^{(n)}(\bar{z}) = d_{i(k)}(\bar{z}) + \mathop{\mathrm{D}}_{r=1}^{n-k} \sum_{i_{k+r}=1}^{N} \frac{c_{i(k+r)}(\bar{z})}{d_{i(k+r)}(\bar{z})}, \quad i(k) \in \mathcal{I},\ 1 \le k \le n-1,\ n \ge 2.$$

It is clear that the following recurrence relations hold

$$Q_{i(k)}^{(n)}(\bar{z}) = d_{i(k)}(\bar{z}) + \sum_{i_{k+1}=1}^{N} \frac{c_{i(k+1)}(\bar{z})}{Q_{i(k+1)}^{(n)}(\bar{z})}, \quad i(k) \in \mathcal{I},\ 1 \le k \le n-1,\ n \ge 2. \quad (4)$$

Definition 1. *The BCF* (1)*, whose elements are functions of N variables, is said to converge uniformly in a certain domain D,* $D \subset \mathbb{C}^N$*, if for each* $\bar{z} \in D$ *at most its approximants* $f_n(\bar{z})$ *have sense and are finite and for a given* $\epsilon > 0$ *there exists* n_ϵ *such that for all* $m, n \geq n_\epsilon$ *and for each* $\bar{z} \in D$ *the following inequality* $|f_m(\bar{z}) - f_n(\bar{z})| < \epsilon$ *is valid.*

Definition 2. *The BCF* (1)*, whose elements are functions of N variables in a domain D,* $D \subset \mathbb{C}^N$*, is said to converge uniformly on a compact subset K of D if there exists* $n(K)$ *such that* $f_n(\bar{z})$ *is holomorphic in some domain containing K for all* $n \geq n(K)$ *and for a given* $\epsilon > 0$ *there exists* $n_\epsilon > n(K)$ *such that* $\sup_{\bar{z}\in K} |f_m(\bar{z}) - f_n(\bar{z})| < \epsilon$ *for* $m, n \geq n_\epsilon$*.*

If $Q_{i(k)}^{(n)}(\bar{z}) \not\equiv 0$ for all $i(k) \in \mathcal{I}$, $1 \leq k \leq n$, $n \geq 1$, the following formula of difference for two approximants of BCF of the form (1) is valid (see [31], p. 28)

$$f_m(\bar{z}) - f_n(\bar{z}) = (-1)^n \sum_{i_1=1}^{N} \cdots \sum_{i_{n+1}=1}^{N} \frac{\prod_{k=1}^{n+1} c_{i(k)}(\bar{z})}{\prod_{k=1}^{n+1} Q_{i(k)}^{(m)}(\bar{z}) \prod_{p=1}^{n} Q_{i(k)}^{(n)}(\bar{z})}, \quad m > n,\ n \geq 1. \quad (5)$$

Note that this formula is used to study the properties of a sequence $\{f_n(\bar{z})\}$.

2. Recurrence Relations for Function $\Phi_D^{(N)}$: Expansions for the Ratios of Function $\Phi_D^{(N)}$ into the Branched Continued Fractions

To construct the expansion of the ratio of hypergeometric series of one or several variables, the recurrence relations between these series are used. Here we give some recurrence relations for multiply power series (2).

We denote $e_i = (\delta_i^1, \delta_i^2, \ldots, \delta_i^{N-1})$, where δ_i^j is the Kronecker delta: $\delta_i^j = 1$, if $i = j$, and $\delta_i^j = 0$, if $i \neq j$.

The recurrence relations for function $\Phi_D^{(N)}$ are valid

$$\begin{aligned}\Phi_D^{(N)}(a,\bar{b};c;\bar{z}) = {} & \Phi_D^{(N)}(a+1,\bar{b};c;\bar{z}) - \sum_{i=1}^{N-1} \frac{b_i z_i}{c} \Phi_D^{(N)}(a+1,\bar{b}+e_i;c+1;\bar{z}) \\ & - \frac{z_N}{c} \Phi_D^{(N)}(a+1,\bar{b};c+1;\bar{z}), \end{aligned} \quad (6)$$

$$\begin{aligned}\Phi_D^{(N)}(a,\bar{b};c;\bar{z}) = {} & \Phi_D^{(N)}(a,\bar{b};c+1;\bar{z}) + \sum_{i=1}^{N-1} \frac{a b_i z_i}{c(c+1)} \Phi_D^{(N)}(a+1,\bar{b}+e_i;c+2;\bar{z}) \\ & + \frac{a z_N}{c(c+1)} \Phi_D^{(N)}(a+1,\bar{b};c+2;\bar{z}), \end{aligned} \quad (7)$$

$$\begin{aligned}\Phi_D^{(N)}(a,\bar{b};c;\bar{z}) = {} & \Phi_D^{(N)}(a,\bar{b}+e_i;c;\bar{z}) \\ & - \frac{a z_i}{c} \Phi_D^{(N)}(a+1,\bar{b}+e_i;c+1;\bar{z}), \quad 1 \leq i \leq N-1. \end{aligned} \quad (8)$$

These formal identities can be derived from (2) by comparing the coefficients of $z_1^{k_1} z_2^{k_2} \ldots z_N^{k_N}$ on both sides of the identities.

From (6)–(8) it follows that

$$
\begin{aligned}
\Phi_D^{(N)}(a,\bar{b};c;\bar{z}) &= \Phi_D^{(N)}(a+1,\bar{b};c;\bar{z}) - \sum_{j=1}^{N-1}\frac{b_j z_j}{c}\Phi_D^{(N)}(a+1,\bar{b}+e_j;c+1;\bar{z}) \\
&\quad - \frac{z_N}{c}\Phi_D^{(N)}(a+1,\bar{b};c+1;\bar{z}) \\
&= \Phi_D^{(N)}(a+1,\bar{b};c;\bar{z}) - \frac{z_N}{c}\Phi_D^{(N)}(a+1,\bar{b};c+1;\bar{z}) \\
&\quad - \sum_{j=1}^{N-1}\frac{b_j z_j}{c}\left(\Phi_D^{(N)}(a+1,\bar{b};c+1;\bar{z}) + \frac{a+1}{c+1}z_j\Phi_D^{(N)}(a+2,\bar{b}+e_j;c+2;\bar{z})\right) \\
&= \Phi_D^{(N)}(a+1,\bar{b};c+1;\bar{z}) - \frac{z_N}{c}\Phi_D^{(N)}(a+1,\bar{b};c+1;\bar{z}) \\
&\quad + \sum_{j=1}^{N-1}\frac{(a+1)b_j z_j}{c(c+1)}\Phi_D^{(N)}(a+2,\bar{b}+e_j;c+2;\bar{z}) \\
&\quad + \frac{(a+1)z_N}{c(c+1)}\Phi_D^{(N)}(a+2,\bar{b};c+2;\bar{z}) \\
&\quad - \sum_{j=1}^{N-1}\frac{b_j}{c}z_j\left(\Phi_D^{(N)}(a+1,\bar{b};c+1;\bar{z}) + \frac{a+1}{c+1}z_j\Phi_D^{(N)}(a+2,\bar{b}+e_j;c+2;\bar{z})\right).
\end{aligned}
$$

So,

$$
\begin{aligned}
\Phi_D^{(N)}(a,\bar{b};c;\bar{z}) &= \Phi_D^{(N)}(a+1,\bar{b};c+1;\bar{z})\left(1 - \frac{z_N}{c} - \sum_{j=1}^{N-1}\frac{b_j}{c}z_j\right) \\
&\quad + \sum_{j=1}^{N-1}\frac{(a+1)b_j}{c(c+1)}z_j(1-z_j)\Phi_D^{(N)}(a+2,\bar{b}+e_j;c+2;\bar{z}) \\
&\quad + \frac{a+1}{c(c+1)}z_N\Phi_D^{(N)}(a+2,\bar{b};c+2;\bar{z}).
\end{aligned} \tag{9}
$$

Using the recurrence relations (8), (9) the expansions of the ratios

$$
\begin{aligned}
X_i(a,\bar{b};c;\bar{z}) &= \frac{\Phi_D^{(N)}(a,\bar{b};c;\bar{z})}{\Phi_D^{(N)}(a+1,\bar{b}+e_i;c+1;\bar{z})}, \quad 1 \le i \le N-1, \\
X_N(a,\bar{b};c;\bar{z}) &= \frac{\Phi_D^{(N)}(a,\bar{b};c;\bar{z})}{\Phi_D^{(N)}(a+1,\bar{b};c+1;\bar{z})},
\end{aligned}
$$

into the branched continued fraction (BCF) of the general form with N branches of branching can be constructed. Indeed, performing the termwise division of the identity (9) by $\Phi_D^{(N)}(a+1,\bar{b};c+1;\bar{z})$, we obtain

$$
\begin{aligned}
X_N(a,\bar{b};c;\bar{z}) &= 1 - \frac{z_N}{c} - \sum_{j=1}^{N-1}\frac{b_j}{c}z_j + \sum_{j=1}^{N-1}\frac{(a+1)b_j}{c(c+1)}\frac{z_j(1-z_j)}{X_j(a+1,\bar{b};c+1;\bar{z})} \\
&\quad + \frac{a+1}{c(c+1)}\frac{z_N}{X_N(a+1,\bar{b};c+1;\bar{z})}.
\end{aligned} \tag{10}
$$

Moreover, from (8) it follows that

$$
X_i(a,\bar{b};c;\bar{z}) = X_N(a,\bar{b}+e_i;c;\bar{z}) - \frac{az_i}{c}, \quad 1 \le i \le N-1. \tag{11}
$$

Taking into account (11), we rewrite formula (10) as follows

$$X_N(a,\bar{b};c;\bar{z}) = 1 - \frac{z_N}{c} - \sum_{j=1}^{N-1}\frac{b_j}{c}z_j + \sum_{j=1}^{N-1}\frac{(a+1)b_j}{c(c+1)}\frac{z_j(1-z_j)}{X_N(a+1,\bar{b}+e_j;c+1;\bar{z}) - \frac{(a+1)z_j}{c+1}} + \frac{a+1}{c(c+1)}\frac{z_N}{X_N(a+1,\bar{b};c+1;\bar{z})}$$

or

$$X_N(a,\bar{b};c;\bar{z}) = 1 - \frac{z_N}{c} - \sum_{j=1}^{N-1}\frac{b_j}{c}z_j + \sum_{i_1=1}^{N}\frac{\frac{(a+1)((1-\delta_{i_1}^N)b_{i_1}+\delta_{i_1}^N)}{c(c+1)}z_{i_1}(1-(1-\delta_{i_1}^N)z_{i_1})}{X_N(a+1,\bar{b}+e_{i_1};c+1;\bar{z}) - (1-\delta_{i_1}^N)\frac{(a+1)z_{i_1}}{c+1}}. \quad (12)$$

Then

$$X_N(a,\bar{b};c;\bar{z}) = 1 - \frac{z_N}{c} - \sum_{j=1}^{N-1}\frac{b_j}{c}z_j + \sum_{i_1=1}^{N}\frac{(a+1)((1-\delta_{i_1}^N)b_{i_1}+\delta_{i_1}^N)}{c(c+1)}z_{i_1}(1-(1-\delta_{i_1}^N)z_{i_1}) \times \left(1 - \frac{z_N}{c+1} - \sum_{j=1}^{N-1}\frac{b_j+\delta_{i_1}^j}{c+1}z_j - (1-\delta_{i_1}^N)\frac{a+1}{c+1}z_{i_1} + \sum_{i_2=1}^{N}\frac{\frac{(a+2)((1-\delta_{i_2}^N)(b_{i_2}+\delta_{i_2}^{i_1})+\delta_{i_2}^N)}{(c+1)(c+2)}z_{i_2} - (1-(1-\delta_{i_2}^N)z_{i_2})}{X_N(a+2,\bar{b}+e_{i_1}+e_{i_2};c+2;\bar{z}) - (1-\delta_{i_2}^N)\frac{a+2}{c+2}z_{i_2}}\right)^{-1}.$$

Substituting expressions for X_N with corresponding parameters into formula (12), after n steps we obtain the expansion for the ratio $X_N(a,\bar{b};c;\bar{z})$ into the finite BCF of the general form with N branches:

$$X_N(a,\bar{b};c;\bar{z}) = 1 - \frac{z_N}{c} - \sum_{j=1}^{N-1}\frac{b_j}{c}z_j + \sum_{i_1=1}^{N}\frac{c_{i(1)}(\bar{z})|}{|d_{i(1)}(\bar{z})} + \sum_{i_2=1}^{N}\frac{c_{i(2)}(\bar{z})|}{|d_{i(2)}(\bar{z})} + \ldots + \sum_{i_n=1}^{N}\frac{c_{i(n)}(\bar{z})|}{|X_N(a+n,\bar{b}+\sum_{p=1}^{n}e_{i_p};c+n;\bar{z}) - (1-\delta_{i_n}^N)\frac{a+n}{c+n}z_{i_n}}, \quad (13)$$

where for $i(k) \in \mathcal{I}, 1 \le k \le n$,

$$c_{i(k)}(\bar{z}) = \begin{cases} \frac{(a+k)(b_{i_k}+\sum_{p=1}^{k-1}\delta_{i_k}^{i_p})}{(c+k-1)(c+k)}z_{i_k}(1-z_{i_k}), & \text{if} \quad 1 \le i_k \le N-1, \\ \frac{a+k}{(c+k-1)(c+k)}z_{i_k}, & \text{if} \quad i_k = N, \end{cases} \quad (14)$$

and for $i(k) \in \mathcal{I}, 1 \leq k \leq n-1$,

$$d_{i(k)}(\bar{z}) = \begin{cases} 1 - \dfrac{z_N}{c+k} - \dfrac{a+k}{c+k} z_{i_k} - \sum\limits_{j=1}^{N-1} \dfrac{b_j + \sum_{p=1}^{k} \delta_j^{i_p}}{c+k} z_j, & \text{if} \quad 1 \leq i_k \leq N-1, \\ 1 - \dfrac{z_N}{c+k} - \sum\limits_{j=1}^{N-1} \dfrac{b_j + \sum_{p=1}^{k} \delta_j^{i_p}}{c+k} z_j, & \text{if} \quad i_k = N. \end{cases} \tag{15}$$

It is easy to prove, by induction, that expansion (13)–(15) is true.

Passing n to ∞, we obtain the formal expansion of $X_n(a, \bar{b}; c; \bar{z})$ into infinite BCF of the form

$$1 - \frac{z_N}{c} - \sum_{j=1}^{N-1} \frac{b_j}{c} z_j + \underset{k=1}{\overset{\infty}{\mathrm{D}}} \sum_{i_k=1}^{N} \frac{c_{i(k)}(\bar{z})}{d_{i(k)}(\bar{z})}. \tag{16}$$

Elements of BCF (16) are defined by Formulas (14) and (15) under $i(k) \in \mathcal{I}, k \geq 1$.

Taking into account Formula (11), we obtain the formal expansion of the ratio $X_{i_0}(a, \bar{b}; c; \bar{z})$, $i_0 \in \{1, \dots, N-1\}$, into such BCF

$$1 - \frac{z_N}{c} - \frac{(a+1)z_{i_0}}{c} - \sum_{j=1}^{N-1} \frac{b_j}{c} z_j + \underset{k=1}{\overset{\infty}{\mathrm{D}}} \sum_{i_k=1}^{N} \frac{l_{i(k)}(\bar{z})}{q_{i(k)}(\bar{z})}, \tag{17}$$

where for $i(k) \in \mathcal{I}, k \geq 1$,

$$l_{i(k)}(\bar{z}) = \begin{cases} \dfrac{(a+k)(b_{i_k} + \sum_{p=0}^{k-1} \delta_{i_k}^{i_p})}{(c+k-1)(c+k)} z_{i_k}(1 - z_{i_k}), & \text{if} \quad 1 \leq i_k \leq N-1, \\ \dfrac{a+k}{(c+k-1)(c+k)} z_{i_k}, & \text{if} \quad i_k = N, \end{cases} \tag{18}$$

$$q_{i(k)}(\bar{z}) = \begin{cases} 1 - \dfrac{z_N}{c+k} - \dfrac{a+k}{c+k} z_{i_k} - \sum\limits_{j=1}^{N-1} \dfrac{b_j + \sum_{p=0}^{k} \delta_j^{i_p}}{c+k} z_j, & \text{if} \quad 1 \leq i_k \leq N-1, \\ 1 - \dfrac{z_N}{c+k} - \sum\limits_{j=1}^{N-1} \dfrac{b_j + \sum_{p=0}^{k} \delta_j^{i_p}}{c+k} z_j, & \text{if} \quad i_k = N. \end{cases} \tag{19}$$

If $z_N = 0$, then the formal expansion of $X_1(a, \bar{b}; c; z_1, \dots, z_{N-1}, 0)$ coincides with the expansion of the ratio of the Lauricella function $F_D^{(N-1)}$

$$\frac{F_D^{(N-1)}(a, \bar{b}; c; z_1, \dots, z_{N-1})}{F_D^{(N-1)}(a+1, \bar{b}+e_1; c+1; z_1, \dots, z_{N-1})}$$

into the $(N-1)$-dimensional analogue of Nörlund's continued fraction [23]. If $z_1 = z_2 = \dots = z_{N-1} = 0$, then the formal expansion of $X_N(a, \bar{b}; c; 0, \dots, 0, z_N)$ coincides with the continued fraction expansion of the ratio of Kummer's confluent function

$$\frac{\Phi(a; c; z_N)}{\Phi(a+1; c+1; z_N)}.$$

3. Convergence of the Branched Continued Fraction Expansions of the Confluent Hypergeometric Function $\Phi_D^{(N)}$ Ratios

Theorem 1. *Let parameters $a, b_1, \dots, b_{N-1}, c$ of the confluent hypergeometric function $\Phi_D^{(N)}$ be real numbers such that*

$$a, b_1, \dots, b_{N-1} \geq 0, \quad 2c > a + b_1 + \dots + b_{N-1} > 0. \tag{20}$$

Then the BCF (16) with elements $c_{i(k)}, d_{i(k)}, i(k) \in \mathcal{I}$, defined by (14), (15), under $k \geq 1$, converges uniformly in the domain

$$G_\epsilon = \left\{ \bar{z} \in \mathbb{R}^N : 0 < z_i < \frac{1}{2} - \epsilon, \; 1 \leq i \leq N-1, \; 0 < z_N < \frac{2c - a - \sum_{j=1}^{N-1} b_j}{2} \right\},$$

where $0 < \epsilon < 1/2$, to the function $X_N(a, \bar{b}; c; \bar{z})$.

Proof. It is obvious that partial numerators $c_{i(k)}(\bar{z})$, $i(k) \in \mathcal{I}$, $k \geq 1$, for all $\bar{z} \in G_\epsilon$ are positive under conditions (20).

We will find lower bound of the denominators $d_{i(k)}(\bar{z})$, $i(k) \in \mathcal{I}, k \geq 1$, for $\bar{z} \in G_\epsilon$. If $1 \leq i_k \leq N-1$, then we have

$$\begin{aligned} d_{i(k)}(\bar{z}) &= 1 - \frac{z_N}{c+k} - \frac{a+k}{c+k} z_{i_k} - \sum_{j=1}^{N-1} \frac{b_j + \sum_{p=1}^{k} \delta_j^{i_p}}{c+k} z_j \\ &> 1 - \frac{2c - a - \sum_{j=1}^{N-1} b_j}{2(c+k)} - \frac{a+k}{c+k}\left(\frac{1}{2} - \epsilon\right) \\ &\quad - \sum_{j=1}^{N-1} \frac{b_j}{c+k}\left(\frac{1}{2} - \epsilon\right) - \sum_{j=1}^{N-1} \frac{\sum_{p=1}^{k} \delta_j^{i_p}}{c+k}\left(\frac{1}{2} - \epsilon\right) \\ &= \frac{k}{2(c+k)} + \epsilon \frac{a + k + \sum_{j=1}^{N-1} b_j}{c+k} - \left(\frac{1}{2} - \epsilon\right) \frac{\sum_{p=1}^{k} \sum_{j=1}^{N-1} \delta_j^{i_p}}{c+k} \\ &\geq \epsilon \frac{a + 2k + \sum_{j=1}^{N-1} b_j}{c+k}. \end{aligned}$$

If $i_k = N$, then

$$\begin{aligned} d_{i(k)}(\bar{z}) &= 1 - \frac{z_N}{c+k} - \sum_{j=1}^{N-1} \frac{b_j + \sum_{p=1}^{k} \delta_j^{i_p}}{c+k} z_j \\ &> 1 - \frac{z_N}{c+k} - \sum_{j=1}^{N-1} \frac{a + k + b_j + \sum_{p=1}^{k} \delta_j^{i_p}}{c+k} z_j \\ &> \epsilon \frac{a + 2k + \sum_{j=1}^{N-1} b_j}{c+k}. \end{aligned}$$

So,

$$Q_{i(k)}^{(n)}(\bar{z}) > d_{i(k)}(\bar{z}) > \epsilon \frac{a + 2k + \sum_{j=1}^{N-1} b_j}{c+k}, \quad i(k) \in \mathcal{I}, \; k \geq 1. \tag{21}$$

We will show that for an arbitrary $\bar{z} \in G_\epsilon$ following inequality

$$|f_m(\bar{z}) - f_n(\bar{z})| < M\left(\frac{\eta}{\eta+1}\right)^n, \quad m > n, \tag{22}$$

where

$$M = \left(\frac{1}{4\epsilon} - \epsilon\right)\frac{a+1}{c} + \frac{2c - a - \sum_{j=1}^{N-1} b_j}{2c\epsilon}, \quad \eta = \left(\frac{1}{4\epsilon^2} - 1\right) + \frac{2c - a - \sum_{j=1}^{N-1} b_j}{2\epsilon^2 (a + \sum_{j=1}^{N-1} b_j)},$$

is valid. Formula (5) can be rewritten as follows

$$f_m(\bar{z}) - f_n(\bar{z}) = (-1)^n \sum_{i_1=1}^{N} \dots \sum_{i_{n+1}=1}^{N} \frac{c_{i(1)}(\bar{z})}{Q^{(q)}_{i(1)}(\bar{z})} \times \prod_{j=1}^{[(n+1)/2]} \frac{c_{i(2j)}(\bar{z})}{Q^{(r)}_{i(2j-1)}(\bar{z}) Q^{(r)}_{i(2j)}(\bar{z})} \prod_{j=1}^{[n/2]} \frac{c_{i(2j+1)}(\bar{z})}{Q^{(q)}_{i(2j)}(\bar{z}) Q^{(q)}_{i(2j+1)}(\bar{z})}, \tag{23}$$

where $q = m$, $r = n$, if $n = 2p$, and $q = n$, $r = m$, if $n = 2p - 1$, $p \geq 1$.

We note, that

$$\sum_{i_{k+1}=1}^{N} \frac{c_{i(k+1)}(\bar{z})}{Q^{(r)}_{i(k)}(\bar{z}) Q^{(r)}_{i(k+1)}(\bar{z})} = \frac{\sum_{i_{k+1}=1}^{N} \frac{c_{i(k+1)}(\bar{z})}{Q^{(r)}_{i(k+1)}(\bar{z})}}{d_{i(k)}(\bar{z}) + \sum_{i_{k+1}=1}^{N} \frac{c_{i(k+1)}(\bar{z})}{Q^{(r)}_{i(k+1)}(\bar{z})}} \leq \frac{\sum_{i_{k+1}=1}^{N} \frac{c_{i(k+1)}(\bar{z})}{d_{i(k)}(\bar{z}) d_{i(k+1)}(\bar{z})}}{1 + \sum_{i_{k+1}=1}^{N} \frac{c_{i(k+1)}(\bar{z})}{d_{i(k)}(\bar{z}) d_{i(k+1)}(\bar{z})}}.$$

Taking into account the inequality (21), we obtain

$$\begin{aligned}
&\sum_{i_{k+1}=1}^{N} \frac{c_{i(k+1)}(\bar{z})}{d_{i(k)}(\bar{z}) d_{i(k+1)}(\bar{z})} \\
&< \frac{(c+k)(c+k+1)}{\epsilon^2 (a + \sum_{j=1}^{N-1} b_j + 2k)(a + \sum_{j=1}^{N-1} b_j + 2k + 2)} \sum_{i_{k+1}=1}^{N} c_{i(k+1)}(\bar{z}) \\
&< \sum_{i_{k+1}=1}^{N-1} \frac{(a+k+1)(b_{i_{k+1}} + \sum_{p=1}^{k} \delta^{i_p}_{i_{k+1}}) z_{i_{k+1}} (1 - z_{i_{k+1}})}{\epsilon^2 (a + \sum_{j=1}^{N-1} b_j + 2k)(a + \sum_{j=1}^{N-1} b_j + 2k + 2)} \\
&+ \frac{(a+k+1) z_N}{\epsilon^2 (a + \sum_{j=1}^{N-1} b_j + 2k)(a + \sum_{j=1}^{N-1} b_j + 2k + 2)} \\
&< \left(\frac{1}{4\epsilon^2} - 1\right) \frac{\sum_{i_{k+1}}^{N-1} (b_{i_{k+1}} + \sum_{p=1}^{k} \delta^{i_p}_{i_{k+1}})}{(a + \sum_{j=1}^{N-1} b_j + 2k)} + \frac{2c - a - \sum_{j=1}^{N-1} b_j}{2\epsilon^2 (a + \sum_{j=1}^{N-1} b_j + k)} \\
&< \left(\frac{1}{4\epsilon} - \epsilon\right) + \frac{2c - a - \sum_{j=1}^{N-1} b_j}{2\epsilon^2 (a + \sum_{j=1}^{N-1} b_j)}.
\end{aligned}$$

We also obtain

$$\begin{aligned}
\sum_{i_1=1}^{N} \frac{c_{i(1)}(\bar{z})}{Q^{(q)}_{i(1)}(\bar{z})} &\leq \frac{c+1}{\epsilon (a + \sum_{j=1}^{N-1} b_j + 2)} \sum_{i_1=1}^{N-1} \frac{(a+1)b}{c(c+1)} \left(\frac{1}{4} - \epsilon^2\right) \\
&+ \frac{c+1}{\epsilon (a + \sum_{j=1}^{N-1} b_j + 2)} \frac{(a+1)(2c - a - \sum_{j=1}^{N-1} b_j)}{2c(c+1)} \\
&< \left(\frac{1}{4\epsilon} - \epsilon\right) \frac{a+1}{c} + \frac{2c - a - \sum_{j=1}^{N-1} b_j}{2c\epsilon}.
\end{aligned}$$

Substituting the above estimates in Formula (23) we obtain inequality (22).

We will consider the difference $X_N(a,\bar{b};c;\bar{z}) - f_n(\bar{z})$. Let

$$\tilde{Q}^{(s)}_{i(s)}(\bar{z}) = X_N\left(a+s,\bar{b}+\sum_{j=1}^{s} e_{i_j};c+s;\bar{z}\right) - (1-\delta^N_{i_s})\frac{a+s}{c+s}z_{i_s},$$

$$\tilde{Q}^{(p)}_{i(k)}(\bar{z}) = d_{i(k)}(\bar{z}) + \sum_{i_{k+1}=1}^{N} \frac{c_{i(k+1)}(\bar{z})|}{|d_{i(k+1)}(\bar{z})} + \sum_{i_{k+2}=1}^{N} \frac{c_{i(k+2)}(\bar{z})|}{|d_{i(k+2)}(\bar{z})}$$
$$+\ldots+\sum_{i_n=1}^{N} \frac{c_{i(n)}(\bar{z})|}{|X_N(a+n,\bar{b}+\sum_{p=1}^{n} e_{i_p};c+n;\bar{z}) - (1-\delta^N_{i_n})\frac{a+n}{c+n}z_{i_n}},$$

where $s \geq 1$, $p \geq 2$, $1 \leq k \leq p-1$. It is clear that the following recurrence relations hold

$$\tilde{Q}^{(p)}_{i(k)}(\bar{z}) = d_{i(k)}(\bar{z}) + \sum_{i_{k+1}=1}^{N} \frac{c_{i(k+1)}(\bar{z})}{\tilde{Q}^{(p)}_{i(k+1)}(\bar{z})}, \quad s \geq 1,\ p \geq 2,\ 1 \leq k \leq p-1.$$

Applying the method suggested in [31], p. 28, for $n \geq 1$ on the first step we obtain

$$X_N(a,\bar{b};c;\bar{z}) - f_n(\bar{z}) = 1 - \frac{z_N}{c} - \sum_{j=1}^{N-1} \frac{b_j}{c} z_j + \sum_{i_1=1}^{N} \frac{c_{i(1)}(\bar{z})}{\tilde{Q}^{(n+1)}_{i(1)}(\bar{z})}$$
$$- \left(1 - \frac{z_N}{c} - \sum_{j=1}^{N-1} \frac{b_j}{c} z_j + \sum_{i_1=1}^{N} \frac{c_{i(1)}(\bar{z})}{Q^{(n)}_{i(1)}(\bar{z})}\right)$$
$$= -\sum_{i_1=1}^{N} \frac{c_{i(1)}(\bar{z})}{\tilde{Q}^{(n+1)}_{i(1)}(\bar{z})Q^{(n)}_{i(1)}(\bar{z})}\left(\tilde{Q}^{(n+1)}_{i(1)}(\bar{z}) - Q^{(n)}_{i(1)}(\bar{z})\right).$$

Let k be an arbitrary natural number and $i(k)$ be an arbitrary multi-index from $\mathcal{I}$; moreover $1 \leq k \leq n-1$, $n \geq 2$. Then we have

$$\tilde{Q}^{(n+1)}_{i(k)}(\bar{z}) - Q^{(n)}_{i(k)}(\bar{z}) = d_{i(k)}(\bar{z}) + \sum_{i_{k+1}=1}^{N} \frac{c_{i(k+1)}(\bar{z})}{\tilde{Q}^{(n+1)}_{i(k+1)}(\bar{z})} - \left(d_{i(k)}(\bar{z}) + \sum_{i_{k+1}=1}^{N} \frac{c_{i(k+1)}(\bar{z})}{Q^{(n)}_{i(k+1)}(\bar{z})}\right)$$
$$= -\sum_{i_{k+1}=1}^{N} \frac{c_{i(k+1)}(\bar{z})}{\tilde{Q}^{(n+1)}_{i(k+1)}(\bar{z})Q^{(n)}_{i(k+1)}(\bar{z})}\left(\tilde{Q}^{(n+1)}_{i(k+1)}(\bar{z}) - Q^{(n)}_{i(k+1)}(\bar{z})\right). \tag{24}$$

Applying recurrence relation (24) and taking into account that

$$\tilde{Q}^{(n+1)}_{i(n)}(\bar{z}) - Q^{(n)}_{i(n)}(\bar{z}) = \sum_{i_{n+1}=1}^{N} \frac{c_{i(n+1)}(\bar{z})}{\tilde{Q}^{(n+1)}_{i(n+1)}(\bar{z})},$$

after nth step we obtain

$$X_N(a,\bar{b};c;\bar{z}) - f_n(\bar{z}) = (-1)^n \sum_{i_1=1}^{N} \ldots \sum_{i_{n+1}=1}^{N} \frac{\prod_{p=1}^{n+1} c_{i(p)}(\bar{z})}{\prod_{p=1}^{n+1} \tilde{Q}^{(n+1)}_{i(p)}(\bar{z}) \prod_{p=1}^{n} Q^{(n)}_{i(p)}(\bar{z})}. \tag{25}$$

From (25) it follows that

$$f_{2m}(\bar{z}) < X_N(\bar{z})(a,\bar{b};c;\bar{z}) < f_{2m-1}(\bar{z}).$$

Since

$$\lim_{m\to\infty} f_{2m}(\bar{z}) = \lim_{m\to\infty} f_{2m-1}(\bar{z}) = f(\bar{z}),$$

then $X_N(\bar{z})(a,\bar{b};c;\bar{z}) = f(\bar{z})$. □

Theorem 2. *Let parameters* $a, b_1, \ldots, b_{N-1}, c$ *of the confluent hypergeometric function* $\Phi_D^{(N)}$ *satisfy conditions* (20). *Then:*

(A) the BCF (16) *with elements* $c_{i(k)}, d_{i(k)}, i(k) \in \mathcal{I}$, *defined by* (14), (15), $i(k) \in \mathcal{I}, k \geq 1$, *converges uniformly on every compact subset of the domain*

$$G = \left\{ \bar{z} \in \mathbb{C}^N : \operatorname{Re} z_i < \frac{1}{2}, \; i = \overline{1, N-1}, \quad |z_N| < \frac{2c - a - \sum_{j=1}^{N-1} b_j}{2} \right\}$$

to a function $f(\bar{z})$ *holomorphic in G;*

(B) $f(\bar{z})$ *is the analytic continuation of the function* $X_N(a,\bar{b};c;\bar{z})$ *which is holomorphic in some neighborhood of the origin in the domain G.*

We will use the following auxiliary lemmas.

Lemma 1 ([23]). *Let elements of the BCF* (1) *be the functions defined in some domain D,* $D \subset \mathbb{C}^N$, *and the following conditions for each* $\bar{z} \in D$ *and for all possible values of multi-indices* $i(k) \in \mathcal{I}$ *are valid:*

(A) $\operatorname{Re} d_{i(k)}(\bar{z}) > 0$;
(B) there exist such functions $g_{i(k)}(\bar{z})$ *given in the domain D that* $0 < g_{i(k)}(\bar{z}) \leq \operatorname{Re} d_{i(k)}(\bar{z})$ *and*

$$\sum_{i_{k+1}=1}^{2} \frac{|c_{i(k+1)}(\bar{z})| - \operatorname{Re} c_{i(k+1)}(\bar{z})}{g_{i(k+1)}(\bar{z})} \leq 2(\operatorname{Re} d_{i(k)}(\bar{z}) - g_{i(k)}(\bar{z})). \tag{26}$$

Then, for each $n \geq 1$,

$$\operatorname{Re}(Q_{i(k)}^{(n)}(\bar{z})) \geq g_{i(k)}(\bar{z}) \quad \text{for all} \quad i(k) \in \mathcal{I}, \; 1 \leq k \leq n, \quad \text{and} \quad \bar{z} \in D, \tag{27}$$

where $Q_{i(k)}^{(n)}(\bar{z}), i(k) \in \mathcal{I}, 1 \leq k \leq n, n \geq 1$, *defined by* (3) *and* (4).

Lemma 2 ([23]). *Let w be a complex number. Then*

$$|w(1-w)| - \operatorname{Re}(w(1-w)) \leq 2\left(\frac{1}{2} - \operatorname{Re} w\right)^2,$$

and equality is achieved only when $\operatorname{Re} w = 1/2$.

In addition, we will use the convergence continuation Theorem 2.17 [31] (see also ([9], Theorem 24.2).

Theorem 3. *Let* $\{f_n(\mathbf{z})\}$ *be a sequence of functions, holomorphic in the domain D,* $D \subset \mathbb{C}^N$, *which is uniformly bounded on every compact subset of D. Let this sequence converge at each point of the set E,* $E \subset D$, *which is the N-dimensional real neighborhood of the point* $\bar{z}^0$, $\bar{z}^0 \in D$. *Then* $\{f_n(\mathbf{z})\}$ *converges uniformly on every compact subset of the domain D to a function holomorphic in D.*

Proof of Theorem 2. We will use the proof scheme from [23]. Let for $k \geq 1$

$$g_{i(k)}(\bar{z}) = \begin{cases} \dfrac{a+k}{c+k}\left(\dfrac{1}{2} - \operatorname{Re} z_{i_k}\right), & \text{if} \quad 1 \leq i_k \leq N-1, \\ \dfrac{a+k}{2(c+k)}, & \text{if} \quad i_k = N. \end{cases} \tag{28}$$

It is obvious that functions $g_{i(k)}(\bar{z})$ are positive. Next we have
(a) for $i_k = N$

$$\begin{aligned} \operatorname{Re} d_{i(k)}(\bar{z}) - g_{i(k)}(\bar{z}) &= 1 - \frac{\operatorname{Re} z_N}{c+k} - \sum_{j=1}^{N-1} \frac{b_j + \sum_{p=1}^{k} \delta_j^{i_p}}{c+k} \operatorname{Re} z_j - \frac{a+k}{2(c+k)} \\ &= \frac{2c-a+k}{2(c+k)} - \frac{\operatorname{Re} z_N}{c+k} - \sum_{j=1}^{N-1} \frac{b_j + \sum_{p=1}^{k} \delta_j^{i_p}}{c+k} \operatorname{Re} z_j \\ &> \frac{2c-a+k}{2(c+k)} - \frac{2c-a-\sum_{j=1}^{N-1} b_j}{2(c+k)} - \sum_{j=1}^{N-1} \frac{b_j + \sum_{p=1}^{k} \delta_j^{i_p}}{2(c+k)} \\ &= \frac{1}{2(c+k)} \left(k - \sum_{j=1}^{N-1} \sum_{p=1}^{k} \delta_j^{i_p} \right) \\ &\geq \frac{1}{2(c+k)}; \end{aligned}$$

(b) for arbitrary $1 \leq i_k \leq N-1$

$$\begin{aligned} \operatorname{Re} d_{i(k)}(\bar{z}) - g_{i(k)}(\bar{z}) &= 1 - \frac{\operatorname{Re} z_N}{c+k} - \frac{a+k}{c+k} \operatorname{Re} z_{i_k} \\ &\quad - \sum_{j=1}^{N-1} \frac{b_j + \sum_{p=1}^{k} \delta_j^{i_p}}{c+k} \operatorname{Re} z_j - \frac{a+k}{c+k} \left(\frac{1}{2} - \operatorname{Re} z_{i_k} \right) \\ &= \frac{2c-a+k}{2(c+k)} - \frac{\operatorname{Re} z_N}{c+k} - \sum_{j=1}^{N-1} \frac{b_j + \sum_{p=1}^{k} \delta_j^{i_p}}{c+k} \operatorname{Re} z_j \\ &> \frac{1}{2(c+k)} \left(k - \sum_{j=1}^{N-1} \sum_{p=1}^{k} \delta_j^{i_p} \right) \geq 0. \end{aligned}$$

Thus, $\operatorname{Re} d_{i(k)}(\bar{z}) \geq g_{i(k)}(\bar{z})$.
On the other hand, taking into account Lemma 2, we obtain

$$\begin{aligned} &\sum_{i_{k+1}=1}^{N} \frac{|c_{i(k+1)}(\bar{z})| - \operatorname{Re} c_{i(k+1)}(\bar{z})}{g_{i(k+1)}(\bar{z})} \\ &\quad = \sum_{i_{k+1}=1}^{N-1} \frac{b_{i_{k+1}} + \sum_{p=1}^{N-1} \delta_{i_{k+1}}^{i_p}}{c+k} \frac{|z_{i_{k+1}}(1-z_{i_{k+1}})| - \operatorname{Re} z_{i_{k+1}}(1-z_{i_{k+1}})}{(1/2 - \operatorname{Re} z_{i_{k+1}})} \\ &\quad + 2\frac{|z_N| - \operatorname{Re} z_N}{c+k} \\ &\quad \leq \sum_{i_{k+1}=1}^{N-1} \frac{b_{i_{k+1}} + \sum_{p=1}^{N-1} \delta_{i_{k+1}}^{i_p}}{c+k} - 2 \sum_{i_{k+1}=1}^{N-1} \frac{b_{i_{k+1}} + \sum_{p=1}^{N-1} \delta_{i_{k+1}}^{i_p}}{(c+k)} \operatorname{Re} z_{i_{k+1}} \\ &\quad + \frac{2c-a-\sum_{j=1}^{N-1} b_j}{c+k} - \frac{2\operatorname{Re} z_N}{c+k} \end{aligned}$$

and

$$2(\operatorname{Re} d_{i(k)}(\bar{z}) - g_{i(k)}(\bar{z})) - \sum_{i_{k+1}=1}^{N} \frac{|c_{i(k+1)}(\bar{z})| - \operatorname{Re} c_{i(k+1)}(\bar{z})}{g_{i(k+1)}(\bar{z})}$$
$$\geq \frac{2c-a+k}{c+k} - \sum_{i_{k+1}=1}^{N-1} \frac{b_{i_{k+1}} + \sum_{p=1}^{N-1} \delta_{i_{k+1}}^{i_p}}{(c+k)} - \frac{2c-a-\sum_{j=1}^{N-1} b_j}{c+k}$$
$$= \frac{1}{2(c+k)} \left(k - \sum_{j=1}^{N-1} \sum_{p=1}^{k} \delta_j^{i_p} \right) \geq 0.$$

Therefore, the conditions (26) of Lemma 1 are satisfied and inequality (27) is valid, where $g_{i(k)}(\bar{z})$ is defined by (28). Thus, $\{f_n(\bar{z})\}$, $n \geq 1$, is a sequence of functions holomorphic in domain G.

Let K be an arbitrary compact subset of G. Then,

$$|f_n(\bar{z})| \leq 1 + \frac{|z_N|}{c} + \sum_{j=1}^{N-1} \frac{b_j}{c}|z_j| + \sum_{i_1=1}^{N} \frac{|c_{i(1)}(\bar{z})|}{g_{i(1)}(\bar{z})}$$
$$\leq 1 + \frac{|z_N|}{c} + \sum_{j=1}^{N-1} \frac{b_j|z_j|}{c} + \sum_{j=1}^{N-1} \frac{b_j|z_j(1-z_j)|}{c(1/2 - \operatorname{Re} z_j)} + \frac{2c - \sum_{j=1}^{N-1} b_j - a}{c}$$
$$\leq 1 + \sup_{\bar{z} \in K} \left(\frac{|z_N|}{c} + \sum_{j=1}^{N-1} \frac{b_j|z_j|}{c} + \sum_{j=1}^{N-1} \frac{b_j|z_j(1-z_j)|}{c(1/2 - \operatorname{Re} z_j)} + \frac{2c - \sum_{j=1}^{N-1} b_j - a}{c} \right)$$
$$= M(K),$$

where constant $M(K)$ depends only on K. Moreover, $G_\epsilon \subset G$. So, sequence of approximants $\{f_n(\bar{z})\}$ of the BCF (16) satisfies the conditions of Theorem 3 and it means that Statement (A) of Theorem 2 is proven.

The series (2) converges for each $\bar{z}$ from domain $\{\bar{z} \in \mathbb{C}^N : |z_i| < 1, 1 \leq i \leq N-1\}$ and $X_N(a, \bar{b}; c; \bar{z})|_{z_1 = \ldots = z_N = 0} = 1$. Therefore, there is such $\delta > 0$ that function $X_N(a, \bar{b}; c; \bar{z})$ is holomorphic in domain $G_\delta = \{\bar{z} \in \mathbb{C}^N : |z_i| < \delta, 1 \leq i \leq N\}$, $G_\delta \subset G$. Since investigated BCF converges uniformly in G_ϵ to $X_N(a, \bar{b}; c; \bar{z})$, then by the principle of analytic continuation ([33], p. 53), Statement (B) follows. □

Let us note that $X_N(0, \bar{b}; c; \bar{z}) = 1/\Phi_D^{(N)}(1, \bar{b}; c+1; \bar{z})$. We assume that $a = 0$ and

$$Q_0^{(0)}(\bar{z}) = 1 - \frac{z_N}{c} - \sum_{j=1}^{N-1} \frac{b_j z_j}{c}, \quad Q_0^{(n)}(\bar{z}) = 1 - \frac{z_N}{c} - \sum_{j=1}^{N-1} \frac{b_j z_j}{c} + \sum_{i_1=1}^{N} \frac{c_{i(1)}(\bar{z})}{Q_{i(1)}^{(n)}(\bar{z})}, \quad n \geq 1.$$

In the proof of the Theorem 2 it is shown that inequality (27) is valid. It can be similarly shown that

$$\operatorname{Re} Q_0^{(n)}(\bar{z}) > g_0(\bar{z}) = 1 - \frac{1}{2c} \sum_{j=1}^{N-1} b_j - \frac{|z_N|}{c} > 0, \quad n \geq 0, \quad \bar{z} \in G. \tag{29}$$

Indeed, for each $\bar{z} \in G$

$$\operatorname{Re} Q_0^{(n)}(\bar{z}) - g_0(\bar{z}) = 1 - \frac{\operatorname{Re} z_N}{c} - \sum_{j=1}^{N-1} \operatorname{Re} \frac{b_j z_j}{c} - \left(1 - \frac{1}{2c}\sum_{j=1}^{N-1} b_- \frac{|z_N|}{c}\right)$$

$$\geq \sum_{j=1}^{N-1} \frac{b_j}{2c}(1 - 2\operatorname{Re} z_j) + \frac{|z_N| - \operatorname{Re} z_N}{c} > 0,$$

$$\sum_{i_1=1}^{N} \frac{|c_{i(1)}(\bar{z})| - \operatorname{Re} c_{i(1)}(\bar{z})}{g_{i(1)}(\bar{z})} = \sum_{i_1=1}^{N-1} \frac{b_{i_1}}{c} \frac{|z_{i_1}(1 - z_{i_1})| - \operatorname{Re} z_{i_1}(1 - z_{i_1})}{(1/2 - \operatorname{Re} z_{i_1})} + 2\frac{|z_N| - \operatorname{Re} z_N}{c}$$

$$\leq \sum_{i_1=1}^{N-1} \frac{b_{i_1}}{c} - 2\sum_{i_1=1}^{N-1} \frac{b_{i_1}}{c} \operatorname{Re} z_{i_1} + 2\frac{|z_N| - \operatorname{Re} z_N}{c},$$

and

$$2\left(1 - \frac{\operatorname{Re} z_N}{c} - \sum_{j=1}^{N-1} \operatorname{Re} \frac{b_j z_j}{c} - g_0(\bar{z})\right) - \sum_{i_1=1}^{N} \frac{|c_{i(1)}(\bar{z})| - \operatorname{Re} c_{i(1)}(\bar{z})}{g_{i(1)}(\bar{z})} \geq 0.$$

From (29) it follows that $\{h_n(\bar{z})\}$, where $h_n(\bar{z}) = (f_n(\bar{z}))^{-1}$, $n \geq 0$, is a sequence of functions holomorphic in G.

Setting $a = 0$, replacing c by $c - 1$ in Theorem 2 and taking into account the above considerations we obtain the corollary.

Corollary 1. *Let parameters $b_1, b_2, \ldots, b_{N-1}, c$ of function $\Phi_D^{(N)}$ satisfy inequalities*

$$b_1, \ldots, b_{N-1} \geq 0, \quad 2c > b_1 + \ldots + b_{N-1} + 2 > 2.$$

Then:
(A) the BCF

$$\left(1 - \frac{z_N}{c-1} - \sum_{j=1}^{N-1} \frac{b_j z_j}{c-1} + \mathop{\mathrm{D}}_{k=1}^{\infty} \sum_{i_k=1}^{N-1} \frac{c_{i(k)}(\bar{z})}{d_{i(k)}(\bar{z})}\right)^{-1} \tag{30}$$

with elements $c_{i(k)}, d_{i(k)}, i(k) \in \mathcal{I}$, defined by

$$c_{i(k)}(\bar{z}) = \begin{cases} \dfrac{k(b_{i_k} + \sum_{p=1}^{k-1} \delta_{i_k}^{i_p})}{(c+k-2)(c+k-1)} z_{i_k}(1 - z_{i_k}), & \text{if} \quad 1 \leq i_k \leq N-1, \\ \dfrac{k}{(c+k-2)(c+k-1)} z_{i_k}, & \text{if} \quad i_k = N, \end{cases} \tag{31}$$

$$d_{i(k)}(\bar{z}) = \begin{cases} 1 - \dfrac{z_N + k z_{i_k}}{c+k-1} - \displaystyle\sum_{j=1}^{N-1} \dfrac{b_j + \sum_{p=1}^{k} \delta_j^{i_p}}{c+k-1} z_j, & \text{if} \quad 1 \leq i_k \leq N-1, \\ 1 - \dfrac{z_N}{c+k-1} - \displaystyle\sum_{j=1}^{N-1} \dfrac{b_j + \sum_{p=1}^{k} \delta_j^{i_p}}{c+k-1} z_j, & \text{if} \quad i_k = N, \end{cases} \tag{32}$$

converges uniformly on every compact subset of H to a function $h(\bar{z})$ holomorphic in H, where

$$H = \left\{\bar{z} \in \mathbb{C}^N : \operatorname{Re} z_i < \frac{1}{2}, \ 1 \leq i \leq N-1, \quad |z_N| < c - 1 - \frac{1}{2}\sum_{j=1}^{N-1} b_j\right\};$$

(B) $h(\bar{z})$ is an analytic continuation of function $\Phi_D^{(N)}(1, \bar{b}; c; \bar{z})$ in domain H.

Example 1. *We set $a = 0$, $b_1 = 0.5$, $b_2 = 1$, $c = 4$. The results of computation of the approximants $h_n(\bar{z})$, $0 \leq n \leq 12$, of BCF (30) with elements $c_{i(k)}, d_{i(k)}, i(k) \in \mathcal{I}$, defined* *by* (31), (32), *and partial sums* $S_n(\bar{z})$, $0 \le n \le 12$, *of* $\Phi_D^{(3)}(1, 0.5, 1; 4; \bar{z})$ *for* $\bar{z} = (0.3, 0.4, 1)$ *and* $\bar{z} = (-0.7, -0.4, 1)$ *are given in Table 1.*

For given parameters and $\bar{z} = (0.3, 0.4, 1)$ *elements of BCF* (30) *are positive and*

$$h_{2m-1}(\bar{z}) < \Phi_D^{(3)}(1, 0.5, 1; 4; \bar{z}) < h_{2m}(\bar{z}), \quad 1 \le m \le 6.$$

If $\bar{z} = (-0.7, -0.4, 1)$, *then*

$$|h_m(\bar{z}) - h_{m-1}(\bar{z})| < |S_m(\bar{z}) - S_{m-1}(\bar{z})|, \quad 1 \le m \le 12.$$

Table 1. Values of $h_n(\bar{z})$, $S_n(\bar{z})$ for different values of $\bar{z} = (z_1, z_2, z_3)$.

n	$h_n(0.3, 0.4, 1)$	$S_n(0.3, 0.4, 1)$	$h_n(-0.7, -0.4, 1)$	$S_n(-0.7, -0.4, 1)$
0	2.0689655172413793	1.0000000000000000	1.0909090909090909	1.0000000000000000
1	1.4560459283938569	1.3875000000000000	1.0798919301578482	1.0625000000000000
2	1.6062420542029685	1.5178750000000000	1.0854460271288587	1.0858750000000000
3	1.5663393776978655	1.5581427083333333	1.0854992029539980	1.0846114583333333
4	1.5774800126642679	1.5700380133928571	1.0855766580493781	1.0858623586309523
5	1.5741237293361620	1.5734982670665922	1.0855849420453230	1.0855849420453230
6	1.5752175755666838	1.5745081593644076	1.0855871865334549	1.0856431331367290
7	1.5748338584710080	1.5748069122651405	1.0855876480094189	1.0855617160131383
8	1.5749774440398022	1.5748968805416772	1.0855877608401303	1.0856005483413065
9	1.5749206724246927	1.5749244851830382	1.0855877888742481	1.0855813521666234
10	1.5749441919671161	1.5749331078713755	1.0855877962018176	1.0855911502163538
11	1.5749340537588600	1.5749358459608639	1.0855877981816782	1.0855860154913730
12	1.5749385748468521	1.5749367284599484	1.0855877987333202	1.0855887673017868

Example 2. *We set* $a = 0$, $b_1 = 1$, $c = 4$. *The results of computation of the approximants* $h_n(\bar{z})$, $0 \le n \le 12$, *of BCF* (30) *with elements* $c_{i(k)}$, $d_{i(k)}$, $i(k) \in \mathcal{I}$, *defined by* (31), (32), *for* $\bar{z} = (-1.2, 1)$ *and* $\bar{z} = (-1.2 + 0.2i, 1 + 0,5i)$ *are given in Table 2. These values of* $\bar{z}$ *do not belong to a convergence domain of double power series for* $\Phi(1, 1; 4; \bar{z})$.

Table 2. Values of $h_n(0, 1; 4; \bar{z})$ for different values of $\bar{z} = (z_1, z_2)$.

$\bar{z}$	$(-1.2, 1)$	$(-1.2 + 0.2i, 1 + 0, 5i)$
$h_0(\bar{z})$	0.9375000000000000	$0.8946877912395153 + 0.1957129543336439i$
$h_1(\bar{z})$	0.9874608150470219	$0.9682330302329962 + 0.1636661528464738i$
$h_2(\bar{z})$	0.9999386478760991	$0.9783495727203259 + 0.1621180086394217i$
$h_3(\bar{z})$	1.0021612335538261	$0.9810777556363008 + 0.1611130234246828i$
$h_4(\bar{z})$	1.0027828150938215	$0.9816708481472565 + 0.1608142450994196i$
$h_5(\bar{z})$	1.0029538035362679	$0.9818431129623030 + 0.1607160062318091i$
$h_6(\bar{z})$	1.0030069414508122	$0.9818931929871372 + 0.1606803796414656i$
$h_7(\bar{z})$	1.0030242918372864	$0.9819087721653132 + 0.1606673323815619i$
$h_8(\bar{z})$	1.0030302600610872	$0.9819137968090410 + 0.1606623598862077i$
$h_9(\bar{z})$	1.0030323958017573	$0.9819154619391862 + 0.1606604197525936i$
$h_{10}(\bar{z})$	1.0030331862564592	$0.9819160242737400 + 0.1606596462158485i$
$h_{11}(\bar{z})$	1.0030334872518964	$0.9819162161393741 + 0.1606593322207231i$
$h_{12}(\bar{z})$	1.0030336047089570	$0.9819162817068529 + 0.1606592028011838i$

The following theorems can be proven in much the same way as Theorems 1 and 2.

Theorem 4. *Let parameters* $a, b_1, \ldots, b_{N-1}, c$ *of the confluent hypergeometric function* $\Phi_D^{(N)}$ *be real numbers such that*

$$a, b_1, \ldots, b_{N-1} \ge 0, \quad 2c > a + b_1 + \ldots + b_{N-1} + 1 > 1. \qquad (33)$$

Then, the BCF (17) *with elements* $l_{i(k)}$, $q_{i(k)}$, $i(k) \in \mathcal{I}$, *defined by* (18), (19), *converges uniformly in the domain*

$$L_\epsilon = \left\{ \bar{z} \in \mathbb{R}^N : \ 0 < z_i < \frac{1}{2} - \epsilon, \ 1 \le i \le N-1, \ 0 < z_N < \frac{2c - a - \sum_{j=1}^{N-1} b_j - 1}{2} \right\},$$

where $0 < \epsilon < 1/2$, *to the function* $X_{i_0}(a, \bar{b}; c; \bar{z})$, $1 \le i_0 \le N-1$.

Theorem 5. *Let parameters* $a, b_1, \ldots, b_{N-1}, c$ *of the confluent hypergeometric function* $\Phi_D^{(N)}$ *satisfy conditions* (33). *Then:*

(A) the BCF (17) *with elements* $l_{i(k)}$, $q_{i(k)}$, $i(k) \in \mathcal{I}$, *defined by* (18), (19), $i(k) \in \mathcal{I}, k \ge 1$, *converges uniformly on every compact subset of the domain*

$$L = \left\{ \bar{z} \in \mathbb{C}^N : \ \mathrm{Re}\, z_i < \frac{1}{2}, \ 1 \le i \le N-1, \ |z_N| < \frac{2c - a - \sum_{j=1}^{N-1} b_j - 1}{2} \right\}$$

to a function $f(\bar{z})$ *holomorphic in* L;

(B) $f(\bar{z})$ *is the analytical continuation of the function* $X_{i_0}(a, \bar{b}; c; \bar{z})$, $1 \le i_0 \le N-1$, *which is holomorphic in some neighborhood of the origin in the domain* L.

4. Conclusions

In the paper we have constructed and investigated the branched continued fraction expansions of the confluent hypergeometric function $\Phi_D^{(N)}$ ratios.

In particular, we have proven that the branched continued fraction expansions converges to the functions which are an analytic continuation of the above-mentioned ratios in some domains. The problem of studying wider convergence domains and establishing estimates of the rate of convergence of the above-mentioned expansions still remains open.

Author Contributions: All authors contributed equally to this work. All authors have read and agreed to the published version of the manuscript.

Funding: This research received no external funding.

Institutional Review Board Statement: Not applicable.

Informed Consent Statement: Not applicable.

Data Availability Statement: Not applicable.

Acknowledgments: The authors were partially supported by the Ministry of Education and Science of Ukraine, project registration number 0122U000857.

Conflicts of Interest: The authors declare no conflict of interest.

References

1. Erdélyi, A.; Magnus, W.; Oberhettinger, F.; Tricomi, F.G. *Higher Transcendental Functions*; McGraw-Hill Book Co.: New York, NY, USA, 1953; Volume 1–2.
2. Erdélyi, A.; Magnus, W.; Oberhettinger, F.; Tricomi, F.G. *Higher Transcendental Functions*; McGraw-Hill Book Co.: New York, NY, USA, 1955; Volume 3.
3. Exton, H. *Multiple Hypergeometric Functions and Applications*; Horwood, E., Ed.; Halsted Press: Chichester, UK, 1976.
4. Horn, J. Hypergeometrische Funktionen zweier Veränderlichen. *Math. Ann.* **1931**, *105*, 381–407. [CrossRef]
5. Sadykov, T. *Hypergeometric Functions in Several Complex Variables*. Doctoral Thesis, Stockholm University, Stockholm, Sweden, 2002.
6. Cuyt, A.A.M.; Petersen, V.; Verdonk, B.; Waadeland, H.; Jones, W.B. *Handbook of Continued Fractions for Special Functions*; Springer: Dordrecht, The Netherlands, 2008.
7. Jones, W.B.; Thron, W.J. *Continued Fractions: Analytic Theory and Applications*; Addison-Wesley Pub. Co.: Reading, MA, USA, 1980.
8. Lorentzen, L.; Waadeland, H. *Continued Fractions with Applications*; Noth Holland: Amsterdam, The Netherlands, 1992.
9. Wall, H.S. *Analytic Theory of Continued Fractions*; D. Van Nostrand Co.: New York, NY, USA, 1948.

10. Antonova, T.M.; Dmytryshyn, R.I. Truncation error bounds for branched continued fraction whose partial denominators are equal to unity. *Mat. Stud.* **2020**, *54*, 3–14. [CrossRef]
11. Bodnar, D.I.; Bilanyk, I.B. Parabolic convergence regions of branched continued fractions of the special form. *Carpathian Math. Publ.* **2021**, *13*, 619–630. [CrossRef]
12. Cuyt, A. A review of multivariate Padé approximation theory. *J. Comput. Appl. Math.* **1985**, *12–13*, 221–232. [CrossRef]
13. Cuyt, A.; Verdonk, B. A review of branched continued fraction theory for the construction of multivariate rational approximants. *Appl. Numer. Math.* **1988**, *4*, 263–271. [CrossRef]
14. Dmytryshyn, R.I. Convergence of multidimensional *A*- and *J*-fractions with independent variables. *Comput. Methods Funct. Theory* **2022**, *22*, 229–242. [CrossRef]
15. Dmytryshyn, R.I. On some of convergence domains of multidimensional *S*-fractions with independent variables. *Carpathian Math. Publ.* **2019**, *11*, 54–58. [CrossRef]
16. Dmytryshyn, R.I. Multidimensional regular *C*-fraction with independent variables corresponding to formal multiple power series. *Proc. R. Soc. Edinb. Sect. A* **2020**, *150*, 1853–1870. [CrossRef]
17. Dmytryshyn, R.I.; Sharyn, S.V. Approximation of functions of several variables by multidimensional *S*-fractions with independent variables. *Carpathian Math. Publ.* **2021**, *13*, 592–607. [CrossRef]
18. Kuchminska, K.Y.; Vozna, S.M. Development of an *N*-multiple power series into an *N*-dimensional regular *C*-fraction. *J. Math. Sci.* **2020**, *246*, 201–208. [CrossRef]
19. Murphy, J.A.; O'Donohoe, M.R. A two-variable generalization of the Stieltjes-type continued fraction. *J. Comput. Appl. Math.* **1978**, *4*, 181–190. [CrossRef]
20. O'Donohoe, M.R. Application of Continued Fractions in One and More Variables. Ph.D. Thesis, Brunel University, Uxbridge, UK, 1974.
21. Antonova, T.; Dmytryshyn, R.; Kravtsiv, V. Branched continued fraction expansions of Horn's hypergeometric function H_3 ratios. *Mathematics* **2021**, *9*, 148. [CrossRef]
22. Antonova, T.; Dmytryshyn, R.; Sharyn, S. Generalized hypergeometric function ${}_3F_2$ ratios and branched continued fraction expansions. *Axioms* **2021**, *10*, 310. [CrossRef]
23. Antonova, T.M.; Hoyenko, N.P. Approximation of Lauricella's functions F_D ratio by Nörlund's branched continued fraction in the complex domain. *Mat. Metody Fiz.-Mekh. Polya* **2004**, *47*, 7–15. (In Ukrainian)
24. Antonova, T.M. On convergence of branched continued fraction expansions of Horn's hypergeometric function H_3 ratios. *Carpathian Math. Publ.* **2021**, *13*, 642–650. [CrossRef]
25. Bodnar, D.I. Expansion of a ratio of hypergeometric functions of two variables in branching continued fractions. *J. Math. Sci.* **1993**, *64*, 1155–1158. [CrossRef]
26. Bodnar, D.I.; Manzii, O.S. Expansion of the ratio of Appel hypergeometric functions F_3 into a branching continued fraction and its limit behavior. *J. Math. Sci.* **2001**, *107*, 3550–3554. [CrossRef]
27. Hoyenko, N.; Hladun, V.; Manzij, O. On the infinite remains of the Nórlund branched continued fraction for Appell hypergeometric functions. *Carpathian Math. Publ.* **2014**, *6*, 11–25. (In Ukrainian) [CrossRef]
28. Manzii, O.S. Investigation of expansion of the ratio of Appel hypergeometric functions F_3 into a branching continued fraction. *Approx. Theor. Its Appl. Pr. Inst. Math. NAS Ukr.* **2000**, *31*, 344–353. (In Ukrainian)
29. Petreolle, M.; Sokal, A.D.; Zhu, B.X. Lattice paths and branched continued fractions: An infinite sequence of generalizations of the Stieltjes-Rogers and Thron-Rogers polynomials, with coefficientwise Hankel-total positivity. *arXiv* **2020**, arXiv:1807.03271v2.
30. Sleshynsky, I.V. Proving the existence of some limits. *Notes Math. Dep. Novorossiysk Soc. Nat.* **1888**, *8*, 129–137. (In Russian)
31. Bodnar, D.I. *Branched Continued Fractions*; Naukova Dumka: Kyiv, Ukraine, 1986. (In Russian)
32. Skorobogatko, V.Y. *Theory of Branched Continued Fractions and Its Applications in Computational Mathematics*; Nauka: Moscow, Russia, 1983. (In Russian)
33. Vladimirov, V.S. *Methods of the Theory of Functions of Several Complex Variables*; Nauka: Moscow, Russia, 1964. (In Russian)

axioms MDPI

Article

Approximation Properties of the Generalized Abel-Poisson Integrals on the Weyl-Nagy Classes

Inna Kal'chuk and **Yurii Kharkevych** *

Faculty of Information Technologies and Mathematics, Lesya Ukrainka Volyn National University, 43025 Lutsk, Ukraine; k.inna.80@gmail.com
* Correspondence: kharkevich.juriy@gmail.com

Abstract: Asymptotic equalities are obtained for the least upper bounds of approximations of functions from the classes $W^r_{\beta,\infty}$ by the generalized Abel-Poisson integrals $P_\gamma(\delta)$, $0 < \gamma \leq 2$, for the case $r > \gamma$ in the uniform metric, which provide the solution to the Kolmogorov–Nikol'skii problem for the given method of approximation on the Weyl-Nagy classes.

Keywords: Weyl-Nagy classes; generalized Abel-Poisson integral; asymptotic equality; Kolmogorov–Nikol'skii problem; uniform metric

MSC: 42A05; 41A60

Citation: Kal'chuk, I.; Kharkevych, Y. Approximation Properties of the Generalized Abel-Poisson Integrals on the Weyl-Nagy Classes. *Axioms* **2022**, *11*, 161. https://doi.org/10.3390/axioms11040161

Academic Editor: Clemente Cesarano

Received: 28 February 2022
Accepted: 28 March 2022
Published: 1 April 2022

1. Introduction

Let L be a space of 2π-periodic summable functions and

$$S[f] = \frac{a_0}{2} + \sum_{k=1}^{\infty}(a_k \cos kx + b_k \sin kx)$$

be the Fourier series of $f \in L$.

Further, let C be a subset of the continuous functions from L with the uniform norm $\|f\|_C = \max_t |f(t)|$; L_∞ be a subset of the functions $f \in L$ with the finite norm $\|f\|_\infty = \operatorname{ess\,sup}_t |f(t)|$.

Let $\Lambda = \{\lambda_\delta(k)\}$ be the set of functions depending on $k \in \mathbb{N} \cup 0$ and on the parameter $\delta \in E_\Lambda \subset \mathbb{R}$, the set E_Λ has at least one limit point and $\lambda_\delta(0) = 1$. Using the set Λ to each function $f \in L$ we can associate the series

$$\frac{a_0}{2} + \sum_{k=1}^{\infty} \lambda_\delta(k)(a_k \cos kx + b_k \sin kx), \quad \delta \in E_\Lambda,$$

which converges for every $\delta \in E_\Lambda$ and all x to the continuous function $U_\delta(f;x;\Lambda)$.

If the series

$$\frac{1}{2} + \sum_{k=1}^{\infty} \lambda_\delta(k) \cos kt$$

is the Fourier series of some summable function, then (similarly to ([1], p. 52)) for almost all $x \in \mathbb{R}$ we have the equality

$$U_\delta(f;x;\Lambda) = \frac{1}{\pi}\int_{-\pi}^{\pi} f(x+t)\Big(\frac{1}{2} + \sum_{k=1}^{\infty} \lambda_\delta(k) \cos kt\Big)dt. \tag{1}$$

Putting in the equality (1) $\lambda_\delta(k) = e^{-\frac{k^\gamma}{\delta}}$, $0 < \gamma \leq 2$, we obtain the quantity

$$U_\delta(f;x;\Lambda) := P_\gamma(\delta;f;x) = \frac{1}{\pi}\int_{-\pi}^{\pi} f(x+t)\left\{\frac{1}{2}+\sum_{k=1}^{\infty} e^{-\frac{k^\gamma}{\delta}}\cos kt\right\}dt,\ \delta > 0,\ 0 < \gamma \leq 2, \quad (2)$$

which is usually called the generalized Abel-Poisson integral of the function f (see, e.g., [2,3]). For $\gamma = 1$ the integral (2) is the Poisson integral (see, e.g., [4]), for $\gamma = 2$ the integral (2) is the Weierstrass integral (see, e.g., [5]).

Let us define the classes of functions that we consider further. Let $f \in L$, $r > 0$ and β be a real number. If the series

$$\sum_{k=1}^{\infty} k^r\left(a_k\cos\left(kx+\frac{\beta\pi}{2}\right)+b_k\sin\left(kx+\frac{\beta\pi}{2}\right)\right)$$

is the Fourier series of a summable function, then it is denoted by f^r_β and is called the (r,β)-derivative of the function f in the Weyl-Nagy sense (see, e.g., [6]). Let $W^r_{\beta,\infty}$ be the classes of the functions f for which $\|f^r_\beta(\cdot)\|_\infty \leq 1$.

In this paper, we consider the problem of asymptotic behavior as $\delta \to \infty$ of the quantity

$$\mathcal{E}(W^r_{\beta,\infty};P_\gamma(\delta))_C = \sup_{f\in W^r_{\beta,\infty}} \|f(\cdot)-P_\gamma(\delta,f,\cdot)\|_C. \quad (3)$$

If the function $g(\delta)$ is found in an explicit form such that

$$\mathcal{E}(W^r_{\beta,\infty};P_\gamma(\delta))_C = g(\delta)+o(g(\delta)), \delta \to \infty,$$

then according to Stepanets [6] we say that the Kolmogorov–Nikol'skii problem is solved for the class $W^r_{\beta,\infty}$ and the generalized Abel-Poisson integral in the uniform metric.

The approximation properties of the generalized Poisson integrals have been studied only in the cases $\gamma = 1$ (Poisson integral) and $\gamma = 1$ (Weierstrass integral). In particular, the Kolmogorov–Nikol'skii problems for the Poisson integral on the different functional classes have been solved in [7–11]. Similar problems for Weierstrass integral have been solved in [5,12–14].

Regarding the results of estimating the approximation rate by the generalized Poisson integrals for $0 < \gamma \leq 2$ we note the work [2], where the approximation properties of the integrals (2) on Zygmund classes $Z_\alpha, 0 \leq \alpha \leq 2$, have been studied.

In this paper, we aim to find asymptotic equations for quantities (3) for arbitrary $0 < \gamma \leq 2$. This will allow us to find such γ for any r, so that the approximation rate of functions from the classes $W^r_{\beta,\infty}$ by the generalized Abel-Poisson integrals, i.e, the rate at which the quantity (3) tends to zero, is equal to $\frac{1}{\delta}$. This approximation rate could not be achieved when approximating by Poisson integrals and Weierstrass integrals.

At present, the extremal problems of the approximation theory, being related to the study of the approximation properties of linear methods for summing Fourier series, become increasingly relevant in applied mathematics, in particular, in the creation of mathematical models [15–19], in signal transmission [20,21], in the decision theory [22] and others. The problem considered in the paper, as well as those close to it [23–25] find practical application in the issues of coding, transmission and reproduction of images.

2. Main Result

Let us define the summing function for the generalized Abel-Poisson integral as follows

$$\tau(u) = \begin{cases} (1-e^{-u^\gamma})\left((\gamma-r-1)\delta^{\frac{r+2}{\gamma}-1}u^{2-\gamma}+(2+r-\gamma)\delta^{\frac{r+1}{\gamma}-1}u^{1-\gamma}\right), 0 \leq u \leq \frac{1}{\sqrt[\gamma]{\delta}}, \\ (1-e^{-u^\gamma})u^{-r}, u \geq \frac{1}{\sqrt[\gamma]{\delta}}, \end{cases} \quad (4)$$

where $0 < \gamma \leq 2,\ \delta > 0$.

Theorem 1. *Let $r > \gamma$. Then the following asymptotic equality holds as $\delta \to \infty$:*

$$\mathcal{E}\Big(W^r_{\beta,\infty}; P_\gamma(\delta)\Big)_C = \frac{1}{\delta} \sup_{f \in W^r_{\beta,\infty}} \|f_0^\gamma(\cdot)\|_C + O(\Upsilon(\delta, r, \gamma)), \tag{5}$$

where $f_0^\gamma(x)$ is (r, β)—derivative in the Weyl-Nagy sense as $r = \gamma,\ \beta = 0$ and

$$\Upsilon(\delta, r, \gamma) = \begin{cases} \frac{1}{(\sqrt[\gamma]{\delta})^r}, & \gamma < r < 2\gamma, \\ \frac{\ln \delta}{\delta^2}, & r = 2\gamma, \\ \frac{1}{\delta^2}, & r > 2\gamma. \end{cases}$$

Proof. Let us rewrite the function $\tau(u)$ given by (4) in the form $\tau(u) = \varphi(u) + \mu(u)$ (see, e.g., [26]), where

$$\varphi(u) = \begin{cases} (\gamma - r - 1)\delta^{\frac{r+2}{\gamma} - 1} u^2 + (2 + r - \gamma)\delta^{\frac{r+1}{\gamma} - 1} u, & 0 \leq u \leq \frac{1}{\sqrt[\gamma]{\delta}}, \\ u^{\gamma - r}, \ u \geq \frac{1}{\sqrt[\gamma]{\delta}}. \end{cases} \tag{6}$$

$$\mu(u) =$$

$$= \begin{cases} (1 - e^{-u^\gamma} - u^\gamma)\Big((\gamma - r - 1)\delta^{\frac{r+2}{\gamma} - 1} u^{2-\gamma} + (2 + r - \gamma)\delta^{\frac{r+1}{\gamma} - 1} u^{1-\gamma}\Big), 0 \leq u \leq \frac{1}{\sqrt[\gamma]{\delta}}, \\ (1 - e^{-u^\gamma} - u^\gamma) u^{-r}, u \geq \frac{1}{\sqrt[\gamma]{\delta}}, \end{cases} \tag{7}$$

Further we show a summability of the transformations of the form

$$\hat{\varphi}_\beta(t) = \hat{\varphi}(t, \beta) = \frac{1}{\pi} \int_0^\infty \varphi(u) \cos\left(ut + \frac{\beta\pi}{2}\right) du, \tag{8}$$

$$\hat{\mu}_\beta(t) = \hat{\mu}(t, \beta) = \frac{1}{\pi} \int_0^\infty \mu(u) \cos\left(ut + \frac{\beta\pi}{2}\right) du. \tag{9}$$

First, prove a convergence of the integral

$$A(\varphi) = \frac{1}{\pi} \int_{-\infty}^\infty |\hat{\varphi}_\beta(t)| dt.$$

Integrating twice by parts and taking into account that $\varphi(0) = 0,\ \lim\limits_{u \to \infty} \varphi(u) = \lim\limits_{u \to \infty} \varphi'(u) = 0$ and $\varphi'(u)$ is continuous on $[0, \infty)$, we have

$$\int_0^\infty \varphi(u) \cos\left(ut + \frac{\beta\pi}{2}\right) du = \frac{1}{t^2}\left(\varphi'(0) \cos \frac{\beta\pi}{2} - \int_0^\infty \varphi''(u) \cos\left(ut + \frac{\beta\pi}{2}\right) du\right).$$

In view of the fact, that the function $\varphi(u)$ is downward closed on $\left[\frac{1}{\sqrt[\gamma]{\delta}}, \infty\right)$, the last relation yields

$$\left|\int_0^\infty \varphi(u) \cos\left(ut + \frac{\beta\pi}{2}\right) du\right| \leq \frac{1}{t^2}\left(|\varphi'(0)| + \left(\int_0^{\frac{1}{\sqrt[\gamma]{\delta}}} + \int_{\frac{1}{\sqrt[\gamma]{\delta}}}^\infty\right) |\varphi''(u)| du\right) =$$

$$= \frac{1}{t^2}\left((2+r-\gamma)\delta^{\frac{r+1}{\gamma}-1} + 2(r+1-\gamma)\delta^{\frac{r+1}{\gamma}-1} + \int_{\frac{1}{\sqrt[\gamma]{\delta}}}^{\infty} \varphi''(u)du\right) =$$

$$= \frac{1}{t^2}\left(K_1\delta^{\frac{r+1}{\gamma}-1} - \varphi'\left(\frac{1}{\sqrt[\gamma]{\delta}}\right)\right) = K_2\delta^{\frac{r+1}{\gamma}-1}\frac{1}{t^2}. \quad (10)$$

Here and below we denote by symbols $K_i, i = 1, 2, \ldots$, some positive constants. From the inequalities (10) it follows that

$$\int_{|t|\geq \sqrt[\gamma]{\delta}} \left| \int_0^{\infty} \varphi(u)\cos\left(ut + \frac{\beta\pi}{2}\right)du \right| dt = O\left(\delta^{\frac{r}{\gamma}-1}\right),\ \delta \to \infty. \quad (11)$$

By virtue of the equality (4.16) from ([1], p. 69), we obtain

$$\int_0^{\sqrt[\gamma]{\delta}} \left| \int_0^{\infty} \varphi(u)\cos\left(ut + \frac{\beta\pi}{2}\right)du \right| dt = \int_0^{\sqrt[\gamma]{\delta}} \left| \int_0^{\frac{1}{\sqrt[\gamma]{\delta}}} + \int_{\frac{1}{\sqrt[\gamma]{\delta}}}^{\infty} \varphi(u)\cos\left(ut + \frac{\beta\pi}{2}\right)du \right| dt \leq$$

$$\leq \sqrt[\gamma]{\delta}\int_0^{\frac{1}{\sqrt[\gamma]{\delta}}} |\varphi(u)|du + \int_0^{\sqrt[\gamma]{\delta}} \int_{\frac{1}{\sqrt[\gamma]{\delta}}}^{\frac{1}{\sqrt[\gamma]{\delta}}+\frac{2\pi}{t}} \varphi(u)dudt \leq K_3\delta^{\frac{r}{\gamma}-1} + \int_0^{\sqrt[\gamma]{\delta}} \int_{\frac{1}{\sqrt[\gamma]{\delta}}}^{\frac{1}{\sqrt[\gamma]{\delta}}+\frac{2\pi}{t}} u^{\gamma-r}dudt. \quad (12)$$

Making a change of variables and integrating by parts in the last integral, we obtain

$$\int_0^{\sqrt[\gamma]{\delta}} \int_{\frac{1}{\sqrt[\gamma]{\delta}}}^{\frac{1}{\sqrt[\gamma]{\delta}}+\frac{2\pi}{t}} u^{\gamma-r}dudt = 2\pi \int_{\frac{2\pi}{\sqrt[\gamma]{\delta}}}^{\infty} \int_{\frac{1}{\sqrt[\gamma]{\delta}}}^{\frac{1}{\sqrt[\gamma]{\delta}}+x} u^{\gamma-r}du\frac{dx}{x^2} =$$

$$= 2\pi\left(-\frac{1}{x}\int_{\frac{1}{\sqrt[\gamma]{\delta}}}^{\frac{1}{\sqrt[\gamma]{\delta}}+x} u^{\gamma-r}du \Bigg|_{\frac{2\pi}{\sqrt[\gamma]{\delta}}}^{\infty} + \int_{\frac{2\pi}{\sqrt[\gamma]{\delta}}}^{\infty} \frac{1}{x}\left(\frac{1}{\sqrt[\gamma]{\delta}} + x\right)^{\gamma-r} dx \right) =$$

$$= 2\pi\Bigg(-\lim_{x\to\infty}\frac{1}{x}\int_{\frac{1}{\sqrt[\gamma]{\delta}}}^{\frac{1}{\sqrt[\gamma]{\delta}}+x} u^{\gamma-r}du + \frac{\sqrt[\gamma]{\delta}}{2\pi}\int_{\frac{1}{\sqrt[\gamma]{\delta}}}^{\frac{(1+2\pi)}{\sqrt[\gamma]{\delta}}} u^{\gamma-r}du +$$

$$+ \delta^{\frac{r}{\gamma}-1}\int_{\frac{2\pi}{\sqrt[\gamma]{\delta}}}^{\infty} \frac{1}{x}\left(1 + \sqrt[\gamma]{\delta}x\right)^{\gamma-r} dx \Bigg). \quad (13)$$

In view of

$$\lim_{x\to\infty}\frac{1}{x}\int_{\frac{1}{\sqrt[\gamma]{\delta}}}^{\frac{1}{\sqrt[\gamma]{\delta}}+x} u^{\gamma-r}du = 0,$$

$$\frac{\sqrt[\gamma]{\delta}}{2\pi}\int_{\frac{1}{\sqrt[\gamma]{\delta}}}^{\frac{(1+2\pi)}{\sqrt[\gamma]{\delta}}} u^{\gamma-r}du = K_4\delta^{\frac{r}{\gamma}-1},$$

$$\delta^{\frac{r}{\gamma}-1}\int\limits_{\frac{2\pi}{\sqrt[\gamma]{\delta}}}^{\infty}\frac{1}{x}\left(1+\sqrt[\gamma]{\delta}x\right)^{\gamma-r}dx=\delta^{\frac{r}{\gamma}-1}\int\limits_{1+2\pi}^{\infty}\frac{y^{\gamma-r}}{y-1}dy=$$

$$=\delta^{\frac{r}{\gamma}-1}\int\limits_{1+2\pi}^{\infty}y^{\gamma-r-1}\left(1+\frac{1}{y-1}\right)dy\leq\left(1+\frac{1}{2\pi}\right)\delta^{\frac{r}{\gamma}-1}\int\limits_{1+2\pi}^{\infty}y^{\gamma-r-1}dy=K_5\delta^{\frac{r}{\gamma}-1},$$

from (13) and (12) we can write that

$$\int\limits_0^{\sqrt[\gamma]{\delta}}\left|\int\limits_0^{\infty}\varphi(u)\cos\left(ut+\frac{\beta\pi}{2}\right)du\right|dt=O\left(\delta^{\frac{r}{\gamma}-1}\right),\ \delta\to\infty. \tag{14}$$

One can analogously show that

$$\int\limits_{-\sqrt[\gamma]{\delta}}^{0}\left|\int\limits_0^{\infty}\varphi(u)\cos\left(ut+\frac{\beta\pi}{2}\right)du\right|dt=O\left(\delta^{\frac{r}{\gamma}-1}\right),\ \delta\to\infty. \tag{15}$$

From the formulas (11), (14) and (15) we obtain

$$A(\varphi)=O\left(\delta^{\frac{r}{\gamma}-1}\right),\ \delta\to\infty.$$

Now we show the convergence of the integral

$$A(\mu)=\frac{1}{\pi}\int\limits_{-\infty}^{\infty}|\hat{\mu}_\beta(t)|dt.$$

Integrating twice by parts and taking into account that $\mu(0)=\mu'(0)=0,\ \lim\limits_{u\to\infty}\mu(u)=\lim\limits_{u\to\infty}\mu'(u)=0$, we have

$$\int\limits_0^{\infty}\mu(u)\cos\left(ut+\frac{\beta\pi}{2}\right)du=-\frac{1}{t^2}\int\limits_0^{\infty}\mu''(u)\cos\left(ut+\frac{\beta\pi}{2}\right)du,$$

and hence

$$\left|\int\limits_0^{\infty}\mu(u)\cos\left(ut+\frac{\beta\pi}{2}\right)du\right|\leq\frac{1}{t^2}\int\limits_0^{\infty}|\mu''(u)|du=\frac{1}{t^2}\left(\left(\int\limits_0^{\frac{1}{\sqrt[\gamma]{\delta}}}+\int\limits_{\frac{1}{\sqrt[\gamma]{\delta}}}^{1}+\int\limits_1^{\infty}\right)|\mu''(u)|du\right). \tag{16}$$

Further we use the notations

$$V(u)=\left(1-e^{-u^\gamma}-u^\gamma\right)u^{2-\gamma},\ W(u)=\left(1-e^{-u^\gamma}-u^\gamma\right)u^{1-\gamma}. \tag{17}$$

Let us differentiate twice the functions $V(u)$ and $W(u)$:

$$V'(u)=\gamma u(e^{-u^\gamma}-1)+(2-\gamma)u^{1-\gamma}(1-e^{-\gamma}-u^\gamma),$$

$$W'(u)=\gamma(e^{-u^\gamma}-1)+(1-\gamma)u^{-\gamma}\left(1-e^{-u^\gamma}-u^\gamma\right),$$

$$V''(u)=\gamma\left(e^{-u^\gamma}(1-\gamma u^\gamma)-1\right)+(2-\gamma)\left((1-\gamma)u^{-\gamma}\left(1-e^{-u^\gamma}-u^\gamma\right)+\gamma(e^{-u^\gamma}-1)\right),$$

$$W''(u) = -\gamma^2 u^{\gamma-1} e^{-u^\gamma} - \gamma(\gamma-1) u^{-\gamma-1}\left(1 - e^{-u^\gamma} - u^\gamma\right) + \gamma(\gamma-1) u^{-1}\left(e^{-u^\gamma} - 1\right).$$

By virtue of the fact, that for $u \in \left[0, \frac{1}{\sqrt[\gamma]{\delta}}\right]$

$$\mu''(u) = (\gamma - r - 1)\delta^{\frac{r+2}{\gamma}-1} V''(u) + (2 + r - \gamma)\delta^{\frac{r+1}{\gamma}-1} W''(u), \quad (18)$$

we obtain

$$\int_0^{\frac{1}{\sqrt[\gamma]{\delta}}} |\mu''(u)| du \leq (r + 1 - \gamma)\delta^{\frac{r+2}{\gamma}-1} \int_0^{\frac{1}{\sqrt[\gamma]{\delta}}} |V''(u)| du + (2 + r - \gamma)\delta^{\frac{r+1}{\gamma}-1} \int_0^{\frac{1}{\sqrt[\gamma]{\delta}}} |W''(u)| du.$$

Taking into account, that for $u \in \left[0, \frac{1}{\sqrt[\gamma]{\delta}}\right]$ $V''(u) \leq 0$, $W''(u) \leq 0$, and also the inequalities

$$1 - e^{-u^\gamma} \leq u^\gamma, \ e^{-u^\gamma} + u^\gamma - 1 \leq \frac{u^{2\gamma}}{2}, \quad (19)$$

we have

$$\int_0^{\frac{1}{\sqrt[\gamma]{\delta}}} |\mu''(u)| du \leq (r + 1 - \gamma)\delta^{\frac{r+2}{\gamma}-1}\left(V'(0) - V'\left(\frac{1}{\sqrt[\gamma]{\delta}}\right)\right) +$$

$$+ (2 + r - \gamma)\delta^{\frac{r+1}{\gamma}-1}\left(W'(0) - W'\left(\frac{1}{\sqrt[\gamma]{\delta}}\right)\right) =$$

$$= (r + 1 - \gamma)\delta^{\frac{r+2}{\gamma}-1}\left(\frac{\gamma}{\sqrt[\gamma]{\delta}}\left(1 - e^{-\frac{1}{\delta}}\right) + \frac{2-\gamma}{\left(\sqrt[\gamma]{\delta}\right)^{1-\gamma}}\left(e^{-\frac{1}{\delta}} + \frac{1}{\delta} - 1\right)\right) +$$

$$+ (2 + r - \gamma)\delta^{\frac{r+1}{\gamma}-1}\left(\gamma\left(1 - e^{-\frac{1}{\delta}}\right) + \frac{1-\gamma}{\left(\sqrt[\gamma]{\delta}\right)^{-\gamma}}\left(e^{-\frac{1}{\delta}} + \frac{1}{\delta} - 1\right)\right) \leq K_6 \delta^{\frac{r+1}{\gamma}-2}. \quad (20)$$

Noting, that for $u \geq \frac{1}{\sqrt[\gamma]{\delta}}$

$$\mu''(u) = r(r+1)\left(1 - e^{-u^\gamma} - u^\gamma\right) u^{-r-2} - 2\gamma u^{\gamma-r-2}\left(e^{-u^\gamma} - 1\right) +$$

$$+ \gamma\left((\gamma-1) u^{\gamma-2}(e^{-u^\gamma} - 1) - \gamma u^{2\gamma-2} e^{-u^\gamma}\right) u^{-r},$$

we can write

$$\int_{\frac{1}{\sqrt[\gamma]{\delta}}}^{1} |\mu''(u)| du \leq r(r+1) \int_{\frac{1}{\sqrt[\gamma]{\delta}}}^{1} (e^{-u^\gamma} + u^\gamma - 1) u^{-r-2} du +$$

$$+ 2\gamma r \int_{\frac{1}{\sqrt[\gamma]{\delta}}}^{1} \left(1 - e^{-u^\gamma}\right) u^{\gamma-r-2} du + \gamma \int_{\frac{1}{\sqrt[\gamma]{\delta}}}^{1} \left|(\gamma-1) u^{\gamma-2}(e^{-u^\gamma} - 1) - \gamma u^{2\gamma-2} e^{-u^\gamma}\right| u^{-r} du.$$

The inequality (19) in combination with

$$\left|(\gamma-1) u^{\gamma-2}(e^{-u^\gamma} - 1) - \gamma u^{2\gamma-2} e^{-u^\gamma}\right| \leq (2\gamma - 1) u^{2\gamma-2}, \ u \in [0, \infty), \quad (21)$$

yields

$$\int_{\frac{1}{\sqrt[\gamma]{\delta}}}^{1} |\mu''(u)|du \le \left(\frac{r(r+1)}{2} + 2\gamma r + \gamma(2\gamma-1)\right) \int_{\frac{1}{\sqrt[\gamma]{\delta}}}^{1} u^{2\gamma-r-2}du \le$$

$$\le \left(\frac{r(r+1)}{2} + 2\gamma r + \gamma(2\gamma-1)\right) \sqrt[\gamma]{\delta} \int_{\frac{1}{\sqrt[\gamma]{\delta}}}^{1} u^{2\gamma-r-1}du = \begin{cases} K_7\delta^{\frac{1}{\gamma}} + K_8\delta^{\frac{r+1}{\gamma}-2}, & r \ne 2\gamma, \\ K_9\delta^{\frac{1}{\gamma}} \ln\delta, & r = 2\gamma, \end{cases} \tag{22}$$

In the case $u \in [1, \infty)$ we obtain

$$\int_1^\infty |\mu''(u)|du \le r(r+1) \int_1^\infty (e^{-u^\gamma} + u^\gamma - 1)u^{-r-2}du +$$

$$+2\gamma r \int_1^\infty \left(1 - e^{-u^\gamma}\right)u^{\gamma-r-2}du + \gamma \int_1^\infty \left|(\gamma-1)u^{\gamma-2}(e^{-u^\gamma} - 1) - \gamma u^{2\gamma-2}e^{-u^\gamma}\right|u^{-r}du.$$

Let $0 < \gamma < 1$, then using the inequalities (19) and (21), we obtain

$$\int_1^\infty |\mu''(u)|du \le \left(\frac{r(r+1)}{2} + 2\gamma r + \gamma(2\gamma-1)\right) \int_1^\infty u^{2\gamma-r-2}du = K_{10}. \tag{23}$$

Let further $1 \le \gamma \le 2$. By virtue of the inequalities

$$(e^{-u^\gamma} + u^\gamma - 1)u^{-2} \le 1, \ \left(1 - e^{-u^\gamma}\right)u^{\gamma-2} \le 1,$$

$$|(\gamma-1)u^{\gamma-2}(e^{-u^\gamma} - 1) - \gamma u^{2\gamma-2}e^{-u^\gamma}| \le 2\gamma - 1,$$

we have

$$\int_1^\infty |\mu''(u)|du \le \left(\frac{r(r+1)}{2} + 2\gamma r + \gamma(2\gamma-1)\right) \int_1^\infty u^{-r}du = K_{11}. \tag{24}$$

Therefore, combining the relations (23), (24), we obtain

$$\int_1^\infty |\mu''(u)|du = O(1), \ \delta \to \infty. \tag{25}$$

In view of (16), taking into account (20), (22) and (25), we obtain

$$\int_{|t| \ge \sqrt[\gamma]{\delta}} \left| \int_0^\infty \mu(u) \cos\left(ut + \frac{\beta\pi}{2}\right)du \right| dt = \begin{cases} O(1), & \gamma < r < 2\gamma, \\ O(\ln\delta), & r = 2\gamma, \\ O(\delta^{\frac{r}{\gamma}-2}), & r > 2\gamma. \end{cases} \tag{26}$$

Let us further consider

$$\int_0^{\sqrt[\gamma]{\delta}} \left| \int_0^\infty \mu(u) \cos\left(ut + \frac{\beta\pi}{2}\right)du \right| dt \le \int_0^{\sqrt[\gamma]{\delta}} \left| \int_0^{\frac{1}{\sqrt[\gamma]{\delta}}} \mu(u) \cos\left(ut + \frac{\beta\pi}{2}\right)du \right| dt +$$

$$+ \int_0^{\sqrt[\gamma]{\delta}} \left| \int_{\frac{1}{\sqrt[\gamma]{\delta}}}^\infty \mu(u) \cos\left(ut + \frac{\beta\pi}{2}\right)du \right| dt. \tag{27}$$

By the inequality (19), one can easily verify that the following relations hold

$$\int_0^{\sqrt[\gamma]{\delta}} \left| \int_0^{\frac{1}{\sqrt[\gamma]{\delta}}} \mu(u) \cos\left(ut + \frac{\beta\pi}{2}\right) du \right| dt \le \int_0^{\sqrt[\gamma]{\delta}} \int_0^{\frac{1}{\sqrt[\gamma]{\delta}}} |\mu(u)| du dt = K_{12}\delta^{\frac{r}{\gamma}-2}. \tag{28}$$

The function $|\mu(u)|$ is monotonically decreasing on the interval $[u_0, \infty], u_0 \ge 1$, non-negative and tends to zero as $u \to \infty$. Then, by the equality (4.16) from ([1], p. 69), we obtain

$$\int_0^{\sqrt[\gamma]{\delta}} \left| \int_{\frac{1}{\sqrt[\gamma]{\delta}}}^{\infty} \mu(u) \cos\left(ut + \frac{\beta\pi}{2}\right) du \right| dt = \int_0^{\sqrt[\gamma]{\delta}} \left| \int_{\frac{1}{\sqrt[\gamma]{\delta}}}^{\infty} |\mu(u)| \cos\left(ut + \frac{\beta\pi}{2}\right) du \right| dt \le$$

$$\le \int_0^{\sqrt[\gamma]{\delta}} \left| \int_{\frac{1}{\sqrt[\gamma]{\delta}}}^{u_0} |\mu(u)| \cos\left(ut + \frac{\beta\pi}{2}\right) du \right| dt + \int_0^{\sqrt[\gamma]{\delta}} \left| \int_{u_0}^{\infty} |\mu(u)| \cos\left(ut + \frac{\beta\pi}{2}\right) du \right| dt \le$$

$$\le \int_0^{\sqrt[\gamma]{\delta}} \int_{\frac{1}{\sqrt[\gamma]{\delta}}}^{u_0} |\mu(u)| du dt + \int_0^{\sqrt[\gamma]{\delta}} \int_{u_0}^{u_0+\frac{2\pi}{t}} |\mu(u)| du dt \le \int_0^{\sqrt[\gamma]{\delta}} \int_{\frac{1}{\sqrt[\gamma]{\delta}}}^{u_0+\frac{2\pi}{t}} |\mu(u)| du dt. \tag{29}$$

Let $n \in \mathbb{N}$ is such that $\frac{1}{\sqrt[\gamma]{\delta}} + \frac{2\pi(n-1)}{t} \le u_0 \le \frac{1}{\sqrt[\gamma]{\delta}} + \frac{2\pi n}{t}$, then

$$\int_0^{\sqrt[\gamma]{\delta}} \int_{\frac{1}{\sqrt[\gamma]{\delta}}}^{u_0+\frac{2\pi}{t}} |\mu(u)| du dt \le \int_0^{\sqrt[\gamma]{\delta}} \int_{\frac{1}{\sqrt[\gamma]{\delta}}}^{\frac{1}{\sqrt[\gamma]{\delta}}+\frac{2\pi(n+1)}{t}} |\mu(u)| du dt. \tag{30}$$

We transform the latter integral using a change of variable and integration by parts (assume that $\delta > (2\pi(n+1)+1)^{\gamma}$)

$$\int_0^{\sqrt[\gamma]{\delta}} \int_{\frac{1}{\sqrt[\gamma]{\delta}}}^{\frac{1}{\sqrt[\gamma]{\delta}}+\frac{2\pi(n+1)}{t}} |\mu(u)| du dt = 2\pi(n+1) \int_{\frac{2\pi(n+1)}{\sqrt[\gamma]{\delta}}}^{\infty} \int_{\frac{1}{\sqrt[\gamma]{\delta}}}^{\frac{1}{\sqrt[\gamma]{\delta}}+x} |\mu(u)| du \frac{dx}{x^2} =$$

$$= 2\pi(n+1) \left(-\left(\frac{1}{x} \int_{\frac{1}{\sqrt[\gamma]{\delta}}}^{\frac{1}{\sqrt[\gamma]{\delta}}+x} |\mu(u)| du \right) \Bigg|_{\frac{2\pi(n+1)}{\sqrt[\gamma]{\delta}}}^{\infty} + \int_{\frac{2\pi(n+1)}{\sqrt[\gamma]{\delta}}}^{\infty} \frac{1}{x} \left| \mu\left(\frac{1}{\sqrt[\gamma]{\delta}} + x \right) \right| dx \right) =$$

$$= 2\pi(n+1) \left(- \lim_{x\to\infty} \frac{1}{x} \int_{\frac{1}{\sqrt[\gamma]{\delta}}}^{\frac{1}{\sqrt[\gamma]{\delta}}+x} \left(e^{-u^{\gamma}} + u^{\gamma} - 1 \right) u^{-r} du + \right.$$

$$+ \frac{\sqrt[\gamma]{\delta}}{2\pi(n+1)} \int_{\frac{1}{\sqrt[\gamma]{\delta}}}^{\frac{1+2\pi(n+1)}{\sqrt[\gamma]{\delta}}} \left(e^{-u^{\gamma}} + u^{\gamma} - 1 \right) u^{-r} du +$$

$$+\int_{\frac{2\pi(n+1)}{\sqrt[\gamma]{\delta}}}^{1-\frac{1}{\sqrt[\gamma]{\delta}}}\frac{1}{x}\left(e^{-\left(\frac{1}{\sqrt[\gamma]{\delta}}+x\right)^{\gamma}}+\left(\frac{1}{\sqrt[\gamma]{\delta}}+x\right)^{\gamma}-1\right)\left(\frac{1}{\sqrt[\gamma]{\delta}}+x\right)^{-r}dx+$$

$$\left.+\int_{1-\frac{1}{\sqrt[\gamma]{\delta}}}^{\infty}\frac{1}{x}\left(e^{-\left(\frac{1}{\sqrt[\gamma]{\delta}}+x\right)^{\gamma}}+\left(\frac{1}{\sqrt[\gamma]{\delta}}+x\right)^{\gamma}-1\right)\left(\frac{1}{\sqrt[\gamma]{\delta}}+x\right)^{-r}dx\right). \quad (31)$$

Obviously,

$$\lim_{x\to\infty}\frac{1}{x}\int_{\frac{1}{\sqrt[\gamma]{\delta}}}^{\frac{1}{\sqrt[\gamma]{\delta}}+x}\left(e^{-u^{\gamma}}+u^{\gamma}-1\right)\psi(\sqrt[\gamma]{\delta}u)du=0. \quad (32)$$

Since the second inequality from (19) holds, then

$$\frac{\sqrt[\gamma]{\delta}}{2\pi(n+1)}\int_{\frac{1}{\sqrt[\gamma]{\delta}}}^{\frac{1+2\pi(n+1)}{\sqrt[\gamma]{\delta}}}\left(e^{-u^{\gamma}}+u^{\gamma}-1\right)u^{-r}du\le$$

$$\le\frac{\sqrt[\gamma]{\delta}}{4\pi(n+1)}\int_{\frac{1}{\sqrt[\gamma]{\delta}}}^{\frac{1+2\pi(n+1)}{\sqrt[\gamma]{\delta}}}u^{2\gamma-r}du\le\frac{\delta^{\frac{r+1}{\gamma}}}{4\pi(n+1)}\int_{\frac{1}{\sqrt[\gamma]{\delta}}}^{\frac{1+2\pi(n+1)}{\sqrt[\gamma]{\delta}}}u^{2\gamma}du\le K_{13}\delta^{\frac{r}{\gamma}-2}. \quad (33)$$

Using the second inequality from (19), we have

$$\int_{\frac{2\pi(n+1)}{\sqrt[\gamma]{\delta}}}^{1-\frac{1}{\sqrt[\gamma]{\delta}}}\frac{1}{x}\left(e^{-\left(\frac{1}{\sqrt[\gamma]{\delta}}+x\right)^{\gamma}}+\left(\frac{1}{\sqrt[\gamma]{\delta}}+x\right)^{\gamma}-1\right)\left(\frac{1}{\sqrt[\gamma]{\delta}}+x\right)^{-r}dx\le$$

$$\le\int_{\frac{2\pi(n+1)}{\sqrt[\gamma]{\delta}}}^{1-\frac{1}{\sqrt[\gamma]{\delta}}}\frac{1}{x}\left(\frac{1}{\sqrt[\gamma]{\delta}}+x\right)^{2\gamma-r}dx=\delta^{\frac{r}{\gamma}-2}\int_{\frac{2\pi(n+1)}{\sqrt[\gamma]{\delta}}}^{1-\frac{1}{\sqrt[\gamma]{\delta}}}\frac{1}{x}\left(1+\sqrt[\gamma]{\delta}x\right)^{2\gamma-r}dx=$$

$$=\delta^{\frac{r}{\gamma}-2}\int_{1+2\pi(n+1)}^{\sqrt[\gamma]{\delta}}\frac{y^{2\gamma-r}}{y-1}dy=\delta^{\frac{r}{\gamma}-2}\int_{1+2\pi(n+1)}^{\sqrt[\gamma]{\delta}}y^{2\gamma-1}\psi(y)\left(1+\frac{1}{y-1}\right)dy\le$$

$$\le\left(1+\frac{1}{2\pi(n+1)}\right)\delta^{\frac{r}{\gamma}-2}\int_{1+2\pi(n+1)}^{\sqrt[\gamma]{\delta}}y^{2\gamma-1-r}dy=\begin{cases}K_{14}+K_{15}\delta^{\frac{r}{\gamma}-2}, & r\neq 2\gamma,\\ K_{16}\ln\delta, & r=2\gamma.\end{cases} \quad (34)$$

Considering the inequality

$$e^{-u^{\gamma}}+u^{\gamma}-1\le u^{\gamma},$$

we have

$$\int_{1-\frac{1}{\sqrt[\gamma]{\delta}}}^{\infty}\frac{1}{x}\left(e^{-\left(\frac{1}{\sqrt[\gamma]{\delta}}+x\right)^{\gamma}}+\left(\frac{1}{\sqrt[\gamma]{\delta}}+x\right)^{\gamma}-1\right)\left(\frac{1}{\sqrt[\gamma]{\delta}}+x\right)^{-r}dx\le$$

$$\leq \int_{1-\frac{1}{\sqrt[\gamma]{\delta}}}^{\infty} \frac{1}{x}\left(\frac{1}{\sqrt[\gamma]{\delta}}+x\right)^{\gamma-r} dx = \delta^{\frac{r}{\gamma}-1} \int_{1-\frac{1}{\sqrt[\gamma]{\delta}}}^{\infty} \frac{1}{x}\left(1+\sqrt[\gamma]{\delta}x\right)^{\gamma-r} dx =$$

$$= \delta^{\frac{r}{\gamma}-1} \int_{\sqrt[\gamma]{\delta}}^{\infty} \frac{y^{\gamma-r}}{y-1} dy = \delta^{\frac{r}{\gamma}-1} \int_{\sqrt[\gamma]{\delta}}^{\infty} y^{\gamma-1-r}\left(1+\frac{1}{y-1}\right) dy \leq$$

$$\leq \left(1+\frac{1}{\sqrt[\gamma]{\delta}-1}\right)\delta^{\frac{r}{\gamma}-1} \int_{\sqrt[\gamma]{\delta}}^{\infty} y^{\gamma-1-r} dy \leq K_{17}\delta^{\frac{r}{\gamma}-1} \int_{\sqrt[\gamma]{\delta}}^{\infty} y^{\gamma-1-r} dy = K_{18}. \tag{35}$$

From (27), taking into account (28) and (29)–(35), we can write the estimation

$$\int_{0}^{\sqrt[\gamma]{\delta}} \left| \int_{0}^{\infty} \mu(u) \cos\left(ut+\frac{\beta\pi}{2}\right) du \right| dt = \begin{cases} O(1), & \gamma < r < 2\gamma, \\ O(\ln\delta), & r = 2\gamma, \\ O(\delta^{\frac{r}{\gamma}-2}), & r > 2\gamma. \end{cases} \tag{36}$$

Similarly, we can show that

$$\int_{-\sqrt[\gamma]{\delta}}^{0} \left| \int_{0}^{\infty} \mu(u) \cos\left(ut+\frac{\beta\pi}{2}\right) du \right| dt = \begin{cases} O(1), & \gamma < r < 2\gamma, \\ O(\ln\delta), & r = 2\gamma, \\ O(\delta^{\frac{r}{\gamma}-2}), & r > 2\gamma. \end{cases} \tag{37}$$

Combining formulas (26), (36) and (37), we obtain

$$A(\mu) = \begin{cases} O(1), & \gamma < r < 2\gamma, \\ O(\ln\delta), & r = 2\gamma, \\ O(\delta^{\frac{r}{\gamma}-2}), & r > 2\gamma. \end{cases} \tag{38}$$

Similarly to [27] we can show that the following equality holds

$$f(x) - P_\gamma(\delta, f, x) = \frac{1}{(\sqrt[\gamma]{\delta})^r} \int_{-\infty}^{\infty} f_\beta^\psi\left(x+\frac{t}{\sqrt[\gamma]{\delta}}\right) \hat{\tau}_\beta(t) dt,$$

where

$$\hat{\tau}_\beta(t) = \hat{\tau}(t,\beta) = \frac{1}{\pi} \int_{0}^{\infty} \tau(u) \cos\left(ut+\frac{\beta\pi}{2}\right) du.$$

Thence

$$\mathcal{E}\left(W^r_{\beta,\infty}; P_\gamma(\delta)\right)_C = \sup_{f\in W^r_{\beta,\infty}} \left\| \frac{1}{(\sqrt[\gamma]{\delta})^r} \int_{-\infty}^{\infty} f_\beta^r\left(x+\frac{t}{\sqrt[\gamma]{\delta}}\right) \hat{\tau}_\beta(t) dt \right\|_C =$$

$$= \sup_{f\in W^r_{\beta,\infty}} \left\| \frac{1}{(\sqrt[\gamma]{\delta})^r} \int_{-\infty}^{\infty} f_\beta^r\left(x+\frac{t}{\sqrt[\gamma]{\delta}}\right) (\hat{\varphi}_\beta(t)+\hat{\mu}_\beta(t)) dt \right\|_C \leq$$

$$\leq \sup_{f\in W^r_{\beta,\infty}} \left\| \frac{1}{(\sqrt[\gamma]{\delta})^r} \int_{-\infty}^{\infty} f_\beta^r\left(x+\frac{t}{\sqrt[\gamma]{\delta}}\right) \hat{\varphi}_\beta(t) dt \right\|_C + \frac{1}{(\sqrt[\gamma]{\delta})^r} \int_{-\infty}^{\infty} |\hat{\mu}_\beta(t)| dt.$$

Therefore,

$$\mathcal{E}\left(W^r_{\beta,\infty}; P_\gamma(\delta)\right)_C = \sup_{f\in W^r_{\beta,\infty}} \left\| \frac{1}{(\sqrt[\gamma]{\delta})^r} \int_{-\infty}^{\infty} f_\beta^r\left(x+\frac{t}{\sqrt[\gamma]{\delta}}\right) \hat{\varphi}_\beta(t) dt \right\|_C + O\left(\frac{1}{(\sqrt[\gamma]{\delta})^r} A(\mu)\right). \tag{39}$$

Similarly to the work [28] , we can show that the Fourier series of the function $f_\varphi(x) = \int\limits_{-\infty}^{\infty} f_\beta^r\left(x + \frac{t}{\sqrt[\gamma]{\delta}}\right)\hat{\varphi}_\beta(t)dt$ has the form:

$$S[f_\varphi] = \sum_{k=1}^{\infty} \frac{k^\gamma}{(\sqrt[\gamma]{\delta})^{\gamma-r}}(a_k \cos kx + b_k \sin kx),$$

where a_k, b_k are the Fourier coefficients of the function f. Therefore

$$\int\limits_{-\infty}^{\infty} f_\beta^r\left(x + \frac{t}{\sqrt[\gamma]{\delta}}\right)\hat{\varphi}_\beta(t)dt = \frac{1}{(\sqrt[\gamma]{\delta})^{\gamma-r}} f_0^\gamma(x), \tag{40}$$

where $f_0^\gamma(x)$ is (r, β)—derivative in the Weyl-Nagy sense for $r = \gamma,\ \beta = 0$.

Substituting (40) into (39), we obtain

$$\mathcal{E}\left(W_{\beta,\infty}^r; P_\gamma(\delta)\right)_C = \frac{1}{\delta} \sup_{f \in W_{\beta,\infty}^r} \|f_0^\gamma(\cdot)\|_C + O\left(\frac{1}{(\sqrt[\gamma]{\delta})^r} A(\mu)\right), \quad \delta \to \infty. \tag{41}$$

Substituting (38) into (41), we obtain the equation (5). The theorem is proved. □

3. Conclusions

One of the extremal problems of approximation theory, namely the problem of studying the asymptotic properties of linear summation methods of Fourier series, has been considered in the paper. Among the linear summation methods, on the one hand, there are methods that are defined by infinite numerical matrices, and on the other hand, methods that are defined by the set of functions of the natural argument that depend on the real parameter δ. This work is devoted to the study of the approximation properties of the methods of the last type, namely, generalized Poisson integrals. The Kolmogorov–Nikol'skii problem takes a special place among the extremal problems of the approximation theory. We have considered the problem of asymptotic equalities finding for the value of the exact upper limits of deviations of generalized Abel-Poisson integrals from functions of the Weyl-Nagy classes in the uniform metric. In particular, the asymptotic equality (5) for arbitrary $r > \gamma$, $0 < \gamma \leq 2$, has been written in the paper, providing the solution of the corresponding Kolmogorov–Nikol'skii problem. The importance of this type of problems in the theory of decision making, in signal transmission, in the study of mathematical models and in the coding and reproduction of images has been noted. Regarding further research in this direction, we note that similar problems can be considered in the broader classes of functions, such as Stepanets classes and classes of non-periodic locally summable functions.

Author Contributions: Conceptualization, I.K. and Y.K.; methodology, I.K. and Y.K.; formal analysis, I.K. and Y.K.; writing—original draft preparation, I.K. and Y.K.; writing—review and editing, I.K. and Y.K. All authors have read and agreed to the published version of the manuscript.

Funding: This work was supported by Grant of the Ministry of Education and Science of Ukraine, 0120U102630.

Institutional Review Board Statement: Not applicable.

Informed Consent Statement: Not applicable.

Data Availability Statement: Not applicable.

Conflicts of Interest: The authors declare no conflict of interest.

References

1. Stepanets, A.I. *Classification and Approximation of Periodic Functions*; Kluwer: Dordrecht, The Netherlands, 1995.
2. Falaleev, L.P. On approximation of functions by generalized Abel-Poisson operators. *Sib. Math. J.* **2001**, *42*, 779–788. [CrossRef]
3. Bugrov, S. Inequalities of the type of Bernstein inequalities and their application to the investigation of the differential properties of the solutions of differential equations of higher order. *Mathematica* **1963**, *5*, 5–25.
4. Natanson, I.P. On the order of approximation of a continuous 2π-periodic function by its Poisson integral. *Dokl. Akad. Nauk SSSR* **1950**, *72*, 11–14. (In Russian)
5. Baskakov, V.A. Some properties of operators of Abel-Poisson type. *Math. Notes* **1975**, *17*, 101–107. [CrossRef]
6. Stepanets, A.I. *Methods of Approximation Theory*; VSP: Leiden, The Netherlands; Boston, MA, USA, 2005.
7. Shtark, E.L. Complete asymptotic expansion for the upper bound of the deviation of functions from Lip1 a singular Abel-Poisson integral. *Math. Notes* **1973**, *13*, 21–28.
8. Timan, A.F. Exact estimate of the remainder as approximation of periodic differentiable functions by Poisson integrals. *Dokl. AN SSSR* **1950**, *74*, 17–20.
9. Kharkevych, Y.I. On approximation of the quasi-smooth functions by their Poisson type integrals. *J. Autom. Inf. Sci.* **2017**, *49*, 74–81. [CrossRef]
10. Zhyhallo, T.V.; Padalko, N.I. On Some Boundary Properties of the Abel-Poisson Integrals. *J. Autom. Inf. Sci.* **2020**, *52*, 73–80. [CrossRef]
11. Kal'chuk, I.V.; Kharkevych, Y.I.; Pozharska K.V. Asymptotics of approximation of functions by conjugate Poisson integrals. *Carpathian Math. Publ.* **2020**, *12*, 138–147. [CrossRef]
12. Korovkin, P.P. On the best approximation of functions of class Z_2 by some linear operators. *Dokl. Akad. Nauk SSSR* **1959**, *127*, 143–149. (In Russian)
13. Bausov, L.I. Approximation of functions of class Z_α by positive methods of summation of Fourier series. *Uspekhi Mat. Nauk* **1961**, *16*, 143–149.
14. Shvai, O.L.; Pozharska, K.V. On some approximation properties of Gauss-Weierstrass singular operators. *J. Math. Sci.* **2022**, *260*, 693–699. [CrossRef]
15. Zhyhallo, K.N. Complete asymptotics of approximations by certain singular integrals in mathematical modeling. *J. Autom. Inf. Sci.* **2020**, *52*, 58–68. [CrossRef]
16. Zhyhallo, T.V. Approximation in the mean of classes of the functions with fractional derivatives by their Abel-Poisson integrals. *J. Autom. Inf. Sci.* **2019**, *51*, 58–69. [CrossRef]
17. Hrabova, U.Z. Uniform approximations by the Poisson threeharmonic integrals on the Sobolev classes. *J. Autom. Inf. Sci.* **2019**, *51*, 46–55. [CrossRef]
18. Fang, X.; Deng, Y. Uniqueness on recovery of piecewise constant conductivity and inner core with one measurement. *Inverse Probl. Imaging* **2018**, *12*, 733–743. [CrossRef]
19. Diao, H.; Cao, X.; Liu, H. On the geometric structures of transmission eigenfunctions with a conductive boundary condition and applications. *Comm. Partial Differ. Equ.* **2021**, *46*, 630–679. [CrossRef]
20. Sobchuk, V.; Kal'chuk, I.; Kharkevych, G.; Laptiev, O.; Kharkevych, Y.; Makarchuk, A. Solving the problem of convergence of the results of analog signals conversion in the process of aircraft control. In Proceedings of the 2021 IEEE 6th International Conference on Actual Problems of Unmanned Aerial Vehicles Development (APUAVD), Kyiv, Ukraine, 19–21 October 2021; pp. 29–32.
21. Cao, X.; Diao, H.; Li, J. Some recent progress on inverse scattering problems within general polyhedral geometry. *Electron. Res. Arch.* **2021**, *29*, 1753–1782. [CrossRef]
22. Hrabova, U.Z. Uniform approximations of functions of Lipschitz class by threeharmonic Poisson integrals. *J. Autom. Inf. Sci.* **2017**, *49*, 57–70. [CrossRef]
23. Serdyuk, A.S.; Stepanyuk, T.A. Uniform approximations by Fourier sums in classes of generalized Poisson integrals. *Anal. Math.* **2019**, *45*, 201–236. [CrossRef]
24. Pozhars'ka, K.V. Estimates for the entropy numbers of the classes $B^{\Omega}_{p,\theta}$ of periodic multivariable functions in the uniform metric. *Ukr. Math. J.* **2018**, *70*, 1439–1455. [CrossRef]
25. Chow, Y.T.; Deng, Y.; He, Y.; Liu, H.; Wang, X. Surface-localized transmission eigenstates, super-resolution imaging, and pseudo surface plasmon modes. *SIAM J. Imaging Sci.* **2021**, *14*, 946–975. [CrossRef]
26. Kal'chuk, I.V.; Kravets, V.I.; Hrabova, U.Z. Approximation of the classes $W^r_\beta H^\alpha$ by three-harmonic Poisson integrals. *J. Math. Sci.* **2020**, *246*, 39–50. [CrossRef]
27. Hrabova, U.Z.; Kal'chuk, I.V. Approximation of the classes $W^r_{\beta,\infty}$ by three-harmonic Poisson integrals. *Carpathian Math. Publ.* **2019** *11*, 321–334. [CrossRef]
28. Abdullayev, F.G., Kharkevych, Y.I. Approximation of the classes $C^\psi_\beta H^\alpha$ by biharmonic Poisson integrals. *Ukr. Math. J.* **2020**, *72*, 21–38. [CrossRef]

axioms

MDPI

Article

Approximate Optimal Control for a Parabolic System with Perturbations in the Coefficients on the Half-Axis

Olena A. Kapustian [1,2], Oleksiy V. Kapustyan [3], Anton Ryzhov [3,*] and Valentyn Sobchuk [3]

1 Faculty of Computer Science and Cybernetics, Taras Shevchenko National University of Kyiv, 4D Academician Glushkov Avenue, 03127 Kyiv, Ukraine; olenakapustian@knu.ua or olena.kapustian@guest.univaq.it

2 Dipartimento di Ingegneria e Scienze dell'Informazione e Matematica, Università degli Studi dell'Aquila, Edificio "Renato Ricamo" (Coppito 1), Via Vetoio, Coppito, 67100 L'Aquila, Italy

3 Faculty of Mechanics and Mathematics, Taras Shevchenko National University of Kyiv, 4E Academician Glushkov Avenue, 03127 Kyiv, Ukraine; kapustyan@knu.ua (O.V.K.); v.v.sobchuk@gmail.com (V.S.)

* Correspondence: ryzhov@knu.ua

Abstract: In this paper, we use the averaging method to find an approximate solution in the optimal control problem of a parabolic system with non-linearity of the form $f(t/\varepsilon, y)$ on an infinite time interval.

Keywords: parabolic system; optimal control; averaging method; approximate solution

Citation: Kapustian, O.A.; Kapustyan, O.V.; Ryzhov, A.; Sobchuk, V. Approximate Optimal Control for a Parabolic System with Perturbations in the Coefficients on the Half-Axis. *Axioms* **2022**, *11*, 175. https://doi.org/10.3390/axioms11040175

Academic Editor: Clemente Cesarano

Received: 17 February 2022
Accepted: 12 April 2022
Published: 14 April 2022

1. Introduction

Many results in the theory of asymptotic approximations have been obtained from 1930 onwards. Indeed, there were a lot of results on integral manifolds, equations with retarded argument, quasi- or almost-periodic equations etc. Earlier work on this theory has been presented in the famous book [1].

Averaging is a valuable method to understand the long-term evolution of dynamical systems characterized by slow dynamics and fast periodic or quasi-periodic dynamics. In [2], a transparent proof of the validity of averaging in the periodic case is presented. Different proofs for both the periodic and the general case are provided by [3,4]. In the last paper, moreover, the relation between averaging and the multiple time-scales method is established.

The averaging method for constructing approximate solutions in the theory of ODEs is presented in [5,6]. In [7], the asymptotic analysis of nonlinear dynamical systems is developed.

The work [8] is devoted to using an asymptotic method for studying the Cauchy problem for a 1D Euler–Poisson system, which represents a physically relevant hydrodynamic model but also a challenging case for a bipolar semiconductor device by considering two different pressure functions. In [9], the averaging results for ordinary differential equations perturbed by a small parameter are proved. Here, authors assume only that the right-hand sides of the equations are bounded by some locally Lebesgue integrable functions with the property that their indefinite integrals satisfy a Lipschitz-type condition.

In [10], the authors prove that averaging can be applied to the extremal flow of optimal control problems with two fast variables, that is considerably more complex because of resonances.

The averaging method is one of the most effective tools for constructing approximate solutions, including optimal control problems for ODEs [11] and PDEs [12], where the autors consider the optimal control problem in coefficients in the so-called class of H-admissible solutions.

The Krasnoselski–Krein theorem and its various modifications [13–15] play an essential role in all such considerations, since it guarantees the limit transition in perturbed problem with fast-oscillating coefficients of the form $a\left(\frac{t}{\varepsilon}\right)$ as $\varepsilon \to 0$.

The typical averaging problem may be defined as follows: one considers an unperturbed problem in which the slow variables remain fixed. Upon perturbation, a slow drift appears in these variables which one would like to approximate independently of the fast variables.

In the present paper we use this approach to nonlinear parabolic system with fast-oscillating (w.r.t. time variable) coefficients $f\left(\frac{t}{\varepsilon}, y\right)$ on an infinite time interval. We prove that the optimal control of the problem with averaging coefficients can be considered to be "approximately" optimal for the initial perturbed system.

2. Statement of the Problem

Let $\Omega \subset \mathbb{R}^d$ be a bounded domain. In cylinders $Q = (0, +\infty) \times \Omega$ we consider an initial boundary-value problem for a parabolic system [16,17]

$$\begin{cases} \frac{\partial y}{\partial t} = A\Delta y + f\left(\frac{t}{\varepsilon}, y\right) + g(y) \cdot u(t,x), (t,x) \in Q, \\ y|_{\partial\Omega} = 0, \\ y|_{t=0} = y_0(x). \end{cases} \tag{1}$$

Here $\varepsilon > 0$ is a small parameter, A is a real $N \times N$ matrix, f is a given vector-valued mapping, g is a given matrix-valued mapping, $y = (y_1, \ldots, y_N)$ is an unknown state function, $u = (u_1, \ldots, u_M)$ is an unknown control function, which are determined by requirements

$$u \in U \subseteq (L^2(Q))^M, \tag{2}$$

$$J(y,u) = \int_Q e^{-\gamma \cdot t} \cdot q(x, y(t,x)) dt dx + \int_Q \sum_{i=1}^{M} \alpha_i \cdot u_i^2(t,x) dt dx \to \inf, \tag{3}$$

where $\gamma, \alpha_1, \ldots, \alpha_M$ are positive constants.

Under the natural assumptions on A, f, g, U, q we prove, that the optimal control problem (1)–(3) has a solution $\{\bar{y}^\varepsilon, \bar{u}^\varepsilon\}$, i.e., for every $u \in U$ and for any solution y^ε of (1) with control u we have

$$J(\bar{y}^\varepsilon, \bar{u}^\varepsilon) \le J(y^\varepsilon, u)$$

In what follows we consider the problem of finding an approximate solution of (1)–(3) by transition to averaged coefficients. For this purpose we assume that uniformly w.r.t. $y \in \mathbb{R}^N$ there exists

$$\bar{f}(y) := \lim_{T \to \infty} \frac{1}{T} \int_0^T f(s,y) ds. \tag{4}$$

We consider the following optimal control problem

$$\begin{cases} \frac{\partial y}{\partial t} = A\Delta y + \bar{f}(y) + g(y) \cdot u(t,x), (t,x) \in Q, \\ y|_{\partial\Omega} = 0, \\ y|_{t=0} = y_0(x), \end{cases} \tag{5}$$

$$u \in U \subseteq (L^2(Q))^M, \tag{6}$$

$$J(y,u) = \int_Q e^{-\gamma \cdot t} \cdot q(x, y(t,x)) dt dx + \int_Q \sum_{i=1}^{M} \alpha_i \cdot u_i^2(t,x) dt dx \to \inf. \tag{7}$$

It should be noted that the transition to the averaging parameters can essentially simplify the problem. In particular, if $\bar{f}$ does not depend on y then in some cases exact solution of (1)–(3) can be found [18,19]. Another approaches for finding exact solutions of optimal control problems and approximate procedures can be found in [20,21].

Assume that $\{\bar{y}, \bar{u}\}$ is a solution of (5)–(7). The main goal of the paper is to prove the limit equality

$$J(\bar{y}^\varepsilon, \bar{u}^\varepsilon) - J(\bar{y}, \bar{u}) \to 0, \varepsilon \to 0. \tag{8}$$

As a consequence of (8) we will prove that the control $\bar{u}$ is approximately optimal for the problem (1)–(3) in the following sense:

$$J(\bar{y}^\varepsilon, \bar{u}^\varepsilon) - J(y^\varepsilon, \bar{u}) \to 0, \varepsilon \to 0,$$

where y^ε is a solution of (1) with control $\bar{u}$.

3. Assumptions, Notations and Basic Results

We assume the following conditions hold.

Assumption 1. $\frac{1}{2}(A + A^*) \geq v \cdot I$, *where* $v > 0$ *and* I *is a unit matrix;*

Assumption 2. $f : \mathbb{R}_+ \times \mathbb{R}^N \mapsto \mathbb{R}^N$ *is continuous and bounded:*

$$\exists C_1 > 0 \quad \forall t \geq 0 \quad \forall y \in \mathbb{R}^N \quad \|f(t, y)\|_{\mathbb{R}^N} \leq C_1;$$

Assumption 3. $g : \mathbb{R}^N \mapsto \mathbb{R}^{N \times M}$ *is continuous and bounded:*

$$\exists C_2 > 0 \quad \forall y \in \mathbb{R}^N \quad \|g(y)\|_{\mathbb{R}^{N \times M}} \leq C_2;$$

Assumption 4. $U \subseteq \left(L^2(Q)\right)^M$ *is closed and convex,* $0 \in U$*;*

Assumption 5. $q : \Omega \times \mathbb{R}^N \mapsto \mathbb{R}$ *is a Carathéodory function,* $\exists K_1, K_2 \in L^1(\Omega)$, $\exists C_3 > 0$ *such that* $\forall x \in \Omega$, $\forall \xi \in \mathbb{R}^N$

$$|q(x, \xi)| \leq C_3 \|\xi\|^2_{\mathbb{R}^N} + K_2(x), \quad q(x, \xi) \geq K_1(x).$$

Here, $\|\xi\|_{\mathbb{R}^N}$ *denotes the Euclidean norm of* $\xi \in \mathbb{R}^N$.

For $u \in U$ and $y_0 \in \left(L^2(\Omega)\right)^N$ we understand solution of (1) in weak (or generalized) sense on every finite time interval, i.e., y is a solution of (1) if

$$y \in L^2_{loc}\left(0, +\infty, (H^1_0(\Omega))^N\right) \bigcap L^\infty_{loc}\left(0, +\infty, (L^2(\Omega))^N\right)$$

such that $\forall T > 0$, $\forall \varphi \in (H^1_0(\Omega))^N$, $\forall \eta \in C^\infty_0(0, T)$ the following equality holds:

$$-\int_0^T (y, \varphi)_H \cdot \eta' dt + \int_0^T (A \nabla y, \nabla \varphi)_H \eta dt = \int_0^T \left(f\left(\frac{t}{\varepsilon}, y\right), \varphi\right)_H \eta dt + \int_0^T (g(y) \cdot u, \varphi)_H \eta dt. \tag{9}$$

Here and after we denote by $\|\cdot\|_H$ and $(\cdot,\cdot)_H$ the classical norm and scalar product in $H := (L^2(\Omega))^N$, by $\|\cdot\|_V$ and $(\cdot,\cdot)_V$ the classical norm and scalar product in $V := (H^1_0(\Omega))^N$, by $\|\cdot\|_U$ the norm in $L^2(Q))^M$, and by V^* the dual space to V.

Due to the Assumptions 1–3, every solution of (1) satisfies

$$\frac{\partial y}{\partial t} \in L^2_{loc}(0, +\infty, V^*).$$

It means that $\forall T > 0$ every solution of (1) is an absolutely continuous function from $[0, T]$ to H, and equality (9) is equivalent to the following one [16]:

$$\frac{d}{dt}(y, \varphi)_H + (A \nabla y, \nabla \varphi)_H = \left(f\left(\frac{t}{\varepsilon}, y\right), \varphi\right)_H + (g(y) \cdot u, \varphi)_H \tag{10}$$

for almost all (a.a.) $t > 0$.

It is known [16,17] that, under Assumptions 1–3, for every $y_0 \in H$, $u \in U$ there exists at least one solution of (1), and for a.a. $t > 0$

$$\frac{1}{2}\frac{d}{dt}\|y(t)\|_H^2 + v \cdot \|y(t)\|_V^2 \leq C_1\|y(t)\|_H + C_2\|y(t)\|_H \cdot \|u(t)\|_{(L^2(\Omega))^M}. \tag{11}$$

Remark 1. *Uniqueness of solution of (1) is not guaranteed. This can be done under some additional assumptions, e.g., [16] $\forall s \geq 0$, $\forall y \in \mathbb{R}^N$, $\forall \omega \in \mathbb{R}^N$*

$$\left(f_y'(s,y)\omega,\omega\right)_{\mathbb{R}^N} \geq -C_4 \cdot \|\omega\|_{\mathbb{R}^N}$$

In the sequel, we denote by $\mathcal{F}^\varepsilon$ (or $\bar{\mathcal{F}}$) a set of all pairs $\{y,u\}$, where y is a solution of (1) (or (5)) with control u.

The following Lemma gives us a result about the solvability of the optimal control problem (1)–(3) and it also provides some useful inequalities.

Lemma 1. *Under the Assumptions 1–5 for every $\varepsilon > 0$ the problem (1)–(3) has a solution $\{\bar{y}^\varepsilon, \bar{u}^\varepsilon\}$, that is,*

$$J(\bar{y}^\varepsilon, \bar{u}^\varepsilon) \leq J(y,u) \quad \forall\{y,u\} \in \mathcal{F}^\varepsilon.$$

Proof of Lemma 1. Fix $\varepsilon > 0$ and suppress index ε throughout the proof. The idea of the proof is to derive a priori estimates for the minimizing sequence. Obtained estimates allow us to pass to the limit in problem (1)–(3).

From (11), Poincare inequality $\|y\|_V^2 \geq \lambda\|y\|_H^2$, $y \in V$, and Young inequality we derive that for some $\delta > 0$, $C_5 > 0$ (not depending on ε) for every $\{y,u\} \in \mathcal{F}^\varepsilon$ for a.a. $t > 0$

$$\frac{d}{dt}\|y(t)\|_H^2 + \delta\|y(t)\|_H^2 \leq C_5\left(1 + \|u(t)\|^2_{(L^2(\Omega))^M}\right).$$

Therefore using Gronwall inequality we get for all $t > 0$

$$\|y(t)\|_H^2 \leq e^{-\delta \cdot t}\left\{\|y_0(t)\|_H^2 + C_5\int_0^t\left(1 + \|u(s)\|^2_{(L^2(\Omega))^M}\right)e^{\delta \cdot s}ds\right\}, \tag{12}$$

$$\|y(t)\|_H^2 \leq e^{-\delta \cdot t}\|y_0\|_H^2 + \frac{C_5}{\delta} + C_5 \cdot \|u\|_U^2. \tag{13}$$

From the inequality (13) and the first inequality from the Assumption 5 we have that for some $C_6 > 0$

$$J(y,u) \leq C_6\left(1 + \|y_0\|_H^2 + \|u\|_U^2\right). \tag{14}$$

Now let $\{y_n, u_n\}$ be a minimizing sequence, that is,

$$\lim_{n\to\infty} J(y_n,u_n) = \inf_{\{y,u\}\in\mathcal{F}^\varepsilon} J(y,u) =: \bar{J}^\varepsilon. \tag{15}$$

Note that due to the Assumption 5 $\forall\{y,u\} \in \mathcal{F}^\varepsilon$

$$J(y,u) \geq \frac{\|K_1\|_{L^1}}{\gamma} \Rightarrow \bar{J}^\varepsilon \geq \frac{\|K_1\|_{L^1}}{\gamma} > -\infty.$$

From (15) for sufficiently large n

$$J(y_n,u_n) \leq \bar{J}^\varepsilon + 1. \tag{16}$$

On the other hand, for $\alpha := \min_{1\le i\le M} \alpha_i > 0$

$$J(y_n, u_n) \ge \frac{\|K_1\|_{L^1}}{\gamma} + \alpha \cdot \|u_n\|_U^2. \tag{17}$$

Inequalities (16) and (17) imply that $\{u_n\}$ is bounded in $(L^2(Q))^M$, so for subsequence

$$u_n \to u \text{ weakly in } (L^2(Q))^M. \tag{18}$$

Due to convexity of U we have inclusion $u \in U$. From (11) over $(0,T)$ and using (13) we we obtain from (5) that $\{y_n\}$ is bounded in

$$L^2(0,T;V)\bigcap L^\infty(0,T;H),$$

$\left\{\frac{\partial y_n}{\partial t}\right\}$ is bounded in $L^2(0,T;V^*)$. Using Compactness Lemma [22] we conclude that up to subsequence $\forall T > 0$

$$\begin{gathered} y_n \to y \text{ weakly in } L^2(0,T;V), \\ y_n \to y \text{ in } L^2(0,T;H), \\ \forall t \ge 0 \;\; y_n(t) \to y(t) \text{ weakly in } H, \\ y_n(t,x) \to y(t,x) \text{ a.a. in } Q. \end{gathered} \tag{19}$$

From (19) and Lebesgue's Dominated Convergence Theorem we can pass to the limit in the equality (9) applied to $\{y_n, u_n\}$, and obtain that $\{y, u\} \in \mathcal{F}^\varepsilon$. Due to pointwise convergence

$$e^{-\gamma\cdot t}\cdot q(x, y_n(t,x)) \to e^{-\gamma\cdot t} q(x, y(t,x)) \text{ a.a. in } Q,$$

Fatou's lemma and weak convergence (18) we have

$$\bar{J}^\varepsilon = \lim_{n\to\infty} J(y_n,u_n) \ge \underline{\lim} \int_Q e^{-\gamma\cdot t} q(x, y_n(t,x))dtdx + \underline{\lim} \int_Q \sum_{i=1}^M \alpha_i (u_i^n(t,x))^2 dtdx \ge J(y,u).$$

Therefore $\{y, u\}$ is a solution of (1)–(3). □

4. Main Results

We assume that $\forall \eta > 0\; \exists \delta > 0\; \forall t \ge 0,\; \forall y, z \in \mathbb{R}^N$

$$\|y - z\|_{\mathbb{R}^N} < \delta \Rightarrow \|f(t,y) - f(t,z)\|_{\mathbb{R}^N} < \eta. \tag{20}$$

Assumption (20) implies that the averaged function $\bar{f} : \mathbb{R}^N \mapsto \mathbb{R}^N$ from (4) is a continuous function and the Assumption 2 holds. It means that under conditions (4), (20) the optimal control problem (5)–(7) has a solution $\{\bar{y}, \bar{u}\}$.

The main result of the paper is the following

Theorem 1. *Suppose that the Assumptions 1–5 and (4), (20) hold and, moreover, the problem (5) has a unique solution for every $u \in U$. Let $\{\bar{y}^\varepsilon, \bar{u}^\varepsilon\}$ be a solution of (1)–(3). Then*

$$J(\bar{y}^\varepsilon, \bar{u}^\varepsilon) \to J(\bar{y}, \bar{u}), \varepsilon \to 0, \tag{21}$$

and up to subsequence

$$\begin{gathered} \bar{y}^\varepsilon \to \bar{y} \text{ in } L^2_{loc}(0,+\infty;H), \\ \bar{u}^\varepsilon \to \bar{u} \text{ in } (L^2(Q))^M, \end{gathered} \tag{22}$$

where $\{\bar{y},\bar{u}\}$ *is a solution of (5)–(7).*

Proof. Let $\varepsilon_n \to 0$, $\{\bar{y}^n,\bar{u}^n\}$ be a solution of (1)–(3) for $\varepsilon = \varepsilon_n$. Due to the optimality of $\{\bar{y}^n,\bar{u}^n\}$ we have

$$J(\bar{y}^n,\bar{u}^n) \le J(y_n,0),$$

where y_n is a solution of (1) with $\varepsilon = \varepsilon_n$ and $u \equiv 0$. Then from (14)

$$\frac{1}{\gamma}\|K_1\|_{L^1} + \alpha\|\bar{u}^n\|_U^2 \le C_6 \cdot (1 + \|y_0\|_H^2).$$

Repeating arguments used in the prof of Lemma 1 conclude that on subsequence for some $\hat{y}$, $\hat{u}$:

$$\bar{u}^n \to \hat{u} \text{ weakly in } (L^2(Q))^M, n \to \infty,$$
$$\bar{y}^n \to \hat{y} \text{ in the sense of (19)}, n \to \infty, \tag{23}$$

Let us prove that $\{\hat{y},\hat{u}\} \in \bar{\mathcal{F}}$, i.e., $\hat{y}$ is a solution of the averaged problem (5) with control $\hat{u}$. For this purpose it is sufficient to make a limit transition in the equality

$$(\bar{y}^n,\varphi)_H - (y_0,\varphi)_H + \int_0^T (A\nabla\bar{y}^n,\nabla\varphi)_H = \int_0^T \left(f\left(\frac{t}{\varepsilon_n},\bar{y}^n\right),\varphi\right)_H + \int_0^T (g(\bar{y}^n)\bar{u}^n,\varphi))_H, \tag{24}$$

for arbitrary $\varphi \in V$ and $T > 0$.

Limit transition in the left part of (24) is a direct consequence of (23). From the Dominated Convergence Theorem we see that

$$g(\bar{y}^n) \to g(\hat{y}) \text{ in } L^2(0,T;H), n \to \infty.$$

Then (23) implies convergence in the last term of (24).

Let us prove that $\forall T > 0, \forall\varphi \in V$

$$\int_{Q_T} \sum_{i=1}^N f_i\left(\frac{t}{\varepsilon_n},\bar{y}^n(t,x)\right)\varphi_i(x)dtdx \to \int_{Q_T} \sum_{i=1}^N \bar{f}_i(\hat{y}(t,x))\varphi_i(x)dtdx, n \to \infty, \tag{25}$$

where $Q_T = (0,T) \times \Omega$. Due to the Dominated Convergence Theorem $\forall 0 < a < b, \forall\psi \in H$

$$\int_a^b\int_\Omega \sum_{i=1}^N \left(f_i\left(\frac{t}{\varepsilon_n},\psi(x)\right) - \bar{f}_i(\psi(x))\right)\varphi_i(x)dxdt \to 0, n \to \infty. \tag{26}$$

Due to Egorov's theorem $\forall\delta > 0\ \exists Q_1^\delta \subset Q_T$ such that $\mu(Q_1^\delta) < \delta$ and

$$\bar{y}^n \to \hat{y} \text{ uniformly on } Q_T \setminus Q_1^\delta \text{ as } n \to \infty. \tag{27}$$

Here μ is Lebesgue's measure on $\mathbb{R}^2$. On the other hand there exists a sequence of step functions

$$y^m(t,x) = \sum_{k=1}^m y_k^m(x)\cdot\chi_{A_k^m}(t), \{y_k^m\} \subset H,$$

$\{A_k^m = (a_k^m,b_k^m)\}$ is a covering of $(0,T)$ such that

$$y^m \to \hat{y} \text{ in } L^2(0,T;H) \text{ and a.e. in } Q_T.$$

Moreover $\forall\delta > 0\ \exists Q_2^\delta \subset Q_T$ such that $\mu(Q_2^\delta) < \delta$ and

$$y^m \to \hat{y} \text{ uniformly on } Q_T \setminus Q_2^\delta \text{ as } m \to \infty.$$

Let us denote

$$I_1^{(n)} := \int\limits_{Q_T} \sum_{i=1}^{N} \left(f_i\left(\frac{t}{\varepsilon_n}, \bar{y}^n(t,x)\right) - f_i\left(\frac{t}{\varepsilon_n}, \hat{y}(t,x)\right)\right) \varphi_i(x) dt dx,$$

$$I_2^{(n)} := \int\limits_{Q_T} \sum_{i=1}^{N} \left(f_i\left(\frac{t}{\varepsilon_n}, \hat{y}(t,x)\right) - \bar{f}(\hat{y}(t,x))\right) \varphi_i(x) dt dx.$$

Then due to (27)

$$I_1^{(n)} \leq \int\limits_{Q_T \setminus Q_1^{\delta}} \left\| f\left(\frac{t}{\varepsilon_n}, \bar{y}^n(t,x)\right) - f\left(\frac{t}{\varepsilon_n}, \hat{y}(t,x)\right)\right\|_{\mathbb{R}^N} \cdot \|\varphi(x)\|_{\mathbb{R}^N} dt dx + 2C_1 \cdot \|\varphi\|_H^{\frac{1}{2}} \cdot \delta^{\frac{1}{2}}. \tag{28}$$

Due to (20) for a given $\delta > 0\ \exists \lambda\ \forall n \geq 1, \forall t \geq 0$

$$\|y - z\|_{\mathbb{R}^N} < \lambda \Rightarrow \left\| f\left(\frac{t}{\varepsilon_n}, y\right) - f\left(\frac{t}{\varepsilon_n}, z\right)\right\| \leq \delta^{\frac{1}{2}}.$$

Therefore, choosing n_1 such that $\forall n \geq n_1$

$$\sup_{(t,x) \in Q_T \setminus Q_1^{\delta}} \|\bar{y}^n(t,x) - \hat{y}(t,x)\|_{\mathbb{R}^N} < \lambda$$

we get from (28) that $\forall n \geq n_1$

$$I_1^{(n)} \leq \delta^{\frac{1}{2}} \cdot \mu^{\frac{1}{2}}(Q_T) \cdot \|\varphi\|_H^{\frac{1}{2}} + 2C_1 \cdot \|\varphi\|_H^{\frac{1}{2}} \cdot \delta^{\frac{1}{2}} \leq C_7(T)\delta^{\frac{1}{2}}. \tag{29}$$

On the other hand, for every step function $y^m(t,x)$ we have due to (26): $\forall m \geq 1$

$$\begin{aligned} &\int\limits_{Q_T} \sum_{i=1}^{N} \left(f_i\left(\tfrac{t}{\varepsilon_n}, y^m(t,x)\right) - \bar{f}_i(y^m(t,x))\right) \varphi_i(x) dt dx \\ &= \sum_{k=1}^{m} \int\limits_{A_k^m} \int\limits_{\Omega} \sum_{i=1}^{N} \left(f_i\left(\frac{t}{\varepsilon_n}, y_k^m(x)\right) - \bar{f}_i(y_k^m(x))\right) \varphi_i(x) dt dx \to 0, n \to \infty. \end{aligned} \tag{30}$$

So $\forall m \geq 1, \exists n_2 = n_2(m), \forall n \geq n_2$

$$\left| \int\limits_{Q_T} \sum_{i=1}^{N} \left(f_i\left(\frac{t}{\varepsilon_n}, y^m(t,x)\right) - \bar{f}_i(y^m(t,x))\right) \varphi_i(x) dt dx \right| < \delta. \tag{31}$$

Furthermore, $\exists m_0, \forall m \geq m_0, \forall n \geq 1$

$$\int\limits_{Q^T \setminus Q_2^{\delta}} \left\| f\left(\frac{t}{\varepsilon_n}, \hat{y}(t,x)\right) - f\left(\frac{t}{\varepsilon_n}, y^m(t,x)\right)\right\|_{\mathbb{R}^N} \cdot \|\varphi(x)\|_{\mathbb{R}^N} dt dx \leq \delta^{\frac{1}{2}} \cdot \mu^{\frac{1}{2}}(Q_T) \cdot \|\varphi\|_H^{\frac{1}{2}}, \tag{32}$$

$$\int\limits_{Q_T \setminus Q_2^{\delta}} \|\bar{f}(\hat{y}(t,x)) - \bar{f}(y^m(t,x))\|_{\mathbb{R}^N} \cdot \|\varphi(x)\|_{\mathbb{R}^N} dt dx \leq \delta^{\frac{1}{2}} \cdot \mu^{\frac{1}{2}}(Q_T) \cdot \|\varphi\|_H^{\frac{1}{2}}. \tag{33}$$

Combining (30)–(33), we obtain $\forall m \geq m_0, \forall n \geq n_2(m)$

$$I_2^{(n)} \leq 2 \cdot \delta^{\frac{1}{2}} \cdot \mu^{\frac{1}{2}}(Q_T) \|\varphi\|_H^{\frac{1}{2}} + \delta \leq C_8(T) \cdot \delta^{\frac{1}{2}}. \tag{34}$$

Inequalities (29), (34) imply (25). So we can pass to the limit in (24) and obtain that $\{\hat{y}, \hat{u}\} \in \bar{\mathcal{F}}$. Now let us prove that $\{\hat{y}, \hat{u}\}$ is an optimal process in (5)–(7).

Fatou's lemma implies
$$\underline{\lim} J(\bar{y}^n, \bar{u}^n) \geq J(\hat{y}, \hat{u}).$$

On the other hand, for every $u \in U$ and any y_n–solution of (1) with control u and $\varepsilon = \varepsilon_n$ we get
$$J(\bar{y}^n, \bar{u}^n) \leq J(\bar{y}_n, u).$$

Using the same arguments as in proof of the Lemma 1 for $\{y_n\}$ we derive that
$$y_n \to y \text{ in the sense of (19)},$$
where y is a unique solution of (5) with control u.

Let us prove that
$$\int_Q e^{-\gamma \cdot t} q(x, y_n(t,x)) dt dx \to \int_Q e^{-\gamma \cdot t} q(x, y(t,x)) dt dx \tag{35}$$

Indeed due to the Assumption 5 and (13) we have
$$\left| e^{-\gamma \cdot t} q(x, y_n(t,x)) \right| \leq C_3 e^{-\gamma \cdot t} \|y_n(t,x)\|^2_{\mathbb{R}^N} + e^{-\gamma \cdot t} \cdot K_2(x). \tag{36}$$

As $y_n \to y$ in $L^2(0,T;H)$ and a.e. in Q, we deduce from Lebesgue's Dominated Convergence theorem:
$$\forall T > 0 \quad \int_{Q_T} e^{-\gamma \cdot t} q(x, y_n(t,x)) dt dx \to \int_{Q_T} e^{-\gamma \cdot t} q(x, y(t,x)) dt dx, n \to \infty. \tag{37}$$

On the other hand, from (12) and (36)
$$\begin{aligned} \int_T^{+\infty} \int_\Omega e^{-\gamma \cdot t} |q(x, y_n(t,x))| dt dx &\leq \int_T^{+\infty} e^{-\gamma \cdot t} \left[C_3 \cdot \|y_n(t)\|^2_H + \|K_2\|_{L^1} \right] dt \\ &\leq \int_T^{+\infty} e^{-\gamma \cdot t} \left[C_3 e^{-\delta \cdot t} \cdot \|y_0(t)\|^2_H + \frac{C_3 \cdot C_5}{\delta} + C_3 \cdot C_5 \cdot \|u\|^2_U + \|K_2\|_{L^1} \right] dt \\ &\leq C_9 \cdot e^{-\gamma \cdot T}, \end{aligned} \tag{38}$$
where C_9 does not depend on T and n. The last inequality together with with (37) leads to (35).

From (35) we conclude the following inequality: $\forall \{y, u\} \in \bar{\mathcal{F}}$
$$J(\hat{y}, \hat{u}) \leq \underline{\lim} J(\bar{y}^n, \bar{u}^n) \leq \underline{\lim} J(y_n, u) = J(y, u). \tag{39}$$

This means that $\{\hat{y}, \hat{u}\}$ is a solution of (5)–(7).

Now we substitute $u = \hat{u}$ in previous arguments. Then $y = \hat{y}$ due to uniqueness. So from (39), we obtain
$$J(\hat{y}, \hat{u}) \leq \underline{\lim} J(\bar{y}^n, \bar{u}^n) \leq J(\hat{y}, \hat{u}).$$

These inequalities mean that up to subsequence
$$J(\bar{y}^n, \bar{u}^n) \to J(\hat{y}, \hat{u}), n \to \infty. \tag{40}$$

Since $J(\hat{y}, \hat{u}) = \inf_{\{y,u\} \in \bar{\mathcal{F}}} J(y, u)$, then convergence in (40) holds for the whole sequence. Therefore (21) is proved.

Moreover, up to subsequence $\bar{y}^n$ tends to $\hat{y}$ in $L^2_{loc}(0, +\infty; H)$. So, repeating arguments (37) and (38) for $\bar{y}^n$, and using boundness of $\{\bar{u}^n\}$, we have

$$\int_Q e^{-\gamma \cdot t} q(x, \bar{y}^n(t,x)) dt dx \to \int_Q e^{-\gamma \cdot t} q(x, \hat{y}(t,x)) dt dx.$$

Then from (40) and weak convergence we deduce (22) □

Corollary 1. *An optimal control $\bar{u} \in U$ of the averaged problem (5)–(7) can serve as an "approximate" optimal control in the initial problem (1), that is:*

$$J(\bar{y}^\varepsilon, \bar{u}^\varepsilon) - J(y^\varepsilon, \bar{u}) \to 0, \varepsilon \to 0, \quad (41)$$

where y^ε is a solution of (1) with control $u = \bar{u}$.

Indeed, for y^{ε_n}, $\varepsilon_n \to 0$, we can repeat arguments of the proof of the Theorem, and due to the uniqueness of the solution of (5) for $u = \bar{u}$ we have up to subsequence

$$y^{\varepsilon_n} \to \bar{y} \text{ in the sense of } (19)$$

Then (35) holds and taking into account strong convergence (22), we obtain (41).

5. Conclusions and Future Research

We sought to obtain a theoretical result that demonstrates the effectiveness of the averaging method of finding an approximate solution of the optimal control problem for a non-linear parabolic system with fast-oscillating coefficients with respect to a time variable. We proved that the optimal control of the problem with averaging coefficients can be considered as an "approximately" optimal for the initial perturbed system. To demonstrate effectiveness of the method we plan to continue research focusing on the practical applications and simulation results using in particular genetic algorithms.

Author Contributions: Conceptualization, O.A.K., O.V.K., A.R. and V.S.; methodology, O.A.K., O.V.K., A.R. and V.S.; formal analysis, O.A.K., O.V.K., A.R. and V.S.; investigation, O.A.K., O.V.K., A.R. and V.S.; writing—original draft preparation, O.A.K., O.V.K., A.R. and V.S.; writing—review and editing, O.A.K., O.V.K., A.R. and V.S. All authors have read and agreed to the published version of the manuscript.

Funding: This research received no external funding.

Institutional Review Board Statement: Not applicable.

Informed Consent Statement: Not applicable.

Data Availability Statement: Not applicable.

Conflicts of Interest: The authors declare no conflict of interest.

References

1. Bogoliubov, N.N.; Mitropolsky, Y.A. *Asymptotic Methods in the Theory of Non-Linear Oscillations*; Gordon and Breach: New York, NY, USA, 1961.
2. Roseau, M. *Vibrations nonlinéaires et théorie de la stabilité*; Springer: Berlin, Germany, 1966.
3. Besjes, J.G. On the asymptotic methods for non-linear differential equations. *J. Mécanique* **1969**, *8*, 357–373.
4. Perko, L.M. Higher order averaging and related methods for perturbed periodic and quasi-periodic systems. *SIAM J. Appl. Math.* **1969**, *17*, 698–724. [CrossRef]
5. Lochak, P.; Meunier, C. *Multiphase Averaging for Classical Systems*; Springer: New York, NY, USA, 1988.
6. Samoilenko, A.M.; Stanzhitskyi, A.N. On averaging differential equations on an infinite interval. *Differ. Uravn.* **2006**, *42*, 476–482. [CrossRef]
7. Sanders, J.A.; Verhulst, F. *Averaging Methods in Nonlinear Dynamical Systems*; Springer: New York, NY, USA, 1985.
8. Donatella Donatelli, D.; Mei, M.; Rubino, B.; Sampalmieri, R. Asymptotic behavior of solutions to Euler–Poisson equations for bipolar hydrodynamic model of semiconductors *J. Differ. Equ.* **2013**, *255*, 3150–3184. [CrossRef]
9. Lakrib, M.; Kherraz, T.; Bourada, A. Averaging for ordinary differential equations perturbed by a small parameter. *Math. Bohem.* **2016**, *141*, 143–151. [CrossRef]

10. Dell'Elce, L.; Caillau, J.-B.; Pomet, J.-B. Considerations on Two-Phase Averaging of Time-Optimal Control Systems. Available online: https://hal.inria.fr/hal-01793704v3 (accessed on 31 March 2022).
11. Nosenko, T.V.; Stanzhytskyi, O.M. Averaging method in some problems of optimal control. *Nonlin. Osc.* **2008**, *11*, 539–547. [CrossRef]
12. Ciro D'Apice, C.; De Maio, U.; Kogut, O.P. Optimal Control Problems in Coefficients for Degenerate Equations of Monotone Type: Shape Stability and Attainability Problems. *SIAM J. Control Optim.* **2012**, *50*, 1174–1199. [CrossRef]
13. Kichmarenko, O.; Stanzhytskyi, O. Sufficient conditions for the existence of optimal control for some classes of functional-differential equations. *Nonlin. Dyn. Syst. Theory* **2018**, *18*, 196–211.
14. Plotnikova, N.V. The Krasnoselskii-Krein theorem for differential inclusions. *Differ. Uravn.* **2005**, *41*, 997–1000.
15. Gamma, R.; Guerman, A.; Smirnov, G. On the asymptotic stability of discontinuous systems via the averaging method. *Nonlin. Ann.* **2011**, *74*, 1513–1522. [CrossRef]
16. Chepyzhov, V.V.; Visnik, M.I. *Attractors for Equations of Mathematical Physics*; AMS: Providence, RI, USA, 2002.
17. Kapustyan, O.V.; Kasyanov, P.O.; Valero, J. Structure of the global attractor for weak solutions of a reaction-diffusion equation. *Appl. Math. Inf. Sci.* **2015**, *9*, 2257–2264.
18. Kapustian, O.A.; Sobchuk, V.V. Approximate homogenized synthesis for disturbed optimal control problem with superposition type cost functional. *Stat. Opt. Inf. Comp.* **2018**, *6*, 233–239.
19. Kapustian, E.A.; Nakonechny, A.G. The minimax problems of pointwise observation for a parabolic boundary-value problem. *J. Autom. Inf. Sci.* **2002**, *34*, 52–63.
20. Pichkur, V.V.; Sobchuk, V.V. Mathematical Model and Control Design of a Functionally Stable Technological Process. *Diff. Eq. App.* **2021**, *29*, 32–41. [CrossRef]
21. Garashchenko, F.G., Pichkur, V.V. Structural optimization of dynamic systems by use of generalized Bellman's principle. *J. Autom. Inf. Sci.* **2000**, *32*, 1–6.
22. Sell, G.R.; You, Y. *Dynamics of Evolutionary Equations*; Springer: New York, NY, USA, 2002.

axioms

MDPI

Article

Some Korovkin-Type Approximation Theorems Associated with a Certain Deferred Weighted Statistical Riemann-Integrable Sequence of Functions

Hari Mohan Srivastava [1,2,3,4,*], Bidu Bhusan Jena [5] and Susanta Kumar Paikray [5]

1 Department of Mathematics and Statistics, University of Victoria, Victoria, BC V8W 3R4, Canada
2 Department of Medical Research, China Medical University Hospital, China Medical University, Taichung 40402, Taiwan
3 Department of Mathematics and Informatics, Azerbaijan University, 71 Jeyhun Hajibeyli Street, Baku AZ1007, Azerbaijan
4 Section of Mathematics, International Telematic University Uninettuno, I-00186 Rome, Italy
5 Department of Mathematics, Veer Surendra Sai University of Technology, Burla 768018, India; bidumath.05@gmail.com (B.B.J.); skpaikray_math@vssut.ac.in (S.K.P.)
* Correspondence: harimsri@math.uvic.ca

Abstract: Here, in this article, we introduce and systematically investigate the ideas of deferred weighted statistical Riemann integrability and statistical deferred weighted Riemann summability for sequences of functions. We begin by proving an inclusion theorem that establishes a relation between these two potentially useful concepts. We also state and prove two Korovkin-type approximation theorems involving algebraic test functions by using our proposed concepts and methodologies. Furthermore, in order to demonstrate the usefulness of our findings, we consider an illustrative example involving a sequence of positive linear operators in conjunction with the familiar Bernstein polynomials. Finally, in the concluding section, we propose some directions for future research on this topic, which are based upon the core concept of statistical Lebesgue-measurable sequences of functions.

Keywords: Riemann and Lebesgue integrals; statistical Riemann and Lebesgue integral; deferred weighted Riemann summability; Banach space; Bernstein polynomials; positive linear operators; Korovkin-type approximation theorems; Lebesgue-measurable sequences of functions

MSC: 40A05; 40G15; 33C45; 41A36

Citation: Srivastava, H.M.; Jena, B.B.; Paikray, S.K. Some Korovkin-Type Approximation Theorems Associated with a Certain Deferred Weighted Statistical Riemann-Integrable Sequence of Functions. *Axioms* **2022**, *11*, 128. https://doi.org/10.3390/axioms11030128

Academic Editor: Yurii Kharkevych

Received: 7 February 2022
Accepted: 11 March 2022
Published: 12 March 2022

1. Introduction and Motivation

The relatively more familiar theory of ordinary convergence is one of the most important topics of study of sequence spaces. It has indeed gradually progressed to a very high level of development. Two prominent researchers, Fast [1] and Steinhaus [2], independently created a new idea in the theory of sequence spaces, which is known as *statistical* convergence. This fruitful concept is extremely valuable for studies in various areas of pure and applied mathematical sciences. It is remarkably more powerful than the traditional convergence and has provided a vital area of research in recent years. Furthermore, such a concept is closely related to the study of Real Analysis, Analytic Probability theory and Number theory, and so on. For some recent related developments on this subject, the reader can see, for example, the works in [3–18].

Suppose that $\mathfrak{C} \subseteq \mathbb{N}$. Moreover, let

$$\mathfrak{C}_k = \{\eta : \eta \leqq k \quad \text{and} \quad \eta \in \mathfrak{C}\}.$$

Then, the natural (or asymptotic) density $d(\mathfrak{E})$ of $\mathfrak{E}$ is

$$d(\mathfrak{E}) = \lim_{k \to \infty} \frac{|\mathfrak{E}_k|}{k} = \tau,$$

where τ is a real and finite number, and $|\mathfrak{E}_k|$ is the cardinality of $\mathfrak{E}_k$.

A sequence (u_n) is said to be statistically convergent to α if, for each $\epsilon > 0$,

$$\mathfrak{E}_\epsilon = \{\eta : \eta \in \mathbb{N} \quad \text{and} \quad |u_\eta - \alpha| \geqq \epsilon\}$$

has zero natural density (see [1,2]). Thus, for every $\epsilon > 0$,

$$d(\mathfrak{E}_\epsilon) = \lim_{k \to \infty} \frac{|\mathfrak{E}_\epsilon|}{k} = 0.$$

We write

$$\text{stat} \lim_{k \to \infty} u_k = \alpha.$$

For a closed and bounded interval $\mathcal{I} := [a, b] \subset \mathbb{R}$, we define the partition of $[a, b]$ as an ordered set that is finite and we denote it as follows:

$$\mathfrak{P} := \{(r_0, r_1, \cdots, r_k) : a = r_0 < r_1 < \cdots < r_k = b\}.$$

We now divide the interval $[a, b]$ into the following non-overlapping subintervals:

$$\mathcal{I}_1 := [r_0, r_1], \quad \mathcal{I}_2 := [r_1, r_2], \quad \cdots, \quad \mathcal{I}_k := [r_{k-1}, r_k].$$

The resulting partition $\mathfrak{P}$ is then given by

$$\mathfrak{P} := \{[r_{i-1}, r_i] : i = 1, 2, 3, \cdots, k\}.$$

Next, in order to find the norm of the partition $\mathfrak{P}$, we have

$$||\mathfrak{P}|| := \max\{r_1 - r_0, r_2 - r_1, r_3 - r_2, \cdots, r_k - r_{k-1}\}.$$

Let $\gamma_i \quad (i = 1, 2, 3, \cdots, k)$ be a point that is chosen arbitrarily from each of the subintervals $(\mathcal{I})_{i=1}^k$. We refer to these points as the tags of the subintervals. We also call the subintervals associated with the tags the tagged partitions of $\mathcal{I}$. We denote it as follows:

$$\mathcal{P} := \{([r_{i-1}, r_i]; \gamma_i) : i = 1, 2, 3, \cdots, k\}.$$

Let $[a, b] \subset \mathbb{R}$. Suppose that, for each $i \in \mathbb{N}$, there is a function $h_i : [a, b] \to \mathbb{R}$. We thus construct the sequence $(h_i)_{i \in \mathbb{N}}$ of functions over the closed interval $[a, b]$.

We now define a subsequence $(h_i)_i^k$ of functions with respect to the Riemann sum associated with a tagged partition $\mathcal{P}$ as follows:

$$\delta(h_i; \mathcal{P}) := \sum_{i=1}^{k} h(\gamma_i)(r_i - r_{i-1}).$$

We next recall the definition of the Riemann integrability.

A sequence $(h_k)_{k \in \mathbb{N}}$ of functions is Riemann-integrable to h on $[a, b]$ if, for each $\epsilon > 0$, there exists $\sigma_\epsilon > 0$ such that, for any tagged partition $\mathcal{P}$ of $[a, b]$ with $||\mathcal{P}|| < \sigma_\epsilon$, we have

$$|\delta(h_k; \mathcal{P}) - h| < \epsilon.$$

The definition of statistically Riemann-integrable functions is given as follows.

Definition 1. *A sequence $(h_k)_{k\in\mathbb{N}}$ of functions is statistically Riemann-integrable to h on $[a,b]$ if, for every $\epsilon > 0$ and for each $x \in [a,b]$, there exists $\sigma_\epsilon > 0$, and for any tagged partition $\mathcal{P}$ of $[a,b]$ with $\|\mathcal{P}\| < \sigma_\epsilon$, the set*

$$\mathfrak{E}_\epsilon = \{\eta : \eta \in \mathbb{N} \quad and \quad |\delta(h_\eta;\mathcal{P}) - h| \geqq \epsilon\}$$

has zero natural density. That is, for every $\epsilon > 0$,

$$d(\mathfrak{E}_\epsilon) = \lim_{k\to\infty} \frac{|\mathfrak{E}_\epsilon|}{k} = 0.$$

We write

$$\mathrm{stat_{Rie}} \lim_{\mathrm{k}\to\infty} \mathrm{ffi}(\mathrm{h_k};\mathcal{P}) = \mathrm{h}.$$

By making use of Definition 1, we first establish an inclusion theorem as Theorem 1 below.

Theorem 1. *If a sequence of functions (h_k) is Riemann-integrable to h over $[a,b]$, then (h_k) is statistically Riemann-integrable to the same function h over $[a,b]$.*

Proof. Given $\epsilon > 0$, there exists $\sigma_\epsilon > 0$. Suppose that $\mathcal{P}$ is any tagged partition of $[a,b]$ such that $\|\mathcal{P}\| < \sigma_\epsilon$. Then

$$|\delta(h_k;\mathcal{P}) - h| < \epsilon.$$

Since, for each $\epsilon > 0$, $\mathcal{P}$ is any tagged partition of $[a,b]$ such that $\|\mathcal{P}\| < \sigma_\epsilon$, so we have

$$\lim_{k\to\infty} \frac{1}{k}|\{\eta : \eta \in \mathbb{N} \quad \text{and} \quad |\delta(h_k;\mathcal{P}) - h| \geqq \epsilon\}| \leqq \lim_{k\to\infty} |\delta(h_k;\mathcal{P}) - h| < \epsilon.$$

Consequently, by Definition 1, we get

$$\mathrm{stat_{Rie}} \lim_{k\to\infty} \delta(h_k;\mathcal{P}) = h,$$

which completes the proof of Theorem 1. □

Remark 1. *In order to demonstrate that the converse of Theorem 1 is not true, we consider Example 1 below.*

Example 1. *Let $h_k : [0,1] \to \mathbb{R}$ be a sequence of functions defined by*

$$h_k(x) = \begin{cases} \dfrac{1}{2} & (x \in \mathbb{Q} \cap [0,1];\ k = j^2,\ j \in \mathbb{N}) \\ \\ \dfrac{1}{n} & (\text{otherwise}). \end{cases} \tag{1}$$

It is easily seen that the sequence (h_k) of functions is statistically Riemann-integrable to 0 over the closed interval $[0,1]$, but it is not Riemann-integrable (in the usual sense) over $[0,1]$.

Motivated mainly by the above-mentioned investigations and developments, we introduce and study the ideas of deferred weighted statistical Riemann integrability and statistical deferred weighted Riemann summability of sequences of real-valued functions. We first prove an inclusion theorem connecting these two potentially useful concepts. We then state and prove two Korovkin-type approximation theorems with algebraic test functions based on the methodologies and techniques that we have adopted here. Furthermore, we consider an illustrative example involving a positive linear operator in conjunction with the familiar Bernstein polynomials, which shows the effectiveness of our findings. Finally, based upon the core concept of statistical Lebesgue-measurable sequences of functions, we suggest some possible directions for future research on this topic in the concluding section of our study.

2. Deferred Weighted Statistical Riemann Integrability

Let (ϕ_k) and (φ_k) be sequences of non-negative integers with the regularity conditions given

$$\phi_k < \varphi_k \quad \text{and} \quad \lim_{k\to\infty} \varphi_k = +\infty.$$

Moreover, let (p_i) be a sequence of non-negative real numbers with

$$P_k = \sum_{i=\phi_k+1}^{\varphi_k} p_i.$$

We then define the deferred weighted summability mean for $\sigma(h_k;\mathcal{P})$ associated with tagged partition $\mathcal{P}$ as follows:

$$\mathcal{W}(\delta(h_k;\mathcal{P})) = \frac{1}{P_k} \sum_{\varrho=\phi_k+1}^{\varphi_k} p_\varrho \delta(h_\varrho;\mathcal{P}). \tag{2}$$

We now present the following definitions for our proposed study.

Definition 2. *A sequence $(h_k)_{k\in\mathbb{N}}$ of functions is said to be deferred weighted statistically Riemann-integrable to h on $[a,b]$ if, for all $\epsilon > 0$, there exists $\sigma_\epsilon > 0$, and for any tagged partition $\mathcal{P}$ of $[a,b]$ with $\|\mathcal{P}\| < \sigma_\epsilon$, the following set*

$$\{\eta : \eta \leqq P_k \quad and \quad p_\eta|\delta(h_\eta;\mathcal{P}) - h| \geqq \epsilon\}$$

has zero natural density. Thus, for every $\epsilon > 0$, we have

$$\lim_{k\to\infty} \frac{|\{\eta : \eta \leqq P_k \quad and \quad p_\eta|\delta(h_\eta;\mathcal{P}) - k| \geqq \epsilon\}|}{P_k} = 0.$$

We write

$$DWR_{\text{stat}} \lim_{k\to\infty} \delta(h_k;\mathcal{P}) = h.$$

Definition 3. *A sequence $(h_k)_{k\in\mathbb{N}}$ of functions is said to statistically deferred weighted Riemann summable to h on $[a,b]$ if, for all $\epsilon > 0 \;\exists\; \sigma_\epsilon > 0$ and for any tagged partition $\mathcal{P}$ of $[a,b]$ with $\|\mathcal{P}\| < \sigma_\epsilon$, the set*

$$\{\eta : \eta \leqq k \quad and \quad |\mathcal{W}(\delta(h_\eta;\mathcal{P})) - h| \geqq \epsilon\}$$

has zero natural density. Thus, for all $\epsilon > 0$, we have

$$\lim_{k\to\infty} \frac{|\{\eta : \eta \leqq k \quad and \quad |\mathcal{W}(\delta(h_\eta;\mathcal{P})) - h| \geqq \epsilon\}|}{k} = 0.$$

We write

$$\text{stat}_{\text{DWR}} \lim_{\text{k}\to\infty} \text{ffi}(\text{h}_\text{k};\mathcal{P}) = \text{h}.$$

An inclusion theorem between the two new potentially useful notions in Definitions 2 and 3 is now given by Theorem 2 below.

Theorem 2. *If the sequence $(h_k)_{k\in\mathbb{N}}$ of functions is deferred weighted statistically Riemann-integrable to a function h over $[a,b]$, then it is statistically deferred weighted Riemann summable to the same function h over $[a,b]$, but not conversely.*

Proof. Suppose that the sequence $(h_k)_{k\in\mathbb{N}}$ is deferred weighted statistically Riemann-integrable to a function h on $[a,b]$. Then, by Definition 2, we have

$$\lim_{k\to\infty}\frac{|\{\eta:\eta\leqq P_k \quad \text{and} \quad p_\eta|\delta(h_\eta;\mathcal{P})-h|\geqq\epsilon\}|}{P_k}=0.$$

Now, if we choose the two sets as follows,

$$\mathcal{O}_\epsilon=\{\eta:\eta\leqq P_k \qquad \text{and} \qquad p_\eta|\delta(h_\eta;\mathcal{P})-h|\geqq\epsilon\}$$

and

$$\mathcal{O}_\epsilon^c=\{\eta:\eta\leqq P_k \qquad \text{and} \qquad p_\eta|\delta(h_\eta;\mathcal{P})-h|<\epsilon\},$$

then we have

$$\begin{aligned}|\mathcal{W}(\delta(h_k;\mathcal{P}))-h| &= \left|\frac{1}{P_k}\sum_{\varrho=\phi_k+1}^{\varphi_k}p_\varrho\delta(h_\varrho;\mathcal{P})-h\right| \\ &\leqq \left|\frac{1}{P_k}\sum_{\varrho=\phi_k+1}^{\varphi_k}p_\varrho\left[\delta(h_\varrho;\mathcal{P})-h\right]\right|+\left|\frac{1}{P_k}\sum_{\varrho=\phi_k+1}^{\varphi_k}p_\varrho h-h\right| \\ &\leqq \frac{1}{P_k}\sum_{\substack{\varrho=\phi_k+1\\(\eta\in\mathcal{O}_\epsilon)}}^{\varphi_k}p_\varrho|\delta(h_\varrho;\mathcal{P})-h|+\frac{1}{P_k}\sum_{\substack{\varrho=\phi_k+1\\(\eta\in\mathcal{O}_\epsilon^c)}}^{\varphi_k}p_\varrho|\delta(h_\varrho;\mathcal{P})-h| \\ &\quad +|h|\left|\frac{1}{P_k}\sum_{\varrho=\phi_k+1}^{\varphi_k}p_\varrho-1\right| \\ &\leqq \frac{1}{P_k}|\mathcal{O}_\epsilon|+\frac{1}{P_k}|\mathcal{O}_\epsilon^c|.\end{aligned}$$

We thus obtain

$$|\mathcal{W}(\delta(h_k;\mathcal{P}))-h|<\epsilon.$$

Hence, clearly, the sequence of functions (h_k) is statistically deferred weighted Riemann-summable to h over $[a,b]$. □

The following example shows that the converse statement of Theorem 2 is not true.

Example 2. *Let $h_k:[0,1]\to\mathbb{R}$ be a sequence of functions of the form given by*

$$h_k(x)=\begin{cases}0 & (x\in\mathbb{Q}\cap[0,1];\ k \text{ is even})\\ \\ 1 & (x\in\mathbb{R}-\mathbb{Q}\cap[0,1];\ k \text{ is odd}),\end{cases} \tag{3}$$

where

$$\phi_k=2k \quad \varphi_k=4k \quad \text{and} \quad p_k=1.$$

The above-specified sequence (h_k) of functions trivially indicates that it is neither Riemann-integrable nor deferred weighted statistically Riemann-integrable. However, as per our proposed mean (2), it is easy to see that

$$\begin{aligned}\mathcal{W}(\delta(h_k;\mathcal{P})) &= \frac{1}{\varphi_k-\phi_k}\sum_{\varrho=\phi_k+1}^{\varphi_k}\delta(h_\varrho;\mathcal{P}) \\ &= \frac{1}{2k}\sum_{m=2k+1}^{4k}\delta(h_\varrho;\mathcal{P})=\frac{1}{2}.\end{aligned}$$

Thus, clearly, the sequence (h_k) *of functions has deferred weighted Riemann sum* $\frac{1}{2}$ *under the tagged partition* $\mathcal{P}$. *Therefore, the sequence* (h_k) *of functions is statistically deferred weighted Riemann-summable to* $\frac{1}{2}$ *over* $[0,1]$, *but it is not deferred weighted statistically Riemann-integrable over* $[0,1]$.

3. Korovkin-Type Approximation Theorems via the $\mathcal{W}(\delta(h_k;\mathcal{P}))$-Mean

Many researchers have worked toward extending (or generalizing) the approximation-theoretic aspects of the Korovkin-type approximation theorems in several different areas of mathematics, such as (for example) probability space, measurable space, sequence spaces, and so on. In Real Analysis, Harmonic Analysis and other related fields, this notion is immensely useful. In this regard, we have chosen to refer the interested reader to the recent works (see, for example, [19–28]).

Let $C[0,1]$ be the space of all continuous real-valued functions defined on $[0,1]$. Suppose also that it is a Banach space with the norm $||.||_\infty$. Then, for $h \in C[0,1]$, the norm of h is given by

$$||h||_\infty = \sup\{|h(\rho)| \,:\, 0 \leqq \rho \leqq 1\}.$$

We say that $\mathfrak{G}_j : C[0,1] \to C[0,1]$ is a sequence of positive linear operators, if

$$\mathfrak{G}_j(h;\rho) \geqq 0 \quad \text{as} \quad h \geqq 0.$$

Now, in view of our above-proposed definitions, we state and prove the following Korovkin-type approximation theorems.

Theorem 3. *Let* $\mathfrak{G}_j : C[0,1] \to C[0,1]$ *be a sequence of positive linear operators. Then, for* $h \in C[0,1]$,

$$\text{DWR}_{\text{stat}} \lim_{j\to\infty} ||\mathfrak{G}_j(h;\rho) - h(\rho)||_\infty = 0 \tag{4}$$

if and only if

$$\text{DWR}_{\text{stat}} \lim_{j\to\infty} ||\mathfrak{G}_j(1;\rho) - 1||_\infty = 0, \tag{5}$$

$$\text{DWR}_{\text{stat}} \lim_{j\to\infty} ||\mathfrak{G}_j(\rho;\rho) - \rho||_\infty = 0 \tag{6}$$

and

$$\text{DWR}_{\text{stat}} \lim_{j\to\infty} ||\mathfrak{G}_j(\rho^2;\rho) - \rho^2||_\infty = 0. \tag{7}$$

Proof. Since each of the following functions

$$h_0(\rho) = 1, \quad h_1(\rho) = 2\rho \quad \text{and} \quad h_2(\rho) = 3\rho^2$$

belongs to $C[0,1]$ and is continuous on $[0,1]$, the implication given by (4) obviously implies (5) to (7).

In order to complete the proof of Theorem 3, we first assume that the conditions (5) to (7) hold true. If $h \in C[0,1]$, then there exists a constant $\mathcal{L} > 0$ such that

$$|h(\rho)| \leqq \mathcal{L} \quad (\forall\, \rho \in [0,1]).$$

We thus find that

$$|h(r) - h(\rho)| \leqq 2\mathcal{L} \quad (r,\rho \in [0,1]). \tag{8}$$

Clearly, for given $\epsilon > 0$, there exists $\delta > 0$ such that

$$|f(r) - f(\rho)| < \epsilon \tag{9}$$

whenever

$$|r - \rho| < \delta \quad \text{for all} \quad r, \rho \in [0,1].$$

If we now choose

$$\mu_1 = \mu_1(r,\rho) = (2r - 2\rho)^2.$$

If

$$|r - \rho| \geqq \delta,$$

then we obtain

$$|h(r) - h(\rho)| < \frac{2\mathcal{L}}{\theta^2}\mu_1(r,\rho). \tag{10}$$

Thus, from Equations (9) and (10), we get

$$|h(r) - h(\rho)| < \epsilon + \frac{2\mathcal{L}}{\theta^2}\mu_1(r,\rho),$$

which implies that

$$-\epsilon - \frac{2\mathcal{L}}{\theta^2}\mu_1(r,\rho) \leqq h(r) - h(\rho) \leqq \epsilon + \frac{2\mathcal{L}}{\theta^2}\mu_1(r,\rho). \tag{11}$$

Now, since $\mathfrak{G}_m(1;\rho)$ is monotone and linear, by applying the operator $\mathfrak{G}_m(1;\rho)$ to the inequality (11), we get

$$\begin{aligned}\mathfrak{G}_m(1;\rho)\left(-\epsilon - \frac{2\mathcal{L}}{\theta^2}\mu_1(r,\rho)\right) &\leqq \mathfrak{G}_m(1;\rho)(h(r) - h(\rho)) \\ &\leqq \mathfrak{G}_m(1;\rho)\left(\epsilon + \frac{2\mathcal{L}}{\theta^2}\mu_1(r,\rho)\right).\end{aligned}$$

We note that ρ is fixed, and so $h(\rho)$ is a constant number. Therefore, we have

$$\begin{aligned}-\epsilon\mathfrak{G}_m(1;\rho) - \frac{2\mathcal{L}}{\theta^2}\mathfrak{G}_m(\mu_1;\rho) \quad &\leqq \mathfrak{G}_m(h;\rho) - h(\rho)\mathfrak{G}_m(1;\rho) \\ &\leqq \epsilon\mathfrak{G}_m(1;\rho) + \frac{2\mathcal{L}}{\theta^2}\mathfrak{G}_m(\mu_1;\rho).\end{aligned} \tag{12}$$

We also know that

$$\mathfrak{G}_m(h;\rho) - h(\rho) = [\mathfrak{G}_m(h;\rho) - h(\rho)\mathfrak{G}_m(1;\rho)] + h(\rho)[\mathfrak{G}_m(1;\rho) - 1]. \tag{13}$$

Thus, by using (12) and (13), we obtain

$$\mathfrak{G}_m(h;\rho) - h(\rho) < \epsilon\mathfrak{G}_m(1;\rho) + \frac{2\mathcal{L}}{\theta^2}\mathfrak{G}_m(\mu_1;\rho) + h(\rho)[\mathfrak{G}_m(1;\rho) - 1]. \tag{14}$$

We now estimate $\mathfrak{G}_m(\mu_1;\rho)$ as follows:

$$\begin{aligned}\mathfrak{G}_m(\mu_1;\rho) &= \mathfrak{G}_m((2r - 2\rho)^2;\rho) = \mathfrak{G}_m(2r^2 - 8\rho r + 4\rho^2;\rho) \\ &= \mathfrak{G}_m(4r^2;\rho) - 8t\mathfrak{G}_m(r;\rho) + 4\rho^2\mathfrak{G}_m(1;\rho) \\ &= 4[\mathfrak{G}_m(r^2;\rho) - \rho^2] - 8t[\mathfrak{G}_m(r;\rho) - \rho] \\ &\quad + 4\rho^2[\mathfrak{G}_m(1;\rho) - 1],\end{aligned}$$

so that, in view of (14), we obtain

$$\begin{aligned}\mathfrak{G}_m(h;\rho)-h(\rho) &< \epsilon\mathfrak{G}_m(1;\rho)+\frac{2\mathcal{L}}{\theta^2}\{4[\mathfrak{G}_m(r^2;\rho)-\rho^2] \\ &\quad -8\rho[\mathfrak{G}_m(r;\rho)-\rho]+4\rho^2[\mathfrak{G}_m(1;\rho)-1]\} \\ &\quad +h(\rho)[\mathfrak{G}_m(1;\rho)-1]. \\ &=\epsilon[\mathfrak{G}_m(1;\rho)-1]+\epsilon+\frac{2\mathcal{L}}{\theta^2}\{4[\mathfrak{G}_m(r^2;\rho)-\rho^2] \\ &\quad -8\rho[\mathfrak{G}_m(r;\rho)-\rho]+4\rho^2[\mathfrak{G}_m(1;\rho)-1]\} \\ &\quad +h(\rho)[\mathfrak{G}_m(1;\rho)-1].\end{aligned}$$

Furthermore, since $\epsilon > 0$ is arbitrary, we can write

$$\begin{aligned}|\mathfrak{G}_m(h;\rho)-h(\rho)| &\leqq \epsilon+\left(\epsilon+\frac{8\mathcal{L}}{\theta^2}+\mathcal{L}\right)|\mathfrak{G}_m(1;\rho)-1| \\ &\quad +\frac{16\mathcal{L}}{\theta^2}|\mathfrak{G}_m(r;\rho)-\rho|+\frac{8\mathcal{L}}{\theta^2}|\mathfrak{G}_m(r^2;\rho)-\rho^2| \\ &\leqq \mathcal{A}(|\mathfrak{G}_m(1;\rho)-1|+|\mathfrak{G}_m(r;\rho)-\rho| \\ &\quad +|\mathfrak{G}_m(r^2;\rho)-\rho^2|),\end{aligned} \tag{15}$$

where

$$\mathcal{A}=\max\left(\epsilon+\frac{8\mathcal{L}}{\theta^2}+\mathcal{L},\frac{16\mathcal{L}}{\theta^2},\frac{8\mathcal{L}}{\theta^2}\right).$$

Now, for a given $\omega > 0$, there exists $\epsilon > 0$ $(\epsilon < \omega)$ such that

$$\mathfrak{T}_m(\rho;\omega)=\{m : m \leqq P_k \quad \text{and} \quad p_m|\mathfrak{G}_m(h;\rho)-h(\rho)| \geqq \omega\}.$$

Furthermore, for $\nu = 0,1,2$, we have

$$\mathfrak{T}_{\nu,m}(\rho;\omega)=\left\{m : m \leqq P_k \quad \text{and} \quad p_m|\mathfrak{G}_m(h;\rho)-h_\nu(\rho)| \geqq \frac{\omega-\epsilon}{3\mathcal{A}}\right\},$$

so that

$$\mathfrak{T}_m(\rho;\omega) \leqq \sum_{\nu=0}^{2}\mathfrak{T}_{\nu,m}(\rho;\omega).$$

Clearly, we obtain

$$\frac{\|\mathfrak{T}_m(\rho;\omega)\|_{C[0,1]}}{P_k} \leqq \sum_{\nu=0}^{2}\frac{\|\mathfrak{T}_{\nu,m}(\rho;\omega)\|_{C[0,1]}}{P_k}. \tag{16}$$

Now, using the above assumption about the implications in (5) to (7) and by Definition 2, the right-hand side of (16) tends to zero as $n \to \infty$. Consequently, we get

$$\lim_{k\to\infty}\frac{\|\mathfrak{T}_m(\rho;\omega)\|_{C[0,1]}}{P_k}=0 \ (\delta,\omega>0).$$

Therefore, the implication (4) holds true. □

Theorem 4. *Let* $\mathfrak{G}_j : C[0,1] \to C[0,1]$ *be a sequence of positive linear operators. Then, for* $h \in C[0,1]$,

$$\text{stat}_{\text{DWR}}\lim_{j\to\infty}\|\mathfrak{G}_j(h;\rho)-h(\rho)\|_\infty=0 \tag{17}$$

if and only if

$$\mathrm{stat_{DWR}} \lim_{j \to \infty} \|\mathfrak{G}_j(1;\rho) - 1\|_\infty = 0, \tag{18}$$

$$\mathrm{stat_{DWR}} \lim_{j \to \infty} \|\mathfrak{G}_j(\rho;\rho) - \rho\|_\infty = 0 \tag{19}$$

and

$$\mathrm{stat_{DWR}} \lim_{j \to \infty} \|\mathfrak{G}_j(\rho^2;\rho) - \rho^2\|_\infty = 0. \tag{20}$$

Proof. The proof of Theorem 4 is similar to the proof of Theorem 3. Therefore, we choose to skip the details involved. □

In view of Theorem 4, here, we consider an illustrative example. In this connection, we now recall the following operator:

$$\rho(1+\rho D) \qquad \left(D = \frac{d}{d\rho}\right), \tag{21}$$

which was used by Al-Salam [29] and, more recently, by Viskov and Srivastava [30].

Example 3. *Consider the Bernstein polynomials $\mathfrak{B}_n(h;\beta)$ on $C[0,1]$ given by*

$$\mathfrak{B}_k(h;\beta) = \sum_{\varrho=0}^{k} f\left(\frac{\varrho}{k}\right)\binom{k}{\varrho}\beta^{\varrho}(1-\beta)^{k-\varrho} \quad (\beta \in [0,1]; k = 0,1,\cdots). \tag{22}$$

Here, in this example, we introduce the positive linear operators on $C[0,1]$ under the composition of the Bernstein polynomials and the operators given by (21) as follows:

$$\mathfrak{G}_\varrho(h;\beta) = [1+h_\varrho]\beta(1+\beta D)\mathfrak{B}_\varrho(h;\beta) \quad (\forall\, h \in C[0,1]), \tag{23}$$

where (h_ϱ) is the same as mentioned in Example 2.

We now estimate the values of each of the testing functions 1, β and β^2 by using our proposed operators (23) as follows:

$$\mathfrak{G}_\varrho(1;\beta) = [1+h_\varrho]\beta(1+\beta D)1 = [1+h_\varrho]\beta,$$

$$\mathfrak{G}_\varrho(t;\beta) = [1+h_\varrho]\beta(1+\beta D)\beta = [1+h_\varrho]\beta(1+\beta)$$

and

$$\begin{aligned}\mathfrak{G}_\varrho(t^2;\beta) &= [1+h_\varrho]\beta(1+\beta D)\left\{\beta^2 + \frac{\beta(1-\beta)}{\varrho}\right\} \\ &= [1+h_\varrho]\left\{\beta^2\left(2 - \frac{3\beta}{\varrho}\right)\right\}.\end{aligned}$$

Consequently, we have

$$\mathrm{stat_{DWR}} \lim_{\varrho \to \infty} \|\mathfrak{G}_\varrho(1;\beta) - 1\|_\infty = 0, \tag{24}$$

$$\mathrm{stat_{DWR}} \lim_{\varrho \to \infty} \|\mathfrak{G}_\varrho(\beta;\beta) - \beta\|_\infty = 0 \tag{25}$$

and

$$\mathrm{stat_{DWR}} \lim_{\varrho \to \infty} \|\mathfrak{G}_\varrho(\beta^2;\beta) - \beta^2\|_\infty = 0, \tag{26}$$

that is, the sequence $\mathfrak{G}_\varrho(h;\beta)$ satisfies the conditions (18) to (20). Therefore, by Theorem 4, we have

$$\mathrm{stat}_{\mathrm{DWR}} \lim_{\varrho\to\infty} \|\mathfrak{G}_\varrho(h;\beta) - h\|_\infty = 0.$$

Hence, the given sequence (h_k) of functions mentioned in Example 2 is statistically deferred weighted Riemann-summable, but not deferred weighted statistically Riemann-integrable. Therefore, our above-proposed operators defined by (23) satisfy Theorem 4. However, they do not satisfy for statistical versions of deferred weighted Riemann-integrable sequence of functions (see Theorem 3).

4. Concluding Remarks and Directions for Further Research

In this concluding section of our present investigation, we further observe the potential usefulness of our Theorem 4 over Theorem 3 as well as over the classical versions of the Korovkin-type approximation theorems.

Remark 2. *Let us consider the sequence $(h_\varrho)_{\varrho\in\mathbb{N}}$ of functions in Example 2. Suppose also that (h_ϱ) is statistically deferred weighted Riemann-summable, so that*

$$\mathrm{stat}_{\mathrm{DWR}} \lim_{\%\to\infty} \mathrm{ffi}(\mathrm{h}_{\%};\mathcal{P}) = \frac{1}{2} \text{ on } [0,1].$$

We then find that

$$\mathrm{stat}_{\mathrm{DWR}} \lim_{\mathrm{k}\to\infty} \|\mathfrak{G}_{\mathrm{k}}(\mathrm{h}_\circ;\text{æ}) - \mathrm{f}_\circ(\text{æ})\|_\infty = 0 \quad (^\circ = 0,1,2). \tag{27}$$

Thus, by Theorem 4, we immediately get

$$\mathrm{stat}_{\mathrm{DWR}} \lim_{\mathrm{j}\to\infty} \|\mathfrak{G}_{\mathrm{k}}(\mathrm{h};\text{æ}) - \mathrm{h}(\text{æ})\|_\infty = 0, \tag{28}$$

where

$$h_0(\rho) = 1, \quad h_1(\rho) = \rho \quad \textit{and} \quad h_2(\rho) = \rho^2.$$

Now, the given sequence (h_k) of functions is statistically deferred weighted Riemann-summable, but neither deferred weighted statistically Riemann-integrable nor classically Riemann-integrable. Therefore, our Korovkin-type approximation Theorem 4 properly works under the operators defined in the Equation (23), but the classical as well as statistical versions of the deferred weighted Riemann-integrable sequence of functions do not work for the same operators. Clearly, this observation leads us to the fact that our Theorem 4 is a non-trivial extension of Theorem 3 as well as the classical Korovkin-type approximation theorem [31].

Remark 3. *Motivated by some recently published results by Jena et al. [32] and Srivastava et al. [33], we choose to draw the attention of the interested readers toward the potential for further research associated with the analogous notion of statistical Lebesgue-measurable sequences of functions.*

Author Contributions: Formal analysis, H.M.S. and S.K.P.; Investigation, B.B.J.; Methodology, S.K.P.; Supervision, H.M.S. and S.K.P.; Writing-original draft, B.B.J.; Writing—review & editing, H.M.S. and S.K.P. All authors have read and agreed to the published version of the manuscript.

Funding: This research received no external funding.

Data Availability Statement: Not applicable.

Conflicts of Interest: The authors declare that they have no conflicts of interest.

References

1. Fast, H. Sur la convergence statistique. *Colloq. Math.* **1951**, 2, 241–244. [CrossRef]
2. Steinhaus, H. Sur la convergence ordinaire et la convergence asymptotique. *Colloq. Math.* **1951**, 2, 73–74.

3. Akdag, S. Weighted equi-statistical convergence of the Korovkin-type approximation theorems. *Results Math.* **2017**, *72*, 1073–1085. [CrossRef]
4. Balcerzak, M.; Dems, K.; Komisarski, A. Statistical convergence and ideal convergence for sequences of functions. *J. Math. Anal. Appl.* **2007**, *328*, 715–729. [CrossRef]
5. Braha, N.L.; Loku, V.; Srivastava, H.M. Λ^2-Weighted statistical convergence and Korovkin and Voronovskaya type theorems. *Appl. Math. Comput.* **2015**, *266*, 675–686. [CrossRef]
6. Et, M.; Baliarsingh, P.; Küçxuxkaslan, H.S.K.M. On μ-deferred statistical convergence and strongly deferred summable functions. *Rev. Real Acad. Cienc. Exactas Fís. Natur. Ser. A Mat. (RACSAM)* **2021**, *115*, 1–14. [CrossRef]
7. Ghosal, S.; Mandal, S. Rough weighted I-$\alpha\beta$-statistical convergence in locally solid Riesz spaces. *J. Math. Anal. Appl.* **2021**, *506*, 125681. [CrossRef]
8. Ghosal, S.; Banerjee, M. Rough weighted statistical convergence on locally solid Riesz spaces. *Positivity* **2021**, *25*, 1789–1804. [CrossRef]
9. Guessab, A.; Schmeisser, G. Convexity results and sharp error estimates in approximate multivariate integration. *Math. Comput.* **2003**, *73*, 1365–1384. [CrossRef]
10. Alotaibi, A. Generalized weighted statistical convergence for double sequences of fuzzy numbers and associated Korovkin-type approximation theorem. *J. Funct. Spaces* **2020**, *2020*, 9298650. [CrossRef]
11. Özger, F. Applications of generalized weighted statistical convergence to approximation theorems for functions of one and two variables. *Numer. Funct. Anal. Optim.* **2020**, *41*, 1990–2006. [CrossRef]
12. Demirci, K.; Dirik, F.; Yıldız, S. Deferred Nörlund statistical relative uniform convergence and Korovkin-type approximation theorem. *Commun. Fac. Sci. Univ. Ank. Ser. A Math. Statist.* **2021**, *70*, 279–289. [CrossRef]
13. Mohiuddine, S.A.; Hazarika, B. On strongly almost generalized difference lacunary ideal convergent sequences of fuzzy numbers. *J. Comput. Anal. Appl.* **2017**, *23*, 925–936.
14. Móricz, F. Tauberian conditions under which statistical convergence follows from statistical summability $(C,1)$. *J. Math. Anal. Appl.* **2002**, *275*, 277–287. [CrossRef]
15. Agrawal, P.N.; Acu, A.-M.; Chauhan, R.; Garg, T. Approximation of Bögel continuous functions and deferred weighted A-statistical convergence by Bernstein-Kantorovich type operators on a triangle. *J. Math. Inequal.* **2021**, *15*, 1695–1711. [CrossRef]
16. Saini, K.; Raj, K.; Mursaleen, M. Deferred Cesàro and deferred Euler equi-statistical convergence and its applications to Korovkin-type approximation theorem. *Internat. J. Gen. Syst.* **2021**, *50*, 567–579. [CrossRef]
17. Söylemez, D. A Korovkin type approximation theorem for Balázs type Bleimann, Butzer and Hahn operators via power series statistical convergence. *Math. Slovaca* **2022**, *72*, 153–164. [CrossRef]
18. Turan, C.; Duman, O. Fundamental properties of statistical convergence and lacunary statistical convergence on time scales. *Filomat* **2017**, *31*, 4455–4467. [CrossRef]
19. Altomare, F. Korovkin-type theorems and approximation by positive linear operators. *Surv. Approx. Theory* **2010**, *5*, 92–164.
20. Braha, N.L. Some weighted equi-statistical convergence and Korovkin-type theorem. *Results Math.* **2016**, *70*, 433–446. [CrossRef]
21. Braha, N.L.; Srivastava, H.M.; Et, M. Some weighted statistical convergence and associated Korovkin and Voronovskaya type theorems. *J. Appl. Math. Comput.* **2021**, *65*, 429–450. [CrossRef]
22. Guessab, A.; Schmeisser, G. Two Korovkin-type theorems in multivariate approximation. *Banach J. Math. Anal.* **2008**, *2*, 121–128. [CrossRef]
23. Jena, B.B.; Paikray, S.K.; Dutta, H. On various new concepts of statistical convergence for sequences of random variables via deferred Cesàro mean. *J. Math. Anal. Appl.* **2020**, *487*, 123950. [CrossRef]
24. Karakuş, S.; Demirci, K.; Duman, O. Equi-statistical convergence of positive linear operators. *J. Math. Anal. Appl.* **2008**, *339*, 1065–1072. [CrossRef]
25. Çınar, S.; Yıldız, S.; Demirci, K. Korovkin type approximation via triangular A-statistical convergence on an infinite interval. *Turk. J. Math. 2021*, **45**, 929–942. [CrossRef]
26. Parida, P.; Paikray, S.K.; Jena, B.B. Generalized deferred Cesàro equi-statistical convergence and analogous approximation theorems. *Proyecciones J. Math.* **2020**, *39*, 307–331. [CrossRef]
27. Srivastava, H.M.; Jena, B.B.; Paikray, S.K. Statistical probability convergence via the deferred Nörlund mean and its applications to approximation theorems. *Rev. Real Acad. Cienc. Exactas Fís. Natur. Ser. A Mat. (RACSAM)* **2020**, *114*, 1–14. [CrossRef]
28. Srivastava, H.M.; Jena, B.B.; Paikray, S.K. Statistical deferred Nörlund summability and Korovkin-type approximation theorem. *Mathematics* **2020**, *8*, 636. [CrossRef]
29. Al-Salam, W.A. Operational representations for the Laguerre and other polynomials. *Duke Math. J.* **1964**, *31*, 127–142. [CrossRef]
30. Viskov, O.V.; Srivastava, H.M. New approaches to certain identities involving differential operators. *J. Math. Anal. Appl.* **1994**, *186*, 1–10. [CrossRef]
31. Korovkin, P.P. Convergence of linear positive operators in the spaces of continuous functions. *Dokl. Akad. Nauk. SSSR (New Ser.)* **1953**, *90*, 961–964. (In Russian)
32. Jena, B.B.; Paikray, S.K.; Dutta, H. A new approach to Korovkin-type approximation via deferred Cesàro statistical measurable convergence. *Chaos Solitons Fractals* **2021**, *148*, 111016.. [CrossRef]
33. Srivastava, H.M.; Jena, B.B.; Paikray, S.K. Statistical Riemann and Lebesgue integrable sequence of functions with Korovkin-type approximation theorems. *Axioms* **2021**, *10*, 229. [CrossRef]

axioms

Article

On Some Generalizations of Reverse Dynamic Hardy Type Inequalities on Time Scales

Ahmed A. El-Deeb [1,*] and **Clemente Cesarano** [2,*]

1 Department of Mathematics, Faculty of Science, Al-Azhar University, Nasr City 11884, Egypt
2 Section of Mathematics, International Telematic University Uninettuno, Corso Vittorio Emanuele II, 39, 00186 Rome, Italy
* Correspondence: ahmedeldeeb@azhar.edu.eg (A.A.E.-D.); c.cesarano@uninettunouniversity.net (C.C.)

Abstract: In the present paper, we prove some new reverse type dynamic inequalities on $\mathbb{T}$. Our main inequalities are proved by using the chain rule and Fubini's theorem on time scales $\mathbb{T}$. Our results extend some existing results in the literature. As special cases, we obtain some new discrete inequalities, quantum inequalities and integral inequalities.

Keywords: reverse Hardy's inequality; dynamic inequality; time scale

MSC: 26D10; 26D15; 34N05; 26E70

Citation: El-Deeb, A.A.; Cesarano, C. On Some Generalizations of Reverse Dynamic Hardy Type Inequalities on Time Scales. *Axioms* **2022**, *11*, 336. https://doi.org/10.3390/axioms11070336

Academic Editor: Yurii Kharkevych

Received: 19 May 2022
Accepted: 8 July 2022
Published: 11 July 2022

1. Introduction

In 1920, the renowned English mathematician Godfrey Harold Hardy [1] proved the following result.

Theorem 1. *Assume that $\{f_n\}_{n=1}^{\infty}$ is a sequence of nonnegative real numbers. If $r > 1$, then*

$$\sum_{n=1}^{\infty} \frac{1}{n^r}\Big(\sum_{k=1}^{n} f_k\Big)^r \leq \Big(\frac{r}{r-1}\Big)^r \sum_{n=1}^{\infty} f_n^r. \tag{1}$$

Inequality (1) is known in the literature as discrete Hardy' inequality.

In 1925, Hardy himself [2] gave the integral analogous of inequality (1) in the following form.

Theorem 2. *Suppose that f is a nonnegative continuous function defined on $[0,\infty)$. If $r > 1$, then*

$$\int_0^{\infty} \frac{1}{\lambda^r}\Big(\int_0^{\lambda} f(\zeta)d\zeta\Big)^r d\lambda \leq \Big(\frac{r}{r-1}\Big)^r \int_0^{\infty} f^r(\lambda)d\lambda. \tag{2}$$

In 1927, Littlewood and Hardy [3] proved the reversed version of inequality (2) in the following manner:

Theorem 3. *Let f be a nonnegative function on $[0,\infty)$. If $0 < r < 1$, then*

$$\int_0^{\infty} \frac{1}{\lambda^r}\Big(\int_{\lambda}^{\infty} f(\zeta)d\zeta\Big)^r d\lambda \geq \Big(\frac{r}{1-r}\Big)^r \int_0^{\infty} f^r(\lambda)d\lambda. \tag{3}$$

In 1928, Hardy [4] established a generalization of inequality (2). He proved that:

Theorem 4. *Suppose that f is a nonnegative continuous function defined on $[0,\infty)$. Then,*

$$\int_0^{\infty} \frac{1}{\lambda^{\gamma}}\Big(\int_0^{\lambda} f(\zeta)d\zeta\Big)^r d\lambda \leq \Big(\frac{r}{\gamma-1}\Big)^r \int_0^{\infty} \lambda^{r-\gamma} f^r(\lambda)d\lambda, \qquad \textit{for} \quad r \geq \gamma > 1, \tag{4}$$

and

$$\int_0^\infty \frac{1}{\lambda^\gamma}\left(\int_\lambda^\infty f(\zeta)d\zeta\right)^r d\lambda \le \left(\frac{r}{1-\gamma}\right)^r \int_0^\infty \lambda^{r-\gamma} f^r(\lambda)d\lambda, \quad for \quad r > 1 > \gamma \ge 0. \tag{5}$$

In 1928, Copson [5] gave the next two discrete inequalities as generalizations of inequality (1).

Theorem 5. *Let $\{f_n\}_{n=1}^\infty$ and $\{\theta_n\}_{n=1}^\infty$ be sequences of nonnegative real numbers. Then,*

$$\sum_{n=1}^\infty \frac{\theta_n\left(\sum_{k=1}^n \theta_k f_k\right)^r}{\left(\sum_{k=1}^n \theta_k\right)^\gamma} \le \left(\frac{r}{\gamma-1}\right)^r \sum_{n=1}^\infty \theta_n f_n^r \left(\sum_{k=1}^n \theta_k\right)^{r-\gamma}, \quad for \quad r \ge \gamma > 1, \tag{6}$$

and

$$\sum_{n=1}^\infty \frac{\theta_n\left(\sum_{k=n}^\infty \theta_k f_k\right)^r}{\left(\sum_{k=1}^n \theta_k\right)^\gamma} \le \left(\frac{r}{1-\gamma}\right)^r \sum_{n=1}^\infty \theta_n f_n^r \left(\sum_{k=1}^n \theta_k\right)^{r-\gamma}, \quad for \quad r > 1 > \gamma \ge 0. \tag{7}$$

In 1970, Leindler [6] explored some discrete Hardy inequality versions (1) and was able to demonstrate that:

Theorem 6. *Let $\{f_n\}_{n=1}^\infty$ and $\{\theta_n\}_{n=1}^\infty$ be sequences of real numbers that are not negative and $r > 1$, then*

$$\sum_{n=1}^\infty \theta_n\left(\sum_{k=1}^n f_k\right)^r \le r^r \sum_{n=1}^\infty \theta_n^{1-r} f_n^r \left(\sum_{k=n}^\infty \theta_k\right)^r, \tag{8}$$

and

$$\sum_{n=1}^\infty \theta_n\left(\sum_{k=n}^\infty f_k\right)^r \le r^r \sum_{n=1}^\infty \theta_n^{1-r} f_n^r \left(\sum_{k=1}^n \theta_k\right)^r. \tag{9}$$

In 1976, Copson [7] gave the inequalities' continuous versions (6) and (7). He arrived at the following conclusion specifically:.

Theorem 7. *Let f and θ be continuous functions that are not negative on $[0,\infty)$. Then,*

$$\int_0^\infty \frac{\theta(\lambda)\left(\int_0^\lambda \theta(\zeta)f(\zeta)d\zeta\right)^r}{\left(\int_0^\lambda \theta(\zeta)d\zeta\right)^\gamma} d\lambda \le \left(\frac{r}{\gamma-1}\right)^r \int_0^\infty \theta(\lambda)f^r(\lambda)\left(\int_0^\lambda \theta(\zeta)d\zeta\right)^{r-\gamma} d\lambda, \quad for \quad r \ge \gamma > 1, \tag{10}$$

and

$$\int_0^\infty \frac{\theta(\lambda)\left(\int_\lambda^\infty \theta(\zeta)f(\zeta)d\zeta\right)^r}{\left(\int_0^\lambda \theta(\zeta)d\zeta\right)^\gamma} d\lambda \le \left(\frac{r}{1-\gamma}\right)^r \int_0^\infty \theta(\lambda)f^r(\lambda)\left(\int_0^\lambda \theta(\zeta)d\zeta\right)^{r-\gamma} d\lambda, \quad for \quad r > 1 > \gamma \ge 0. \tag{11}$$

In 1982, Lyon [8] discovered a reverse version of the discrete Hardy inequality (1) for the special case when $r = 2$. According to his conclusion:

Theorem 8. *Let $\{f_n\}_{n=0}^\infty$ be a nonincreasing sequence of real numbers that are nonnegative. Then,*

$$\sum_{n=0}^\infty \left(\frac{1}{n+1}\sum_{k=0}^n f_k\right)^2 \ge \frac{\pi^2}{6}\sum_{n=0}^\infty f_n^2. \tag{12}$$

In 1986, Renaud [9] proved the following two results.

Theorem 9. *Assume that $\{f_n\}_{n=1}^{\infty}$ is a nonincreasing sequence of nonnegative real numbers. If $r > 1$, then,*

$$\sum_{n=1}^{\infty}\left(\sum_{k=n}^{\infty} f_k\right)^r \geq \sum_{n=1}^{\infty} n^r f_n^r. \tag{13}$$

Theorem 10. *Assume that f is a nonincreasing nonnegative function defined on $[0,\infty)$. If $r > 1$, then,*

$$\int_0^{\infty}\left(\int_{\lambda}^{\infty} f(\zeta)d\zeta\right)^p dx \geq \int_0^{\infty} \lambda^p f^r(\lambda)d\lambda. \tag{14}$$

In 1990, the reverses of inequalities (8) and (9) were demonstrated by Leindler in [10] as the following:

Theorem 11. *If $\{f_n\}_{n=1}^{\infty}$ and $\{\theta_n\}_{n=1}^{\infty}$ are sequences of nonnegative real numbers and $0 < r \leq 1$, then,*

$$\sum_{n=1}^{\infty}\theta_n\left(\sum_{k=1}^{n} f_k\right)^r \geq r^r \sum_{n=1}^{\infty} \theta^{1-r}(n) f_n^r \left(\sum_{k=n}^{\infty}\theta_k\right)^r, \tag{15}$$

and

$$\sum_{n=1}^{\infty}\theta_n\left(\sum_{k=n}^{\infty} f_k\right)^r \geq r^r \sum_{n=1}^{\infty} \theta_n^{1-r} f_n^r \left(\sum_{k=1}^{n}\theta_k\right)^r. \tag{16}$$

Hilger, in his Ph.D. thesis [11], was the first one to accomplish the unification and extension of differential equations, difference equations, q-difference equations, and so on to the encompassing theory of dynamic equations on time scales.

Throughout this work, a knowledge and understanding of time scales and time-scale notation is assumed; for an excellent introduction to the calculus on time scales, see Bohner and Peterson [12,13].

In 2005, Řehák [14] was a forerunner in extending Hardy-type inequalities to time scales. He expanded the original Hardy inequalities (1) and (2) to a time scale of our choosing, and so, he combined them into a single form, as illustrated below.

Theorem 12. *Suppose $\mathbb{T}$ is a time scale, and $f \in C_{rd}([a,\infty)_{\mathbb{T}}, [0,\infty))$. If $r \geq 1$, then,*

$$\int_a^{\infty}\left(\frac{\int_a^{\sigma(\eta)} f(\zeta)\Delta\zeta}{\sigma(\eta)-a}\right)^r \Delta\eta < \left(\frac{r}{r-1}\right)^r \int_a^{\infty} f^r(\eta)\Delta\eta, \tag{17}$$

unless $f \equiv 0$.

In 2017, Agarwal et al. [15] presented the next dynamic inequality.

Theorem 13. *Let $\mathbb{T}$ be a time scale such that $0 \in \mathbb{T}$. Moreover, assume f is a nonincreasing nonnegative function on $[0,\infty)_{\mathbb{T}}$. If $r > 1$, then,*

$$\int_0^{\infty}\frac{1}{\eta^r}\left(\int_0^{\eta} f(\zeta)\Delta\zeta\right)^r\Delta\eta \geq \frac{r}{r-1}\int_0^{\infty} f^r(\eta)\Delta\eta. \tag{18}$$

Very recently, El-Deeb et al. [16] established the next dynamic inequalities.

Theorem 14. *Suppose $\mathbb{T}$ is a time scale with $a \in [0,\infty)_{\mathbb{T}}$. Additionally, suppose that $f > 0$ and $\theta > 0$ are rd-continuous functions on $[a,\infty)_{\mathbb{T}}$ and f is nonincreasing.*

(*i*) *If* $r \geq 1$ *and* $\gamma \geq 0$, *then*

$$\int_a^\infty \frac{\theta(\eta)\left(\int_\eta^\infty \theta(\zeta)f(\zeta)\Delta\zeta\right)^r}{\left(\int_a^{\sigma(\eta)} \theta(\zeta)\Delta\zeta\right)^\gamma}\Delta\eta \geq \int_a^\infty \frac{\theta(\eta)\left(\int_a^\eta \theta(\zeta)\Delta\zeta\right)^r f^r(\eta)}{\left(\int_a^{\sigma(\eta)} \theta(\zeta)\Delta\zeta\right)^\gamma}\Delta\eta. \tag{19}$$

(*ii*) *If* $r \geq 1$ *and* $\gamma > 1$, *then*

$$\int_a^\infty \frac{\theta(\eta)\left(\int_\eta^\infty \theta(\zeta)f(\zeta)\Delta\zeta\right)^r}{\left(\int_\eta^\infty \theta(\zeta)\Delta\zeta\right)^\gamma}\Delta\eta \geq \frac{r}{\gamma-1}\int_a^\infty \theta(\eta)\left(\int_\eta^\infty \theta(\zeta)\Delta\zeta\right)^{r-\gamma} f^r(\eta)\Delta\eta. \tag{20}$$

(*iii*) *If* $r \geq 1$ *and* $\gamma > 1$, *then*

$$\int_a^\infty \frac{\theta(\eta)\left(\int_a^\eta \theta(\zeta)f(\zeta)\Delta\zeta\right)^r}{\left(\int_a^\eta \theta(\zeta)\Delta\zeta\right)^\gamma}\Delta\eta \geq \frac{r}{\gamma-1}\int_a^\infty \theta(\eta)\left(\int_a^\eta \theta(\zeta)\Delta\zeta\right)^{r-\gamma} f^r(\eta)\Delta\eta. \tag{21}$$

(*iv*) *If* $r \geq 1$ *and* $0 \leq \gamma < 1$, *then*

$$\int_a^\infty \frac{\theta(\eta)\left(\int_a^\eta \theta(\zeta)f(\zeta)\Delta\zeta\right)^r}{\left(\int_{\sigma(\eta)}^\infty \theta(\zeta)\Delta\zeta\right)^\gamma}\Delta\eta \geq \frac{r}{1-\gamma}\int_a^\infty \theta(\eta)\left(\int_a^\eta \theta(\zeta)\Delta\zeta\right)^{r-1}\left(\int_\eta^\infty \theta(\zeta)\Delta\zeta\right)^{1-\gamma} f^r(\eta)\Delta\eta. \tag{22}$$

For more details on Hardy-type inequalities and other types on time scales, we suggest [17–29] for the reader.

Theorem 15 (Fubini's Theorem, see [Theorem 1.1, Page 300] [30]). *Assume that* $(\lambda, \Sigma_1, \mu_\Delta)$ *and* $(Y, \Sigma_2, \nu_\Delta)$ *are two finite-dimensional time scales measure spaces. Moreover, suppose that* $f : \lambda \times Y \to \mathbb{R}$ *is a delta integrable function and define the functions*

$$\Phi(y) = \int_\lambda f(\lambda, y)d\mu_\Delta(\lambda), \quad y \in Y,$$

and

$$\hat{\Psi}(\lambda) = \int_Y f(\lambda, y)d\nu_\Delta(y), \quad \lambda \in \lambda.$$

Then, Φ *is delta integrable on* Y *and* $\hat{\Psi}$ *is delta integrable on* λ *and*

$$\int_\lambda d\mu_\Delta(\lambda)\int_Y f(\lambda, y)d\nu_\Delta(y) = \int_Y d\nu_\Delta(y)\int_\lambda f(\lambda, y)d\mu_\Delta(\lambda).$$

The basic theorems that will be required in the proof of our results are presented next.

Theorem 16 (Chain rule on time scales, see [Theorem 1.87, Page 31] [12]). *Assume* $g : \mathbb{R} \to \mathbb{R}$, $g : \mathbb{T} \to \mathbb{R}$ *is delta differentiable on* $\mathbb{T}^\kappa$, *and* $f : \mathbb{R} \to \mathbb{R}$ *is continuously differentiable. Then, there exists* $c \in [\eta, \sigma(\eta)]$ *with*

$$(f \circ g)^\Delta(\eta) = f'(g(c))g^\Delta(\eta). \tag{23}$$

Theorem 17 (Chain rule on time scales, see [Theorem 1.90, Page 32] [12]). *Let $f : \mathbb{R} \to \mathbb{R}$ be continuously differentiable and suppose $g : \mathbb{T} \to \mathbb{R}$ is delta differentiable. Then, $f \circ g : \mathbb{T} \to \mathbb{R}$ is delta differentiable and the formula*

$$(f \circ g)^{\Delta}(\eta) = \left\{ \int_0^1 \left[f'(hg^{\sigma}(\eta) + (1-h)g(\eta)) \right] dh \right\} g^{\Delta}(\eta),$$

holds.

In this manuscript, we show and prove some new dynamic Hardy-type which are reverse inequalities on time scales. The dynamic Hardy-type inequalities we obtained are entirely original, and as a result, we could obtain some integral and discrete inequalities of Hardy-type that are new. Furthermore, our findings generalize inequities (19)–(22). This paper is organized in the following way: Some basic concepts of the calculus on time scales and useful lemmas are introduced in Section 1. In Section 2, we state and prove the main results. In Section 3, we state the conclusion.

2. Main Results

The version of inequality (14) on time scales is given as a special case of the following theorem.

Theorem 18. *Assume that $\mathbb{T}$ is a time scale with $0 \le a \in \mathbb{T}$. Additionally, let f, g, $\check{\xi}$ and θ be nonnegative functions defined on $[0, \infty)_{\mathbb{T}}$ such that f and g are nonincreasing. Moreover, let $\check{\Psi} : \mathbb{R}_+ \to \mathbb{R}_+$ be a differentiable function such that $\check{\Psi}'$ is nondecreasing and $\check{\Psi}'(xy) = \check{\Psi}'(x)\check{\Psi}'(y)$ for all $x, y \in \mathbb{R}_+$. If $\gamma \ge 0$, then*

$$\int_a^{\infty} \frac{\check{\xi}(\eta) g(\eta) \check{\Psi}\left(\int_{\eta}^{\infty} \check{\xi}(\zeta) f(\zeta) \Delta\zeta \right)}{\left(\int_a^{\sigma(\eta)} \theta(\zeta) \Delta\zeta \right)^{\gamma}} \Delta\eta \ge \int_a^{\infty} \frac{\check{\xi}(\eta) g(\eta) \check{\Psi}\left(\int_a^{\eta} \check{\xi}(\zeta) \Delta\zeta \right) \check{\Psi}'(f(\eta)) f(\eta)}{\left(\int_a^{\sigma(\eta)} \theta(\zeta) \Delta\zeta \right)^{\gamma}} \Delta\eta. \quad (24)$$

Proof. Owing to nonincreasity of f, we have for $\lambda \ge \eta \ge a$

$$\int_{\eta}^{\lambda} \check{\xi}(\zeta) f(\zeta) \Delta\zeta \ge f(\lambda) \int_{\eta}^{\lambda} \check{\xi}(\zeta) \Delta\zeta,$$

then, since $\check{\Psi}'$ is nondecreasing,

$$\check{\Psi}'\left(\int_{\eta}^{\lambda} \check{\xi}(\zeta) f(\zeta) \Delta\zeta \right) \ge \check{\Psi}'\left(f(\lambda) \int_{\eta}^{\lambda} \check{\xi}(\zeta) \Delta\zeta \right) = \check{\Psi}'(f(\lambda)) \check{\Psi}'\left(\int_{\eta}^{\lambda} \check{\xi}(\zeta) \Delta\zeta \right). \quad (25)$$

Applying the chain rule (23), there exists $c \in [\lambda, \sigma(\lambda)]$ such that

$$\left[\check{\Psi}\left(\int_{\eta}^{\lambda} \check{\xi}(\zeta) f(\zeta) \Delta\zeta \right) \right]^{\Delta_\lambda} = \check{\Psi}'\left(\int_{\eta}^{c} \check{\xi}(\zeta) f(\zeta) \Delta\zeta \right) \left(\int_{\eta}^{\lambda} \check{\xi}(\zeta) f(\zeta) \Delta\zeta \right)^{\Delta_\lambda}.$$

Since $c \ge \lambda$, $\check{\Psi}'$ is nondecreasing, and $\left(\int_{\eta}^{\lambda} \check{\xi}(\zeta) f(\zeta) \Delta\zeta \right)^{\Delta_\lambda} = \check{\xi}(\lambda) f(\lambda) \ge 0$, we have

$$\left[\check{\Psi}\left(\int_{\eta}^{\lambda} \check{\xi}(\zeta) f(\zeta) \Delta\zeta \right) \right]^{\Delta_\lambda} \ge \check{\xi}(\lambda) f(\lambda) \check{\Psi}'\left(\int_{\eta}^{\lambda} \check{\xi}(\zeta) f(\zeta) \Delta\zeta \right). \quad (26)$$

Combining (25) with (26) yields

$$\left[\check{\Psi}\left(\int_{\eta}^{\lambda} \check{\xi}(\zeta) f(\zeta) \Delta\zeta \right) \right]^{\Delta_\lambda} \ge \check{\xi}(\lambda) \check{\Psi}'\left(\int_{\eta}^{\lambda} \check{\xi}(\zeta) \Delta\zeta \right) \check{\Psi}'(f(\lambda)) f(\lambda),$$

and so

$$\frac{\check{\xi}(\eta)g(\eta)\left[\check{\Psi}\left(\int_{\eta}^{\lambda}\check{\xi}(\zeta)f(\zeta)\Delta\zeta\right)\right]^{\Delta_\lambda}}{\left(\int_a^{\sigma(\eta)}\theta(\zeta)\Delta\zeta\right)^{\gamma}} \geq \frac{\check{\xi}(\eta)g(\eta)\check{\xi}(\lambda)\check{\Psi}'\left(\int_{\eta}^{\lambda}\check{\xi}(\zeta)\Delta\zeta\right)\check{\Psi}'(f(\lambda))f(\lambda)}{\left(\int_a^{\sigma(\eta)}\theta(\zeta)\Delta\zeta\right)^{\gamma}}.$$

Considering that $\lambda \geq \eta$ implies: (i) $\sigma(\lambda) \geq \sigma(\eta)$ and hence $\int_a^{\sigma(\lambda)}\theta(\zeta)\Delta\zeta \geq \int_a^{\sigma(\eta)}\theta(\zeta)\Delta\zeta$; (ii) $g(\lambda) \leq g(\eta)$, we obtain

$$\frac{\check{\xi}(\eta)g(\eta)\left[\check{\Psi}\left(\int_{\eta}^{\lambda}\check{\xi}(\zeta)f(\zeta)\Delta\zeta\right)\right]^{\Delta_\lambda}}{\left(\int_a^{\sigma(\eta)}\theta(\zeta)\Delta\zeta\right)^{\gamma}} \geq \frac{\check{\xi}(\eta)\check{\xi}(\lambda)g(\lambda)\check{\Psi}'\left(\int_{\eta}^{\lambda}\check{\xi}(\zeta)\Delta\zeta\right)\check{\Psi}'(f(\lambda))f(\lambda)}{\left(\int_a^{\sigma(\lambda)}\theta(\zeta)\Delta\zeta\right)^{\gamma}}.$$

If we integrate both sides with respect to λ over $[\eta,\infty)_{\mathbb{T}}$, we obtain

$$\frac{\check{\xi}(\eta)g(\eta)\check{\Psi}\left(\int_{\eta}^{\infty}\check{\xi}(\zeta)f(\zeta)\Delta\zeta\right)}{\left(\int_a^{\sigma(\eta)}\theta(\zeta)\Delta\zeta\right)^{\gamma}} \geq \int_{\eta}^{\infty}\frac{\check{\xi}(\eta)\check{\xi}(\lambda)g(\lambda)\check{\Psi}'\left(\int_{\eta}^{\lambda}\check{\xi}(\zeta)\Delta\zeta\right)\check{\Psi}'(f(\lambda))f(\lambda)}{\left(\int_a^{\sigma(\lambda)}\theta(\zeta)\Delta\zeta\right)^{\gamma}}\Delta\lambda.$$

If we integrate both sides once more, but with respect to η over $[a,\infty)_{\mathbb{T}}$, we obtain

$$\int_a^{\infty}\frac{\check{\xi}(\eta)g(\eta)\check{\Psi}\left(\int_{\eta}^{\infty}\check{\xi}(\zeta)f(\zeta)\Delta\zeta\right)}{\left(\int_a^{\sigma(\eta)}\theta(\zeta)\Delta\zeta\right)^{\gamma}}\Delta\eta \geq \int_a^{\infty}\check{\xi}(\eta)\left(\int_{\eta}^{\infty}\frac{\check{\xi}(\lambda)g(\lambda)\check{\Psi}'\left(\int_{\eta}^{\lambda}\check{\xi}(\zeta)\Delta\zeta\right)\check{\Psi}'(f(\lambda))f(\lambda)}{\left(\int_a^{\sigma(\lambda)}\theta(\zeta)\Delta\zeta\right)^{\gamma}}\Delta\lambda\right)\Delta\eta. \quad (27)$$

By Using Fubini's theorem on time scales, (27) can be rewritten as

$$\int_a^{\infty}\frac{\check{\xi}(\eta)g(\eta)\check{\Psi}\left(\int_{\eta}^{\infty}\check{\xi}(\zeta)f(\zeta)\Delta\zeta\right)}{\left(\int_a^{\sigma(\eta)}\theta(\zeta)\Delta\zeta\right)^{\gamma}}\Delta\eta \geq \int_a^{\infty}\frac{\check{\xi}(\lambda)g(\lambda)\check{\Psi}'(f(\lambda))f(\lambda)\left(\int_a^{\lambda}\check{\xi}(\eta)\check{\Psi}'\left(\int_{\eta}^{\lambda}\check{\xi}(\zeta)\Delta\zeta\right)\Delta\eta\right)}{\left(\int_a^{\sigma(\lambda)}\theta(\zeta)\Delta\zeta\right)^{\gamma}}\Delta\lambda. \quad (28)$$

Now, from the chain rule (23), one can see that there exists $c \in [\eta, \sigma(\eta)]$ with

$$\left[-\check{\Psi}\left(\int_{\eta}^{\lambda}\check{\xi}(\zeta)\Delta\zeta\right)\right]^{\Delta_\eta} = -\check{\Psi}'\left(\int_{c}^{\lambda}\check{\xi}(\zeta)\Delta\zeta\right)\left(\int_{\eta}^{\lambda}\check{\xi}(\zeta)\Delta\zeta\right)^{\Delta_\eta}.$$

Since $c \geq \eta$, $\check{\Psi}'$ is nondecreasing, $r \geq 1$ and $\left(\int_{\eta}^{\lambda}\check{\xi}(\zeta)\Delta\zeta\right)^{\Delta_\eta} = -\check{\xi}(\eta) \leq 0$, we have

$$\left[-\check{\Psi}\left(\int_{\eta}^{\lambda}\check{\xi}(\zeta)\Delta\zeta\right)\right]^{\Delta_\eta} \leq \check{\xi}(\eta)\check{\Psi}'\left(\int_{\eta}^{\lambda}\check{\xi}(\zeta)\Delta\zeta\right). \quad (29)$$

Substituting (29) into (28) leads to

$$\begin{aligned}
&\int_a^\infty \frac{\check{\xi}(\eta)g(\eta)\Psi\left(\int_\eta^\infty \check{\xi}(\zeta)f(\zeta)\Delta\zeta\right)}{\left(\int_a^{\sigma(\eta)}\theta(\zeta)\Delta\zeta\right)^\gamma}\Delta\eta \\
&\geq \int_a^\infty \frac{\check{\xi}(\lambda)g(\lambda)\Psi'(f(\lambda))f(\lambda)\left(\int_a^\lambda \left[-\Psi\left(\int_\eta^\lambda \check{\xi}(\zeta)\Delta\zeta\right)\right]^{\Delta_\eta}\Delta\eta\right)}{\left(\int_a^{\sigma(\lambda)}\theta(\zeta)\Delta\zeta\right)^\gamma}\Delta\lambda \\
&= \int_a^\infty \frac{\check{\xi}(\lambda)g(\lambda)\Psi\left(\int_a^\lambda \check{\xi}(\zeta)\Delta\zeta\right)\Psi'(f(\lambda))f(\lambda)}{\left(\int_a^{\sigma(\lambda)}\theta(\zeta)\Delta\zeta\right)^\gamma}\Delta\lambda.
\end{aligned}$$

This shows the validity of (24). □

Remark 1. *In Theorem 18, if we take* $\check{\Psi}(\eta) = \eta^r$, $r \geq 1$, $\check{\xi}(\eta) = \theta(\eta)$ *and* $g(\eta) = 1$, *then inequality* (24) *reduces to inequality* (19).

Corollary 1. *In Theorem 18, if we take* $\check{\Psi}(\eta) = \eta^r$, $\check{\xi}(\eta) = g(\eta) = 1$ *and* $a = \gamma = 0$, *then inequality* (24) *reduces to*

$$\int_0^\infty \left(\int_\eta^\infty f(\zeta)\Delta\zeta\right)^r \Delta\eta \geq \int_0^\infty \left(\int_0^\eta \check{\xi}(\zeta)\Delta\zeta\right)^r f^r(\eta)\Delta\eta,$$

which is the time scales version of (14).

Corollary 2. *If* $\mathbb{T} = \mathbb{R}$ *in Theorem 18, then inequality* (24) *reduces to*

$$\int_a^\infty \frac{\check{\xi}(\eta)g(\eta)\Psi\left(\int_\eta^\infty \check{\xi}(\zeta)f(\zeta)d\zeta\right)}{\left(\int_a^\eta \theta(\zeta)d\zeta\right)^\gamma}d\eta \geq \int_a^\infty \frac{\check{\xi}(\eta)g(\eta)\Psi\left(\int_a^\eta \check{\xi}(\zeta)d\zeta\right)\Psi'(f(\eta))f(\eta)}{\left(\int_a^\eta \theta(\zeta)d\zeta\right)^\gamma}d\eta.$$

Remark 2. *In Corollary 2, if we take* $\check{\Psi}(\eta) = \eta^r$, $\check{\xi}(\eta) = g(\eta) = 1$, $a = \gamma = 0$, *then we reclaim inequality* (14).

Corollary 3. *If* $\mathbb{T} = h\mathbb{Z}$ *in Theorem 18, then inequality* (24) *is reduced to*

$$\sum_{n=\frac{a}{h}}^\infty \frac{\check{\xi}(nh)g(nh)\Psi\left(h\sum_{m=\frac{n}{\theta}}^\infty \check{\xi}(mh)f(mh)\right)}{\left(\sum_{m=\frac{a}{h}}^{\frac{n}{h}}\theta(mh)\right)^\gamma} \geq \sum_{n=\frac{a}{h}}^\infty \frac{\check{\xi}(nh)g(nh)\Psi\left(h\sum_{m=\frac{a}{h}}^{\frac{n}{\theta}-1}\check{\xi}(mh)\right)\Psi'(f(nh))f(nh)}{\left(\sum_{m=\frac{a}{h}}^{\frac{n}{h}}\theta(mh)\right)^\gamma}.$$

Corollary 4. *In Corollary 3, if we take* $h = 1$, *then, inequality* (24) *will be reduced to*

$$\sum_{n=a}^\infty \frac{\check{\xi}(n)g(n)\Psi\left(\sum_{m=n}^\infty \check{\xi}(m)f(m)\right)}{\left(\sum_{m=a}^n \theta(m)\right)^\gamma} \geq \sum_{n=a}^\infty \frac{\check{\xi}(n)g(n)\Psi\left(\sum_{m=a}^{n-1}\check{\xi}(m)\right)\Psi'(f(n))f(n)}{\left(\sum_{m=a}^n \theta(m)\right)^\gamma}.$$

Remark 3. In Corollary 4, if we take $\check{\Psi}(\eta) = \eta^r$, $\check{\xi}(\eta) = g(\eta) = 1$, $a = 1$ and $\gamma = 0$, then we reclaim inequality (13).

Corollary 5. *If* $\mathbb{T} = \overline{q^{\mathbb{Z}}}$ *in Theorem 18, then*

$$\sum_{n=(\log_q a)}^{\infty} \frac{q^n \check{\xi}(q^n) g(q^n) \check{\Psi}\left((q-1)\sum_{m=(\log_q n)}^{\infty} q^m \check{\xi}(q^m) f(q^m)\right)}{\left(\sum_{m=(\log_q a)}^{(\log_q qn)-1} q^m h(q^m)\right)^{\gamma}}$$

$$\geq \sum_{n=(\log_q a)}^{\infty} \frac{q^n \check{\xi}(q^n) g(q^n) \check{\Psi}\left((q-1)\sum_{m=(\log_q a)}^{(\log_q n)-1} q^m \check{\xi}(q^m)\right) \check{\Psi}'(f(q^n)) f(q^n)}{\left(\sum_{m=(\log_q a)}^{(\log_q qn)-1} q^m h(q^m)\right)^{\gamma}}.$$

Now, as a new result, we are interested in discussing the inequality (24) in the case of the extrema of integration $\int_a^{\eta} \theta(s) \Delta s$ being replaced to be from η to ∞. In fact, that is what we will do in the following theorem.

Theorem 19. *Assume that* $\mathbb{T}$ *is a time scale with* $0 \leq a \in \mathbb{T}$. *Additionally, let* f, g, θ *and* $\check{\xi}$ *be nonnegative functions defined on* $[0, \infty)_{\mathbb{T}}$ *such that* f *and* g *are nonincreasing. Furthermore, let* $\check{\Psi} : \mathbb{R}_+ \to \mathbb{R}_+$ *be a differentiable function such that* $\check{\Psi}'$ *is nondecreasing and* $\check{\Psi}'(xy) = \check{\Psi}'(x)\check{\Psi}'(y)$ *for all* $x, y \in \mathbb{R}_+$. *If* $\gamma > 1$, *then*

$$\int_a^{\infty} \frac{\check{\xi}(\eta) g(\eta) \check{\Psi}\left(\int_{\eta}^{\infty} \theta(\zeta) f(\zeta) \Delta \zeta\right)}{\left(\int_{\eta}^{\infty} \check{\xi}(\zeta) \Delta \zeta\right)^{\gamma}} \Delta \eta \geq \frac{1}{\gamma - 1} \int_a^{\infty} \frac{\theta(\eta) g(\eta) \check{\Psi}'\left(\int_{\eta}^{\infty} \theta(\zeta) \Delta \zeta\right) \check{\Psi}'(f(\eta)) f(\eta)}{\left(\int_{\eta}^{\infty} \check{\xi}(\zeta) \Delta \zeta\right)^{\gamma-1}} \Delta \eta. \qquad (30)$$

Proof. Because of nonincreasity of f, we have for $\eta \geq \lambda \geq a$

$$\int_{\lambda}^{\infty} \theta(\zeta) f(\zeta) \Delta \zeta \leq f(\lambda) \int_{\lambda}^{\infty} \theta(\zeta) \Delta \zeta,$$

therefore, because $\check{\Psi}'$ is nondecreasing,

$$\check{\Psi}'\left(\int_{\lambda}^{\infty} \theta(\zeta) f(\zeta) \Delta \zeta\right) \geq \check{\Psi}'\left(f(\lambda) \int_{\lambda}^{\infty} \theta(\zeta) \Delta \zeta\right) = \check{\Psi}'(f(\lambda)) \check{\Psi}'\left(\int_{\lambda}^{\infty} \theta(\zeta) \Delta \zeta\right). \qquad (31)$$

From the chain rule (23), we see that there is $c \in [\lambda, \sigma(\lambda)]$ with

$$\left[\check{\Psi}\left(\int_{\lambda}^{\infty} \theta(\zeta) f(\zeta) \Delta \zeta\right)\right]^{\Delta} = \check{\Psi}'\left(\int_c^{\infty} \theta(\zeta) f(\zeta) \Delta \zeta\right) \left(\int_{\lambda}^{\infty} \theta(\zeta) f(\zeta) \Delta \zeta\right)^{\Delta}.$$

Since $c \geq \lambda$, $\check{\Psi}'$ is nondecreasing, $r \geq 1$ and $\left(\int_{\lambda}^{\infty} \theta(\zeta) f(\zeta) \Delta \zeta\right)^{\Delta} = -\theta(\lambda) f(\lambda) \leq 0$, we have

$$\left[\check{\Psi}\left(\int_{\lambda}^{\infty} \theta(\zeta) f(\zeta) \Delta \zeta\right)\right]^{\Delta} \geq -\theta(\lambda) f(\lambda) \check{\Psi}'\left(\int_{\lambda}^{\infty} \theta(\zeta) f(\zeta) \Delta \zeta\right) \qquad (32)$$

Combining (31) with (32) yields

$$\left[\check{\Psi}\left(\int_{\lambda}^{\infty} \theta(\zeta) f(\zeta) \Delta \zeta\right)\right]^{\Delta} \geq -\theta(\lambda) \check{\Psi}'\left(\int_{\lambda}^{\infty} \theta(\zeta) \Delta \zeta\right) \check{\Psi}'(f(\lambda)) f(\lambda),$$

which implies

$$\frac{\check{\xi}(\eta)g(\eta)\left[\Psi\left(\int_{\lambda}^{\infty}\theta(\zeta)f(\zeta)\Delta\zeta\right)\right]^{\Delta}}{\left(\int_{\eta}^{\infty}\check{\xi}(\zeta)\Delta\zeta\right)^{\gamma}} \geq \frac{-\check{\xi}(\eta)g(\eta)\theta(\lambda)\Psi'\left(\int_{\lambda}^{\infty}\theta(\zeta)\Delta\zeta\right)\Psi'(f(\lambda))f(\lambda)}{\left(\int_{\eta}^{\infty}\check{\xi}(\zeta)\Delta\zeta\right)^{\gamma}}.$$

As g is nonincreasing and $\lambda \leq \eta$, we have $g(\lambda) \geq g(\eta)$ and hence,

$$\frac{\check{\xi}(\eta)g(\eta)\left[\Psi\left(\int_{\lambda}^{\infty}\theta(\zeta)f(\zeta)\Delta\zeta\right)\right]^{\Delta}}{\left(\int_{\eta}^{\infty}\check{\xi}(\zeta)\Delta\zeta\right)^{\gamma}} \geq \frac{-\check{\xi}(\eta)\theta(\lambda)g(\lambda)\Psi'\left(\int_{\lambda}^{\infty}\theta(\zeta)\Delta\zeta\right)\Psi'(f(\lambda))f(\lambda)}{\left(\int_{\eta}^{\infty}\check{\xi}(\zeta)\Delta\zeta\right)^{\gamma}}.$$

Now, after both sides are integrated with respect to λ over $[a,\eta]_{\mathbb{T}}$, we could have

$$\begin{aligned}&\frac{\check{\xi}(\eta)g(\eta)\left[\Psi\left(\int_{\eta}^{\infty}\theta(\zeta)f(\zeta)\Delta\zeta\right)-\Psi\left(\int_{a}^{\infty}\theta(\zeta)f(\zeta)\Delta\zeta\right)\right]}{\left(\int_{\eta}^{\infty}\check{\xi}(\zeta)\Delta\zeta\right)^{\gamma}}\\ &\geq \int_{a}^{\eta}\frac{-\check{\xi}(\eta)\theta(\lambda)g(\lambda)\Psi'\left(\int_{\lambda}^{\infty}\theta(\zeta)\Delta\zeta\right)\Psi'(f(\lambda))f(\lambda)}{\left(\int_{\eta}^{\infty}\check{\xi}(\zeta)\Delta\zeta\right)^{\gamma}}\Delta\lambda.\end{aligned}$$

Since $\Psi\left(\int_{\eta}^{\infty}\theta(\zeta)f(\zeta)\Delta\zeta\right) \geq \Psi\left(\int_{\eta}^{\infty}\theta(\zeta)f(\zeta)\Delta\zeta\right) - \Psi\left(\int_{a}^{\infty}\theta(\zeta)f(\zeta)\Delta\zeta\right)$, we have

$$\frac{\check{\xi}(\eta)g(\eta)\Psi\left(\int_{\eta}^{\infty}\theta(\zeta)f(\zeta)\Delta\zeta\right)}{\left(\int_{\eta}^{\infty}\check{\xi}(\zeta)\Delta\zeta\right)^{\gamma}} \geq -\int_{a}^{\eta}\check{\xi}(\eta)\theta(\lambda)g(\lambda)\Psi'\left(\int_{\lambda}^{\infty}\theta(\zeta)\Delta\zeta\right)\left(\int_{\eta}^{\infty}\check{\xi}(\zeta)\Delta\zeta\right)^{-\gamma}\Psi'(f(\lambda))f(\lambda)\Delta\lambda.$$

Afterwards, if both sides are integrated with respect to η over $[a,\infty)_{\mathbb{T}}$, we obtain

$$\begin{aligned}&\int_{a}^{\infty}\frac{\check{\xi}(\eta)g(\eta)\Psi\left(\int_{\eta}^{\infty}\theta(\zeta)f(\zeta)\Delta\zeta\right)}{\left(\int_{\eta}^{\infty}\check{\xi}(\zeta)\Delta\zeta\right)^{\gamma}}\Delta\eta\\ &\geq -\int_{a}^{\infty}\check{\xi}(\eta)\left(\int_{\eta}^{\infty}\check{\xi}(\zeta)\Delta\zeta\right)^{-\gamma}\left(\int_{a}^{\eta}\theta(\lambda)g(\lambda)\Psi'\left(\int_{\lambda}^{\infty}\theta(\zeta)\Delta\zeta\right)\Psi'(f(\lambda))f(\lambda)\Delta\lambda\right)\Delta\eta.\end{aligned} \tag{33}$$

Using Fubini's theorem on time scales, (33) can be rewritten as

$$\begin{aligned}&\int_{a}^{\infty}\frac{\check{\xi}(\eta)g(\eta)\Psi\left(\int_{\eta}^{\infty}\theta(\zeta)f(\zeta)\Delta\zeta\right)}{\left(\int_{\eta}^{\infty}\check{\xi}(\zeta)\Delta\zeta\right)^{\gamma}}\Delta\eta\\ &\geq -\int_{a}^{\infty}\theta(\lambda)g(\lambda)\Psi'\left(\int_{\lambda}^{\infty}\theta(\zeta)\Delta\zeta\right)\Psi'(f(\lambda))f(\lambda)\left(\int_{\lambda}^{\infty}\check{\xi}(\eta)\left(\int_{\eta}^{\infty}\check{\xi}(\zeta)\Delta\zeta\right)^{-\gamma}\Delta\eta\right)\Delta\lambda.\end{aligned} \tag{34}$$

If we take a look at the chain rule, (23), we could say that there exists $c \in [\eta, \sigma(\eta)]$ such that

$$\left[-\left(\int_{\eta}^{\infty}\check{\xi}(\zeta)\Delta\zeta\right)^{1-\gamma}\right]^{\Delta}=-(1-\gamma)\left(\int_{c}^{\infty}\check{\xi}(\zeta)\Delta\zeta\right)^{-\gamma}\left(\int_{\eta}^{\infty}\check{\xi}(\zeta)\Delta\zeta\right)^{\Delta}.$$

Since $c \geq \eta$, $\gamma > 1$ and $\left(\int_{\eta}^{\infty}\check{\xi}(\zeta)\Delta\zeta\right)^{\Delta} = -\check{\xi}(\eta) \leq 0$, we get

$$\left[-\left(\int_{\eta}^{\infty}\check{\xi}(\zeta)\Delta\zeta\right)^{1-\gamma}\right]^{\Delta}\geq-(\gamma-1)\check{\xi}(\eta)\left(\int_{\eta}^{\infty}\check{\xi}(\zeta)\Delta\zeta\right)^{-\gamma}. \tag{35}$$

Substituting (35) into (34) leads to

$$\begin{aligned}
&\int_{a}^{\infty}\frac{\check{\xi}(\eta)g(\eta)\check{\Psi}\left(\int_{\eta}^{\infty}\theta(\zeta)f(\zeta)\Delta\zeta\right)}{\left(\int_{\eta}^{\infty}\check{\xi}(\zeta)\Delta\zeta\right)^{\gamma}}\Delta\eta\\
&\geq\frac{1}{\gamma-1}\int_{a}^{\infty}\theta(\lambda)g(\lambda)\check{\Psi}'\left(\int_{\lambda}^{\infty}\theta(\zeta)\Delta\zeta\right)\check{\Psi}'(f(\lambda))f(\lambda)\left(\int_{\lambda}^{\infty}\left[-\left(\int_{\eta}^{\infty}\check{\xi}(\zeta)\Delta\zeta\right)^{1-\gamma}\right]^{\Delta}\Delta\eta\right)\Delta\lambda\\
&=\frac{1}{\gamma-1}\int_{a}^{\infty}\theta(\lambda)g(\lambda)\check{\Psi}'\left(\int_{\lambda}^{\infty}\theta(\zeta)\Delta\zeta\right)\left(\int_{\lambda}^{\infty}\check{\xi}(\zeta)\Delta\zeta\right)^{1-\gamma}\check{\Psi}'(f(\lambda))f(\lambda)\Delta\lambda,
\end{aligned}$$

from which inequality (30) follows. □

Remark 4. *In Theorem 19, if we take* $\check{\Psi}(\eta) = \eta^{r}$, $\check{\xi}(\eta) = \theta(\eta)$ *and* $g(\eta) = 1$, *then inequality* (30) *reduces to inequality* (20).

Corollary 6. *If* $\mathbb{T} = \mathbb{R}$ *in Theorem 19, then, inequality* (30) *will be reduced to*

$$\int_{a}^{\infty}\frac{\check{\xi}(\eta)g(\eta)\check{\Psi}\left(\int_{\eta}^{\infty}\theta(\zeta)f(\zeta)d\zeta\right)}{\left(\int_{\eta}^{\infty}\check{\xi}(\zeta)d\zeta\right)^{\gamma}}d\eta\geq\frac{1}{\gamma-1}\int_{a}^{\infty}\frac{\theta(\eta)g(\eta)\check{\Psi}'\left(\int_{\eta}^{\infty}\theta(\zeta)d\zeta\right)\check{\Psi}'(f(\eta))f(\eta)}{\left(\int_{\eta}^{\infty}\check{\xi}(\zeta)d\zeta\right)^{\gamma-1}}d\eta.$$

Corollary 7. *If* $\mathbb{T} = h\mathbb{Z}$ *in Theorem 19, then inequality* (30) *is reduced to*

$$\sum_{n=\frac{a}{h}}^{\infty}\frac{\check{\xi}(nh)g(nh)\check{\Psi}\left(h\sum_{m=\frac{n}{h}}^{\infty}\theta(mh)f(mh)\right)}{\left(h\sum_{m=\frac{n}{h}}^{\infty}\check{\xi}(mh)\right)^{\gamma}}\geq\frac{1}{\gamma-1}\sum_{n=\frac{a}{h}}^{\infty}\frac{\theta(nh)g(nh)\check{\Psi}'\left(h\sum_{m=\frac{n}{h}}^{\infty}\theta(mh)\right)\check{\Psi}'(f(nh))f(nh)}{\left(h\sum_{m=\frac{n}{h}}^{\infty}\check{\xi}(mh)\right)^{\gamma-1}}.$$

Corollary 8. *In Corollary 7, if we take* $h = 1$, *then inequality* (30) *reduces to*

$$\sum_{n=a}^{\infty}\frac{\check{\xi}(n)g(n)\check{\Psi}\left(\sum_{m=n}^{\infty}\theta(m)f(m)\right)}{\left(\sum_{m=n}^{\infty}\check{\xi}(m)\right)^{\gamma}}\geq\frac{1}{\gamma-1}\sum_{n=a}^{\infty}\frac{\theta(n)g(n)\check{\Psi}'\left(\sum_{m=n}^{\infty}\theta(m)\right)\check{\Psi}'(f(n))f(n)}{\left(\sum_{m=n}^{\infty}\check{\xi}(m)\right)^{\gamma-1}}.$$

Corollary 9. *If* $\mathbb{T} = \overline{q^{\mathbb{Z}}}$ *in Theorem 19, then inequality* (30) *will be reduced to*

$$\sum_{n=(\log_q a)}^{\infty} \frac{q^n \check{\xi}(q^n) g(q^n) \Psi\left((q-1) \sum_{m=(\log_q n)}^{\infty} q^m h(q^m) f(q^m)\right)}{\left((q-1) \sum_{m=(\log_q n)}^{\infty} q^m \check{\xi}(q^m)\right)^{\gamma}}$$

$$\geq \frac{1}{\gamma - 1} \sum_{n=(\log_q a)}^{\infty} \frac{q^n h(q^n) g(q^n) \Psi'\left((q-1) \sum_{m=(\log_q n)}^{\infty} q^m h(q^m)\right) \Psi'(f(q^n)) f(q^n)}{\left((q-1) \sum_{m=(\log_q n)}^{\infty} q^m \check{\xi}(q^m)\right)^{\gamma - 1}}.$$

In the next theorem, we make a broad popularization of Theorem 13.

Theorem 20. *Let* $\mathbb{T}$ *be a time scale with* $0 \leq a \in \mathbb{T}$. *Moreover, suppose that* f, g, θ *and* $\check{\xi}$ *are nonnegative functions defined on* $[0, \infty)_{\mathbb{T}}$ *such that* f *is nonincreasing and* g *is nondecreasing. In addition, let* $\Psi : \mathbb{R}_+ \to \mathbb{R}_+$ *be a differentiable function such that* Ψ' *is nondecreasing and* $\Psi'(xy) = \Psi'(x)\Psi'(y)$ *for all* $x, y \in \mathbb{R}_+$. *If* $\gamma > 1$, *then*

$$\int_a^{\infty} \frac{\check{\xi}(\eta) g(\eta) \Psi\left(\int_0^{\eta} \theta(\zeta) f(\zeta) \Delta\zeta\right)}{\left(\int_0^{\eta} \check{\xi}(\zeta) \Delta\zeta\right)^{\gamma}} \Delta\eta \geq \frac{1}{\gamma - 1} \int_a^{\infty} \frac{\theta(\eta) g(\eta) \Psi'\left(\int_0^{\eta} \theta(\zeta) \Delta\zeta\right) \Psi'(f(\eta)) f(\eta)}{\left(\int_0^{\eta} \check{\xi}(\zeta) \Delta\zeta\right)^{\gamma - 1}} \Delta\eta. \tag{36}$$

Proof. As a result of of the nonincreasity of f, we have for $\eta \geq \lambda \geq 0$

$$\int_0^{\lambda} \theta(\zeta) f(\zeta) \Delta\zeta \geq f(\lambda) \int_0^{\lambda} \theta(\zeta) \Delta\zeta,$$

then, since Ψ' is nondecreasing,

$$\Psi'\left(\int_0^{\lambda} \theta(\zeta) f(\zeta) \Delta\zeta\right) \geq \Psi'\left(f(\lambda) \int_0^{\lambda} \theta(\zeta) \Delta\zeta\right) = \Psi'(f(\lambda)) \Psi'\left(\int_0^{\lambda} \theta(\zeta) \Delta\zeta\right). \tag{37}$$

Using the chain rule (23), there exists $c \in [\lambda, \sigma(\lambda)]$ such that

$$\left[\Psi\left(\int_0^{\lambda} \theta(\zeta) f(\zeta) \Delta\zeta\right)\right]^{\Delta} = \Psi'\left(\int_0^{c} \theta(\zeta) f(\zeta) \Delta\zeta\right) \left(\int_0^{\lambda} \theta(\zeta) f(\zeta) \Delta\zeta\right)^{\Delta}.$$

Since $c \geq \lambda$, Ψ' is nondecreasing, $r \geq 1$ and $\left(\int_0^{\lambda} \theta(\zeta) f(\zeta) \Delta\zeta\right)^{\Delta} = \theta(\lambda) f(\lambda) \geq 0$, we have

$$\left[\Psi\left(\int_0^{\lambda} \theta(\zeta) f(\zeta) \Delta\zeta\right)\right]^{\Delta} \geq \theta(\lambda) f(\lambda) \Psi'\left(\int_0^{\lambda} \theta(\zeta) f(\zeta) \Delta\zeta\right). \tag{38}$$

By using (37) and (38) together we could have

$$\left[\Psi'\left(\int_0^{\lambda} \theta(\zeta) f(\zeta) \Delta\zeta\right)\right]^{\Delta} \geq \theta(\lambda) \Psi'\left(\int_0^{\lambda} \theta(\zeta) \Delta\zeta\right) \Psi'(f(\lambda)) f(\lambda).$$

and thus

$$\frac{\check{\xi}(\eta) g(\eta) \left[\Psi\left(\int_0^{\lambda} \theta(\zeta) f(\zeta) \Delta\zeta\right)\right]^{\Delta}}{\left(\int_0^{\eta} \check{\xi}(\zeta) \Delta\zeta\right)^{\gamma}} \geq \frac{\check{\xi}(\eta) g(\eta) \theta(\lambda) \Psi'\left(\int_0^{\lambda} \theta(\zeta) \Delta\zeta\right) \Psi'(f(\lambda)) f(\lambda)}{\left(\int_0^{\eta} \check{\xi}(\zeta) \Delta\zeta\right)^{\gamma}}.$$

As g is nondecreasing and $\lambda \leq \eta$, we have $g(\lambda) \leq g(\eta)$ and hence,

$$\frac{\check{\xi}(\eta)g(\eta)\left[\Psi\left(\int_0^\lambda \theta(\zeta)f(\zeta)\Delta\zeta\right)\right]^\Delta}{\left(\int_0^\eta \check{\xi}(\zeta)\Delta\zeta\right)^\gamma} \geq \frac{\check{\xi}(\eta)g(\lambda)\theta(\lambda)\Psi'\left(\int_0^\lambda \theta(\zeta)\Delta\zeta\right)\Psi'(f(\lambda))f(\lambda)}{\left(\int_0^\eta \check{\xi}(\zeta)\Delta\zeta\right)^\gamma}.$$

Integrating both sides of the last inequality with respect to λ over $[0,\eta]_{\mathbb{T}}$ gives

$$\begin{aligned}&\frac{\check{\xi}(\eta)g(\eta)\left[\Psi\left(\int_0^\eta \theta(\zeta)f(\zeta)\Delta\zeta\right)-\Psi\left(\int_0^a \theta(\zeta)f(\zeta)\Delta\zeta\right)\right]}{\left(\int_0^\eta \check{\xi}(\zeta)\Delta\zeta\right)^\gamma}\\ &\geq \int_a^\eta \frac{\check{\xi}(\eta)\theta(\lambda)g(\lambda)\Psi'\left(\int_0^\lambda \theta(\zeta)\Delta\zeta\right)\Psi'(f(\lambda))f(\lambda)}{\left(\int_0^\eta \check{\xi}(\zeta)\Delta\zeta\right)^\gamma}\Delta\lambda.\end{aligned}$$

Since $\Psi\left(\int_0^\eta \theta(\zeta)f(\zeta)\Delta\zeta\right) \geq \Psi\left(\int_0^\eta \theta(\zeta)f(\zeta)\Delta\zeta\right) - \Psi\left(\int_0^a \theta(\zeta)f(\zeta)\Delta\zeta\right)$, we obtain

$$\frac{\check{\xi}(\eta)g(\eta)\Psi\left(\int_0^\eta \theta(\zeta)f(\zeta)\Delta\zeta\right)}{\left(\int_0^\eta \check{\xi}(\zeta)\Delta\zeta\right)^\gamma} \geq \int_a^\eta \check{\xi}(\eta)\theta(\lambda)g(\lambda)\Psi'\left(\int_0^\lambda \theta(\zeta)\Delta\zeta\right)\left(\int_0^\eta \check{\xi}(\zeta)\Delta\zeta\right)^{-\gamma}\Psi'(f(\lambda))f(\lambda)\Delta\lambda,$$

After integrating both sides with respect to η over $[a,\infty)_{\mathbb{T}}$,

$$\begin{aligned}&\int_a^\infty \frac{\check{\xi}(\eta)g(\eta)\Psi\left(\int_0^\eta \theta(\zeta)f(\zeta)\Delta\zeta\right)}{\left(\int_0^\eta \check{\xi}(\zeta)\Delta\zeta\right)^\gamma}\Delta\eta\\ &\geq \int_a^\infty \check{\xi}(\eta)\left(\int_0^\eta \check{\xi}(\zeta)\Delta\zeta\right)^{-\gamma}\left(\int_a^\eta \theta(\lambda)g(\lambda)\Psi'\left(\int_0^\lambda \theta(\zeta)\Delta\zeta\right)\Psi'(f(\lambda))f(\lambda)\Delta\lambda\right)\Delta\eta. \qquad (39)\end{aligned}$$

Employing Fubini's theorem on time scales, (39) can be rewritten as

$$\begin{aligned}&\int_a^\infty \frac{\check{\xi}(\eta)g(\eta)\Psi\left(\int_0^\eta \theta(\zeta)f(\zeta)\Delta\zeta\right)}{\left(\int_0^\eta \check{\xi}(\zeta)\Delta\zeta\right)^\gamma}\Delta\eta\\ &\geq \int_a^\infty \theta(\lambda)g(\lambda)\Psi'\left(\int_0^\lambda \theta(\zeta)\Delta\zeta\right)\Psi'(f(\lambda))f(\lambda)\left(\int_\lambda^\infty \check{\xi}(\eta)\left(\int_0^\eta \check{\xi}(\zeta)\Delta\zeta\right)^{-\gamma}\Delta\eta\right)\Delta\lambda. \qquad (40)\end{aligned}$$

Additionally, by taking a look at the chain rule (23), we can say that there exists $c \in [\eta,\sigma(\eta)]$ such that

$$\left[-\left(\int_0^\eta \check{\xi}(\zeta)\Delta\zeta\right)^{1-\gamma}\right]^\Delta = -(1-\gamma)\left(\int_0^c \check{\xi}(\zeta)\Delta\zeta\right)^{-\gamma}\left(\int_0^\eta \check{\xi}(\zeta)\Delta\zeta\right)^\Delta.$$

Since $c \geq \eta$, $\gamma > 1$ and $\left(\int_0^\eta \check{\xi}(\zeta)\Delta\zeta\right)^\Delta = \check{\xi}(\eta) \geq 0$, we get

$$\left[-\left(\int_0^\eta \check{\xi}(\zeta)\Delta\zeta\right)^{1-\gamma}\right]^\Delta \leq (\gamma-1)\check{\xi}(\eta)\left(\int_0^\eta \check{\xi}(\zeta)\Delta\zeta\right)^{-\gamma}. \tag{41}$$

Substituting (41) into (40) leads to

$$\begin{aligned}
&\int_a^\infty \frac{\check{\xi}(\eta)g(\eta)\check{\Psi}\left(\int_0^\eta \theta(\zeta)f(\zeta)\Delta\zeta\right)}{\left(\int_0^\eta \check{\xi}(\zeta)\Delta\zeta\right)^\gamma}\Delta\eta \\
&\geq \frac{1}{\gamma-1}\int_a^\infty \theta(\lambda)g(\lambda)\check{\Psi}'\left(\int_0^\lambda \theta(\zeta)\Delta\zeta\right)\check{\Psi}'(f(\lambda))f(\lambda)\left(\int_\lambda^\infty \left[-\left(\int_0^\eta \check{\xi}(\zeta)\Delta\zeta\right)^{1-\gamma}\right]^\Delta \Delta\eta\right)\Delta\lambda \\
&= \frac{1}{\gamma-1}\int_a^\infty \theta(\lambda)g(\lambda)\check{\Psi}'\left(\int_0^\lambda \theta(\zeta)\Delta\zeta\right)\left(\int_0^\lambda \check{\xi}(\zeta)\Delta\zeta\right)^{1-\gamma}\check{\Psi}'(f(\lambda))f(\lambda)\Delta\lambda.
\end{aligned}$$

This concludes the proof. □

Remark 5. *In Theorem 20, if we make* $\check{\Psi}(\eta) = \eta^r$, $\check{\xi}(\eta) = \theta(\eta)$ *and* $g(\eta) = 1$, *then inequality* (36) *reduces to inequality* (21).

Remark 6. *In Theorem 20, if we make* $\check{\Psi}(\eta) = \eta^r$, $\check{\xi}(\eta) = \theta(\eta) = g(\eta) = 1$, $r = \gamma$ *and* $a = 0$, *then we reclaim Theorem 13.*

Corollary 10. *If* $\mathbb{T} = \mathbb{R}$ *in Theorem 20, then, inequality* (36) *boils down to*

$$\int_a^\infty \frac{\check{\xi}(\eta)g(\eta)\check{\Psi}\left(\int_0^\eta \theta(\zeta)f(\zeta)d\zeta\right)}{\left(\int_0^\eta \check{\xi}(\zeta)d\zeta\right)^\gamma}d\eta \geq \frac{1}{\gamma-1}\int_a^\infty \frac{\theta(\eta)g(\eta)\check{\Psi}'\left(\int_0^\eta \theta(\zeta)d\zeta\right)\check{\Psi}'(f(\eta))f(\eta)}{\left(\int_0^\eta \check{\xi}(\zeta)d\zeta\right)^{\gamma-1}}d\eta.$$

Corollary 11. *If* $\mathbb{T} = h\mathbb{Z}$ *in Theorem 20, then, inequality* (36) *boils down to*

$$\sum_{n=\frac{a}{h}}^\infty \frac{\check{\xi}(nh)g(nh)\check{\Psi}\left(h\sum_{m=0}^{\frac{n}{h}-1}\theta(mh)f(mh)\right)}{\left(h\sum_{m=0}^{\frac{n}{h}-1}\check{\xi}(mh)\right)^\gamma} \geq \frac{1}{\gamma-1}\sum_{n=\frac{a}{h}}^\infty \frac{\theta(nh)g(nh)\check{\Psi}'\left(h\sum_{m=0}^{\frac{n}{h}-1}\theta(mh)\right)\check{\Psi}'(f(nh))f(nh)}{\left(h\sum_{m=0}^{\frac{n}{h}-1}\check{\xi}(mh)\right)^{\gamma-1}}.$$

Corollary 12. *In Corollary 11, if we take* $\mathbb{T} = \mathbb{Z}$, *and inequality* (36) *abbreviates to*

$$\sum_{n=a}^\infty \frac{\check{\xi}(n)g(n)\check{\Psi}\left(\sum_{m=0}^{n-1}\theta(m)f(m)\right)}{\left(\sum_{m=0}^{n-1}\check{\xi}(m)\right)^\gamma} \geq \frac{1}{\gamma-1}\sum_{n=a}^\infty \frac{\theta(n)g(n)\check{\Psi}'\left(\sum_{m=0}^{n-1}\theta(m)\right)\check{\Psi}'(f(n))f(n)}{\left(\sum_{m=0}^{n-1}\check{\xi}(m)\right)^{\gamma-1}}.$$

Corollary 13. *If* $\mathbb{T} = \overline{q^{\mathbb{Z}}}$ *in Theorem 20, and inequality* (36) *abbreviates to*

$$\sum_{n=(\log_q a)}^{\infty} \frac{q^n \check{\xi}(q^n) g(q^n) \check{\Psi}\Big((q-1) \sum_{m=0}^{(\log_q n)-1} q^m h(q^m) f(q^m) \Big)}{\Big((q-1) \sum_{m=0}^{(\log_q n)-1} q^m \check{\xi}(q^m) \Big)^{\gamma}}$$
$$\geq \frac{1}{\gamma-1} \sum_{n=(\log_q a)}^{\infty} \frac{q^n h(q^n) g(q^n) \check{\Psi}'\Big((q-1) \sum_{m=0}^{(\log_q n)-1} q^m h(q^m) \Big) \check{\Psi}'(f(q^n)) f(q^n)}{\Big((q-1) \sum_{m=0}^{(\log_q n)-1} q^m \check{\xi}(q^m) \Big)^{\gamma-1}}.$$

Now, as a new result, we are interested in discussing the results in Theorem (20) in the case of the extrema of integration $\int_a^{\eta} \check{\xi} \Delta s$ being replaced to be from η to ∞. In fact, that is exactly what we shall accomplish in the next theorem.

Theorem 21. *Suppose that* $\mathbb{T}$ *is a time scale with* $0 \leq a \in \mathbb{T}$. *Moreover, assume that* f, g, θ *and* $\check{\xi}$ *are nonnegative functions defined on* $[0, \infty)_{\mathbb{T}}$ *such that* f *is nonincreasing and* g *is nondecreasing. Moreover, let* $\check{\Psi} : \mathbb{R}_+ \to \mathbb{R}_+$ *be a differentiable function such that* $\check{\Psi}'$ *is nondecreasing and* $\check{\Psi}'(xy) = \check{\Psi}'(x)\check{\Psi}'(y)$ *for all* $x, y \in \mathbb{R}_+$. *If* $0 \leq \gamma < 1$, *then*

$$\int_a^{\infty} \frac{\check{\xi}(\eta) g(\eta) \check{\Psi}\Big(\int_0^{\eta} \theta(\zeta) f(\zeta) \Delta\zeta \Big)}{\Big(\int_{\sigma(\eta)}^{\infty} \check{\xi}(\zeta) \Delta\zeta \Big)^{\gamma}} \Delta\eta \geq \frac{1}{1-\gamma} \int_a^{\infty} \frac{\theta(\eta) g(\eta) \check{\Psi}'\Big(\int_0^{\eta} \theta(\zeta) \Delta\zeta \Big) \check{\Psi}'(f(\eta)) f(\eta)}{\Big(\int_{\eta}^{\infty} \check{\xi}(\zeta) \Delta\zeta \Big)^{\gamma-1}} \Delta\eta. \tag{42}$$

Proof. Due to nonincreasity of f, we have for $\eta \geq \lambda \geq 0$

$$\int_0^{\lambda} \theta(\zeta) f(\zeta) \Delta\zeta \geq f(\lambda) \int_0^{\lambda} \theta(\zeta) \Delta\zeta,$$

and thus,

$$\check{\Psi}\Big(\int_0^{\lambda} \theta(\zeta) f(\zeta) \Delta\zeta \Big) \geq \check{\Psi}\Big(f(\lambda) \int_0^{\lambda} \theta(\zeta) \Delta\zeta \Big) = \check{\Psi}(f(\lambda)) \check{\Psi}\Big(f(\lambda) \int_0^{\lambda} \theta(\zeta) \Delta\zeta \Big). \tag{43}$$

Applying the chain rule (23), there exists $c \in [\lambda, \sigma(\lambda)]$ such that

$$\Big[\check{\Psi}\Big(\int_0^{\lambda} \theta(\zeta) f(\zeta) \Delta\zeta \Big) \Big]^{\Delta} = \check{\Psi}'\Big(\int_0^{c} \theta(\zeta) f(\zeta) \Delta\zeta \Big) \Big(\int_0^{\lambda} \theta(\zeta) f(\zeta) \Delta\zeta \Big)^{\Delta}.$$

Since $c \geq \lambda$, $\check{\Psi}'$ is nondecreasing, $r \geq 1$ and $\Big(\int_0^{\lambda} \theta(\zeta) f(\zeta) \Delta\zeta \Big)^{\Delta} = \theta(\lambda) f(\lambda) \geq 0$, we get

$$\Big[\check{\Psi}\Big(\int_0^{\lambda} \theta(\zeta) f(\zeta) \Delta\zeta \Big) \Big]^{\Delta} \geq \theta(\lambda) f(\lambda) \check{\Psi}'\Big(\int_0^{\lambda} \theta(\zeta) f(\zeta) \Delta\zeta \Big). \tag{44}$$

Combining (43) with (44) gives

$$\Big[\check{\Psi}\Big(\int_0^{\lambda} \theta(\zeta) f(\zeta) \Delta\zeta \Big) \Big]^{\Delta} \geq \theta(\lambda) \check{\Psi}'\Big(\int_0^{\lambda} \theta(\zeta) \Delta\zeta \Big) \check{\Psi}'(f(\lambda)) f(\lambda),$$

and then

$$\frac{\check{\xi}(\eta)g(\eta)\left[\Psi\left(\int_0^\lambda \theta(\zeta)f(\zeta)\Delta\zeta\right)\right]^\Delta}{\left(\int_{\sigma(\eta)}^\infty \check{\xi}(\zeta)\Delta\zeta\right)^\gamma} \geq \frac{\check{\xi}(\eta)g(\eta)\theta(\lambda)\Psi'\left(\int_0^\lambda \theta(\zeta)\Delta\zeta\right)\Psi'(f(\lambda))f(\lambda)}{\left(\int_{\sigma(\eta)}^\infty \check{\xi}(\zeta)\Delta\zeta\right)^\gamma}.$$

Since g is nondecreasing and $\lambda \leq \eta$, we have $g(\lambda) \leq g(\eta)$ and thus,

$$\frac{\check{\xi}(\eta)g(\eta)\left[\Psi\left(\int_0^\lambda \theta(\zeta)f(\zeta)\Delta\zeta\right)\right]^\Delta}{\left(\int_{\sigma(\eta)}^\infty \check{\xi}(\zeta)\Delta\zeta\right)^\gamma} \geq \frac{\check{\xi}(\eta)g(\lambda)\theta(\lambda)\Psi'\left(\int_0^\lambda \theta(\zeta)\Delta\zeta\right)\Psi'(f(\lambda))f(\lambda)}{\left(\int_{\sigma(\eta)}^\infty \check{\xi}(\zeta)\Delta\zeta\right)^\gamma}.$$

Therefore,

$$\frac{\check{\xi}(\eta)g(\eta)\Psi\left(\int_0^\eta \theta(\zeta)f(\zeta)\Delta\zeta\right)}{\left(\int_{\sigma(\eta)}^\infty \check{\xi}(\zeta)\Delta\zeta\right)^\gamma} \geq \int_a^\eta \frac{\check{\xi}(\eta)\theta(\lambda)g(\lambda)\Psi'\left(\int_0^\lambda \theta(\zeta)\Delta\zeta\right)\Psi'(f(\lambda))f(\lambda)}{\left(\int_{\sigma(\eta)}^\infty \check{\xi}(\zeta)\Delta\zeta\right)^\gamma}\Delta\lambda.$$

Hence,

$$\begin{aligned}
&\int_a^\infty \frac{\check{\xi}(\eta)g(\eta)\Psi\left(\int_0^\eta \theta(\zeta)f(\zeta)\Delta\zeta\right)}{\left(\int_{\sigma(\eta)}^\infty \check{\xi}(\zeta)\Delta\zeta\right)^\gamma}\Delta\eta \\
&\geq \int_a^\infty \check{\xi}(\eta)\left(\int_{\sigma(\eta)}^\infty \check{\xi}(\zeta)\Delta\zeta\right)^{-\gamma}\left(\int_a^\eta \theta(\lambda)g(\lambda)\Psi'\left(\int_0^\lambda \theta(\zeta)\Delta\zeta\right)\Psi'(f(\lambda))f(\lambda)\Delta\lambda\right)\Delta\eta. \qquad (45)
\end{aligned}$$

Equation (45) can be reformulated as follows by using Fubini's theorem on time scales:

$$\begin{aligned}
&\int_a^\infty \frac{\check{\xi}(\eta)g(\eta)\Psi\left(\int_0^\eta \theta(\zeta)f(\zeta)\Delta\zeta\right)}{\left(\int_{\sigma(\eta)}^\infty \check{\xi}(\zeta)\Delta\zeta\right)^\gamma}\Delta\eta \\
&\geq \int_a^\infty \theta(\lambda)g(\lambda)\Psi'\left(\int_0^\lambda \theta(\zeta)\Delta\zeta\right)\Psi'(f(\lambda))f(\lambda)\left(\int_\lambda^\infty \check{\xi}(\eta)\left(\int_{\sigma(\eta)}^\infty \check{\xi}(\zeta)\Delta\zeta\right)^{-\gamma}\Delta\eta\right)\Delta\lambda. \qquad (46)
\end{aligned}$$

By recalling the chain rule (23), we can say there exists $c \in [\eta, \sigma(\eta)]$ such that

$$\left[-\left(\int_\eta^\infty \check{\xi}(\zeta)\Delta\zeta\right)^{1-\gamma}\right]^\Delta = -(1-\gamma)\left(\int_c^\infty \check{\xi}(\zeta)\Delta\zeta\right)^{-\gamma}\left(\int_\eta^\infty \check{\xi}(\zeta)\Delta\zeta\right)^\Delta.$$

Since $c \leq \sigma(\eta)$, $0 \leq \gamma < 1$ and $\left(\int_\eta^\infty \check{\xi}(\zeta)\Delta\zeta\right)^\Delta = -\check{\xi}(\eta) \leq 0$, we get

$$\left[-\left(\int_\eta^\infty \check{\xi}(\zeta)\Delta\zeta\right)^{1-\gamma}\right]^\Delta \leq (1-\gamma)\check{\xi}(\eta)\left(\int_{\sigma(\eta)}^\infty \check{\xi}(\zeta)\Delta\zeta\right)^{-\gamma}. \qquad (47)$$

Substituting (47) into (46) leads to

$$\int_a^\infty \frac{\check{\xi}(\eta)g(\eta)\Psi\left(\int_0^\eta \theta(\zeta)f(\zeta)\Delta\zeta\right)}{\left(\int_{\sigma(\eta)}^\infty \check{\xi}(\zeta)\Delta\zeta\right)^\gamma}\Delta\eta$$

$$\geq \frac{1}{1-\gamma}\int_a^\infty \theta(\lambda)g(\lambda)\Psi'\left(\int_0^\lambda \theta(\zeta)\Delta\zeta\right)\Psi'(f(\lambda))f(\lambda)\left(\int_\lambda^\infty \left[-\left(\int_\eta^\infty \check{\xi}(\zeta)\Delta\zeta\right)^{1-\gamma}\right]^\Delta \Delta\eta\right)\Delta\lambda$$

$$= \frac{1}{1-\gamma}\int_a^\infty \theta(\lambda)g(\lambda)\Psi'\left(\int_0^\lambda \theta(\zeta)\Delta\zeta\right)\Psi'(f(\lambda))f(\lambda)\left(\int_\lambda^\infty \check{\xi}(\zeta)\Delta\zeta\right)^{1-\gamma}\Delta\lambda,$$

which is our desired inequality (42). □

Remark 7. *In Theorem 21, if we take $\Psi(\eta) = \eta^r$, $\check{\xi}(\eta) = \theta(\eta)$ and $g(\eta) = 1$, then inequality* (42) *reduces to inequality* (22).

Corollary 14. *If $\mathbb{T} = \mathbb{R}$ in Theorem 21, and by considering, inequality* (42) *abbreviates to*

$$\int_a^\infty \frac{\check{\xi}(\eta)g(\eta)\Psi\left(\int_0^\eta \theta(\zeta)f(\zeta)d\zeta\right)}{\left(\int_\eta^\infty \check{\xi}(\zeta)d\zeta\right)^\gamma}d\eta \geq \frac{1}{1-\gamma}\int_a^\infty \frac{\theta(\eta)g(\eta)\Psi'\left(\int_0^\eta \theta(\zeta)d\zeta\right)\Psi'(f(\eta))f(\eta)}{\left(\int_\eta^\infty \check{\xi}(\zeta)d\zeta\right)^{\gamma-1}}d\eta.$$

Corollary 15. *If $\mathbb{T} = h\mathbb{Z}$ in Theorem 21, and by considering, inequality* (42) *abbreviates to*

$$\sum_{n=\frac{a}{h}}^\infty \frac{\check{\xi}(nh)g(nh)\Psi\left(h\sum_{m=0}^{\frac{n}{h}-1}\theta(mh)f(mh)\right)}{\left(h\sum_{m=\frac{n}{h}+1}^\infty \check{\xi}(mh)\right)^\gamma} \geq \frac{1}{1-\gamma}\sum_{n=\frac{a}{h}}^\infty \frac{\theta(nh)g(nh)\Psi'\left(h\sum_{m=0}^{\frac{a}{h}-1}\theta(mh)\right)\Psi'(f(nh))f(nh)}{\left(h\sum_{m=\frac{n}{h}}^\infty \check{\xi}(mh)\right)^{\gamma-1}}.$$

Corollary 16. *In Corollary 15, if we take $h = 1$, then, inequality* (42) *boils down to*

$$\sum_{n=a}^\infty \frac{\check{\xi}(n)g(n)\Psi\left(\sum_{m=0}^{n-1}\theta(m)f(m)\right)}{\left(\sum_{m=n+1}^\infty \check{\xi}(m)\right)^\gamma} \geq \frac{1}{1-\gamma}\sum_{n=a}^\infty \frac{\theta(n)g(n)\Psi'\left(\sum_{m=0}^{n-1}\theta(m)\right)\Psi'(f(n))f(n)}{\left(\sum_{m=n}^\infty \check{\xi}(m)\right)^{\gamma-1}}.$$

Corollary 17. *If $\mathbb{T} = \overline{q^{\mathbb{Z}}}$ in Theorem 21, and by considering, inequality* (42) *abbreviates to*

$$\sum_{n=(\log_q a)}^\infty \frac{q^n\check{\xi}(q^n)g(q^n)\Psi\left((q-1)\sum_{m=0}^{(\log_q n)-1} q^m h(q^m)f(q^m)\right)}{\left((q-1)\sum_{m=(\log_q n)+1}^\infty q^m\check{\xi}(q^m)\right)^\gamma}$$

$$\geq \frac{1}{1-\gamma}\sum_{n=(\log_q a)}^\infty \frac{q^n h(q^n)g(q^n)\Psi'\left((q-1)\sum_{m=0}^{(\log_q n)-1} q^m h(q^m)\right)\Psi'(f(q^n))f(q^n)}{\left((q-1)\sum_{m=(\log_q n)}^\infty q^m\check{\xi}(q^m)\right)^{\gamma-1}}.$$

3. Conclusions

In this paper, with the help of Fubini's theorem as well as a straightforward outcome of Keller's chain rule on time scales, we generalized some reverse Hardy-type inequalities to a general time scale. Moreover, we generalized a number of other inequalities to a general time scale. We obtained the discrete and the continuous inequalities as special cases of our main results.

Author Contributions: Conceptualization, A.A.E.-D. and C.C.; formal analysis, A.A.E.-D. and C.C.; investigation, A.A.E.-D. and C.C.; writing—original draft preparation, A.A.E.-D. and C.C.; writing—review and editing, A.A.E.-D. and C.C. All authors have read and agreed to the published version of the manuscript.

Funding: This research received no external funding.

Institutional Review Board Statement: Not applicable.

Informed Consent Statement: Not applicable.

Data Availability Statement: Not applicable.

Conflicts of Interest: The authors declare no conflict of interest.

References

1. Hardy, G.H. Note on a theorem of Hilbert. *Math. Z.* **1920**, *6*, 314–317. [CrossRef]
2. Hardy, G.H. Notes on some points in the integral calculus (LX). *Messenger Math.* **1925**, *54*, 150–156.
3. Littlewood, J.E.; Hardy, G.H. Elementary theorems concerning power series with positive coefficients and moment constants of positive functions. *J. Reine Angew. Math.* **1927**, *157*, 141–158.
4. Hardy, G.H. Notes on some points in the integral calculus (LXIT). *Messenger Math.* **1928**, *57*, 12–16.
5. Copson, E.T. Note on Series of Positive Terms. *J. Lond. Math. Soc.* **1928**, *3*, 49–51. [CrossRef]
6. Leindler, L. Generalization of inequalities of Hardy and Littlewood. *Acta Sci. Math.* **1970**, *31*, 279–285.
7. Copson, E.T. Some integral inequalities. *Proc. R. Soc. Edinb. Sect. A* **1976**, *75*, 157–164. [CrossRef]
8. Lyons, R. A lower bound on the Cesàro operator. *Proc. Am. Math. Soc.* **1982**, *86*, 694. [CrossRef]
9. Renaud, P.F. A reversed Hardy inequality. *Bull. Austral. Math. Soc.* **1986**, *34*, 225–232. [CrossRef]
10. Leindler, L. Further sharpening of inequalities of Hardy and Littlewood. *Acta Sci. Math.* **1990**, *54*, 285–289.
11. Hilger, S. Analysis on measure chains–a unified approach to continuous and discrete calculus. *Results Math.* **1990**, *18*, 18–56. [CrossRef]
12. Bohner, M.; Peterson, A. *Dynamic Equations on Time Scales. An Introduction with Applications*; Birkhäuser Boston, Inc.: Boston, MA, USA, 2001; p. x+358.
13. Bohner, M.; Peterson, A. (Eds.) *Advances in Dynamic Equations on Time Scales*; Birkhäuser Boston, Inc.: Boston, MA, USA, 2003; p. xii+348.
14. Řehák, P. Hardy inequality on time scales and its application to half-linear dynamic equations. *J. Inequal. Appl.* **2005**, *2005*, 495–507. [CrossRef]
15. Agarwal, R.P.; Mahmoud, R.R.; O'Regan, D.; Saker, S.H. Some reverse dynamic inequalities on time scales. *Bull. Aust. Math. Soc.* **2017**, *96*, 445–454. [CrossRef]
16. El-Deeb, A.A.; El-Sennary, H.A.; Khan, Z.A. Some reverse inequalities of Hardy type on time scales. *Adv. Differ. Equ.* **2020**, *2020*, 402. [CrossRef]
17. Donchev, T.; Nosheen, A.; Pečarić, J. Hardy-type inequalities on time scale via convexity in several variables. *ISRN Math. Anal.* **2013**, *2013*, 903196. [CrossRef]
18. Agarwal, R.P.; O'Regan, D.; Saker, S.H. *Hardy Type Inequalities on Time Scales*; Springer: Cham, Switzerland, 2016; p. x+305.
19. El-Deeb, A.A.; Makharesh, S.D.; Askar, S.S.; Awrejcewicz, J. A variety of Nabla Hardy's type inequality on time scales. *Mathematics* **2022**, *10*, 722. [CrossRef]
20. El-Deeb, A.A.; Baleanu, D. Some new dynamic Gronwall-Bellman-Pachpatte type inequalities with delay on time scales and certain applications. *J. Inequal. Appl.* **2022**, *2022*, 45. [CrossRef]
21. El-Deeb, A.A.; Moaaz, O.; Baleanu, D.; Askar, S.S. A variety of dynamic α-conformable Steffensen-type inequality on a time scale measure space. *AIMS Math.* **2022**, *7*, 11382–11398. [CrossRef]
22. El-Deeb, A.A.; Akin, E.; Kaymakcalan, B. Generalization of Mitrinović-Pečarić inequalities on time scales. *Rocky Mt. J. Math.* **2021**, *51*, 1909–1918. [CrossRef]
23. El-Deeb, A.A.; Makharesh, S.D.; Nwaeze, E.R.; Iyiola, O.S.; Baleanu, D. On nabla conformable fractional Hardy-type inequalities on arbitrary time scales. *J. Inequal. Appl.* **2021**, *2021*, 192. [CrossRef]
24. El-Deeb, A.A.; Awrejcewicz, J. Novel Fractional Dynamic Hardy–Hilbert-Type Inequalities on Time Scales with Applications. *Mathematics* **2021**, *9*, 2964. [CrossRef]
25. Kh, F.M.; El-Deeb, A.A.; Abdeldaim, A.; Khan, Z.A. On some generalizations of dynamic Opial-type inequalities on time scales. *Adv. Differ. Equ.* **2019**, *2019*, 323. [CrossRef]

26. Tian, Y.; El-Deeb, A.A.; Meng, F. Some nonlinear delay Volterra-Fredholm type dynamic integral inequalities on time scales. *Discret. Dyn. Nat. Soc.* **2018**, *2018*, 5841985. [CrossRef]
27. El-Deeb, A.A. Some Gronwall-Bellman type inequalities on time scales for Volterra-Fredholm dynamic integral equations. *J. Egypt. Math. Soc.* **2018**, *26*, 1–17. [CrossRef]
28. El-Deeb, A.A.; Rashid, S. On some new double dynamic inequalities associated with Leibniz integral rule on time scales. *Adv. Differ. Equ.* **2021**, *2021*, 125. [CrossRef]
29. El-Deeb, A.A.; Xu, H.; Abdeldaim, A.; Wang, G. Some dynamic inequalities on time scales and their applications. *Adv. Differ. Equ.* **2019**, *2019*, 130. [CrossRef]
30. Bibi, R.; Bohner, M.; Pečarić, J.; Varošanec, S. Minkowski and Beckenbach-Dresher inequalities and functionals on time scales. *J. Math. Inequal.* **2013**, *7*, 299–312. [CrossRef]

axioms

MDPI

Article

Pointwise Wavelet Estimations for a Regression Model in Local Hölder Space

Junke Kou, Qinmei Huang and Huijun Guo *

School of Mathematics and Computational Science, Guilin University of Electronic Technology, Guilin 541004, China; kjkou@guet.edu.cn (J.K.); hqm353474937@163.com (Q.H.)
* Correspondence: gkmath17@163.com

Abstract: This paper considers an unknown functional estimation problem in a regression model with multiplicative and additive noise. A linear wavelet estimator is first constructed by a wavelet projection operator. The convergence rate under the pointwise error of linear wavelet estimators is studied in local Hölder space. A nonlinear wavelet estimator is provided by the hard thresholding method in order to obtain an adaptive estimator. The convergence rate of the nonlinear estimator is the same as the linear estimator up to a logarithmic term. Finally, it should be pointed out that the convergence rates of two wavelet estimators are consistent with the optimal convergence rate on pointwise nonparametric estimation.

Keywords: nonparametric estimation; pointwise error; local Hölder space; wavelet

MSC: 62G07; 62G20; 42C40

Citation: Kou, J.; Huang, Q.; Guo, H. Pointwise Wavelet Estimations for a Regression Model in Local Hölder Space. *Axioms* **2022**, *11*, 466. https://doi.org/10.3390/axioms11090466

Academic Editor: Yurii Kharkevych

Received: 26 July 2022
Accepted: 6 September 2022
Published: 10 September 2022

1. Introduction

The classical regression model plays an important role in many practical applications. The definition of this model is shown by $Y_i = f(X_i) + \varepsilon_i, i \in \{1, \ldots, n\}$. The aim of this conventional regression model is to estimate the unknown regression function $f(x)$ by observed data $(X_1, Y_1), \ldots, (X_n, Y_n)$. For this classical regression model, many important and interesting results have been obtained by Hart [1], Kerkyacharian and Picard [2], Chesneau [3], Reiß [4], Yuan and Zhou [5], and Wang and Politis [6].

Recently, Chesneau et al. [7] studied the following regression model

$$Y_i = f(X_i)U_i + V_i, i \in \{1, \ldots, n\}, \tag{1}$$

where $(X_1, Y_1), \ldots, (X_n, Y_n)$ are independent and identically distributed random variables, f is an unknown function defined on $\Delta \subseteq \mathbb{R}$, $U_1, \ldots, U_n$ are n identically distributed random vectors, $X_1, \ldots, X_n$ and $V_1, \ldots, V_n$ are identically distributed random variables. Moreover, X_i and U_i are independent, U_i and V_i are independent for any $i \in \{1, \ldots, n\}$. The aim of this model is to estimate the unknown function $r(x) (r := f^2)$ by the observed data $(X_1, Y_1), \ldots, (X_n, Y_n)$.

For the above model (1), it reduces to the classical regression model when $U_i \equiv 1$. In other words, (1) can be viewed as an extension of the classical regression problem. In addition, model (1) becomes the classical heteroscedastic regression model when V_i is a function of X_i ($V_i = g(X_i)$). Then, the function $r(x) (r := f^2)$ is called a variance function in a heteroscedastic regression model, which plays a crucial role in financial and economic fields (Cai and Wang [8], Alharbi and Patili [9]). Furthermore, the regression model (1) is also widely used in Global Positioning Systems (Huang et al. [10]), Image processing (Kravchenko et al. [11], Cui [12]), and so on.

For this regression model, Chesneau et al. [7] propose two wavelet estimators and discuss convergence rates under the mean integrated square error over Besov space. However, this study only focuses on the global error of wavelet estimators. There is a lack of pointwise risk estimation for this model. In this paper, two new wavelet estimators are constructed, and the convergence rates over the pointwise error of wavelet estimators in local Hölder space are considered. More importantly, those wavelet estimators can all obtain the optimal convergence rate under pointwise error.

2. Assumptions, Local Hölder Space and Wavelet

In this paper, we will consider model (1) with $\Delta = [0,1]$. Additional technical assumptions are formulated below.

- A1:Y_i is bounded for any $i \in \{1, \ldots, n\}$.
- A2:$X_1 \sim U(0,1)$.
- A3:$U_1 \sim N(0,1)$.
- A4:V_1 has a moment of order 2.
- A5:X_i and V_i are independent for any $i \in \{1, \ldots, n\}$.
- A6:$V_i = g(X_i)$, where $g\colon [0,1] \to \mathbb{R}$ is known and bounded.

For the above assumptions, it is easy to see that A5 and A6 are reversed. Hence, we will define the following two sets, H1 and H2, of the above assumptions

H1:={A1,A2,A3,A4,A5},
H2:={A1,A2,A3,A4,A6}.

Note that the difference between H1 and H2 is the relationship between V_i and X_i. Since the above assumptions are separated into two sets, H1 and H2; the estimators of the function $r(x)$ should be constructed under different condition sets, respectively.

This paper will consider nonparametric pointwise estimation in local Hölder space. Now, we introduce the concept of local Hölder space. Recall the classic Hölder condition $H^\delta(\mathbb{R})(0 < \delta < 1)$,

$$|f(y) - f(x)| \leq C|y - x|^\delta, x, y \in \mathbb{R}.$$

Let Ω_{x_0} be a neighborhood of $x_0 \in \mathbb{R}$ and a function space $H^\delta(\Omega_{x_0})(0 < \delta \leq 1)$ be defined as

$$H^\delta(\Omega_{x_0}) = \left\{f\colon |f(y) - f(x)| \leq C|y - x|^\delta, x, y \in \Omega_{x_0}\right\},$$

where $C > 0$ is a fixed constant. Clearly, $f \in H^\delta(\mathbb{R})$ must be contained in $H^\delta(\Omega_{x_0})$. However, the converse does not hold.

For $s = N + \delta > 0$ with $\delta \in (0,1]$ and $N \in \mathbb{N}$ (the nonnegative integer set), we define the local Hölder space as

$$H^s(\Omega_{x_0}) = \left\{f\colon f^{(N)} \in H^\delta(\Omega_{x_0})\right\}.$$

Furthermore, it follows from the definition of $H^s(\Omega_{x_0})$ that $H^s(\Omega_{x_0}) \subseteq L^2(\mathbb{R})$.

In order to construct wavelet estimators in later sections, we introduce some basic theories of wavelets.

Definition 1. *A multiresolution analysis (MRA) is a sequence of closed subspaces $\{V_j\}_{j\in\mathbb{Z}}$ of the square-integrable function space $L^2(\mathbb{R})$ satisfying the following properties:*
(i) $V_j \subseteq V_{j+1}$;
(ii) $\overline{\bigcup_{j\in\mathbb{Z}} V_j} = L^2(\mathbb{R})$(the space $\bigcup_{j\in\mathbb{Z}} V_j$ is dense in $L^2(\mathbb{R})$);
(iii) $f(2\cdot) \in V_{j+1}$ if and only if $f(\cdot) \in V_j$ for each $j \in \mathbb{Z}$;
(iv) There exists $\phi \in L^2(\mathbb{R})$ (scaling function) such that $\{\phi(\cdot - k), k \in \mathbb{Z}\}$ forms an orthonormal basis of $V_0 = \overline{span}\{\phi(\cdot - k)\}$.

Let ϕ be a scaling function, and ψ be a wavelet function such that

$$\{\phi_{j_*,k}, \psi_{j,k}, j \geq j_*, k \in \mathbb{Z}\}$$

constitutes an orthonormal basis of $L^2(\mathbb{R})$, *where* j_* *is a positive integer,* $\phi_{j_*,k} = 2^{\frac{j_*}{2}}\phi(2^{j_*}x - k)$ *and* $\psi_{j,k} = 2^{\frac{j}{2}}\psi(2^j x - k)$. *In this paper, we choose the Daubechies wavelets. Then for any* $h(x) \in H^s(\Omega_{x_0})$, *it has the following expansion*

$$h(x) = \sum_{k\in\mathbb{Z}} \alpha_{j_*,k}\phi_{j_*,k}(x) + \sum_{j\geq j_*}\sum_{k\in\mathbb{Z}} \beta_{j,k}\psi_{j,k}(x),$$

where $\alpha_{j,k} = \langle h, \phi_{j,k}\rangle$, $\beta_{j,k} = \langle h, \psi_{j,k}\rangle$. *Further details can be found in Meyer [13] and Daubechies [14].*

Let P_j *be the orthogonal projection operator from* $L^2(\mathbb{R})$ *onto the space* V_j *with the orthonormal basis* $\left\{\phi_{j,k}(\cdot) = 2^{\frac{j}{2}}\phi(2^j\cdot - k), k \in \mathbb{Z}\right\}$. *Then for* $h(x) \in H^s(\Omega_{x_0})$ *and* $\alpha_{j,k} = \langle h, \phi_{j,k}\rangle$,

$$P_j h(x) = \sum_{k\in Z} \alpha_{j,k}\phi_{j,k}(x).$$

In this position, we give an important lemma, which will be used in later discussions. Here and after, we adopt the following symbol: $A \lesssim B$ *denotes* $A \leq cB$ *for some constant* $c > 0$; $A \gtrsim B$ *means* $B \lesssim A$; $A \sim B$ *stand for both* $A \lesssim B$ *and* $B \lesssim A$.

Lemma 1 (Liu and Wu [15]). *If* $f \in H^s(\Omega_{x_0})$, $s > 0$ *with* $s = N + \delta(0 < \delta \leq 1)$, *then for* $x \in \Omega_{x_0}$ *and* $j_* \in \mathbb{N}$,

(i) $\sup\limits_{f\in H^s(\Omega_{x_0})} \sum\limits_{k\in\mathbb{Z}} \left|\beta_{j,k}\psi_{j,k}(x)\right| \lesssim 2^{-js}$;

(ii) $f(x) = \sum\limits_{k\in\mathbb{Z}} \alpha_{j_*,k}\phi_{j_*,k}(x) + \sum\limits_{j\geq j_*}\sum\limits_{k\in\mathbb{Z}} \beta_{j,k}\psi_{j,k}$;

(iii) $\sup\limits_{f\in H^s(\Omega_{x_0})} \left|f(x) - P_{j_*}f(x)\right| \lesssim 2^{-j_* s}$.

3. Linear Wavelet Estimator

In this section, a linear wavelet estimator is given by using the wavelet method, and the order of pointwise convergence of this estimator is studied in local Hölder space. Now we define our linear wavelet estimator

$$\hat{r}_n^{lin}(x) = \sum_k \hat{\alpha}_{j_*,k}\phi_{j_*,k}(x), \tag{2}$$

where

$$\hat{\alpha}_{j_*,k} = \frac{1}{n}\sum_{i=1}^{n} Y_i^2\phi_{j_*,k}(X_i) - v_{j_*,k}, \tag{3}$$

$$v_{j_*,k} = \begin{cases} \mathbb{E}[V_1^2]2^{-j_*/2}, & \text{A5}, \\ \int_0^1 g^2(x)\phi_{j_*,k}(x)dx, & \text{A6}. \end{cases} \tag{4}$$

According to the definition of $v_{j_*,k}$, it is clear that the structure of this linear wavelet estimator depends on the reverse conditions of A5 and A6. Some of the lemmas needed in this section and their proofs are given below.

Lemma 2. *For model (1), if H1 or H2 hold,*

$$\mathbb{E}[\hat{\alpha}_{j_*,k}] = \alpha_{j_*,k}. \tag{5}$$

Proof. According to the definition of $\hat{\alpha}_{j_*,k}$,

$$\begin{aligned}\mathbb{E}[\hat{\alpha}_{j_*,k}] &= \mathbb{E}\left[\frac{1}{n}\sum_{i=1}^{n} Y_i^2\phi_{j_*,k}(X_i) - v_{j_*,k}\right] \\ &= \mathbb{E}\left[Y_1^2\phi_{j_*,k}(X_1)\right] - v_{j_*,k} \\ &= \mathbb{E}\left[r(X_1)U_1^2\phi_{j_*,k}(X_1)\right] + 2\mathbb{E}[f(X_1)U_1V_1\phi_{j_*,k}(X_1)] + \mathbb{E}\left[V_1^2\phi_{j_*,k}(X_1)\right] - v_{j_*,k}.\end{aligned}$$

Since U_i is independent from X_i and V_i, respectively,

$$\mathbb{E}[f(X_1)U_1V_1\phi_{j_*,k}(X_1)] = \mathbb{E}[U_1]\mathbb{E}[f(X_1)V_1\phi_{j_*,k}(X_1)].$$

In addition, condition A3 implies that $\mathbb{E}[U_1] = 0$. Then one gets

$$\mathbb{E}[f(X_1)U_1V_1\phi_{j_*,k}(X_1)] = 0.$$

It follows from A5, A2 and A4 that

$$\mathbb{E}[V_1^2]\mathbb{E}[\phi_{j_*,k}(X_1)] = \mathbb{E}\left[V_1^2\right]\int_0^1 \phi_{j_*,k}(x)dx = \mathbb{E}[V_1^2]2^{-\frac{j_*}{2}} = v_{j_*,k}.$$

On the other hand, we obtain

$$\mathbb{E}\left[V_1^2\phi_{j_*,k}(X_1)\right] = \int_0^1 g^2(x)\phi_{j_*,k}(x)dx = v_{j_*,k}$$

with condition A6.

Finally, according to the assumption of A3 and A2,

$$\mathbb{E}[\hat{\alpha}_{j_*,k}] = \mathbb{E}[U_1^2]\mathbb{E}[r(X_1)\phi_{j_*,k}(X_1)] = \int_0^1 r(x)\phi_{j_*,k}(x)dx = \alpha_{j_*,k}.$$

□

In order to estimate $\mathbb{E}\left[\left|\hat{\alpha}_{j_*,k} - \alpha_{j_*,k}\right|^p\right]$, we need the following Rosenthal's inequality.

Rosenthal's inequality Let $X_1, \ldots, X_n$ be independent random variables such that $\mathbb{E}[X_i] = 0$ and $|X_i| \leq M (i = 1, 2, \ldots, n)$,

(i) $\mathbb{E}\left[\left|\sum\limits_{i=1}^{n} X_i\right|^p\right] \lesssim \left(M^{p-2}\sum\limits_{i=1}^{n}\mathbb{E}[X_i^2] + \left(\sum\limits_{i=1}^{n}\mathbb{E}[X_i^2]\right)^{p/2}\right), p > 2;$

(ii) $\mathbb{E}\left[\left|\sum\limits_{i=1}^{n} X_i\right|^p\right] \lesssim \left(\sum\limits_{i=1}^{n}\mathbb{E}[X_i^2]\right)^{p/2}, 0 < p \leq 2.$

Lemma 3. *Let $\hat{\alpha}_{j_*,k}$ be defined by (3). If H1 or H2 hold and $2^{j_*} \leq n$, then for $1 \leq p < \infty$,*

$$\mathbb{E}\left[\left|\hat{\alpha}_{j_*,k} - \alpha_{j_*,k}\right|^p\right] \lesssim n^{-p/2}. \tag{6}$$

Proof. By (5) and the definition of $\hat{\alpha}_{j_*,k}$,

$$\begin{aligned}|\hat{\alpha}_{j_*,k} - \alpha_{j_*,k}| &= \left|\frac{1}{n}\sum_{i=1}^{n} Y_i^2\phi_{j_*,k}(X_i) - v_{j_*,k} - \mathbb{E}\left[\frac{1}{n}\sum_{i=1}^{n} Y_i^2\phi_{j_*,k}(X_i) - v_{j_*,k}\right]\right| \\ &= \frac{1}{n}\left|\sum_{i=1}^{n}(Y_i^2\phi_{j_*,k}(X_i) - \mathbb{E}\left[Y_i^2\phi_{j_*,k}(X_i)\right])\right| = \frac{1}{n}\left|\sum_{i=1}^{n} Z_i\right| \end{aligned} \tag{7}$$

with $Z_i := Y_i^2\phi_{j_*,k}(X_i) - \mathbb{E}[Y_i^2\phi_{j_*,k}(X_i)]$. It is clear that $\mathbb{E}[Z_i] = 0$. Using the definition of Z_i and A1, there exists a constant $c > 0$ such that

$$|Z_i| = \left|Y_i^2\phi_{j_*,k}(X_i) - \mathbb{E}\left[Y_i^2\phi_{j_*,k}(X_i)\right]\right| \leq \left|Y_i^2\phi_{j_*,k}(X_i)\right| + \left|\mathbb{E}\left[Y_i^2\phi_{j_*,k}(X_i)\right]\right| \leq c2^{\frac{j_*}{2}} \lesssim 2^{\frac{j_*}{2}}.$$

When $p > 2$, according to Rosenthal's inequality,

$$\begin{aligned}\mathbb{E}\left[\left|\sum_{i=1}^{n} Z_i\right|^p\right] &\lesssim \left(M^{p-2}\sum_{i=1}^{n}\mathbb{E}\left[Z_i^2\right] + \left(\sum_{i=1}^{n}\mathbb{E}\left[Z_i^2\right]\right)^{\frac{p}{2}}\right) \\ &\lesssim (2^{\frac{j_*}{2}})^{p-2}\sum_{i=1}^{n}\mathbb{E}\left[Z_i^2\right] + \left(\sum_{i=1}^{n}\mathbb{E}\left[Z_i^2\right]\right)^{\frac{p}{2}}. \end{aligned} \tag{8}$$

Note that $\mathbb{E}\left[Z_i^2\right] = Var[Z_i] = Var\left[Y_i^2\phi_{j_*,k}(X_i) - \mathbb{E}[Y_i^2\phi_{j_*,k}(X_i)]\right] = Var\left[Y_i^2\phi_{j_*,k}(X_i)\right] \leq \mathbb{E}\left[Y_i^4\phi_{j_*,k}^2(X_i)\right]$. Furthermore, it follows from A1 and the property of $\phi_{j_*,k}$ that

$$\mathbb{E}\left[Z_i^2\right] \lesssim \mathbb{E}\left[Y_i^4\phi_{j_*,k}^2(X_i)\right] \lesssim 1.$$

Then it can be easily seen that

$$\left(\sum_{i=1}^{n}\mathbb{E}\left[Z_i^2\right]\right)^{p/2} \lesssim n^{\frac{p}{2}}. \tag{9}$$

By (8) and (9), we obtain

$$\mathbb{E}\left[\left|\sum_{i=1}^{n} Z_i\right|^p\right] \lesssim (2^{\frac{j_*}{2}})^{p-2}n + n^{\frac{p}{2}}. \tag{10}$$

When $1 \leq p < 2$,

$$\mathbb{E}\left[\left|\sum_{i=1}^{n} Z_i\right|^p\right] \lesssim \left(\sum_{i=1}^{n}\mathbb{E}\left[Z_i^2\right]\right)^{p/2}.$$

Hence,

$$\mathbb{E}\left[\left|\sum_{i=1}^{n} Z_i\right|^p\right] \lesssim n^{\frac{p}{2}}. \tag{11}$$

It follows from (7), (10) and (11) that

$$\mathbb{E}\left[|\hat{\alpha}_{j_*,k} - \alpha_{j_*,k}|^p\right] \lesssim \mathbb{E}\left[\left(\frac{1}{n}\left|\sum_{i=1}^{n} Z_i\right|\right)^p\right] = \frac{1}{n^p}\mathbb{E}\left[\left|\sum_{i=1}^{n} Z_i\right|^p\right].$$

Hence,

$$\mathbb{E}\left[|\hat{\alpha}_{j_*,k} - \alpha_{j_*,k}|^p\right] \lesssim \begin{cases} \frac{1}{n^p}[(2^{\frac{j_*}{2}})^{p-2} \cdot n + n^{\frac{p}{2}}], & p \geq 2, \\ n^{-\frac{p}{2}}, & 1 \leq p < 2. \end{cases} \tag{12}$$

This with $2^{j_*} \leq n$ implies that

$$\mathbb{E}[|\hat{\alpha}_{j_*,k} - \alpha_{j_*,k}|^p] \lesssim n^{-\frac{p}{2}}.$$

□

Now the convergence rate of the linear wavelet estimator is proved in the following.

Theorem 1. *Let $r \in H^s(\Omega_{x_0})$ with $s > 0$. Then for each $1 \le p < \infty$, the linear wavelet estimator $\hat{r}_n^{lin}(x)$ defined in (2) with $2^{j_*} \sim n^{\frac{1}{2s+1}}$ satisfies*

$$\sup_{r \in H^s(\Omega_{x_0})} \left\{ \mathbb{E}\left[|\hat{r}_n^{lin}(x_0) - r(x_0)|^p \right] \right\}^{\frac{1}{p}} \lesssim n^{-\frac{s}{2s+1}}.$$

Remark 1. *Note that $n^{-\frac{s}{2s+1}}$ is the optimal convergence rate over pointwise error for nonparametric functional estimation (Brown and Low [16]). The above result yields that the linear wavelet estimator can obtain the optimal convergence rate.*

Proof. The triangular inequality gives

$$\begin{aligned} \left\{ \mathbb{E}\left[\left| \hat{r}_n^{lin}(x_0) - r(x_0) \right|^p \right] \right\}^{\frac{1}{p}} &\lesssim \left\{ \mathbb{E}\left[\left| \hat{r}_n^{lin}(x_0) - P_{j_*} r(x_0) \right|^p + \left| P_{j_*} r(x_0) - r(x_0) \right|^p \right] \right\}^{\frac{1}{p}} \\ &\lesssim \left\{ \mathbb{E}\left[\left| \hat{r}_n^{lin}(x_0) - P_{j_*} r(x_0) \right|^p \right] \right\}^{\frac{1}{p}} \\ &\quad + \left| P_{j_*} r(x_0) - r(x_0) \right|. \end{aligned} \tag{13}$$

- The bias term $\left| P_{j_*} r(x_0) - r(x_0) \right|$. According to Lemma 1,

$$\left| P_{j_*} r(x_0) - r(x_0) \right| \lesssim 2^{-j_* s}. \tag{14}$$

- The stochastic term $\left\{ \mathbb{E}\left[\left| \hat{r}_n^{lin}(x_0) - P_{j_*} r(x_0) \right|^p \right] \right\}^{\frac{1}{p}}$. Note that

$$\begin{aligned} \mathbb{E}\left[\left| \hat{r}_n^{lin}(x_0) - P_{j_*} r(x_0) \right|^p \right] &= \mathbb{E}\left[\left| \sum_{k \in \Lambda_{j_*}} \left(\hat{\alpha}_{j_*,k} - \alpha_{j_*,k} \right) \phi_{j_*,k}(x_0) \right|^p \right] \\ &\le \mathbb{E}\left[\left\{ \sum_{k \in \Lambda_{j_*}} \left| \hat{\alpha}_{j_*,k} - \alpha_{j_*,k} \right| \left| \phi_{j_*,k}(x_0) \right|^{\frac{1}{p}} \left| \phi_{j_*,k}(x_0) \right|^{\frac{1}{p'}} \right\}^p \right] \end{aligned}$$

with $\frac{1}{p} + \frac{1}{p'} = 1$. According to the Hölder inequality, Lemma 3 and $\sum_{k \in \Lambda_{j_*}} \left| \phi_{j_*,k} \right| \lesssim 2^{j_*/2}$, the above inequality reduces to

$$\begin{aligned} &\mathbb{E}\left[\left| \hat{r}_n^{lin}(x_0) - P_{j_*} r(x_0) \right|^p \right] \\ &\le \mathbb{E}\left[\left\{ \left(\sum_{k \in \Lambda_{j_*}} \left| \hat{\alpha}_{j_*,k} - \alpha_{j_*,k} \right|^p \left| \phi_{j_*,k}(x_0) \right| \right)^{\frac{1}{p}} \left(\sum_{k \in \Lambda_{j_*}} \left| \phi_{j_*,k}(x_0) \right| \right)^{\frac{1}{p'}} \right\}^p \right] \\ &\lesssim \sum_{k \in \Lambda_{j_*}} \mathbb{E}\left[\left| \hat{\alpha}_{j_*,k} - \alpha_{j_*,k} \right|^p \left| \phi_{j_*,k}(x_0) \right| \right] 2^{\frac{j_* p}{2p'}} \\ &\lesssim \left(\frac{1}{n} \right)^{\frac{p}{2}} 2^{\frac{j_*}{2}\left(1 + \frac{p}{p'}\right)} = \left(\frac{2^{j_*}}{n} \right)^{\frac{p}{2}} \end{aligned} \tag{15}$$

Combining (13), (14) and (15), one has

$$\left\{ \mathbb{E}\left[\left| \hat{r}_n^{lin}(x_0) - r(x_0) \right|^p \right] \right\}^{1/p} \le 2^{-j_* s} + \left(\frac{2^{j_*}}{n} \right)^{\frac{1}{2}}.$$

Furthermore, by the given choice $2^{j_*} \sim n^{\frac{1}{2s+1}}$,

$$\sup_{r\in H^s(\Omega_{x_0})} \left\{\mathbb{E}\left[|\hat{r}_n^{lin}(x_0) - r(x_0)|^p\right]\right\}^{\frac{1}{p}} \lesssim n^{-\frac{s}{2s+1}}.$$

□

4. Nonlinear Wavelet Estimator

According to the definition of the linear wavelet estimator, we can easily find that the scale parameter j_* of the linear wavelet estimator depends on the smooth parameter s of the function $r(x)$ to be estimated, so the linear estimator is not adaptive. In this section, we will solve this problem by constructing a nonlinear wavelet estimator with the hard thresholding method.

Now we define our nonlinear wavelet estimator

$$\hat{r}_n^{non}(x) = \sum_{k\in\Lambda_{j_*}} \hat{\alpha}_{j_*,k}\phi_{j_*,k}(x) + \sum_{j=j_*}^{j_1}\sum_{k\in\Lambda_j} \hat{\beta}_{j,k} I_{\{|\hat{\beta}_{j,k}|\geq \kappa t_n\}}\psi_{j,k}(x), x \in [0,1], \tag{16}$$

where $\hat{\alpha}_{j_*,k}$ is defined by (3),

$$\hat{\beta}_{j,k} := \frac{1}{n}\sum_{i=1}^{n} Y_i^2 \psi_{j,k}(X_i) - w_{j,k}, \tag{17}$$

$$w_{j,k} := \begin{cases} 0, & \text{A5}, \\ \int_0^1 g^2(x)\psi_{j,k}(x)dx, & \text{A6}, \end{cases} \tag{18}$$

and $t_n = \sqrt{\ln n/n}$, I_G denotes the indicator function over an event G. The positive integer j_*, j_1, and κ will be given in Theorem 2.

Remark 2. *Compared with the structure of $\hat{\beta}_{j,k}$ in Chesneau et al. [7], the definition of $\hat{\beta}_{j,k}$ in this paper does not need a thresholding algorithm. In other words, this paper reduces the complexity of the nonlinear wavelet estimator.*

Lemma 4. *For model (1), if H1 or H2 hold, then*

$$\mathbb{E}\left[\hat{\beta}_{j,k}\right] = \beta_{j,k}.$$

Lemma 5. *Let $\hat{\beta}_{j,k}$ be defined by (17). If H1 or H2 hold and $2^j \leq n$, then for $1 \leq p < \infty$,*

$$\mathbb{E}\left[|\hat{\beta}_{j,k} - \beta_{j,k}|^p\right] \lesssim n^{-p/2}.$$

The proof methods of Lemmas 4 and 5 are similar to that of Lemmas 2 and 3, so the proofs are omitted here. For nonlinear wavelet estimation, Bernstein's inequality plays a crucial role.

Bernstein's inequality Let $X_1, \ldots, X_n$ be independent random variables such that $\mathbb{E}[X_i] = 0$, $|X_i| \leq M$ and $\mathbb{E}[X_i^2] = \sigma^2$, then for each $v > 0$

$$\mathbb{P}\left(\frac{1}{n}\left|\sum_{i=1}^{n} X_i\right| \geq v\right) \leq 2\exp\left\{-\frac{nv^2}{2(\sigma^2 + \frac{vM}{3})}\right\}.$$

Lemma 6. *Let $\hat{\beta}_{j,k}$ be defined by (17), $t_n = \sqrt{\frac{\ln n}{n}}$ and $2^j \leq \frac{n}{\ln n}$. If H1 or H2 hold, then for each $w > 0$, there exists a constant $\kappa > 1$ such that*

$$\mathbb{P}(|\hat{\beta}_{j,k} - \beta_{j,k}| \geq \kappa t_n) \lesssim 2^{-wj}.$$

Proof. According to the definition of $\hat{\beta}_{j,k}$,

$$\begin{aligned}
|\hat{\beta}_{j,k} - \beta_{j,k}| &= \left|\frac{1}{n}\sum_{i=1}^{n} Y_i^2 \psi_{j,k}(X_i) - w_{j,k} - \mathbb{E}\left[\frac{1}{n}\sum_{i=1}^{n} Y_i^2 \psi_{j,k}(X_i) - w_{j,k}\right]\right| \\
&= \left|\frac{1}{n}\sum_{i=1}^{n} Y_i^2 \psi_{j,k}(X_i) - \mathbb{E}\left[\frac{1}{n}\sum_{i=1}^{n} Y_i^2 \psi_{j,k}(X_i)\right]\right| \\
&= \frac{1}{n}\left|\sum_{i=1}^{n}\left(Y_i^2 \psi_{j,k}(X_i) - \mathbb{E}\left[Y_i^2 \psi_{j,k}(X_i)\right]\right)\right| = \frac{1}{n}\left|\sum_{i=1}^{n} D_i\right|
\end{aligned}$$

with $D_i = Y_i^2 \psi_{j,k}(X_i) - \mathbb{E}[Y_i^2 \psi_{j,k}(X_i)]$. Clearly, $\mathbb{E}[D_i] = 0$. Furthermore, by A1 and the property of $\psi_{j,k}$, $\mathbb{E}[D_i^2] = Var[D_i] \leq \mathbb{E}[Y_i^4 \psi_{j,k}^2(X_i)] \lesssim 1$ and $|D_i| \leq 2^{\frac{j}{2}}$.

Note that

$$\left\{|\hat{\beta}_{j,k} - \beta_{j,u}| \geq \kappa t_n\right\} \subseteq \left\{\frac{1}{n}\left|\sum_{i=1}^{n} D_i\right| \geq \kappa t_n\right\}.$$

Hence,

$$\mathbb{P}(|\hat{\beta}_{j,k} - \beta_{j,k}| \geq \kappa t_n) \leq \mathbb{P}\left(\frac{1}{n}\left|\sum_{i=1}^{n} D_i\right| \geq \kappa t_n\right).$$

Using Bernstein's inequality, $t_n = \sqrt{\frac{\ln n}{n}}$ and $2^j \leq \frac{n}{\ln n}$,

$$\mathbb{P}\left(\frac{1}{n}\left|\sum_{i=1}^{n} D_i\right| \geq \kappa t_n\right) \lesssim \exp\left\{-\frac{n(\kappa t_n)^2}{2(1 + \frac{\kappa t_n 2^{j/2}}{3})}\right\} \lesssim \exp\left\{-\frac{\kappa^2 \ln n}{2(1 + \frac{\kappa}{3})}\right\}.$$

Then one chooses a large enough $\kappa > 1$ such that

$$\mathbb{P}(|\hat{\beta}_{j,k} - \beta_{j,k}| \geq \kappa t_n) \leq \mathbb{P}\left(\frac{1}{n}\left|\sum_{i=1}^{n} D_i\right| \geq \kappa t_n\right) \lesssim 2^{-wj}.$$

□

Theorem 2. *Let $r \in H^s(\Omega_{x_0})$ with $s > 0$. Then for each $1 \leq p < \infty$, the nonlinear wavelet estimator $\hat{r}_n^{non}(x)$ defined in (16) with $2^{j_*} \sim n^{\frac{1}{2m+1}}$ $(s < m)$ and $2^{j_1} \sim \frac{n}{\ln n}$ satisfies*

$$\sup_{r \in H^s(\Omega_{x_0})} \left\{\mathbb{E}[|\hat{r}_n^{non}(x_0) - r(x_0)|^p]\right\}^{\frac{1}{p}} \lesssim (\ln n)^{1-\frac{1}{p}} \left(\frac{\ln n}{n}\right)^{s/(2s+1)}. \quad (19)$$

Remark 3. *Compared with the linear wavelet estimator, the nonlinear wavelet estimator does not depend on the smooth parameter of $r(x)$. Hence, the nonlinear estimator is adaptive. More importantly, the nonlinear estimator can also achieve the optimal convergence rate up to an $\ln n$ factor.*

Proof. By the definition of $\hat{r}_n^{lin}(x)$ and $\hat{r}_n^{non}(x)$, one has

$$\hat{r}_n^{non}(x_0) - r(x_0) = [\hat{r}_n^{lin}(x_0) - P_{j_*}r(x_0)] - [r(x_0) - P_{j_1+1}r(x_0)] + \sum_{j=j_*}^{j_1}\sum_{k\in\Lambda_j}\left(\hat{\beta}_{j,k}I_{\{|\hat{\beta}_{j,k}|\geq\kappa t_n\}} - \beta_{j,k}\right)\psi_{j,k}(x_0).$$

Hence,

$$\{\mathbb{E}[|\hat{r}_n^{non}(x_0) - r(x_0)|^p]\}^{\frac{1}{p}} \lesssim T_1 + T_2 + Q,$$

where

$$T_1 = \left\{\mathbb{E}\left[\left|\hat{r}_n^{lin}(x_0) - P_{j_*}r(x_0)\right|^p\right]\right\}^{\frac{1}{p}},$$

$$T_2 = \left|P_{j_1+1}r(x_0) - r(x_0)\right|,$$

$$Q = \left\{\mathbb{E}\left[\left(\sum_{j=j_*}^{j_1}\sum_{k\in\Lambda_j}\left|\left(\hat{\beta}_{j,k}I_{\{|\hat{\beta}_{j,k}|\geq\kappa t_n\}} - \beta_{j,k}\right)\psi_{j,k}(x_0)\right|\right)^p\right]\right\}^{\frac{1}{p}}.$$

- For T_1. It follows from (15) and $2^{j_*} \sim n^{\frac{1}{2m+1}}\,(s < m)$ that

$$T_1 = \left\{\mathrm{E}\left[\left|\hat{r}_n^{lin}(x_0) - P_{j_*}r(x_0)\right|^p\right]\right\}^{\frac{1}{p}} \lesssim \left(\frac{2^{j_*}}{n}\right)^{1/2} \lesssim n^{-\frac{m}{2m+1}} < n^{-\frac{s}{2s+1}}. \quad (20)$$

- For T_2. Using Lemma 1 and $2^{j_1} \sim \frac{n}{\ln n}$, one gets

$$T_2 = \left|P_{j_1+1}r(x_0) - r(x_0)\right| \lesssim 2^{-j_1 s} \lesssim \left(\frac{\ln n}{n}\right)^s < \left(\frac{\ln n}{n}\right)^{\frac{s}{2s+1}}. \quad (21)$$

Then equality (19) will be proven if we can show

$$Q \lesssim (\ln n)^{1-\frac{1}{p}}\left(\frac{\ln n}{n}\right)^{s/(2s+1)}.$$

According to Hölder inequality,

$$Q \lesssim \left\{(j_1 - j_* + 1)^{p-1}\sum_{j=j_*}^{j_1}\mathrm{E}\left[\left(\sum_{k\in\Lambda_j}\left|\left(\hat{\beta}_{j,k}I_{\{|\hat{\beta}_{j,k}|\geq\kappa t_n\}} - \beta_{j,k}\right)\psi_{j,k}(x_0)\right|\right)^p\right]\right\}^{1/p}.$$

It is obvious that

$$|\hat{\beta}_{j,k}I_{\{|\hat{\beta}_{j,k}|\geq\kappa t_n\}} - \beta_{j,k}| = |\hat{\beta}_{j,k} - \beta_{j,k}|\left[I_{\{|\hat{\beta}_{j,k}|\geq\kappa t_n, |\beta_{j,k}|<\frac{\kappa t_n}{2}\}} + I_{\{|\hat{\beta}_{j,k}|\geq\kappa t_n, |\beta_{j,k}|\geq\frac{\kappa t_n}{2}\}}\right] + |\beta_{j,k}|\left[I_{\{|\hat{\beta}_{j,k}|<\kappa t_n, |\beta_{j,k}|>2\kappa t_n\}} + I_{\{|\hat{\beta}_{j,k}|<\kappa t_n, |\beta_{j,k}|\leq 2\kappa t_n\}}\right].$$

Moreover,

$$\left\{|\hat{\beta}_{j,k}| \geq \kappa t_n, |\beta_{j,k}| < \frac{\kappa t_n}{2}\right\} \subseteq \left\{|\hat{\beta}_{j,k} - \beta_{j,k}| > \frac{\kappa t_n}{2}\right\},$$

$$\left\{|\hat{\beta}_{j,k}| < \kappa t_n, |\beta_{j,k}| > 2\kappa t_n\right\} \subseteq \left\{|\hat{\beta}_{j,k} - \beta_{j,k}| > \frac{\kappa t_n}{2}\right\},$$

$$|\hat{\beta}_{j,k} - \beta_{j,k}| \geq |\beta_{j,k}| - |\hat{\beta}_{j,k}| \geq \frac{\kappa t_n}{2}.$$

Hence, one can obtain that

$$Q \lesssim (j_1 - j_* + 1)^{1-\frac{1}{p}}(Q_1 + Q_2 + Q_3),$$

where

$$Q_1 = \left\{ \sum_{j=j_*}^{j_1} \mathbb{E}\left[\left(\sum_{k\in\Lambda_j} \left|\hat{\beta}_{j,k} - \beta_{j,k}\right| I_{\{|\hat{\beta}_{j,k}-\beta_{j,k}|>\frac{\kappa t_n}{2}\}} \left|\psi_{j,k}(x_0)\right| \right)^p \right] \right\}^{1/p},$$

$$Q_2 = \left\{ \sum_{j=j_*}^{j_1} \mathbb{E}\left[\left(\sum_{k\in\Lambda_j} \left|\hat{\beta}_{j,k} - \beta_{j,k}\right| I_{\{|\beta_{j,k}|\geq\frac{\kappa t_n}{2}\}} \left|\psi_{j,k}(x_0)\right| \right)^p \right] \right\}^{1/p},$$

$$Q_3 = \sum_{j=j_*}^{j_1} \sum_{k\in\Lambda_j} \left|\beta_{j,k}\right| I_{\{|\beta_{j,k}|\leq 2\kappa t_n\}} \left|\psi_{j,k}(x_0)\right|.$$

- For Q_1. By Hölder inequality ($\frac{1}{p} + \frac{1}{p'} = 1$) and $\sum_k \left|\psi_{j,k}(x_0)\right| \lesssim 2^{j/2}$

$$\begin{aligned}
&\mathbb{E}\left[\left(\sum_{k\in\Lambda_j} \left|\hat{\beta}_{j,k} - \beta_{j,k}\right| I_{\{|\hat{\beta}_{j,k}-\beta_{j,k}|>\frac{\kappa t_n}{2}\}} \left|\psi_{j,k}(x_0)\right| \right)^p \right] \\
&= \mathbb{E}\left[\left(\sum_{k\in\Lambda_j} \left|\hat{\beta}_{j,k} - \beta_{j,k}\right| I_{\{|\hat{\beta}_{j,k}-\beta_{j,k}|>\frac{\kappa t_n}{2}\}} \left|\psi_{j,k}(x_0)\right|^{1/p} \left|\psi_{j,k}(x_0)\right|^{1/p'} \right)^p \right] \\
&\leq \mathbb{E}\left[\sum_{k\in\Lambda_j} \left|\hat{\beta}_{j,k} - \beta_{j,k}\right|^p I_{\{|\hat{\beta}_{j,k}-\beta_{j,k}|>\frac{\kappa t_n}{2}\}} \left|\psi_{j,k}(x_0)\right| \right] \left(\sum_k \left|\psi_{j,k}(x_0)\right| \right)^{p/p'} \\
&\leq \mathbb{E}\left[\sum_{k\in\Lambda_j} \left|\hat{\beta}_{j,k} - \beta_{j,k}\right|^p I_{\{|\hat{\beta}_{j,k}-\beta_{j,k}|>\frac{\kappa t_n}{2}\}} \left|\psi_{j,k}(x_0)\right| \right] 2^{\frac{jp}{2p'}}.
\end{aligned} \tag{22}$$

Furthermore, using the Cauchy–Schwarz inequality, Lemmas 5 and 6, one has

$$\begin{aligned}
&\mathbb{E}\left[\left|\hat{\beta}_{j,k} - \beta_{j,k}\right|^p I_{\{|\hat{\beta}_{j,k}-\beta_{j,k}|>\frac{\kappa t_n}{2}\}} \right] \\
&\leq \left(\mathbb{E}\left[\left|\hat{\beta}_{j,k} - \beta_{j,k}\right|^{2p} \right] \right)^{1/2} \left(\mathbb{E}\left[I_{\{|\hat{\beta}_{j,k}-\beta_{j,k}|>\frac{\kappa t_n}{2}\}} \right] \right)^{1/2} \lesssim n^{-\frac{p}{2}} 2^{-\frac{wj}{2}}.
\end{aligned} \tag{23}$$

This with (22) yields that

$$\begin{aligned}
&\mathbb{E}\left[\left(\sum_{k\in\Lambda_j} \left|\hat{\beta}_{j,k} - \beta_{j,k}\right| I_{\{|\hat{\beta}_{j,k}-\beta_{j,k}|>\frac{\kappa t_n}{2}\}} \left|\psi_{j,k}(x_0)\right| \right)^p \right] \\
&\lesssim 2^{\frac{jp}{2}} \mathbb{E}\left[\left|\hat{\beta}_{j,k} - \beta_{j,k}\right|^p I_{\{|\hat{\beta}_{j,k}-\beta_{j,k}|>\frac{\kappa t_n}{2}\}} \right] \lesssim n^{-\frac{p}{2}} 2^{-\frac{wj}{2}} 2^{\frac{jp}{2}}.
\end{aligned} \tag{24}$$

Hence,

$$Q_1 \lesssim \left(\sum_{j=j_*}^{j_1} 2^{\frac{jp}{2}} n^{-\frac{p}{2}} 2^{-\frac{wj}{2}} \right)^{\frac{1}{p}} = \left(n^{-\frac{p}{2}} \sum_{j=j_*}^{j_1} 2^{j(\frac{p}{2}-\frac{w}{2})} \right)^{\frac{1}{p}} \lesssim \left(n^{-\frac{p}{2}} 2^{j_*\frac{p}{2}} \right)^{\frac{1}{p}} = \left(\frac{2^{j_*}}{n} \right)^{\frac{1}{2}},$$

where κ is chosen to be large enough such that $w > p$ in Lemma 6. This with the choice $2^{j_*} \sim n^{\frac{1}{2m+1}}$ $(s < m)$ shows that

$$Q_1 \lesssim n^{-\frac{m}{2m+1}} \lesssim n^{-\frac{s}{2s+1}}. \tag{25}$$

- For Q_2. Let us first define
$$2^{j'} \sim \left(\frac{n}{\ln n}\right)^{1/(2s+1)}.$$
Clearly, $2^{j_*} \sim n^{\frac{1}{2m+1}} \leq 2^{j'} \sim \left(\frac{n}{\ln n}\right)^{1/(2s+1)} \leq 2^{j_1} \sim \frac{n}{\ln n}$. Note that
$$\begin{aligned} Q_2 &= \left\{\sum_{j=j_*}^{j_1} \mathbb{E}\left[\left(\sum_{k\in\Lambda_j} \left|\hat{\beta}_{j,k} - \beta_{j,k}\right| I_{\{|\beta_{j,k}|\geq \frac{\kappa t_n}{2}\}} \left|\psi_{j,k}(x_0)\right|\right)^p\right]\right\}^{1/p} \\ &\leq \left\{\sum_{j=j_*}^{j'} \mathbb{E}\left[\left(\sum_{k\in\Lambda_j} \left|\hat{\beta}_{j,k} - \beta_{j,k}\right|\left|\psi_{j,k}(x_0)\right|\right)^p\right]\right\}^{1/p} \\ &+ \left\{\sum_{j=j'+1}^{j_1} \mathbb{E}\left[\left(\sum_{k\in\Lambda_j} \left|\hat{\beta}_{j,k} - \beta_{j,k}\right| \frac{\left|\beta_{j,k}\right|}{t_n}\left|\psi_{j,k}(x_0)\right|\right)^p\right]\right\}^{1/p}. \end{aligned}$$
Similar to the argument of (15), one gets
$$\left\{\sum_{j=j_*}^{j'} \mathbb{E}\left[\left(\sum_{k\in\Lambda_j} \left|\hat{\beta}_{j,k} - \beta_{j,k}\right|\left|\psi_{j,k}(x_0)\right|\right)^p\right]\right\}^{1/p} \lesssim \left(\sum_{j=j_*}^{j'} n^{-\frac{p}{2}} 2^{\frac{jp}{2}}\right)^{\frac{1}{p}} \lesssim \left(\frac{2^{j'}}{n}\right)^{1/2}. \tag{26}$$
On the other hand, by Hölder inequality ($\frac{1}{p} + \frac{1}{p'} = 1$) and Lemma 1
$$\begin{aligned} &\mathbb{E}\left[\left(\sum_{k\in\Lambda_j} \left|\hat{\beta}_{j,k} - \beta_{j,k}\right| \frac{\left|\beta_{j,k}\right|}{t_n}\left|\psi_{j,k}(x_0)\right|\right)^p\right] \\ &= \mathbb{E}\left[\left(\sum_{k\in\Lambda_j} \left|\hat{\beta}_{j,k} - \beta_{j,k}\right| \frac{\left|\beta_{j,k}\right|^{1/p}}{t_n^{1/p}}\left|\psi_{j,k}(x_0)\right|^{1/p} \frac{\left|\beta_{j,k}\right|^{1/p'}}{t_n^{1/p'}}\left|\psi_{j,k}(x_0)\right|^{1/p'}\right)^p\right] \\ &\leq \mathbb{E}\left[\sum_{k\in\Lambda_j} \left|\hat{\beta}_{j,k} - \beta_{j,k}\right|^p \frac{\left|\beta_{j,k}\right|}{t_n}\left|\psi_{j,k}(x_0)\right|\right]\left(\sum_{k\in\Lambda_j} \frac{\left|\beta_{j,k}\right|}{t_n}\left|\psi_{j,k}(x_0)\right|\right)^{p/p'} \\ &\lesssim n^{-p/2} t_n{}^{-p} 2^{-jps} \lesssim (\ln n)^{-\frac{p}{2}} 2^{-jps}. \end{aligned}$$
Hence,
$$\left[\sum_{j=j'+1}^{j_1} (\ln n)^{-\frac{p}{2}} 2^{-jps}\right]^{1/p} \lesssim (\ln n)^{-\frac{1}{2}} 2^{-j's}. \tag{27}$$
Combing (26), (27) and $2^{j'} \sim \left(\frac{n}{\ln n}\right)^{1/(2s+1)}$, one gets
$$Q_2 \lesssim \left(\frac{2^{j'}}{n}\right)^{1/2} + (\ln n)^{-\frac{1}{2}} 2^{-j's} \lesssim \left(\frac{\ln n}{n}\right)^{s/(2s+1)}. \tag{28}$$

- For Q_3. Note that
$$Q_3 = \left(\sum_{j=j_*}^{j'} + \sum_{j=j'+1}^{j_1}\right) \sum_{k\in\Lambda_j} \left|\beta_{j,k}\right| I_{\{|\beta_{j,k}|\leq 2\kappa t_n\}} \left|\psi_{j,k}(x_0)\right| =: Q_{31} + Q_{32}.$$

It is easy to show that

$$Q_{31} = \sum_{j=j_*}^{j'} \sum_{k\in\Lambda_j} \left|\beta_{j,k}\right| I_{\{|\beta_{j,k}|\le 2\kappa t_n\}} \left|\psi_{j,k}(x_0)\right|$$
$$\lesssim \sum_{j=j_*}^{j'} \sum_{k\in\Lambda_j} \left|\beta_{j,k}\right| \frac{2\kappa t_n}{\left|\beta_{j,k}\right|} \left|\psi_{j,k}(x_0)\right| \lesssim \sum_{j=j_*}^{j'} 2^{\frac{j}{2}} t_n \lesssim 2^{\frac{j'}{2}} \sqrt{\frac{\ln n}{n}}. \tag{29}$$

In addition,

$$Q_{32} = \sum_{j=j'+1}^{j_1} \sum_{k\in\Lambda_j} \left|\beta_{j,k}\right| I_{\{|\beta_{j,k}|\le 2\kappa t_n\}} \left|\psi_{j,k}(x_0)\right|$$
$$\lesssim \sum_{j=j'+1}^{j_1} \sum_{k\in\Lambda_j} \left|\beta_{j,k}\psi_{j,k}(x_0)\right| \lesssim \sum_{j=j'+1}^{j_1} 2^{-js} \lesssim 2^{-j's}. \tag{30}$$

Then according to (29), (30) and $2^{j'} \sim \left(\frac{n}{\ln n}\right)^{1/(2s+1)}$, one can obtain

$$Q_3 \lesssim 2^{\frac{j'}{2}} \sqrt{\frac{\ln n}{n}} + 2^{-j's} \lesssim \left(\frac{\ln n}{n}\right)^{s/(2s+1)}. \tag{31}$$

Furthermore, together with (25) and (28), this yields

$$Q \lesssim (\ln n)^{1-\frac{1}{p}} \left(n^{-\frac{s}{2s+1}} + \left(\frac{\ln n}{n}\right)^{s/(2s+1)} + \left(\frac{\ln n}{n}\right)^{s/(2s+1)} \right)$$
$$\lesssim (\ln n)^{1-\frac{1}{p}} \left(\frac{\ln n}{n}\right)^{s/(2s+1)}. \tag{32}$$

Finally, it follows from (20), (21) and (32) that

$$\sup_{r\in H^s(\Omega_{x_0})} \left\{ E\left[|\hat{r}_n^{non}(x_0) - r(x_0)|^p \right] \right\}^{\frac{1}{p}} \lesssim (\ln n)^{1-\frac{1}{p}} \left(\frac{\ln n}{n}\right)^{s/(2s+1)},$$

which completes the proof of Theorem 2. □

5. Conclusions

This paper studies the pointwise estimations of an unknown function in a regression model with multiplicative and additive noise. Under some different assumptions, linear and nonlinear wavelet estimators are constructed. It is clear that those wavelet estimators have diverse forms with different conditions. The convergence rates over the pointwise risk of two wavelet estimators are proposed by Theorems 1 and 2. It should be pointed out that the linear and nonlinear wavelet estimators can all obtain the optimal convergence rate of pointwise nonparametric estimation. More importantly, the nonlinear wavelet estimator is adaptive. In other words, the conclusions of asymptotic and theoretical performance are clear in this paper. However, it is a difficult problem to give numerical experiments, which need more investigations and new skills. We will study it in the future.

Author Contributions: Writing—original draft, J.K. and Q.H.; Writing—review and editing, H.G. All authors have read and agreed to the published version of the manuscript.

Funding: Junke Kou is supported by the National Natural Science Foundation of China (12001133) and Guangxi Natural Science Foundation (2019GXNSFFA245012). Huijun Guo is supported by the National Natural Science Foundation of China (12001132), and Guangxi Colleges and Universities Key Laboratory of Data Analysis and Computation.

Institutional Review Board Statement: Not applicable.

Informed Consent Statement: Not applicable.

Data Availability Statement: Not applicable.

Acknowledgments: The authors would like to thank the anonymous reviewers for their helpful comments.

Conflicts of Interest: The authors state that there is no conflict of interest.

References

1. Hart, J.D. Kernel regression estimation with time series errors. *J. R. Stat. Soc. Ser. B* **1991**, *53*, 173–187.
2. Kerkyacharian, G.; Picard, D. Regression in random design and warped wavelets. *Bernoulli* **2004**, *10*, 1053–1105. [CrossRef]
3. Chesneau, C. Regression with random design: A minimax study. *Stat. Probab. Lett.* **2007**, *77*, 40–53. [CrossRef]
4. Reiß, M. Asymptotic equivalence for nonparametric regression with multivariate and random design. *Ann. Stat.* **2008**, *36*, 1957–1982. [CrossRef]
5. Yuan, M.; Zhou, D.X. Minimax optimal rates of estimation in high dimensional additive models. *Ann. Stat.* **2016**, *44*, 2564–2593. [CrossRef]
6. Wang, L.; Politis, D.N. Asymptotic validity of bootstrap confidence intervals in nonparametric regression without an additive model. *Electron. J. Stat.* **2021**, *15*, 392–426. [CrossRef]
7. Chesneau, C.; Kolei, S.E.; Kou, J.K.; Navarro, F. Nonparametric estimation in a regression model with additive and multiplicative noise. *J. Comput. Appl. Math.* **2020**, *380*, 112971. [CrossRef]
8. Cai, T.T.; Wang, L. Adaptive variance function estimation in heteroscedastic nonparametric regression. *Ann. Stat.* **2008**, *36*, 2025–2054. [CrossRef]
9. Alharbi, Y.F.; Patili, P.N. Error variance function estimation in nonparametric regression models. *Commun. Stat. Simul. Comput.* **2018**, *47*, 1479–1491. [CrossRef]
10. Huang, P.; Pi, Y.; Progri, I. GPS signal detection under multiplicative and additive noise. *J. Navig.* **2013**, *66*, 479–500. [CrossRef]
11. Kravchenko, V.F.; Ponomaryov, V.I.; Pustovoit, V.I.; Palacios-Enriquez, A. 3D Filtering of images corrupted by additive-multiplicative noise. *Dokl. Math.* **2020**, *102*, 414–417. [CrossRef]
12. Cui, G. Application of addition and multiplication noise model parameter estimation in INSAR image Processing. *Math. Probl. Eng.* **2022**, *2022*, 3164513. [CrossRef]
13. Meyer, Y. *Wavelets and Operators*; Cambridge University Press: Cambridge, UK, 1992.
14. Daubechies, I. *Ten Lecture on Wavelets*; SIAM: Philadelphia, PA, USA, 1992.
15. Liu, Y.M.; Wu, C. Point-wise estimation for anisotropic densities. *J. Multivar. Anal.* **2019**, *171*, 112–125. [CrossRef]
16. Brown, L.D.; Low, M.G. A constrained risk inequality with applications to nonparametric functional estimation. *Ann. Stat.* **1996**, *24*, 2524–2535. [CrossRef]

axioms

MDPI

Article

Fixed Point Results on Partial Modular Metric Space

Dipankar Das [1], Santanu Narzary [1], Yumnam Mahendra Singh [2], Mohammad Saeed Khan [3] and Salvatore Sessa [4,*]

1 Department of Mathematical Sciences, Bodoland University, Kokrajhar 783370, Assam, India; dipankardasguw@yahoo.com (D.D.); narzarysantanu1@gmail.com (S.N.)
2 Department of Humanities and Basic Sciences, Manipur Institute of Technology, A Constitute College of Manipur University, Takyepat 795004, Manipur, India; ymahenmit@rediffmail.com
3 Department of Mathematics and Applied Mathematics, Sefako Makgatho Health Sciences University, Gauteng 0208, South Africa; drsaeed9@gmail.com
4 Department of Architecture, Federico II Naples University, Via Toledo 402, 80134 Naples, Italy
* Correspondence: sessa@unina.it

Abstract: In the present paper, we refine the notion of the partial modular metric defined by Hosseinzadeh and Parvaneh to eliminate the occurrence of discrepancies in the non-zero self-distance and triangular inequality. In support of this, we discuss non-trivial examples. Finally, we prove a common fixed-point theorem for four self-mappings in partial modular metric space and an application to our result; the existence of a solution for a system of Volterra integral equations is discussed.

Keywords: fixed point; partial metric space; modular space; partial modular space; weakly compatible mappings; C-class function; Volterra integral equation

MSC: 47H10; 54H25

Citation: Das, D.; Narzary, S.; Singh, Y.M.; Khan, M.S.; Sessa, S. Fixed Point Results on Partial Modular Metric Space. *Axioms* **2022**, *11*, 62. https://doi.org/10.3390/axioms11020062

Academic Editor: Yurii Kharkevych

Received: 9 November 2021
Accepted: 28 January 2022
Published: 1 February 2022

1. Introduction

In 1992, Matthews [1] initiated the idea of non-zero self-distance by introducing the notion of the partial metric as a part of the study of the denotational semantics of data flow programming languages in a topological model in computer sciences and also extended Banach's contraction principle [2] in such space. Subsequently, many authors have begun to report its topological properties and obtained many fixed-point theorems in this space (for more details and references, we refer to [3–8]). On the other hand, in 1950, Nakano [9] introduced the concept of the modular in connection with the theory of order spaces, which was later developed by Musielak and Orlicz [10], Khamsi [11] and Kozlowski [12] as modular function space.

In 2006, Chistyakov [13] introduced the notion of the metric modular on an arbitrary set and the corresponding modular space, which is more general than a metric space, and, based on this, he further studied Lipschitz continuity and a class of superposition (or Nemytskii) operators on modular metric space (see also [14,15]). Recently, Hosseinzadeh and Parvaneh [16] introduced the notion of partial modular metric spaces as a generalization partial metric space and gave some fixed-point results.

In this paper, we refine the concept of the partial modular metric to eliminate the occurrence of discrepancies in the non-zero self-distance and triangular inequality and prove a common fixed-point theorem for four self-mappings with a suitable example. As an application of our result, the existence of a solution for a system of Volterra integral equations is discussed.

2. Preliminaries

In this section, we recall some definitions and properties to use in our result.

Definition 1 ([1])**.** *Let $X \neq \emptyset$. A function $p : X \times X \to [0, \infty)$ is called a partial metric on X if it satisfies:*
$(p_1) : 0 \leq p(x, y),\ \forall x, y \in X$ *and* $p(x, y) = p(x, x) = p(y, y) \Longleftrightarrow x = y$;
$(p_2) : p(x, x) \leq p(x, y),\ \forall x, y \in X$;
$(p_3) : p(x, y) = p(y, x),\ \forall x, y \in X$;
$(p_4) : p(x, y) \leq p(x, z) + p(z, y) - p(z, z),\ \forall x, y, z \in X.$
Then, the pair (X, p) is called a partial metric space.

Obviously, if $p(x, y) = 0$, then, from (p_1) and (p_2), we have $x = y$, but the converse may not be true. Moreover, if (X, p) is a partial metric space, then the function $d^p : X \times X \to [0, \infty)$ defined by

$$d^p(x, y) = 2p(x, y) - p(x, x) - p(y, y)$$

is a metric on X.

Example 1 ([1])**.** *Let $X \neq \emptyset$ and $c \geq 0$. Define $p(x, y) = |x - y| + c$; the p is a partial metric on X and the corresponding metric is $d_p(x, y) = 2|x - y|,\ \forall x, y \in X$.*

Every partial metric p on X generates a T_0 topology τ_p on X with a base, which is defined by the family of open $p-$ balls $\{B_p(x, \epsilon) : x \in X,\ \epsilon > 0\}$, where $B_p(x, \epsilon) = \{u : p(x, u) < p(x, x) + \epsilon\},\ \forall x \in X$ and $\epsilon > 0$.

Definition 2 ([13–15])**.** *Let $X \neq \emptyset$. A function $\omega : (0, +\infty) \times X \times X \to [0, \infty)$, defined by $\omega(\lambda, x, y) = \omega_\lambda(x, y)$, is called a modular metric on X if it satisfies the following:*
$(\omega_1) : \omega_\lambda(x, y) = 0 \Longleftrightarrow x = y,\ \forall \lambda > 0$;
$(\omega_2) : \omega_\lambda(x, y) = \omega_\lambda(y, x),\ \forall x, y \in X$ *and* $\forall \lambda > 0$;
$(\omega_3) : \omega_{\lambda+\mu}(x, y) \leq \omega_\lambda(x, z) + \omega_\mu(z, y)\ \forall x, y, z \in X$ *and* $\forall \lambda, \mu > 0$.

If in lieu of (ω_1), we write

$$(\omega_{1'}) :\ \omega_\lambda(x, x) = 0,\ \forall \lambda > 0,$$

and then ω is called the pseudomodular metric on X. Note that the function $\lambda \longmapsto \omega_\lambda \in [0, \infty)$ is non-decreasing. Indeed, $\forall x, y \in X$ and $\forall \lambda, \mu >$ such that $0 < \mu < \lambda$; from (ω_1) and (ω_3), we obtain

$$\omega_\lambda(x, y) \leq \omega_{\lambda-\mu}(x, x) + \omega_\mu(x, y) = \omega_\mu(x, y).$$

Moreover, we say that ω is convex if it satisfies the axioms (ω_1), (ω_2) of Definition 2 and the following:

$$(\omega_4) :\ \omega_{\lambda+\mu}(x, y) \leq \frac{\lambda}{\lambda + \mu}\omega_\lambda(x, z) + \frac{\mu}{\lambda + \mu}\omega_\mu(z, y),\ \forall x, y, z \in X \text{ and } \forall \lambda, \mu > 0.$$

Now, we define the following definition, a general form of convex modular metric on X.

Definition 3. *A modular metric ω defined on a non-empty set X is said to be a weak convex modular if it satisfies the axioms (ω_1), (ω_2) of Definition 2 such that there exists a function $\alpha : (0, \infty) \times (0, \infty) \to (0, 1)$ satisfying the following:*

$$(\omega_{4'}) :\ \omega_{\lambda+\mu}(x, y) \leq \alpha(\lambda, \mu)\omega_\lambda(x, z) + (1 - \alpha(\lambda, \mu))\omega_\mu(z, y),$$

$\forall x, y, z \in X$ *and* $\forall \lambda, \mu > 0$.

Obviously, every convex modular metric is a weak convex modular metric but the converse may not be true. Moreover, every (weak) convex modular metric is a modular metric but the converse may not be true. In fact, by setting $\alpha = \frac{\lambda}{\lambda+\mu}$, then $0 < \alpha < 1$ and $0 < 1 - \alpha = \frac{\mu}{\lambda+\mu} < 1$, so (ω_4) and $(\omega_{4'})$ infer directly the axiom (ω_3) of Definition 2.

Let $X \neq \emptyset$ be an arbitrary set. For given $x_0 \in X$, we define

$$X_\omega(x_0) = \{x \in X : \lim_{\lambda \to +\infty} \omega_\lambda(x_0, x) = 0\}$$

and

$$X^*_\omega(x_0) = \{x \in X : \exists \lambda = \lambda(x) > 0,\ \omega_\lambda(x_0, x) < \infty\}.$$

Then, the two sets X_ω and X^*_ω are called modular spaces centered at x_0. It is obvious that $X_\omega \subseteq X^*_\omega$. If $x_0 \in X$ is an arbitrary, then $X_\omega(x_0)$ and $X^*_\omega(x_0)$ are written as X_ω and X^*_ω. If ω is a modular metric on X, then the modular space X_ω is a metric space equipped with a non-trivial metric given by

$$d_\omega(x, y) = \inf\{\lambda : \omega_\lambda(x, y) \leq \lambda\},\ \forall x, y \in X_\omega.$$

Further, if ω is a convex modular on X, then $X_\omega = X^*_\omega$, and this common space can be equipped with a metric d^*_ω defined by

$$d^*_\omega(x, y) = \inf\{\lambda : \omega_\lambda(x, y) \leq 1\},\ \forall x, y \in X_\omega.$$

If a modular metric ω on X is finite and $\omega_\lambda(x, y) = \omega_\mu(x, y)$,$\forall x, y \in X$ and $\forall \lambda, \mu > 0$, then $d(x, y) = \omega_\lambda(x, y)$ is a metric on X.

Example 2 ([17]). *Let (X, d) be a metric space. Define $\omega_\lambda(x, y) = \frac{d(x,y)}{\lambda}$, $\forall x, y \in X$ and $\forall \lambda > 0$. Then, ω is a modular metric on X. Moreover, ω is convex and hence it is a weak convex modular metric on X.*

Lemma 1 ([14]). *Let ω be a modular metric on a set X, given a sequence $\{x_n\}_{n \in \mathbb{N}}$ in X_ω and $x \in X_\omega$. Then, $d_\omega(x_n, x) \to 0$ as $n \to \infty$ if and only if $\omega_\lambda(x_n, x) \to 0$ as $n \to \infty$, $\forall \lambda > 0$. A similar assertion holds for Cauchy sequences.*

Example 3. *Define $\omega_\lambda(x, y) = \frac{e^{-\lambda}|x-y|}{c}$, $c > 0$ $\forall x, y \in X$ and $\forall \lambda > 0$. Obviously, ω satisfies the axioms (ω_1), (ω_2) and (ω_3) of Definition 2. Therefore, ω is a modular metric but not a convex modular metric on X.*

In fact, $\forall \lambda, \mu > 0$, and we have

$$\begin{aligned} \omega_{\lambda+\mu}(x, y) \leq & \frac{e^{-(\lambda+\mu)}}{c}[|x - z| + |z - y|] \\ = & \frac{e^\lambda}{e^{\lambda+\mu}} \frac{e^{-\lambda}|x - z|}{c} + \frac{e^\mu}{e^{\lambda+\mu}} \frac{e^{-\mu}|z - y|}{c} \\ = & \frac{e^\lambda}{e^{\lambda+\mu}} \omega_\lambda(x, z) + \frac{e^\mu}{e^{\lambda+\mu}} \omega_\mu(z, y). \end{aligned}$$

Note that $0 < \frac{\lambda}{\lambda+\mu} < \frac{e^\lambda}{e^{\lambda+\mu}} < 1$ and $0 < \frac{\mu}{\lambda+\mu} < \frac{e^\mu}{e^{\lambda+\mu}} < 1$. Thus, ω is not a convex modular metric on X.

Definition 4 ([16]). *Let $X \neq \emptyset$ and $\omega^p : (0, +\infty) \times X \times X \to [0, \infty)$ be a function defined by $\omega^p(\lambda, x, y) = \omega^p_\lambda(x, y)$, which is called a partial modular metric on X if it satisfies the following axioms:*
(ω^p_1): $\omega^p_\lambda(x, y) = \omega^p_\lambda(x, x) = \omega^p_\lambda(y, y) \iff x = y,\ \forall \lambda > 0$;
(ω^p_2) : $\omega^p_\lambda(x, x) \leq \omega^p_\lambda(x, y)$, $\forall\ x, y \in X$ *and* $\forall \lambda > 0$;
(ω^p_3) : $\omega^p_\lambda(x, y) = \omega^p_\lambda(y, x)$, $\forall x, y \in X$ *and* $\forall \lambda > 0$;

(ω_4^p) : $\omega_{\lambda+\mu}^p(x,y) \leq \omega_\lambda^p(x,z) + \omega_\mu^p(z,y) - \frac{\omega_\lambda^p(x,x)+\omega_\lambda^p(z,z)+\omega_\mu^p(z,z)+\omega_\lambda^p(y,y)}{2}$, $\forall x,y \in X$ *and* $\forall \lambda,\mu > 0$.

As in Definition 1, the self-distance in Definition 4 of a partial modular metric need not be restricted to zero, i.e., $\omega_\lambda^p(x,x) = 0$. Note that if $x = y = z$, $\forall \lambda,\mu > 0$, then, from (ω_4^p), it follows that $\omega_\lambda^p(x,x) = 0$. In order to avoid this limitation, we modify the axioms (ω_1^p) and (ω_4^p) in Definition 4 and restate them as follows.

Definition 5. *Let* $X \neq \emptyset$ *and* $\omega^p : (0,+\infty) \times X \times X \to [0,\infty)$ *be a function defined by* $\omega^p(\lambda,x,y) = \omega_\lambda^p(x,y)$*, which is called a partial modular metric on X if it retains the axioms* (ω_2^p) *and* (ω_3^p) *of Definition 4 with the following:*
$(\omega_{1'}^p) : \omega_\lambda^p(x,x) = \omega_\mu^p(x,x)$ *and* $\omega_\lambda^p(x,x) = \omega_\lambda^p(x,y) = \omega_\lambda^p(y,y) \iff x = y$, $\forall \lambda,\mu > 0$;
$(\omega_{4'}^p) : \omega_{\lambda+\mu}^p(x,y) \leq \omega_\lambda^p(x,z) + \omega_\mu^p(z,y) - \omega_\lambda^p(z,z)$, $\forall x,y \in X$ *and* $\forall \lambda,\mu > 0$.

Obviously, if $\omega_\lambda^p(x,y) = 0$, then, from $(\omega_{1'}^p)$ and (ω_2^p), we have $x = y$, but the converse may not be true. It is not difficult to see that a partial modular metric ω^p on X is a modular metric but the converse may not be true. If a partial modular metric ω^p on X possesses a finite value and is independent of the parameter $\lambda > 0$ that is $\omega_\lambda^p(x,y) = \omega_\mu^p(x,y)$, $\forall \lambda,\mu > 0$, then $p(x,y) = \omega_\lambda^p(x,y)$ is a partial metric on X.

Definition 6. *A partial modular metric* ω^p *on X is said to be convex if, in addition to the axioms* $(\omega_{1'}^p)$, (ω_2^p) *and* (ω_3^p)*, it satisfies the following:*

$$(\omega_5^p): \ \omega_{\lambda+\mu}^p(x,y) \leq \frac{\lambda}{\lambda+\mu}\omega_\lambda^p(x,y) + \frac{\mu}{\lambda+\mu}\omega_\mu^p(z,y) - \frac{\lambda}{\lambda+\mu}\omega_\lambda^p(z,z),$$

$\forall x,y,z \in X$ *and* $\forall \lambda,\mu > 0$.

Definition 7. *A partial modular metric* ω^p *on X is said to be weakly convex if it satisfies the axioms* $(\omega_{1'}^p)$, (ω_2^p), (ω_3^p) *and the following:*

$$(\omega_{5'}^p): \ \omega_{\lambda+\mu}^p(x,y) \leq \alpha(\lambda,\mu)\omega_\lambda^p(x,y) + (1-\alpha(\lambda,\mu))\omega_\mu^p(z,y) - \alpha(\lambda,\mu)\omega_\lambda^p(z,z),$$

$\forall x,y,z \in X$ *and* $\forall \lambda,\mu > 0$*, where* $\alpha : (0,\infty) \times (0,\infty) \to (0,1)$ *is a function.*

Now, we define the following definitions as in the modular metric:

Definition 8. *Let* ω^p *be a partial modular metric on a set X. For given* $x_0 \in X$*, we define*

$$X_{\omega^p}(x_0) = \{x \in X : \lim_{\lambda \to +\infty} \omega_\lambda^p(x_0,x) = c\},$$

for some $c \geq 0$ *and*

$$X_{\omega^p}^*(x_0) = \{x \in X : \exists \lambda = \lambda(x) > 0,\ \omega_\lambda^p(x_0,x) < \infty\}.$$

Then, two sets X_{ω^p} *and* $X_{\omega^p}^*$ *are called partial modular spaces centered at* x_0*. It is obvious that* $X_{\omega^p} \subset X_{\omega^p}^*$*. We write* $X_{\omega^p} \equiv X_{\omega^p}(x_0)$ *and* $X^* \equiv X_{\omega^p}^*(x_0)$*, if* $x_0 \in X$ *is arbitrary.*

Remark 1. *For every* $x,y \in X$*, the function* $\lambda \longmapsto \omega_\lambda^p \in [0,\infty)$ *is non-increasing. Indeed,* $\forall x \in X$ *and* $0 < \mu < \lambda$*, from* $(\omega_{1'}^p)$ *and* $(\omega_{4'}^p)$*, and we obtain*

$$\omega_\lambda^p(x,y) \leq \omega_{\lambda-\mu}^p(x,x) + \omega_\mu^p(x,y) - \omega_{\lambda-\mu}^p(x,x) = \omega_\mu^p(x,y).$$

Lemma 2. *Let ω^p be a partial modular metric on a non-empty set X. Define*

$$\omega^s_\lambda(x,y) = 2\omega^p_\lambda(x,y) - \omega^p_\lambda(x,x) - \omega^p_\lambda(y,y).$$

Then, ω^s is a modular metric on X.

Proof. Obviously, ω^s holds (ω_2) of Definition 2. For (ω_1) and (ω_3), we have
(ω_1) : If $x = y$, then $\omega^s_\lambda(x,y) = 0,\ \forall\lambda > 0$. Suppose $\omega^s_\lambda(x,y) = 0,\ \forall\lambda > 0$, then

$$2\omega^p_\lambda(x,y) = \omega^p_\lambda(x,x) + \omega^p_\lambda(y,y).$$

From (ω^p_2) of Definition 5, we obtain

$$2\omega^p_\lambda(x,x) \le 2\omega^p_\lambda(x,y) = \omega^p_\lambda(x,x) + \omega^p_\lambda(y,y) \implies \omega^p_\lambda(x,x) \le \omega^p_\lambda(y,y).$$

Similarly, we obtain

$$2\omega^p_\lambda(y,y) \le 2\omega^p_\lambda(x,y) = \omega^p_\lambda(x,x) + \omega^p_\lambda(y,y) \implies \omega^p_\lambda(y,y) \le \omega^p_\lambda(x,x).$$

Consequently, we obtain

$$\omega^p_\lambda(x,y) = \omega^p_\lambda(x,x) = \omega^p_\lambda(y,y).$$

Thus, by the second part of $(\omega^p_{1'})$ of Definition 5, $x = y$.
(ω_3) : From $(\omega^p_{1'})$ of Definition 5, we obtain
$\omega^p_{\lambda+\mu}(x,x) = \omega^p_\lambda(x,x)$ and $\omega^p_{\lambda+\mu}(y,y) = \omega^p_\lambda(y,y), \forall x,y \in X$ and $\forall\lambda,\mu > 0$.
Now, by $(\omega^p_{4'})$ of Definition 5, we have

$$\begin{aligned}
\omega^s_{\lambda+\mu}(x,y) &= 2\omega^p_{\lambda+\mu}(x,y) - \omega^p_{\lambda+\mu}(x,x) - \omega^p_{\lambda+\mu}(y,y) \\
&= 2\omega^p_{\lambda+\mu}(x,y) - \omega^p_\lambda(x,x) - \omega^p_\mu(y,y) \\
&\le 2\Big(\omega^p_\lambda(x,z) + \omega^p_\mu(z,y) - \omega^p_\lambda(z,z))\Big) - \omega^p_\lambda(x,x) - \omega^p_\mu(y,y) \\
&= \Big(2\omega^p_\lambda(x,z) - \omega^p_\lambda(x,x) - \omega^p_\lambda(z,z)\Big) + \Big(2\omega^p_\mu(z,y) - \omega^p_\lambda(z,z)) - \omega^p_\mu(y,y)\Big) \\
&= \omega^s_\lambda(x,z) + \omega^s_\mu(z,y).
\end{aligned}$$

Thus, ω^s satisfies the axioms $(\omega_1), (\omega_2)$ and (ω_3) of Definition 2 and hence ω^s is a modular metric. □

Remark 2. *(i) Let ω^s be a modular metric induced by partial modular metric ω^p on a non-empty set X, and then X_{ω^s} shall denote the modular space with respect to modular metric ω^s.*
(ii) Let ω be a modular metric on X and $c \ge 0$; then,

$$\omega^p_\lambda(x,y) = \omega_\lambda(x,y) + c$$

defines a partial modular metric on X and the corresponding modular metric is $\omega^s_\lambda(x,y) = 2\omega_\lambda(x,y)$ or $\omega^s_\lambda(x,y) = 2(\omega^p_\lambda(x,y) - c)$. Moreover, ω^p is (weakly) convex if ω is a (weakly) convex modular metric with $c = 0$ on X.

Example 4. *Let $X = \mathbb{R}$. Define a function $\omega^p_\lambda : (0,\infty) \times X \times X \to [0,\infty)$ by*

$$\omega^p_\lambda(x,y) = e^{-\lambda}|x-y| + c,$$

where $c \ge 0$, $\lambda > 0$ and $\forall x,y \in X$. Then, ω^p is a partial modular metric on X.

Example 5. *Let (X,d) be a metric space and a function ω^p be defined by*

$$\omega^p_\lambda(x,y) = \frac{d(x,y)+c}{\lambda}, \ \forall x,y \in X, \text{ and } \forall \lambda > 0$$

where $c \geq 0$. We see that $\lim_{\lambda\to+\infty} \omega^p_\lambda(x,y) = 0$, $\forall x,y \in X$. However, ω^p is not a partial modular metric on X. Indeed, by the first part of $(\omega^p_{1'})$ of Definition 5, $\omega^p_\lambda(x,x) \neq \omega^p_\mu(x,x)$, $\forall x \in X$ and $\forall \lambda, \mu > 0, \lambda \neq \mu$.

Example 6. *Let $X = \mathbb{R}$. Define*

$$\omega^p_\lambda(x,y) = e^{-\lambda}|x-y| + |x| + |y|, \ \forall x,y \in X \text{ and } \forall \lambda > 0.$$

Then, ω^p is a partial modular metric on X. It is obvious that $(\omega^p_{1'})$, (ω^p_2) and (ω^p_3) of Definition 5 hold. For $(\omega^p_{4'})$, $\forall \lambda, \mu > 0$ and $\forall x,y,z \in X$, we have

$$\begin{aligned}
\omega^p_{\lambda+\mu}(x,y) &= e^{-(\lambda+\mu)}|x-y| + |x| + |y| \\
&\leq e^{-(\lambda+\mu)}\Big(|x-z| + |z-y|\Big) + |x| + |y| \\
&= \Big(e^{-(\lambda+\mu)}|x-z| + |x|\Big) + \Big(e^{-(\lambda+\mu)}|z-y| + |y|\Big) \\
&\leq \Big(e^{-\lambda}|x-z| + |x| + |z|\Big) + \Big(e^{-\mu}|z-y| + |z| + |y|\Big) - 2|z| \\
&= \omega^p_\lambda(x,z) + \omega^p_\mu(z,y) - \omega^p_\lambda(z,z).
\end{aligned}$$

Thus, ω^p is a partial modular metric on X.

Example 7. *Let $X \neq \emptyset$ be a set. Define $\omega^p_\lambda(x,y) = \frac{|x-y|}{\lambda} + c, c > 0$, $\forall x,y \in X$ and $\forall \lambda > 0$. It is obvious that $(\omega^p_{1'})$, (ω^p_2) and (ω^p_3) of Definition 5 hold. Now, we show that ω^p is a partial modular metric and but not (weakly) convex on X.*
For $(\omega^p_{4'})$, $\forall x,y,z \in X$ and $\forall \lambda, \mu > 0$, we have

$$\begin{aligned}
\omega^p_{\lambda+\mu}(x,y) &= \frac{|x-y|}{\lambda+\mu} + c \\
&\leq \frac{1}{\lambda+\mu}\Big(|x-z| + |z-y|\Big) + c \\
&\leq \Big(\frac{|x-z|}{\lambda} + c\Big) + \Big(\frac{|z-y|}{\mu} + c\Big) - c \\
&= \omega^p_\lambda(x,z) + \omega^p_\mu(z,y) - \omega^p_\mu(z,z).
\end{aligned}$$

Then, ω^p is a partial modular metric on X. On the other hand, $\forall \lambda, \mu > 0$ and $\forall x.y,z \in X$, and we have

$$\begin{aligned}
\omega^p_{\lambda+\mu}(x,y) &\leq \frac{1}{\lambda+\mu}\Big(|x-z| + |z-y|\Big) + c \\
&= \frac{\lambda}{\lambda+\mu}\Big(\frac{|x-z|}{\lambda} + c\Big) + \frac{\mu}{\lambda+\mu}\Big(\frac{|z-y|}{\mu} + c\Big) \\
&= \frac{\lambda}{\lambda+\mu}\omega^p_\lambda(x,z) + \frac{\mu}{\lambda+\mu}\omega^p_\mu(z,y).
\end{aligned}$$

To show that ω^p is not convex on X, $\forall\lambda, \mu > 0$, taking $x = 4, y = 1, z = 2$, then

$$\begin{aligned}&\Big(\frac{\lambda}{\lambda+\mu}\omega^p_\lambda(x,z) + \frac{\mu}{\lambda+\mu}\omega^p_\mu(z,y) - \frac{\lambda}{\lambda+\mu}\omega^p_\mu(z,z)\Big) - \omega^p_{\lambda+\mu}(x,y)\\ &= \Big(\frac{3}{\lambda+\mu} + c - \frac{\lambda}{\lambda+\mu}c\Big) - \Big(\frac{3}{\lambda+\mu} + c\Big)\\ &= -\frac{\lambda}{\lambda+\mu}c < 0.\end{aligned}$$

This shows that ω^p is not convex and, hence, it is not a weakly convex partial modular metric on X.

Example 8. *Let ω^p be a partial modular metric on a non-empty set X. Define $\omega^p_\lambda(x,y) = \frac{\omega_\lambda(x,y)}{\lambda}$, $\forall x, y \in X$ and $\forall\lambda > 0$. Then, ω^p is convex and hence it is a weakly convex partial modular metric on X.*

Example 9. *For any non-empty set X, define $\omega^p_\lambda(x,y) = e^{-\lambda}\omega_\lambda(x,y)$, $\forall x, y \in X$ and $\forall\lambda > 0$. Then, ω^p is weakly convex but is not a convex partial modular metric on X.*

Definition 9. *Let ω^p be a partial modular metric on a non-empty set X and $\{x_n\}$ be a sequence in a partial modular space X_{ω^p}; then,*

(i) *$\{x_n\}$ is said to be convergent to a point $x \in X_{\omega^p}$, if and only if, for every $\epsilon > 0$, there exists $n_0 \in \mathbb{N} \cup \{0\}$ such that*
$$|\omega^p_\lambda(x_n, x) - \omega^p_\lambda(x,x)| \leq \epsilon,$$
$\forall n \geq n_0$ and $\forall\lambda > 0$. We write $\lim_{n\to+\infty} \omega^p_\lambda(x_n, x) = \omega^p_\lambda(x,x)$, $\forall\lambda > 0$;

(ii) *a sequence $\{x_n\}$ is a Cauchy in X_{ω^p} if $\lim_{n,m\to+\infty} \omega^p_\lambda(x_n, x_m) = c$, $\forall\lambda > 0$, for some $c \geq 0$. In this case, $\lim_{n\to+\infty} \omega^p_\lambda(x_n, x_n) = \lim_{m\to+\infty} \omega^p_\lambda(x_m, x_m) = c$. Thus, if $\{x_n\}$ is a Cauchy sequence in X_{ω^s}, then $c = 0$;*

(iii) *a partial modular space X_{ω^p} is said to be complete if every Cauchy sequence converges to a point $x \in X_{\omega^p}$ such that*
$$\lim_{n,m\to+\infty} \omega^p_\lambda(x_n, x_m) = \omega^p_\lambda(x,x),\ \forall\lambda > 0.$$

Remark 3. (i) *If $\{x_n\}$ is a Cauchy sequence in X_{ω^s}, i.e., $\lim_{n,m\to+\infty} \omega^s_\lambda(x_n, x_m) = 0$, then*
$$\lim_{n,m\to+\infty} \omega^p_\lambda(x_n, x_m) = \lim_{n\to+\infty} \omega^p_\lambda(x_n, x_n) = \lim_{m\to+\infty} \omega^p_\lambda(x_m, x_m).$$

(ii) *If $\{x_n\}$ is a Cauchy sequence in X_{ω^s} that converges to some point $x \in X_{\omega^s}$, then*
$$\lim_{n,m\to+\infty} \omega^p_\lambda(x_n, x_m) = \lim_{n\to+\infty} \omega^p_\lambda(x_n, x_n) = \omega^p_\lambda(x,x).$$

(iii) *A sequence $\{x_n\}$ in X_{ω^p} is a Cauchy sequence if it is a Cauchy sequence in X_{ω^s}, i.e., $\lim_{n,m\to+\infty} \omega^s_\lambda(x_n, x_m) = 0$.*

Lemma 3. *Let ω^p be a partial modular on X and $\{x_n\}$ be a sequence in X_{ω^p}. Then,*

(i) *$\{x_n\}$ is a Cauchy sequence in X_{ω^p} if it is a Cauchy sequence in the modular space X_{ω^s} induced by partial modular metric ω^p;*

(ii) *a partial modular space X_{ω^p} is complete if and only if the modular space X_{ω^s} induced by ω^p is complete. Furthermore,*
$$\lim_{n\to+\infty} \omega^s_\lambda(x_n, x) = 0 \iff \lim_{n\to\infty}[2\omega^p_\lambda(x_n, x) - \omega^p_\lambda(x_n, x_n) - \omega^p_\lambda(x.x)] = 0$$

or

$$\lim_{n\to\infty} \omega^s_\lambda(x_n, x) = 0 \Longleftrightarrow \lim_{n\to+\infty} \omega^p_\lambda(x_n, x) = \lim_{n\to+\infty} \omega^p_\lambda(x_n, x_n) = \omega^p_\lambda(x, x),\ \forall\lambda > 0.$$

Definition 10 ([18]). *A continuous function $\mathcal{F} : [0,\infty) \times [0,\infty) \to \mathbb{R}$ is called a $C-$ class function if, for any $s, t \in \mathbb{R}$, the following conditions hold:*

(i) $\mathcal{F}(s,t) \leq s$;
(ii) $\mathcal{F}(s,t) = s$ *implies* $s = 0$ *or* $t = 0$.

Example 10 ([18]). *The following are examples of the $C-$class function:*

(i) $\mathcal{F}(s,t) = \alpha s,\ \alpha \in (0,1)$;
(ii) $\mathcal{F}(s,t) = \frac{s}{(1+t)^r},\ r \in (0,\infty)$;
(iii) $\mathcal{F}(s,t) = \frac{\log(t+\alpha^s)}{(1+t)},\ \alpha > 1$.

Definition 11 ([19]). *A control function $\psi : [0,\infty) \to [0,\infty)$ is called an altering distance if the following conditions hold:*

(i) ψ *is non-decreasing and continuous;*
(ii) $\psi(t) = 0$ *if and only if* $t = 0$.

We denote by Ψ the set of all altering distance functions.

Example 11 ([20]). *The following examples are the altering distance functions:*

(i) $\psi(t) = e^{\alpha t} + \beta t - 1$;
(ii) $\psi(t) = \alpha t^2 + \ln(\beta t + 1)$, *where* $\alpha, \beta > 0$.

Definition 12 ([18]). *A control function $\varphi : [0,\infty) \to [0,\infty)$ is called an ultra-altering distance if the following conditions hold:*

(i) φ *is continuous;*
(ii) $\varphi(t) > 0,\ t > 0$ *and* $\varphi(0) \geq 0$.

Φ denotes the set of all ultra-altering distance functions.

Definition 13 ([21]). *A triplet $(\psi, \varphi, \mathcal{F})$, where $\psi \in \Psi$, $\varphi \in \Phi$ and $\mathcal{F} \in C$ is monotonically increasing if*

$$\forall x, y \in [0,\infty),\ x \leq y \Longrightarrow \mathcal{F}(\psi(x), \varphi(x)) \leq \mathcal{F}(\psi(y), \varphi(y)).$$

Further, we say that the triplet $(\psi, \varphi, \mathcal{F})$ is strictly monotonically increasing if

$$\forall x, y \in [0,\infty)\ x < y \Longrightarrow \mathcal{F}(\psi(x), \varphi(x)) < \mathcal{F}(\psi(y), \varphi(y)).$$

Example 12 ([21]). *Consider a $C-$ class function $\mathcal{F}(s,t) = s - t$. Define $\psi, \varphi : [0,\infty) \to [0,\infty)$ by $\varphi(x) = \sqrt{x}$ and*

$$\psi(x) = \begin{cases} \sqrt{x}, & 0 \leq x \leq 1; \\ x^2, & x > 1. \end{cases}$$

Obviously, the triplet $(\psi, \varphi, \mathcal{F})$ is monotonically increasing.

Definition 14 ([22]). *Let $\mathcal{P}$ and $\mathcal{Q}$ be two self-mappings on a non-empty set X; then, they are said to be weakly compatible if they commute at their coincidence points, i.e., $\mathcal{P}\mathcal{Q}x = \mathcal{Q}\mathcal{P}x$, for some $x \in X$.*

Definition 15 ([23]). *Let $X \neq \emptyset$ and $\mathcal{P}, \mathcal{Q} : X \to X$ be two self-mappings. If $u = \mathcal{P}x = \mathcal{Q}x$, for some $x \in X$, then x is called a coincidence point of $\mathcal{P}$ and $\mathcal{Q}$, and u is called a point of coincidence (briefly, poc) of $\mathcal{P}$ and $\mathcal{Q}$.*

Lemma 4 ([23]). *If $\mathcal{P}$ and $\mathcal{Q}$ are weakly compatible self-mappings on a non-empty set X, and if $\mathcal{P}$ and $\mathcal{Q}$ have a unique point of coincidence $u = \mathcal{P}x = \mathcal{Q}x$, then u is the unique common fixed-point $\mathcal{P}$ and $\mathcal{Q}$.*

3. Main Results

Let ω^p be a partial modular metric on a non-empty set X and X_{ω^p} be a partial modular space. Suppose that $\mathcal{P}, \mathcal{Q}, \mathcal{R}, \mathcal{S} : X_{\omega^p} \to X_{\omega^p}$ are four self-mappings such that

$$\mathcal{P}X_{\omega^p} \subseteq \mathcal{Q}X_{\omega^p} \text{ and } \mathcal{R}X_{\omega^p} \subseteq \mathcal{S}X_{\omega^p}. \tag{1}$$

Let $x_0 \in X_{\omega^p}$ be any point. By virtue of (1), the two sequences $\{x_n\}$ and $\{y_n\}$ in X_{ω^p} are defined as follows:

$$y_{2n} = \mathcal{P}x_{2n} = \mathcal{Q}x_{2n+1} \text{ and } y_{2n+1} = \mathcal{R}x_{2n+1} = \mathcal{S}x_{2n+2}, \forall n \in \mathbb{N} \cup \{0\}. \tag{2}$$

Inspired by Chandok et al. [4], we are ready to prove the following lemma, which plays a crucial role in the subsequent results.

Lemma 5. *Let ω^p be a partial modular metric on a non-empty set X and X_{ω^p} be a partial modular space. Suppose that $\mathcal{P}, \mathcal{Q}, \mathcal{R}, \mathcal{S} : X_{\omega^p} \to X_{\omega^p}$ are four self-mappings satisfying the condition (1). If there exist $\psi \in \Psi$, $\varphi \in \Phi$ and $\mathcal{F} \in \mathcal{C}$ such that the triplet $(\psi, \varphi, \mathcal{F})$ is a monotonically increasing function satisfying the following:*

$$\psi(\omega^p_\lambda(\mathcal{P}x, \mathcal{R}y)) \leq \mathcal{F}(\psi(\mathcal{M}(x,y)), \varphi(\mathcal{M}(x,y))), \tag{3}$$

where

$$\begin{aligned}\mathcal{M}(x,y) = \ &\max\{\omega^p_\lambda(\mathcal{S}x, \mathcal{Q}y), \omega^p_\lambda(\mathcal{S}x, \mathcal{P}x), \omega^p_\lambda(\mathcal{Q}y, \mathcal{R}y), \\ &\frac{1}{2}[\omega^p_{2\lambda}(\mathcal{Q}y, \mathcal{P}x) + \omega^p_{2\lambda}(\mathcal{S}x, \mathcal{R}y)]\},\end{aligned}$$

$\forall \lambda > 0$ and $\forall x, y \in X_{\omega^p}$. Then, the sequence $\{y_n\}$ defined by (2) is a Cauchy sequence in X_{ω^p}.

Proof. From (2), we recall that

$$y_{2n} = \mathcal{P}x_{2n} = \mathcal{Q}x_{2n+1} \text{ and } y_{2n+1} = \mathcal{R}x_{2n+1} = \mathcal{S}x_{2n+2}, \forall n \in \mathbb{N} \cup \{0\}.$$

Using (3), we obtain

$$\begin{aligned}\psi(\omega^p_\lambda(y_{2n}, y_{2n+1})) &= \psi(\omega^p_\lambda(\mathcal{P}x_{2n}, \mathcal{R}x_{2n+1})) \\ &\leq \mathcal{F}(\psi(\mathcal{M}(x_{2n}, x_{2n+1})), \varphi(\mathcal{M}(x_{2n}, x_{2n+1}))),\end{aligned} \tag{4}$$

where

$$\begin{aligned}\mathcal{M}(x_{2n}, x_{2n+1}) = \ &\max\{\omega^p_\lambda(\mathcal{S}x_{2n}, \mathcal{Q}x_{2n+1}), \omega^p_\lambda(\mathcal{S}x_{2n}, \mathcal{P}x_{2n}), \omega^p_\lambda(\mathcal{Q}x_{2n+1}, \mathcal{R}x_{2n+1}), \\ &\frac{1}{2}[\omega^p_{2\lambda}(\mathcal{Q}x_{2n+1}, \mathcal{P}x_{2n}) + \omega^p_{2\lambda}(\mathcal{S}x_{2n}, \mathcal{R}x_{2n+1})]\} \\ = \ &\max\{\omega^p_\lambda(y_{2n-1}, y_{2n}), \omega^p_\lambda(y_{2n-1}, y_{2n}), \omega^p_\lambda(y_{2n}, y_{2n+1}), \\ &\frac{1}{2}[\omega^p_{2\lambda}(y_{2n}, y_{2n}) + \omega^p_{2\lambda}(y_{2n-1}, y_{2n+1})]\}.\end{aligned} \tag{5}$$

and by $(\omega^p_{1'})$ and $(\omega^p_{4'})$, we have

$$\begin{aligned}&\frac{1}{2}[\omega^p_{2\lambda}(y_{2n}, y_{2n}) + \omega^p_{2\lambda}(y_{2n-1}, y_{2n+1})] \\ &\leq \frac{1}{2}[\omega^p_{\lambda}(y_{2n}, y_{2n}) + \omega^p_{\lambda}(y_{2n-1}, y_{2n}) + \omega^p_{\lambda}(y_{2n}, y_{2n+1}) - \omega^p_{\lambda}(y_{2n}, y_{2n})] \\ &= \frac{1}{2}[\omega^p_{\lambda}(y_{2n-1}, y_{2n}) + \omega^p_{\lambda}(y_{2n}, y_{2n+1})].\end{aligned} \tag{6}$$

Using (5), (6) and the monotonicity of the triplet $(\psi, \varphi, \mathcal{F})$, (4) becomes

$$\begin{aligned}\psi(\omega^p_{\lambda}(y_{2n}, y_{2n+1})) \leq \mathcal{F}(&\psi(\max\{\omega^p_{\lambda}(y_{2n-1}, y_{2n}), \omega^p_{\lambda}(y_{2n}, y_{2n+1})\}), \\ &\varphi(\max\{\omega^p_{\lambda}(y_{2n-1}, y_{2n}), \omega^p_{\lambda}(y_{2n}), y_{2n+1})\})),\end{aligned} \tag{7}$$

From the above inequality, the following cases arise:

Case (I): Suppose $\omega^p_{\lambda}(y_{2n-1}, y_{2n}) < \omega^p_{\lambda}(y_{2n}, y_{2n+1})$; then, from (7) and by the strict monotonicity of $(\psi, \varphi, \mathcal{F})$, we obtain

$$\begin{aligned}\psi(\omega^p_{\lambda}(y_{2n}, y_{2n+1})) &< \mathcal{F}(\psi(\omega^p_{\lambda}(y_{2n}, y_{2n+1}), \varphi(\omega^p_{\lambda}(y_{2n}, y_{2n+1}))) \\ &\leq \psi(\omega^p_{\lambda}(y_{2n}, y_{2n+1})).\end{aligned}$$

Therefore, $\omega^p_{\lambda}(y_{2n}, y_{2n+1}) < \omega^p_{\lambda}(y_{2n}, y_{2n+1})$. This is a contradiction.

Case (II): Suppose $\omega^p_{\lambda}(y_{2n}, y_{2n+1}) \leq \omega^p_{\lambda}(y_{2n-1}, y_{2n})$; then, from (7), we obtain

$$\psi(\omega^p_{\lambda}(y_{2n}, y_{2n+1})) \leq \mathcal{F}(\psi(\omega^p_{\lambda}(y_{2n-1}, y_{2n})), \varphi(\omega^p_{\lambda}(y_{2n-1}, y_{2n})). \tag{8}$$

Since ψ is a non-increasing function, then, from (8), we have

$$\psi(\omega^p_{\lambda}(y_{2n}, y_{2n+1})) \leq \psi(\omega^p_{\lambda}(y_{2n-1}, y_{2n})) \Longrightarrow \omega^p_{\lambda}(y_{2n}, y_{2n+1})) \leq \quad \omega^p_{\lambda}(y_{2n-1}, y_{2n}).$$

This shows that $\{\omega^p_{\lambda}(y_{2n}, y_{2n+1})\}$ is a non-increasing sequence of non-negative real numbers. Thus, there exists $\epsilon \geq 0$ such that

$$\lim_{n \to +\infty} \omega^p_{\lambda}(y_{2n}, y_{2n+1}) = \epsilon, \ \forall \lambda > 0.$$

Taking the limit as $n \to +\infty$ in (8), we obtain

$$\psi(\epsilon) \leq \mathcal{F}(\psi(\epsilon), \varphi(\epsilon)) \leq \psi(\epsilon) \Longrightarrow \mathcal{F}(\psi(\epsilon), \varphi(\epsilon)) = \psi(\epsilon),$$

so $\psi(\epsilon) = 0$ or $\varphi(\epsilon) = 0$ and hence $\epsilon = 0$, i.e.,

$$\lim_{n \to +\infty} \omega^p_{\lambda}(y_{2n}, y_{2n+1}) = 0, \ \forall \lambda > 0. \tag{9}$$

Now, we show that $\{y_n\}$ is a Cauchy sequence in X_{ω^p}. By Lemma 3, it is sufficient to prove that a subsequence $\{y_{2n}\}$ of $\{y_n\}$ is a Cauchy sequence in X_{ω^s}.

From (ω^p_2) of Definition 4, we have

$$0 \leq \omega^p_{\lambda}(y_{2n}, y_{2n}) \leq \omega^p_{\lambda}(y_{2n}, y_{2n+1}), \ \forall \lambda > 0,$$

so from (9), it follows that

$$\lim_{n \to +\infty} \omega^p_{\lambda}(y_{2n}, y_{2n}) = 0. \tag{10}$$

Similarly, $\lim_{n \to +\infty} \omega^p_{\lambda}(y_{2n+1}, y_{2n+1}) = 0, \ \forall \lambda > 0$.

If possible, let $\{y_{2n}\}$ be not a Cauchy in X_{ω^s}, and then there exists $\delta > 0$ such that, for each even $+ve$ integer k, we can find subsequence $\{y_{2m(k)}\}$ and $\{y_{2n(k)}\}$ of $\{y_{2n}\}$ with $2n(k) > 2m(k) \geq k$ such that

$$\omega_\lambda^s(y_{2m(k)}, y_{2n(k)}) > \delta, \ \forall\, \lambda > 0. \tag{11}$$

Now, we choose $2n(k)$ corresponding to $2m(k)$ such that it is the smallest even integer with $2n(k) > 2m(k)$ and satisfies Inequality (11). Hence,

$$\omega_\lambda^s(y_{2m(k)}, y_{2n(k)-1}) \leq \delta, \ \forall\, \lambda > 0. \tag{12}$$

By triangular inequality (ω_3) and (12), we have

$$\begin{aligned} \omega_\lambda^s(y_{2m(k)}, y_{2n(k)}) &\leq \omega_{\frac{\lambda}{2}}^s(y_{2m(k)}, y_{2n(k)-1}) + \omega_{\frac{\lambda}{2}}^s(y_{2n(k)-1}, y_{2n(k)})| \\ &\leq \delta + \omega_{\frac{\lambda}{2}}^s(y_{2n(k)-1}, y_{2n(k)}). \end{aligned} \tag{13}$$

On the other hand, by Lemma 2, $\forall \lambda > 0$, we have

$$\begin{aligned} \omega_\lambda^s(y_{2n(k)-1}, y_{2n(k)}) = 2\omega_\lambda^p(y_{2n(k)-1}, y_{2n(k)}) - \omega_\lambda^p(y_{2n(k)-1}, y_{2n(k)-1}) \\ - \omega_\lambda^p(y_{2n(k)}, y_{2n(k)}). \end{aligned} \tag{14}$$

Letting $k \to +\infty$ on (14), then from (9) and (10) , $\forall \lambda > 0$, we have

$$\lim_{k \to +\infty} \omega_\lambda^s(y_{2n(k)-1}, y_{2n(k)}) = 0, \ \forall \lambda > 0. \tag{15}$$

From (13), using (11) and (15), we have

$$\delta < \lim_{k \to \infty} \omega_\lambda^s(y_{2m(k)}, y_{2n(k)}) \leq \delta, \ \forall \lambda > 0.$$

This implies

$$\lim_{k \to +\infty} \omega_\lambda^s(y_{2m(k)}, y_{2n(k)}) = \delta. \tag{16}$$

Again, using the triangular inequality (ω_3), we have

$$\begin{aligned} \omega_\lambda^s(y_{2n(k)}, y_{2m(k)}) &\leq \omega_{\frac{\lambda}{2}}^s(y_{2n(k)}, y_{2n(k)-1}) + \omega_{\frac{\lambda}{2}}^s(y_{2n(k)-1}, y_{2m(k)}) \\ &\leq \omega_{\frac{\lambda}{2}}^s(y_{2n(k)}, y_{2n(k)-1}) + \omega_{\frac{\lambda}{4}}^s(y_{2n(k)-1}, y_{2m(k)-1}) \\ &\quad + \omega_{\frac{\lambda}{4}}^s(y_{2m(k)-1}, y_{2m(k)}). \end{aligned} \tag{17}$$

Furthermore, we have

$$\begin{aligned} \omega_\lambda^s(y_{2n(k)-1}, y_{2m(k)-1}) \leq \omega_{\frac{\lambda}{2}}^s(y_{2n(k)-1}, y_{2n(k)}) + \omega_{\frac{\lambda}{4}}^s(y_{2n(k)}, y_{2m(k)}) \\ + \omega_{\frac{\lambda}{4}}^s(y_{2m(k)}, y_{2m(k)-1}) \end{aligned} \tag{18}$$

Letting the limit as $k \to +\infty$ in (17) and (18), using (15) and (16), we obtain

$$\lim_{k \to \infty} \omega_\lambda^s(y_{2n(k)-1}, y_{2m(k)-1}) = \delta.$$

Further, we have

$$\omega_\lambda^s(y_{2n(k)+1}, y_{2m(k)}) \leq \omega_{\frac{\lambda}{2}}^s(y_{2n(k)+1}, y_{2n(k)}) + \omega_{\frac{\lambda}{2}}^s(y_{2n(k)}, y_{2m(k)}). \tag{19}$$

However,

$$\omega^s_{2\lambda}(y_{2n(k)}, y_{2m(k)}) \leq \omega^s_\lambda(y_{2n(k)}, y_{2n(k)+1}) + \omega^s_\lambda(y_{2n(k)+1}, y_{2m(k)}). \tag{20}$$

Taking the limit on (19) and (20) as $k \to +\infty$ and using (15) and (16), we obtain

$$\lim_{k\to+\infty} \omega^s_\lambda(y_{2n(k)+1}, y_{2m(k)}) = \delta. \tag{21}$$

Since $\forall\lambda > 0$, we have

$$\begin{aligned}\omega^s_\lambda(y_{2n(k)}, y_{2m(k)}) = {} & [2\omega^p_\lambda(y_{2n(k)}, y_{2m(k)}) - \omega^p_\lambda(y_{2n(k)}, y_{2n(k)}) \\ & - \omega^p_\lambda(y_{2m(k)}, y_{2m(k)})].\end{aligned}$$

Taking the limit on the above equation as $k \to +\infty$, and then using (9) and (16), we obtain

$$\lim_{k\to+\infty} \omega^p_\lambda(y_{2n(k)}, y_{2m(k)}) = \frac{\delta}{2} = d \text{ (say)} \tag{22}$$

Similarly, we obtain

$$\lim_{k\to+\infty} \omega^p_\lambda(y_{2n(k)}, y_{2m(k)-1}) = \frac{\delta}{2} = d \text{ and } \lim_{k\to+\infty} \omega^p_\lambda(y_{2n(k)+1}, y_{2m(k)}) = \frac{\delta}{2} = d. \tag{23}$$

Now, from (3), we obtain

$$\begin{aligned}\psi(\omega^p_\lambda(y_{2m(k)}, y_{2n(k)+1})) &= \psi(\omega^p_\lambda(\mathcal{P}x_{2m(k)}, \mathcal{R}x_{2n(k)+1})) \\ &\leq \mathcal{F}(\psi(\mathcal{M}(x_{2m(k)}, x_{2n(k)+1})), \varphi(\mathcal{M}(x_{2m(k)}, x_{2n(k)+1}))),\end{aligned} \tag{24}$$

where

$$\begin{aligned}\mathcal{M}(x_{2m(k)}, x_{2n(k)+1}) = {} & \max\{\omega^p_\lambda(Sx_{2m(k)}, Qx_{2n(k)+1}), \omega^p_\lambda(Sx_{2m(k)}, Px_{2m(k)}), \\ & \omega^p_\lambda(Qx_{2n(k)+1}, Rx_{2n(k)+1}), \\ & \frac{1}{2}[\omega^p_{2\lambda}(Qx_{2n(k)+1}, Px_{2m(k)}) + \omega^p_{2\lambda}(Sx_{2m(k)}, Rx_{2n(k)+1})]\} \\ = {} & \max\{\omega^p_\lambda(y_{2m(k)-1}, y_{2n(k)}), \omega^p_\lambda(y_{2m(k)-1}, y_{2m(k)}), \\ & \omega^p_\lambda(y_{2n(k)}, y_{2n(k)+1}), \\ & \frac{1}{2}[\omega^p_{2\lambda}(y_{2n(k)}, y_{2m(k)}) + \omega^p_{2\lambda}(y_{2m(k)-1}, y_{2n(k)+1})]\}\end{aligned}$$

and by $(\omega^p_{4'})$, we have

$$\begin{aligned}& \frac{1}{2}[\omega^p_{2\lambda}(y_{2n(k)}, y_{2m(k)}) + \omega^p_{2\lambda}(y_{2m(k)-1}, y_{2n(k)+1})] \\ & = \frac{1}{2}\omega^p_{2\lambda}(y_{2n(k)}, y_{2m(k)}) + \frac{1}{2}[\omega^p_\lambda(y_{2m(k)-1}, y_{2m(k)}) + \omega^p_\lambda(y_{2m(k)}, y_{2n(k)+1}) \\ & - \omega^p_\lambda(y_{2m(k)}, y_{2m(k)})].\end{aligned}$$

Taking the limit as $k \to +\infty$ on (24), and then using (9), (10), (20), (22) and (23), we obtain

$$\psi(d) \leq \mathcal{F}(\psi(d), \varphi(d)) \leq \psi(d) \Longrightarrow \mathcal{F}(\psi(d), \varphi(d)) = \psi(d),$$

which implies $\psi(d) = 0$ or $\varphi(d) = 0$; then, $d = 0$. This is a contradiction. Therefore, $\{y_n\}$ is a Cauchy sequence in the modular space X_{ω^s} and hence the sequence $\{y_n\}$ is a Cauchy sequence in X_{ω^p}. $\square$

Theorem 1. *Suppose $\mathcal{P},\mathcal{Q},\mathcal{R},\mathcal{S}: X_{\omega^p} \to X_{\omega^p}$ to be four self-mappings defined on a complete partial modular space satisfying (1) and (3). Then, $poc(\mathcal{P},\mathcal{S}) \neq \emptyset$ and $poc(\mathcal{Q},\mathcal{R}) \neq \emptyset$. Further, if the pairs $(\mathcal{P},\mathcal{S})$ and $(\mathcal{Q},\mathcal{R})$ are weakly compatible in X_{ω^p}, then $\mathcal{P},\mathcal{Q},\mathcal{R}$ and $\mathcal{S}$ have a unique common fixed point in X_{ω^p}.*

Proof. By Lemma 5, $\{y_n\}$ is a Cauchy sequence in the partial modular space X_{ω^p}. Since X_{ω^p} is complete, $\{y_n\}$ converges in X_{ω^p}. Then, there exists $z \in X_{\omega^p}$ such that

$$\lim_{n\to+\infty} \omega^p_\lambda(y_n,z) = \lim_{n\to+\infty} \omega^p_\lambda(y_n,x_n) = \omega^p_\lambda(z,z),\ \forall\lambda > 0.$$

By Lemma 3 and from (9), we obtain

$$\lim_{n\to+\infty} \omega^p_\lambda(y_n,z) = 0 \text{ and } \omega^p_\lambda(z,z) = 0,\ \forall\lambda > 0. \tag{25}$$

Since X_{ω^p} is complete, the subsequences $\{\mathcal{P}x_{2n}\}, \{\mathcal{Q}x_{2n+1}\}, \{\mathcal{R}x_{2n+1}\}$ and $\{\mathcal{S}x_{2n+2}\}$, $\forall n \in \mathbb{N}\cup\{0\}$ converge to $z \in X_{\omega^p}$. Now, we show that $poc(\mathcal{P},\mathcal{S}) \neq \emptyset$ and $poc(\mathcal{Q},\mathcal{R}) \neq \emptyset$. Since $\{\mathcal{S}x_{2n+2}\}$ converges to $z \in X_{\omega^p}$, there exists $u \in X_{\omega^p}$ such that $z = \mathcal{S}u$. We claim that $\mathcal{P}u = \mathcal{S}u$. Using (3), we obtain

$$\begin{aligned}\psi(\omega^p_\lambda(\mathcal{P}u,y_{2n+1})) =&\psi(\omega^p_\lambda(\mathcal{P}u,\mathcal{R}x_{2n+1}))\\ \leq&\mathcal{F}(\psi(\mathcal{M}(u,x_{2n+1})),\varphi(\mathcal{M}(u,x_{2n+1}))),\end{aligned} \tag{26}$$

where

$$\begin{aligned}\mathcal{M}(u,x_{2n+1}) =&\ \max\{\omega^p_\lambda(\mathcal{S}u,\mathcal{Q}x_{2n+1}),\omega^p_\lambda(\mathcal{S}u,\mathcal{P}u),\omega^p_\lambda(\mathcal{Q}x_{2n+1},\mathcal{R}x_{2n+1}),\\ &\ \frac{1}{2}[\omega^p_{2\lambda}(\mathcal{Q}x_{2n+1},\mathcal{P}u)+\omega^p_{2\lambda}(\mathcal{S}u,\mathcal{R}x_{2n+1})]\}\\ =&\ \max\{\omega^p_\lambda(z,y_{2n}),\omega^p_\lambda(z,\mathcal{P}u),\omega^p_\lambda(y_{2n},y_{2n+1}),\\ &\ \frac{1}{2}[\omega^p_{2\lambda}(y_{2n},\mathcal{P}u)+\omega^p_{2\lambda}(z,y_{2n+1})]\}\end{aligned}$$

and

$$\omega^p_{2\lambda}(y_{2n},\mathcal{P}u) \leq \omega^p_\lambda(y_{2n},z) + \omega^p_\lambda(z,\mathcal{P}u) - \omega^p_\lambda(z,z).$$

Taking the limit as $n \to +\infty$ on (26), and then using (9), (25) and (27), and by the definition of $(\psi,\varphi,\mathcal{F})$, we obtain

$$\psi(\omega^p_\lambda(\mathcal{P}u,z)) \leq \lim_{n\to+\infty} \mathcal{F}(\psi(\mathcal{M}(u,x_{2n+1})),\varphi(\mathcal{M}(u,x_{2n+1}))),$$

where

$$\lim_{n\to+\infty} \mathcal{M}(u,x_{2n+1}) = \max\{\omega^p_\lambda(z,\mathcal{P}u),\frac{1}{2}\lim_{n\to+\infty}\omega^p_{2\lambda}(y_{2n},\mathcal{P}u)\}$$

and

$$\begin{aligned}\lim_{n\to+\infty} \omega^p_{2\lambda}(y_{2n},\mathcal{P}u) \leq& \lim_{n\to+\infty}[\omega^p_\lambda(y_{2n},z) + \omega^p_\lambda(z,\mathcal{P}u) - \omega^p_\lambda(z,z)]\\ \leq&\omega^p_\lambda(z,\mathcal{P}u).\end{aligned} \tag{27}$$

Therefore,

$$\begin{aligned}\psi(\omega_\lambda^p(\mathcal{P}u,z)) \leq & \lim_{n\to+\infty}\mathcal{F}(\psi(\mathcal{M}(u,x_{2n+1})),\varphi(\mathcal{M}(u,x_{2n+1}))) \\ \leq & \lim_{n\to+\infty}\mathcal{F}(\psi(\omega_\lambda^p(z,\mathcal{P}u)),\varphi(\omega_\lambda^p(z,\mathcal{P}u))) \\ \leq & \psi(\omega_\lambda^p(z,\mathcal{P}u)).\end{aligned}$$

It follows that

$$\mathcal{F}(\psi(\omega_\lambda^p(z,\mathcal{P}u)),\varphi(\omega_\lambda^p(z,\mathcal{P}u))) = \psi(\omega_\lambda^p(z,\mathcal{P}u)),$$

so $\psi(\omega_\lambda^p(z,\mathcal{P}u)) = 0$ or $\varphi(\omega_\lambda^p(z,\mathcal{P}u))$; then, $\omega_\lambda^p(z,\mathcal{P}u) = 0$ and hence $\mathcal{P}u = \mathcal{S}u = z$, i.e., $poc(\mathcal{P},\mathcal{S}) \neq \emptyset$.

Since $\mathcal{P}X_{\omega^p} \subset \mathcal{Q}X_{\omega^p}$ and $u \in poc(\mathcal{P},\mathcal{S})$, i.e., $\mathcal{P}u = \mathcal{S}u = z$, then there exists $v \in \mathcal{Q}X_{\omega^p}$ such that $\mathcal{P}u = \mathcal{Q}v = z$. Now, we show that $\mathcal{R}v = \mathcal{Q}v$. For this, from (3), we obtain

$$\psi(\omega_\lambda^p(z,\mathcal{R}v)) = \psi(\omega_\lambda^p(\mathcal{P}u,\mathcal{R}v)) \leq \mathcal{F}(\psi(\mathcal{M}(u,v)),\varphi(\mathcal{M}(u,v))), \tag{28}$$

where

$$\begin{aligned}\mathcal{M}u,v) = & \max\{\omega_\lambda^p(\mathcal{S}u,\mathcal{Q}v),\omega_\lambda^p(\mathcal{S}u,\mathcal{P}u),\omega_\lambda^p(\mathcal{Q}v,\mathcal{R}v), \\ & \frac{1}{2}[\omega_{2\lambda}^p(\mathcal{Q}v,\mathcal{P}u)+\omega_{2\lambda}^p(\mathcal{S}u,\mathcal{R}v)]\} \\ = & \max\{\omega_\lambda^p(z,z),\omega_\lambda^p(z,z),\omega_\lambda^p(z,\mathcal{R}v), \\ & \frac{1}{2}[\omega_{2\lambda}^p(z,z)+\omega_{2\lambda}^p(z,\mathcal{R}v)]\}.\end{aligned}$$

Then, (28) becomes

$$\psi(\omega_\lambda^p(z,\mathcal{R}v)) \leq \mathcal{F}(\psi(\omega_\lambda^p(z,\mathcal{R}v)),\varphi(\omega_\lambda^p(z,\mathcal{R}v))) \leq \psi(\omega_\lambda^p(z,\mathcal{R}v)).$$

Therefore,

$$\mathcal{F}(\psi(\omega_\lambda^p(z,\mathcal{R}v)),\varphi(\omega_\lambda^p(z,\mathcal{R}v))) = \psi(\omega_\lambda^p(z,\mathcal{R}v)),$$

yielding $\psi(\omega_\lambda^p(z,\mathcal{R}v)) = 0$ or $\varphi(\omega_\lambda^p(z,\mathcal{R}v)) = 0$; then, $\omega_\lambda^p(z,\mathcal{R}v) = 0$ and hence $\mathcal{R}v = z = \mathcal{Q}v$. Thus, $poc(\mathcal{R},\mathcal{Q}) \neq \emptyset$.

Since $(\mathcal{P},\mathcal{S})$ and $(\mathcal{R},\mathcal{Q})$ are weakly compatible, then $\mathcal{P}z = \mathcal{P}\mathcal{S}u = \mathcal{S}\mathcal{P}u = \mathcal{S}z$ and $\mathcal{R}z = \mathcal{R}\mathcal{Q}v = \mathcal{Q}\mathcal{R}v = \mathcal{Q}z$. Now, we claim that the pairs $(\mathcal{P},\mathcal{S})$ and $(\mathcal{R},\mathcal{Q})$ have a unique common point of coincidence. Suppose, if possible, that there exist $r,r^* \in X_{\omega^p}$, $r \neq r^*$ such that $\mathcal{P}z = \mathcal{S}z = r$ and $\mathcal{R}z = \mathcal{Q}z = r^*$.

From (3), we obtain

$$\psi(\omega_\lambda^p(r,r^*)) = \psi(\omega_\lambda^p(\mathcal{P}z,\mathcal{R}z)) \leq \mathcal{F}(\psi(\mathcal{M}(z,z)),\varphi(\mathcal{M}(z,z)))$$

where

$$\begin{aligned}\mathcal{M}(z,z) = & \max\{\omega_\lambda^p(\mathcal{S}z,\mathcal{Q}z),\omega_\lambda^p(\mathcal{S}z,\mathcal{P}z),\omega_\lambda^p(\mathcal{Q}z,\mathcal{R}z), \\ & \frac{1}{2}[\omega_{2\lambda}^p(\mathcal{Q}z,\mathcal{P}z)+\omega_{2\lambda}^p(\mathcal{S}z,\mathcal{R}z)]\} \\ = & \max\{\omega_\lambda^p(r,r^*),\omega_\lambda^p(r,r),\omega_\lambda^p(r^*,r^*), \\ & \frac{1}{2}[\omega_{2\lambda}^p(r^*,r)+\omega_{2\lambda}^p(r,r^*)]\}.\end{aligned}$$

From the above inequality, we obtain

$$\psi(\omega_\lambda^p(r,r^*)) \le \mathcal{F}(\psi(\omega_\lambda^p(r^*,r)),\varphi(\omega_\lambda^p(r^*,r))) \le \psi(\omega_\lambda^p(r^*,r))$$

It follows that

$$\mathcal{F}(\psi(\omega_\lambda^p(r^*,r)),\varphi(\omega_\lambda^p(r^*,r))) = \psi(\omega_\lambda^p(r^*,r))$$

giving $\psi(\omega_\lambda^p(r^*,r)) = 0$ or $\varphi(\omega_\lambda^p(r^*,r)) = 0$. Then, $\omega_\lambda^p(r^*,r) = 0$ and hence $r = r^*$. This is a contradiction. Therefore, by Lemma 4, the pairs $(\mathcal{P},\mathcal{S})$ and $(\mathcal{R},\mathcal{Q})$ have a unique common fixed point in X_{ω^p}. □

Example 13. *Let $X = [0,\infty)$ and define $\omega_\lambda^p(x,y) = e^{-\lambda}|x-y| + |x| + |y|$; then, ω^p is a partial modular metric on X. Moreover, we can verify that X_{ω^p} is a complete partial modular space. Let $\mathcal{P},\mathcal{Q},\mathcal{R},\mathcal{S} : X_{\omega^p} \to X_{\omega^p}$ be self-mappings defined by*

$$\mathcal{P}x = \frac{1}{2}x,\ \mathcal{Q}x = \frac{1}{3}x,\ \mathcal{S}x = x \text{ and } \mathcal{R}x = \frac{1}{6}x,\ \forall x \in X_{\omega^p}.$$

Clearly, $\mathcal{P}X_{\omega^p} \subset \mathcal{Q}X_{\omega^p}$ and $\mathcal{R}X_{\omega^p} \subset \mathcal{S}X_{\omega^p}$. Moreover, the pairs $(\mathcal{P},\mathcal{S})$ and $(\mathcal{Q},\mathcal{R})$ are weakly compatible. Setting $\psi(r) = \varphi(r) = kr$ and $\mathcal{F}(s,t) = k^2 s$, where $k = \frac{1}{2}$. Then, the triplet $(\psi,\varphi,\mathcal{F})$ is monotonically increasing. Now, $\forall x,y \in X_{\omega^p}$ and $\forall\lambda > 0$, and we have

$$\begin{aligned}
\omega_\lambda^p(\mathcal{P}x,\mathcal{R}y) &= e^{-\lambda}|\frac{1}{2}x - \frac{1}{6}y| + |\frac{1}{2}x| + |\frac{1}{6}y| \\
&= \frac{1}{2}\Big(e^{-\lambda}|x - \frac{1}{3}y| + |x| + |\frac{1}{3}y|\Big) \\
&= \frac{1}{2}\Big(e^{-\lambda}|\mathcal{S}x - \mathcal{Q}y| + |\mathcal{S}x| + |\mathcal{Q}y|\Big) \\
&\le \frac{1}{2}\mathcal{M}(x,y).
\end{aligned}$$

Therefore,

$$\begin{aligned}
\psi(\omega_\lambda^p(\mathcal{P}x,\mathcal{R}y)) &= k\omega_\lambda^p(\mathcal{P}x,\mathcal{R}y) \le k^2 M(x,y) \\
&\le \mathcal{F}(\psi(\mathcal{M}(x,y)),\varphi(\mathcal{M}(x,y))),\ \forall x,y \in X_{\omega^p} \text{ and } \forall\lambda > 0.
\end{aligned}$$

Thus, all the conditions of Theorem 1 are satisfied and 0 is the unique fixed point of $\mathcal{P},\mathcal{Q},\mathcal{R}$ and $\mathcal{S}$ in X_{ω^p}.

The following theorem is the direct consequence of Theorem 1, which is a counterpart of Banach's contraction in metric space.

Theorem 2. *Let ω^p be a partial modular metric on a non-empty set X and X_{ω^p} be a complete partial modular metric space. Suppose $\mathcal{P} : X_{\omega^p} \to X_{\omega^p}$ to be a self-mapping satisfying*

$$\omega_\lambda^p(\mathcal{P}x,\mathcal{P}y) \le k\omega_\lambda^p(x,y),\ \forall\ x,y \in X_{\omega^p} \text{ and } \forall\lambda > 0,$$

where $0 \le k < 1$; then, $\mathcal{P}$ has a unique fixed point in X_{ω^p}.

4. Application

In this section, inspired by Pant et al. [6], we establish the existence of a solution of a system of Volterra-type integral equations.

Consider a set of Volterra-type integral equations

$$x(t) = q(t) + \int_0^t \mathcal{K}_i(t,s,x(t))ds, \tag{29}$$

where $t \in [0,k] = I \subset \mathbb{R}$, $\mathcal{K}_i : [0,k] \times [0,k] \times \mathbb{R} \to \mathbb{R}, i = \{1,2,3,4\}$ and $q : [0,k] \to \mathbb{R}$ are continuous functions.

Let $X = C(I, \mathbb{R})$ be the space of real continuous functions defined on I. Define ω^p on X by

$$\omega^p_\lambda(x,y) = \max_{t\in[0,k]} \left[e^{-\lambda}|x(t) - y(t)| + |x(t)| + |y(t)|\right], \ \forall \lambda > 0.$$

Then, X_{ω^p} is a complete modular space. Suppose $\mathcal{H}_i : X_{\omega^p} \to X_{\omega^p}$ to be a self-mapping defined by

$$\mathcal{H}_i x(t) = q(t) + \int_0^t \mathcal{K}_i(t,s,x(t))ds, \forall x \in X_{\omega^p} \text{ and } \forall t \in I, i = \{1,2,3,4\}.$$

Clearly, $x(t)$ is a solution of (29) if and only if it is a common fixed point of $\mathcal{H}_i$ for $i = \{1,2,3,4\}$.

Theorem 3. *Under the above conditions, assume that the following hypotheses hold:*
(h_1): *For any $x \in X_{\omega^p}$, there exist $u, v \in X_{\omega^p}$ such that*

$$\mathcal{H}_1 x = \mathcal{H}_3 u, \ \mathcal{H}_2 x = \mathcal{H}_4 v;$$

(h_2): *For any $t \in I$, there exist $u, v \in X_{\omega^p}$ such that*

$$\mathcal{H}_1\mathcal{H}_4 u(t) = \mathcal{H}_4\mathcal{H}_1 u(t), \text{ if } \mathcal{H}_1 u(t) = \mathcal{H}_4 u(t)$$

and

$$\mathcal{H}_2\mathcal{H}_3 v(t) = \mathcal{H}_3\mathcal{H}_2 v(t), \text{ if } \mathcal{H}_2 v(t) = \mathcal{H}_3 v(t);$$

(h_3): *There exists a continuous function $f : I \times I \to \mathbb{R}^+$ such that*

$$\begin{aligned}|\mathcal{K}_1(t,s,x(s)) - \mathcal{K}_3(t,s,y(s))| \leq & f(t,s)\Big[|\mathcal{H}_4 x(s) - \mathcal{H}_2 y(s)| + e^\lambda(|\mathcal{H}_4 x(s)| \\ & + |\mathcal{H}_2 y(s)|) - 2e^\lambda(|\mathcal{H}_1 x(s)| + |\mathcal{H}_3 y(s)|)\Big]\end{aligned}$$

$\forall\ \lambda > 0$ and $\forall x, y \in X_{\omega^p}$, where $t, s \in I$;
(h_4): $\max_{t\in[0,k]} \int_0^t f(t,s)ds \leq \frac{1}{2}$.

Then, the system (29) of integral equations has a unique common solution in X_{ω^p}.

Proof. From (h_1), $\mathcal{H}_1 X_{\omega^p} \subseteq \mathcal{H}_3 X_{\omega^p}$ and $\mathcal{H}_2 X_{\omega^p} \subseteq \mathcal{H}_4 X_{\omega^p}$.

From (h_2), the pairs $(\mathcal{H}_1, \mathcal{H}_4)$ and $(\mathcal{H}_2, \mathcal{H}_3)$ are weakly compatible. Now, from (h_3), we have

$$\begin{aligned}\omega^p_\lambda(\mathcal{H}_1 x, \mathcal{H}_3 y) &= \max_{t\in[0,k]} \left[e^{-\lambda}|\mathcal{H}_1 x(t) - \mathcal{H}_3 y(t)| + |\mathcal{H}_1 x(t)| + |\mathcal{H}_3 y(t)|\right] \\ &\leq \max_{t\in[0,k]} \left[e^{-\lambda} \int_0^t |\mathcal{K}_1(t,s,r(s)) - \mathcal{K}_3(t,s,r(s))|ds + |\mathcal{H}_1 x(t)| + |\mathcal{H}_3 y(t)|\right] \\ &\leq e^{-\lambda} \max_{t\in[0,k]} \int_0^t f(t,s)ds\Big[|\mathcal{H}_4 x - \mathcal{H}_2 y| + e^\lambda(|\mathcal{H}_4 x| + |\mathcal{H}_2 y|) \\ &\quad - 2e^\lambda(|\mathcal{H}_1 x| + |\mathcal{H}_3 y|)\Big] + \Big(|\mathcal{H}_1 x| + |\mathcal{H}_3 y|\Big) \\ &\leq \frac{1}{2}\left[e^{-\lambda}|\mathcal{H}_4 x - \mathcal{H}_2 y| + |\mathcal{H}_4 x| + |\mathcal{H}_2 y|\right] \\ &= \frac{1}{2}\omega^p_\lambda(\mathcal{H}_4 x, \mathcal{H}_2 y) \\ &\leq \frac{1}{2}\mathcal{M}(x,y),\end{aligned}$$

where

$$\mathcal{M}(x,y) = \max\Big\{\omega_\lambda^p(\mathcal{H}_4x,\mathcal{H}_2y),\omega_\lambda^p(\mathcal{H}_4x,\mathcal{H}_1x),\omega_\lambda^p(\mathcal{H}_2y,\mathcal{H}_3y), \frac{\omega_{2\lambda}^p(\mathcal{H}_2x,\mathcal{H}_1x)+\omega_{2\lambda}^p(\mathcal{H}_4x,\mathcal{H}_3y)}{2}\Big\}.$$

Setting $\psi(t) = \varphi(t) = t$ and $\mathcal{F}(s,t) = \frac{1}{2}t$, then the triplet $(\psi,\varphi,\mathcal{F})$ is monotonically increasing. Therefore,

$$\omega_\lambda^p(\mathcal{H}_1x,\mathcal{H}_3y) \leq \mathcal{F}(\psi(\mathcal{M}(x,y)),\varphi(\mathcal{M}(x,y))),\ \forall x,y \in X_{\omega^p} \text{ and } \forall\lambda > 0.$$

Thus, all the conditions of Theorem 1 are satisfied, and hence the system (29) has a unique solution in X_{ω^p}. □

5. Conclusions

We propose a refinement of the notion of the partial modular metric to eliminate the occurrence of discrepancies in the non-zero self-distance and triangular inequality. Using the altering distance functions, a common fixed-point theorem for four self-mappings via the $\mathcal{C}-$ class function is proven in such space. In addition, we apply our results to establish the existence of a solution for a system of Volterra integral equations as an application.

Author Contributions: D.D., S.N. and Y.M.S. contributed to the methodology and the original draft preparation. Y.M.S., M.S.K. and S.S. reviewed and edited the manuscript. S.S. designed the research and supported funding acquisition. All authors have read and agreed to the published version of the manuscript.

Funding: This research received no external funding.

Data Availability Statement: Not applicable.

Acknowledgments: The authors thank the anonymous referees for their valuable constructive comments and suggestions, which improved the quality of this paper in the present form.

Conflicts of Interest: The authors declare no conflicts of interest.

References

1. Matthews, S. Partial metric topology, Proc. 8th Summer conference on general topology and applications. *Ann. N. Y. Acad. Sci.* **1994**, *728*, 183–197. [CrossRef]
2. Banach, S. Sur les operations dans les ensembles abstracts et leur application aux equations integrales. *Fund. Math.* **1922**, *3*, 133–181. [CrossRef]
3. Bukatin, M.; Kopperman, R.; Matthews, S.; Pajoohesh, H. Partial metric spaces. *Am. Math. Mon.* **2009**, *116*, 708–718. [CrossRef]
4. Chandok, S.; Kumar, D.; Park, C. C^*-algebra-valued partial metric space and fixed point theorems. *Indian Acad. Sci. (Math. Sci.)* **2019**, *37*, 1–9.
5. Kumar, S.; Rugumisa, T. Common Fixed Point of non-self mappings satisfying implicit relations in partial metric spaces. *J. Anal.* **2020**, *28*, 363–375 [CrossRef]
6. Nazam, M.; Arshad, M.; Abbas, M. Existence of common fixed points of improved F-contraction on partial metric spaces. *Appl. Gen. Topol.* **2017**, *18*, 277–287. [CrossRef]
7. Paesano, D.; Vetro, P. Fixed Points and completeness on partial metric spaces. *Miskolc Math. Notes* **2015**, *16*, 369–383. [CrossRef]
8. Pant, R.; Shukla, R.; Nashine, H.K.; Panicker, R. Some new fixed point theorems in partial metric spaces with applications. *J. Funct. Spaces* **2017**, *2017*, 1–13. [CrossRef]
9. Nakano, H. *Modulared Semi-Ordered Linear Spaces*; Maruzen Co., Ltd.: Tokyo, Japan, 1950.
10. Musielak, J.; Orlicz, W. On modular spaces. *Stud. Math.* **1959**, *18*, 49–65. [CrossRef]
11. Khamsi, M.A. A convexity property in modular function spaces. *Math. Japan.* **1996**, *44*, 269–279.
12. Kozlowski, W.M. *Modular Function Spaces, Monographs and Textbooks in Pure and Applied Mathematics*; Marcel Dekker Inc.: New York, NY, USA, 1988; Volume 122, p. 252.
13. Chistyakov, V.V. Metric modular and their applications. *Dokl. Akad. Nauk* **2006**, *406*, 165–168. [CrossRef]
14. Chistyakov, V.V. Modular metric spaces I: Basic concepts. *Nonlinear Anal.* **2010**, *72*, 1–14. [CrossRef]
15. Chistyakov, V.V. Modular metric spaces, II: Application to superposition operators. *Nonlinear Anal.* **2010**, *72*, 15–30. [CrossRef]

16. Hosseinzadeh, H.; Parvaneh, V. Meir-Keeler type contractive mappings in modular and partial modular metric spaces. *Asian-Eur. J. Math.* **2020**, *13*, 1–18. [CrossRef]
17. Abobaker, H.; Ryan, R.A. Modular Metric Spaces. *Irish Math. Soc. Bull.* **2017**, *80*, 35–44. [CrossRef]
18. Ansari, A.H. φ-ψ-contractive type mappings and related fixed point. In *The 2nd Regional Conference on Mathematics and Applications;* Payame Noor University: Tehran, Iran, 2014; pp. 377–380.
19. Khan, M.S.; Swaleh, M.; Sessa, S. Fixed point theorems by altering distances between the points. *Bull. Aust. Math. Soc.* **1984**, *30*, 1–9. [CrossRef]
20. Khan, M.S.; Mahendra Singh, Y.; Karapınar, E. On the interpolative (φ, ψ)-type Z-contraction. *UPB Sci. Bull. Ser. A* **2021**, *83*, 25–38.
21. Ansari, A.H.; Saleem, N.; Fisher, B.; Khan, M.S. $C-$ class function on Khan type fixed point theorems in generalized metric Space. *Filomat* **2017**, *31*, 3483–3494. [CrossRef]
22. Jungck, G. Common fixed points for noncontinuous non-self maps on non-metric spaces. *Far East J. Math. Sci.* **1996**, *4*, 199–215.
23. Abbas, M.; Jungck, G. Common fixed point results for non-commuting mappings without continuity in cone metric spaces. *J. Math. Anal. Appl.* **2008**, *341*, 416–420. [CrossRef]

axioms

MDPI

Article

Quadratic Lyapunov Functions for Stability of the Generalized Proportional Fractional Differential Equations with Applications to Neural Networks

Ricardo Almeida [1], Ravi P. Agarwal [2], Snezhana Hristova [3,*] and Donal O'Regan [4]

[1] Center for Research and Development in Mathematics and Applications, Department of Mathematics, University of Aveiro, 3810-193 Aveiro, Portugal; ricardo.almeida@ua.pt
[2] Department of Mathematics, Texas A&M University-Kingsville, Kingsville, TX 78363, USA; Ravi.Agarwal@tamuk.edu
[3] Faculty of Mathematics and Informatics, University of Plovdiv "Paisii Hilendarski", 4000 Plovdiv, Bulgaria
[4] School of Mathematical and Statistical Sciences, National University of Ireland, H91 TK33 Galway, Ireland; donal.oregan@nuigalway.ie
* Correspondence: snehri@uni-plovdiv.bg

Abstract: A fractional model of the Hopfield neural network is considered in the case of the application of the generalized proportional Caputo fractional derivative. The stability analysis of this model is used to show the reliability of the processed information. An equilibrium is defined, which is generally not a constant (different than the case of ordinary derivatives and Caputo-type fractional derivatives). We define the exponential stability and the Mittag–Leffler stability of the equilibrium. For this, we extend the second method of Lyapunov in the fractional-order case and establish a useful inequality for the generalized proportional Caputo fractional derivative of the quadratic Lyapunov function. Several sufficient conditions are presented to guarantee these types of stability. Finally, two numerical examples are presented to illustrate the effectiveness of our theoretical results.

Keywords: generalized Caputo proportional fractional derivative; stability; exponential stability; Mittag–Leffler stability; quadratic Lyapunov functions; Hopfield neural networks

Citation: Almeida, R.; Agarwal, R.P.; Hristova, S.; O'Regan, D. Quadratic Lyapunov Functions for Stability of the Generalized Proportional Fractional Differential Equations with Applications to Neural Networks. *Axioms* **2021**, *10*, 322. https://doi.org/10.3390/axioms10040322

Academic Editor: Yurii Kharkevych

Received: 29 October 2021
Accepted: 25 November 2021
Published: 27 November 2021

1. Introduction

In [1], Jarad, Abdeljawad, and Alzabut introduced a new type of fractional derivative, the so-called generalized proportional fractional derivative. This type of derivative preserves the semigroup property, possesses a nonlocal character, and converges to the original function and its derivative upon limiting cases [2]. Some stability properties of the Ulam type for generalized proportional fractional differential equations were studied in [3] and in [4]. We emphasize that the regular stability has not been investigated yet. In this paper, we develop some necessary tools for the generalized Caputo proportional fractional derivatives, starting with an important inequality concerning an estimate of that derivative of quadratic functions. We derive some inequalities for quadratic Lyapunov functions and some connections between the solutions and the Lyapunov functions. These results are applied to study the stability properties of the Hopfield neural network with time-variable coefficients and Lipschitz activation functions. Due to its long-term memory, nonlocality, and weak singularity characteristics, fractional calculus has been successfully applied to various models of neural networks. For instance, Boroomand constructed the Hopfield neural networks based on fractional calculus [5], Kaslik analyzed the stability of Hopfield neural networks [6], Wang applied the fractional steepest descent algorithm to train BP neural networks and proved the monotonicity and convergence of a three-layer example [7]. The three features for the generalized proportional fractional derivative—the kernel of the fractional operator, the semi-group property of the generated fractional integrals, and obtaining the Riemann–Liouville and Caputo fractional derivatives as a special case—offers a possibility for more adequate modeling of some properties of the neural network.

The equilibrium of the studied model as well as its exponential stability and the Mittag–Leffler stability are defined and investigated.

The paper is organized as follows. In Section 2, some basic definitions and results are given. In Section 3, we present several auxiliary results for the generalized Caputo proportional fractional derivatives of the quadratic Lyapunov function. Section 4 contains the main results. The Hopfield neural model with time-variable coefficients and the generalized proportional fractional derivatives of the Caputo type are set up. The equilibrium is defined in an appropriate way. Exponential stability and Mittag–Leffler stability are defined, and several sufficient conditions are obtained. The paper concludes with Section 5, in which some detailed examples of neural networks are presented and simulated.

2. Preliminary Results

We recall that the generalized proportional fractional operators of a function $u \in C^1([a,b],\mathbb{R})$, ($a < b \le \infty$ are real numbers, and in the case of $b = \infty$, the interval is open) are defined respectively by (see [2]):

- the generalized proportional fractional integral

$$({}_a\mathscr{I}^{\alpha,\rho}u)(t) = \frac{1}{\rho^\alpha\Gamma(\alpha)}\int_a^t e^{\frac{\rho-1}{\rho}(t-s)}(t-s)^{\alpha-1}u(s)\,ds, \text{ for } t \in (a,b],\ \alpha > 0;$$

- the generalized proportional Caputo fractional derivative

$$\begin{aligned}({}_a^C\mathscr{D}^{\alpha,\rho}u)(t) &= ({}_a\mathscr{I}^{1-\alpha,\rho}(\mathscr{D}^{1,\rho}u))(t)\\ &= \frac{1}{\rho^{1-\alpha}\Gamma(1-\alpha)}\int_a^t e^{\frac{\rho-1}{\rho}(t-s)}(t-s)^{-\alpha}(\mathscr{D}^{1,\rho}u)(s)\,ds, \text{ for } t \in (a,b],\ \alpha \in (0,1),\ \rho \in (0,1],\end{aligned} \tag{1}$$

where $(\mathscr{D}^{1,\rho}u)(t) = (\mathscr{D}^{\rho}u)(t) = (1-\rho)u(t) + \rho u'(t)$ and $\rho \in (0,1]$ are fixed parameters.

Remark 1. *The generalized proportional Caputo fractional derivative defined by* (1) *is a generalization of the Caputo fractional derivative (with $\rho = 1$).*

Remark 2. *Note that, in some works (for example, see [8–10]), the so-called tempered fractional integral and tempered fractional derivative are applied and defined by the following:*

$${}_aI_t^{\alpha,\lambda}x(t) = \frac{1}{\Gamma(\alpha)}\int_a^t e^{-\lambda(t-s)}(t-s)^{\alpha-1}x(s)ds, \text{ for } \alpha > 0$$

and

$${}_a^CD_t^{\alpha,\lambda}x(t) = \frac{e^{-\lambda t}}{\Gamma(1-\alpha)}\int_a^t \frac{e^{\lambda s}}{(t-s)^\alpha}(\lambda x(s) + x'(s))ds, \text{ for } \alpha \in (0,1),$$

where $\lambda \ge 0$ is a fixed parameter. Tempered fractional integrals and tempered fractional derivatives are similar to the generalized proportional fractional integrals and derivatives (if $\lambda = (1-\rho)/\rho$, $\rho \in (0,1]$, then ${}_aI_t^{\alpha,\frac{1-\rho}{\rho}}u(t) = \rho^\alpha({}_a\mathscr{I}^{\alpha,\rho}u)(t)$ and $\rho^\alpha\,{}_a^CD_t^{\alpha,\frac{1-\rho}{\rho}}u(t) = ({}_a^C\mathscr{D}^{\alpha,\rho}u)(t)$).

Proposition 1 (Proposition 5.2, [1]). *Let $\alpha \in (0,1)$ and $\rho \in (0,1]$. Then,*

$$({}_a^C\mathscr{D}^{\alpha,\rho}u)(t) = 0,\ t > a \quad \textit{with}\ u(s) = e^{\frac{\rho-1}{\rho}s},\ s > a.$$

There is an explicit formula for the solution in the scalar linear case provided in Example 5.7 [1], which is (with an appropriate correction):

Proposition 2. *The solution of the linear Caputo proportional fractional initial value problem*

$$ {}_{a}^{C}\mathscr{D}^{\alpha,\rho}x(t) = \rho^{\alpha}\lambda x(t) + f(t), \quad x(a) = x_0, \tag{2}$$

is given by

$$x(t) = x_0 e^{\frac{\rho-1}{\rho}(t-a)} E_{\alpha}(\lambda(t-a)^{\alpha}) + \rho^{-\alpha}\int_a^t e^{\frac{\rho-1}{\rho}(s-a)}(s-a)^{\alpha-1}E_{\alpha,\alpha}(\lambda(s-a)^{\alpha})f(s)ds, \tag{3}$$

where

$$E_{\alpha}(Az) = \sum_{k=0}^{\infty}\frac{(Az)^k}{\Gamma(1+k\alpha)} \quad \textit{and} \quad E_{\alpha,\beta}(Az) = \sum_{k=0}^{\infty}\frac{(Az)^k}{\Gamma(\beta+k\alpha)}$$

are Mittag–Leffler functions with one parameter and two parameters, respectively.

3. Quadratic Lyapunov Functions and Their Generalized Proportional Derivatives

Initially, we will prove the following results for scalar functions:

Lemma 1. *Let the function $u \in C^1([a,b],\mathbb{R})$ with $a, b \in \mathbb{R}$, $b \le \infty$ (if $b = \infty$, then the interval is half open) and $\alpha \in (0,1)$, $\rho \in (0,1]$ be two reals. Then,*

$$({}_{a}^{C}\mathscr{D}^{\alpha,\rho}u^2)(t) \le 2u(t)({}_{a}^{C}\mathscr{D}^{\alpha,\rho}u)(t), \quad t \in (a,b]. \tag{4}$$

Proof. From definition (1), we have that for any $t \in (a,b]$,

$$\begin{aligned}
&({}_{a}^{C}\mathscr{D}^{\alpha,\rho}u^2)(t) - 2u(t)({}_{a}^{C}\mathscr{D}^{\alpha,\rho}u)(t)\\
&= \frac{1}{\rho^{1-\alpha}\Gamma(1-\alpha)}\int_a^t e^{\frac{\rho-1}{\rho}(t-s)}(t-s)^{-\alpha}\Big\{(1-\rho)[(u(s))^2 - 2u(t)u(s) + u^2(t) - u^2(t)]\\
&+ 2\rho\Big[(u(s))'(u(s)) - (u(s))'u(t)\Big]\Big\}\,ds\\
&= \frac{1}{\rho^{1-\alpha}\Gamma(1-\alpha)}\int_a^t (t-s)^{-\alpha}\Big\{(1-\rho)e^{-\frac{1-\rho}{\rho}t}e^{\frac{1-\rho}{\rho}s}[(u(s)-u(t))^2 - u^2(t)]\\
&+ 2\rho e^{-\frac{1-\rho}{\rho}t}e^{\frac{1-\rho}{\rho}s}u(s)'[u(s)-u(t)]\Big\}\,ds\\
&\le \frac{e^{-\frac{1-\rho}{\rho}t}}{\rho^{1-\alpha}\Gamma(1-\alpha)}\int_a^t (t-s)^{-\alpha}\Big\{(1-\rho)e^{\frac{1-\rho}{\rho}s}[u(s)-u(t)]^2 + 2\rho e^{\frac{1-\rho}{\rho}s}u(s)'[u(s)-u(t)]\Big\}\,ds.
\end{aligned} \tag{5}$$

Use integration by parts and obtain the following:

$$\begin{aligned}
&({}_{a}^{C}\mathscr{D}^{\alpha,\rho}(u)^2)(t) - 2u(t)({}_{a}^{C}\mathscr{D}^{\alpha,\rho}u)(t)\\
&\le \frac{e^{-\frac{1-\rho}{\rho}t}}{\rho^{1-\alpha}\Gamma(1-\alpha)}\Big\{\rho\int_a^t (t-s)^{-\alpha}[u(s)-u(t)]^2 de^{\frac{1-\rho}{\rho}s} + 2\rho\int_a^t (t-s)^{-\alpha}e^{\frac{1-\rho}{\rho}s}u(s)'[u(s)-u(t)]ds\Big\}\\
&= \frac{e^{-\frac{1-\rho}{\rho}t}}{\rho^{1-\alpha}\Gamma(1-\alpha)}\Big\{\rho\left(\frac{[u(s)-u(t)]^2 e^{\frac{1-\rho}{\rho}s}}{(t-s)^{\alpha}}\right)\Big|_{s=a}^{s=t} - \rho\int_a^t e^{\frac{1-\rho}{\rho}s}d\Big((t-s)^{-\alpha}[u(s)-u(t)]^2\Big)\\
&+ 2\rho\int_a^t (t-s)^{-\alpha}e^{\frac{1-\rho}{\rho}s}u(s)'[u(s)-u(t)]ds\Big\}\\
&= \frac{e^{-\frac{1-\rho}{\rho}t}}{\rho^{1-\alpha}\Gamma(1-\alpha)}\Big\{\rho\left(\frac{[u(s)-u(t)]^2 e^{\frac{1-\rho}{\rho}s}}{(t-s)^{\alpha}}\right)\Big|_{s=a}^{s=t} - \rho\alpha\int_a^t e^{\frac{1-\rho}{\rho}s}(t-s)^{1-\alpha}[u(s)-u(t)]^2 ds\\
&- 2\rho\int_a^t e^{\frac{1-\rho}{\rho}s}(t-s)^{-\alpha}u'(s)[u(s)-u(t)]ds + 2\rho\int_a^t (t-s)^{-\alpha}e^{\frac{1-\rho}{\rho}s}u(s)'[u(s)-u(t)]ds\Big\}\\
&= \frac{e^{-\frac{1-\rho}{\rho}t}}{\rho^{1-\alpha}\Gamma(1-\alpha)}\Big\{\rho\left(\frac{[u(s)-u(t)]^2 e^{\frac{1-\rho}{\rho}s}}{(t-s)^{\alpha}}\right)\Big|_{s=a}^{s=t} - \rho\alpha\int_a^t e^{\frac{1-\rho}{\rho}s}(t-s)^{-1-\alpha}[u(s)-u(t)]^2 ds.
\end{aligned} \tag{6}$$

The integral

$$\int_a^t e^{\frac{1-\rho}{\rho}s}(t-s)^{-1-\alpha}[u(s)-u(t)]^2 ds$$

has a singularity at the upper limit t, but it is a removable singularity because by the L'Hopital rule, we obtain the following:

$$\lim_{s\to t^-}\frac{[u(s)-u(t)]^2}{(t-s)^{1+\alpha}} = \lim_{s\to t^-}\frac{2u'(s)(u(s)-u(t))}{-(1+\alpha)(t-s)^{\alpha}} = \lim_{s\to t^-}\frac{2(u'(s)(u(s)-u(t)))'}{(1+\alpha)\alpha}(t-s)^{1-\alpha} = 0.$$

Thus,

$$\begin{aligned}&({}_a^C\mathscr{D}^{\alpha,\rho}(u)^2)(t) - 2u(t)({}_a^C\mathscr{D}^{\alpha,\rho}u)(t) \le \frac{\rho^{\alpha}e^{-\frac{1-\rho}{\rho}t}}{\Gamma(1-\alpha)}\left(\frac{[u(s)-u(t)]^2e^{\frac{1-\rho}{\rho}s}}{(t-s)^{\alpha}}\right)\Bigg|_{s=a}^{s=t} \\ &= \frac{\rho^{\alpha}e^{-\frac{1-\rho}{\rho}t}}{\Gamma(1-\alpha)}\left(\lim_{s\to t}\frac{[u(s)-u(t)]^2e^{\frac{1-\rho}{\rho}s}}{(t-s)^{\alpha}} - \frac{[u(a)-u(t)]^2e^{\frac{1-\rho}{\rho}a}}{(t-a)^{\alpha}}\right).\end{aligned} \tag{7}$$

By the L'Hopital rule we get the following:

$$\begin{aligned}&({}_a^C\mathscr{D}^{\alpha,\rho}(u)^2)(t) - 2u(t)({}_a^C\mathscr{D}^{\alpha,\rho}u)(t) \le \frac{\rho^{\alpha}e^{-\frac{1-\rho}{\rho}t}}{\Gamma(1-\alpha)}\lim_{s\to t}\frac{[u(s)-u(t)]^2e^{\frac{1-\rho}{\rho}s}}{(t-s)^{\alpha}} \\ &= -\frac{\rho^{\alpha}e^{-\frac{1-\rho}{\rho}t}}{\Gamma(1-\alpha)}\lim_{s\to t}\frac{2u'(s)[u(s)-u(t)]e^{\frac{1-\rho}{\rho}s} + \frac{1-\rho}{\rho}[u(s)-u(t)]^2e^{\frac{1-\rho}{\rho}s}}{\alpha(t-s)^{\alpha-1}} \\ &= -\frac{\rho^{\alpha}e^{-\frac{1-\rho}{\rho}t}}{\Gamma(1-\alpha)\alpha}\lim_{s\to t}\left(2u'(s)[u(s)-u(t)]e^{\frac{1-\rho}{\rho}s} + \frac{1-\rho}{\rho}[u(s)-u(t)]^2e^{\frac{1-\rho}{\rho}s}\right)(t-s)^{1-\alpha} = 0.\end{aligned} \tag{8}$$

Inequality (8) proves the claim of Lemma 1. □

Inequality (4) is true in the vector case:

Corollary 1. *Let the function $u \in C^1([a,b],\mathbb{R}^n)$ with $a,b \in \mathbb{R}$, $b \le \infty$ (if $b = \infty$, then the interval is half open) and $\alpha \in (0,1)$, $\rho \in (0,1]$. Then,*

$$({}_a^C\mathscr{D}^{\alpha,\rho}u^T(t)u(t)) \le 2u^T(t)({}_a^C\mathscr{D}^{\alpha,\rho}u)(t), \quad t \in (a,b]. \tag{9}$$

The proof follows from the decomposition of the scalar product $u^T(t)u(t)$ into a sum of products and the application of Lemma 1.

Remark 3. *In the case of the Caputo fractional derivative, i.e., $\rho = 1$, the results of Lemma 1 and Corollary 1 are reduced to Lemma 1 [11] and Remark 1 [11].*

Consider the following system of nonlinear fractional differential equations with the generalized proportional Caputo fractional derivative:

$$\begin{aligned}&({}_{t_0}^C\mathscr{D}^{\alpha,\rho}u)(t) = F(t,u(t)), \quad \text{for } t > t_0, \\ &u(t_0) = u_0,\end{aligned} \tag{10}$$

where $t_0 \ge 0$, $({}_{t_0}^C\mathscr{D}^{\alpha,\rho}u)(t)$ is the generalized proportional Caputo fractional derivative of the function $u \in C^1([t_0,\infty),\mathbb{R}^n)$, $\rho \in (0,1]$, $\alpha \in (0,1)$ are two reals, and $F : [t_0,\infty) \times \mathbb{R}^n \to \mathbb{R}^n$ is a function.

Remark 4. *We will assume that for any initial value u_0, the initial value problem* (10) *has a solution $u(t;t_0,u_0)$ defined for $t \ge t_0$.*

Next, we will obtain two types of bounds for the solutions of (10).

Lemma 2. *Assume that:*

1. *The function $u(\cdot) = u(\cdot; t_0, u_0) \in C^1([t_0,\infty), \mathbb{R}^n)$ is a solution of the IVP for the nonlinear system of generalized proportional Caputo fractional differential equations (10);*
2. *For any point $t \geq t_0$, the inequality*

$$ {}_{t_0}^{C}\mathscr{D}^{\alpha,\rho}(\|u(t)\|^2) \leq 0 \tag{11}$$

holds.

Then,

$$\|u(t)\| \leq \|u_0\| e^{\frac{\rho-1}{2\rho}(t-t_0)}, \quad \text{for } t \geq t_0. \tag{12}$$

Proof. Define the function $m(t) = u^T(t)u(t) = \|u(t)\|^2 : [t_0, \infty) \to \mathbb{R}_+$. Let $\varepsilon > 0$ be an arbitrary number. We will prove that

$$m(t) < (\|u_0\|^2 + \varepsilon)e^{\frac{\rho-1}{\rho}(t-t_0)}, \quad t \geq t_0. \tag{13}$$

For $t = t_0$, we get

$$m(t_0) = \|u_0\|^2 < (\|u_0\|^2 + \varepsilon) = (\|u_0\|^2 + \varepsilon)e^{\frac{\rho-1}{\rho}(t_0-t_0)},$$

i.e., inequality (13) is true for $t = t_0$.

Now, assume that (13) is not true. Then there exist $t^* \in (t_0, \infty)$, such that

$$m(t) < (\|u_0\|^2 + \varepsilon)e^{\frac{\rho-1}{\rho}(t-t_0)}, \ t \in [t_0, t^*), \quad m(t^*) = (\|u_0\|^2 + \varepsilon)e^{\frac{\rho-1}{\rho}(t^*-t_0)}. \tag{14}$$

Denote $\eta(t) = \|u(t)\|^2 - (\|u_0\|^2 + \varepsilon)e^{\frac{\rho-1}{\rho}(t-t_0)} : [t_0, t^*] \to (-\infty, 0]$. From (14), it follows that $\eta(t^*) = 0$, $\eta(t) < 0$ for $t \in [t_0, t^*)$. Therefore,

$$\begin{aligned}
({}_{t_0}^{C}\mathscr{D}^{\alpha,\rho}\eta)(t)\Big|_{t=t^*} &= \frac{1}{\rho^{1-\alpha}\Gamma(1-\alpha)} \int_{t_0}^{t^*} e^{\frac{\rho-1}{\rho}(t^*-s)}(t^*-s)^{-\alpha}\Big((1-\rho)\eta(s) + \rho\eta'(s)\Big)\, ds \\
&= \frac{1}{\rho^{1-\alpha}\Gamma(1-\alpha)} \Big[\rho \int_{t_0}^{t^*} (t^*-s)^{-\alpha}\eta(s) d e^{\frac{\rho-1}{\rho}(t-s)} + \rho \int_{t_0}^{t^*} e^{\frac{\rho-1}{\rho}(t^*-s)}(t^*-s)^{-\alpha}\eta'(s) ds, \\
&= \frac{1}{\rho^{1-\alpha}\Gamma(1-\alpha)} \Big[\rho(t^*-s)^{-\alpha}\eta(s)e^{\frac{\rho-1}{\rho}(t^*-s)}\Big|_{s=t_0}^{s=t^*} - \rho \int_{t_0}^{t^*} e^{\frac{\rho-1}{\rho}(t^*-s)} d((t^*-s)^{-\alpha}\eta(s)) \\
&\quad + \rho \int_{t_0}^{t^*} e^{\frac{\rho-1}{\rho}(t^*-s)}(t^*-s)^{-\alpha}\eta'(s) ds.
\end{aligned} \tag{15}$$

Thus, by the L'Hopital rule, we get the following:

$$(t^*-s)^{-\alpha}\eta(s)e^{\frac{\rho-1}{\rho}(t^*-s)}\Big|_{s=t^*} = \lim_{s\to t^*-0} \frac{\eta(s)e^{\frac{\rho-1}{\rho}(t^*-s)}}{(t^*-s)^{\alpha}} = \lim_{s\to t^*-0} \frac{\eta'(s)e^{\frac{\rho-1}{\rho}(t^*-s)} - \frac{\rho-1}{\rho}\eta(s)e^{\frac{\rho-1}{\rho}(t^*-s)}}{\alpha}(t^*-s)^{1-\alpha} = 0. \tag{16}$$

From (15) and (16), we obtain the following:

$$\begin{aligned}
({}_{t_0}^{C}\mathscr{D}^{\alpha,\rho}\eta)(t)\Big|_{t=t^*} &= \frac{1}{\rho^{1-\alpha}\Gamma(1-\alpha)} \Bigg[-\rho(t^*-t_0)^{-\alpha}\eta(t_0)e^{\frac{\rho-1}{\rho}(t-t_0)} - \rho\alpha \int_{t_0}^{t^*} e^{\frac{\rho-1}{\rho}(t^*-s)} \frac{\eta(s)}{(t^*-s)^{1+\alpha}} ds \\
&\quad - \rho \int_{t_0}^{t^*} e^{\frac{\rho-1}{\rho}(t^*-s)}(t^*-s)^{-\alpha}\eta'(s) ds + \rho \int_{t_0}^{t^*} e^{\frac{\rho-1}{\rho}(t-s)}(t^*-s)^{-\alpha}\eta'(s) ds \Bigg] \\
&= \frac{1}{\rho^{1-\alpha}\Gamma(1-\alpha)} \Bigg[-\rho\eta(t_0)\frac{e^{\frac{\rho-1}{\rho}(t^*-t_0)}}{(t^*-t_0)^{\alpha}} - \rho\alpha \int_{t_0}^{t^*} \frac{e^{\frac{\rho-1}{\rho}(t^*-s)}}{(t^*-s)^{1+\alpha}}\eta(s) ds \Bigg] > 0.
\end{aligned} \tag{17}$$

From Proposition 1, inequality (17), and condition 2 for $t = t^*$, we obtain the equation below:

$$0 < ({}_{t_0}^{C}\mathscr{D}^{\alpha,\rho}\eta)(t)\Big|_{t=t^*} = {}_{t_0}^{C}\mathscr{D}^{\alpha,\rho}(\|u(t)\|^2 - (\|u_0\|^2 + \varepsilon)e^{\frac{\rho-1}{\rho}(t-t_0)})\Big|_{t=t^*}$$
$$= {}_{t_0}^{C}\mathscr{D}^{\alpha,\rho}\|u(t)\|^2\Big|_{t=t^*} - (\|u_0\|^2 + \varepsilon)e^{\frac{1-\rho}{\rho}t_0}{}_{t_0}^{C}\mathscr{D}^{\alpha,\rho}e^{\frac{\rho-1}{\rho}t}\Big|_{t=t^*} = {}_{t_0}^{C}\mathscr{D}^{\alpha,\rho}\|u(t)\|^2\Big|_{t=t^*} \leq 0. \tag{18}$$

The obtained contradiction proves the validity of (13) for any $\varepsilon > 0$. Therefore,

$$\|u(t)\|^2 < \|u_0\|^2 e^{\frac{\rho-1}{\rho}(t-t_0)},$$

i.e., the claim of Lemma 2 is true. □

Corollary 2. *Assume that the conditions of Lemma 2 are satisfied. Then, $\|x(t)\| \leq \|u_0\|$ for all $t \geq t_0$.*

The proof follows from inequality (12), $\rho \in (0,1]$, and the inequality $e^{\frac{\rho-1}{2\rho}(t-t_0)} \leq 1$.

Lemma 3. *Assume that:*

1. *The function $u(\cdot) = u(\cdot; t_0, u_0) \in C^1([t_0,\infty), \mathbb{R}^n)$ is a solution of the IVP for the nonlinear system of generalized proportional Caputo fractional differential equations (10);*
2. *There exists a positive constant $K > 0$, such that at any point $t \geq t_0$, the inequality*

$$ {}_{t_0}^{C}\mathscr{D}^{\alpha,\rho}\left(\|u(t)\|^2\right) \leq -K\|u(t)\|^2 \tag{19}$$

holds.

Then,

$$\|u(t)\| \leq \|u_0\| e^{\frac{\rho-1}{2\rho}(t-t_0)}\sqrt{E_\alpha\left(\frac{-K}{\rho^\alpha}t^\alpha\right)} \quad \text{for } t \geq t_0. \tag{20}$$

Proof. Define the function $m(t) = u^T(t)u(t) = \|u(t)\|^2 : [t_0,\infty) \to \mathbb{R}_+$. From inequality (19), it follows that there exists a function $\xi : [t_0,\infty) \to [0,\infty)$, such that

$$({}_{t_0}^{C}\mathscr{D}^{\alpha,\rho}m)(t) \leq -Km(t) - \xi(t),\ t \geq t_0. \tag{21}$$

According to Proposition 2, with $a = 0$, $\lambda = -K/\rho^\alpha$, $f(t) = -\xi(t)$, and $x_0 = m(0)$, the solution of the linear Caputo proportional fractional initial value problem (21) is given by

$$m(t) = m(0)e^{\frac{\rho-1}{\rho}t}E_\alpha\left(\frac{-K}{\rho^\alpha}t^\alpha\right) - \rho^{-\alpha}\int_0^t e^{\frac{\rho-1}{\rho}s}s^{\alpha-1}E_{\alpha,\alpha}\left(\frac{-K}{\rho^\alpha}s^\alpha\right)\xi(s)ds \leq m(0)e^{\frac{\rho-1}{\rho}t}E_\alpha\left(\frac{-K}{\rho^\alpha}t^\alpha\right). \tag{22}$$

□

4. Stability of Neural Networks with a Generalized Proportional Caputo Fractional Derivative

The fractional-order Hopfield neural networks with the generalized proportional Caputo fractional derivative is described by the following equation:

$$({}_{0}^{C}\mathscr{D}^{\alpha,\rho}x_i)(t) = -a_i(t)x_i(t) + \sum_{k=1}^{n} b_{i,k}(t)f_k(x_k(t)) + I_i(t),\ \ t > 0,\ i = 1,2,\ldots,n, \tag{23}$$

where n is the number of units in a neural network, ${}_{0}^{C}\mathscr{D}^{\alpha,\rho}$ denotes the generalized proportional Caputo fractional derivative of order $\alpha \in (0,1)$, $\rho \in (0,1]$, $x_i(t)$ is the state of the i-th unit at time t, $f_k(u)$ denotes the activation function of the k-th neuron, $b_{i,k}(t) : [0,\infty) \to \mathbb{R}$ denotes the connection weight of the k-th neuron on the i-th neuron at time t, $a_i(t) : [0,\infty) \to (0,\infty)$ represents the rate at which the i-th neuron resets its potential to the resting state when disconnected from the network at time t, and $I_i(t)$ denotes the external inputs at time t.

We will now define the equilibrium of the neural network (23). Different than the classical case of ordinary derivatives and the Caputo fractional derivatives, in the general case, the equilibrium of (23) could not be a constant because the generalized proportional derivative of a nonzero constant is not 0. Applying Proposition 1, we define the equilibrium of (23):

Definition 1. *The function* $x^*(t) = Ce^{\frac{\rho-1}{\rho}t} : C = (C_1, C_2, \ldots, C_n) \in \mathbb{R}^n$, $c_i = const$, $i = 1,2,\ldots,n$, *is called an equilibrium of* (23) *if*

$$a_i(t)C_i e^{\frac{\rho-1}{\rho}t} = \sum_{k=1}^{n} b_{i,k}(t) f_k(C_k e^{\frac{\rho-1}{\rho}t}) + I_i(t),\ t \geq 0,\ \ i = 1,2\ldots,n.$$

Remark 5. *The constant vector* $C \in \mathbb{R}^n$ *in Definition 1 could be a zero vector (zero equilibrium) or a nonzero vector (nonzero equilibrium).*

Remark 6. *The zero vector is an equilibrium of* (23) *if* $f_k(0) = 0$ *and* $I_k(t) \equiv 0$ *for all* $k = 1,2,\ldots,n$.

Let $x^*(t) = Ce^{\frac{\rho-1}{\rho}t}$ be an equilibrium of (23). Consider the change in the variables $u(t) = x(t) - x^*(t)$, $t \geq 0$, in system (23), use Proposition 1 and obtain the following:

$$\begin{aligned}
&({}_0^C\mathscr{D}^{\alpha,\rho}u_i)(t) = ({}_0^C\mathscr{D}^{\alpha,\rho}x_i)(t) - ({}_0^C\mathscr{D}^{\alpha,\rho}x_i^*)(t) = ({}_0^C\mathscr{D}^{\alpha,\rho}x_i)(t) \\
&= -a_i(t)(u_i(t) + x_i^*(t)) + \sum_{k=1}^{n} b_{i,k}(t) f_k(u_k(t) + x_k^*(t)) + I_i(t) \\
&= -a_i(t)u_i(t) + \sum_{k=1}^{n} b_{i,k}(t)[f_k(u_k(t) + x_k^*(t)) - f_k(x_k^*(t))] - a_i(t)x_i^*(t) + \sum_{k=1}^{n} b_{i,k}(t) f_k(x_k^*(t)) + I_i(t) \\
&= -a_i(t)u_i(t) + \sum_{k=1}^{n} b_{i,k}(t) F_k(t, u_k(t)),\ \ t > 0,\ i = 1,2,\ldots,n,
\end{aligned} \tag{24}$$

where $F_k(t,v) = f_k(v + x_k^*(t)) - f_k(x_k^*(t))$, i.e., if $x^*(t)$ is an equilibrium of (23), then the system

$$({}_0^C\mathscr{D}^{\alpha,\rho}u_i)(t) = -a_i(t)u_i(t) + \sum_{k=1}^{n} b_{i,k}(t) F_k(t, u_k(t)),\ \ t > 0,\ i = 1,2,\ldots,n, \tag{25}$$

has a zero solution, and vice versa.

Definition 2. *Let* $\alpha \in (0,1)$ *and* $\rho \in (0,1)$. *The equilibrium* $x^*(\cdot)$ *of* (23) *is called exponentially stable if, for any solution* $x(t)$ *of* (23), *the inequality*

$$\|x(t) - x^*(t)\| \leq m(\|x(0) - x^*(0)\|) e^{\lambda\frac{\rho-1}{\rho}t},\ t \geq 0,$$

holds, where $\lambda > 0$ *is a constant, and* $m(s) \geq 0$, $m(0) = 0$, *is a given locally Lipschitz function.*

Remark 7. *Note that the exponential stability is defined only for* $\rho \in (0,1)$.

Remark 8. *The exponential stability of the equilibrium* $x^*(\cdot)$ *implies that every solution* $x(\cdot)$ *of* (23) *satisfies* $\lim_{t\to\infty} \|x(t) - x^*(t)\| = 0$.

Definition 3. *Let $\alpha \in (0,1)$ and $\rho \in (0,1]$. The equilibrium $x^*(\cdot)$ of (23) is called generalized Mittag–Leffler stable if there exist the positive constants λ, μ, and γ, such that for any solution $x(\cdot)$ of (23), the inequality*

$$\|x(t) - x^*(t)\| \leq m(\|x(0) - x^*(0)\|)e^{\lambda\frac{\rho-1}{\rho}t}\Big(E_\alpha(-\mu t^\alpha)\Big)^\gamma, \; t \geq 0,$$

holds, where $E_\alpha(z)$ is the Mittag–Leffler function with one parameter, $m(s) \geq 0$, $m(0) = 0$, is a given locally Lipschitz function.

Remark 9. *Note that the generalized Mittag–Leffler stability is defined for $\rho \in (0,1]$ and for $\rho = 1$, and it generalizes the corresponding results for the Caputo fractional differential equations [6,12–15].*

Remark 10. *Note that the Mittag–Leffler stability for the Hopfield neural network with tempered fractional derivatives is studied in [10,16], but only for zero equilibrium, zero internal perturbations, and constant coefficients.*

Remark 11. *The generalized Mittag–Leffler stability of the equilibrium $x^*(\cdot)$ implies that every solution $x(\cdot)$ of (23) satisfies $\lim_{t\to\infty} \|x(t) - x^*(t)\| = 0$.*

Theorem 1 (Exponential stability). *Let the following assumptions hold:*

1. *$\alpha \in (0,1)$ and $\rho \in (0,1)$;*
2. *The functions $a_i \in C(\mathbb{R}_+, (0,\infty))$, $b_{i,k}, I_i \in C(\mathbb{R}_+, \mathbb{R})$, $i,k = 1,2,\dots,n$;*
3. *There exist positive constants M_i, $i = 1,2,\dots,n$, such that the activation functions $f_i \in C(\mathbb{R},\mathbb{R})$ satisfy $|f_i(v) - f_k(w)| \leq M_i|v - w|$ for $v, w \in \mathbb{R}$;*
4. *Equation (23) has an equilibrium $x^*(\cdot) = (x_1^*(\cdot), x_2^*(\cdot), \dots, x_n^*(\cdot))$;*
5. *The inequality*

$$2a_i(t) \geq \sum_{k=1}^{n}\Big(|b_{i,k}(t)| + M_i^2|b_{k,i}(t)|\Big), \; t \geq 0, \; i = 1,2,\dots,n$$

holds.

Then, the equilibrium $x^*(\cdot)$ of (23) is exponentially stable.

Proof. Let $x(\cdot)$ be a solution of (23), and consider the system (25) with $u(t) = x(t) - x^*(t)$, $t \geq 0$. From condition 3, we have the following equation:

$$|F_k(t,v)| = |f_k(v + x_k^*(t)) - f_k(0 + x_k^*(t))| \leq M_k|v|,$$

for $v \in \mathbb{R}$, $t \geq 0$. Then,

$$\begin{aligned} u_i(t)({}_0^C\mathscr{D}^{\alpha,\rho}u_i)(t) &= -a_i(t)u_i^2(t) + \sum_{k=1}^{n} b_{i,k}(t)(u_i(t)F_k(t,u_k(t))) \\ &\leq -a_i(t)u_i^2(t) + \sum_{k=1}^{n}|b_{i,k}(t)|0.5(u_i^2(t) + F_k^2(t,u_k(t))) \leq 0.5\Big(-2a_i(t) + \sum_{k=1}^{n}|b_{i,k}(t)|\Big)u_i^2(t) + 0.5\sum_{k=1}^{n}|b_{i,k}(t)M_k^2u_k^2(t), \end{aligned} \tag{26}$$

and by applying Condition 5, we get the following:

$$\begin{aligned}
&({}_0^C\mathscr{D}^{\alpha,\rho}(u^T(t)u(t)) \le 2u^T(t)({}_0^C\mathscr{D}^{\alpha,\rho}u)(t) = 2\sum_{i=1}^n u_i(t)({}_0^C\mathscr{D}^{\alpha,\rho}u_i)(t) \\
&\le 0.5\sum_{i=1}^n\Big(-2a_i(t)+\sum_{k=1}^n|b_{i,k}(t)|\Big)u_i^2(t)+\sum_{i=1}^n\sum_{k=1}^n|b_{i,k}(t)M_k^2u_k^2(t) \\
&= 0.5\sum_{i=1}^n\Big(-2a_i(t)+\sum_{k=1}^n|b_{i,k}(t)|\Big)u_i^2(t)+0.5\sum_{i=1}^n M_i^2u_i^2(t)\sum_{k=1}^n|b_{k,i}(t)| \\
&= 0.5\sum_{i=1}^n\Big[-2a_i(t)+\sum_{k=1}^n\Big(|b_{i,k}(t)|+M_i^2|b_{k,i}(t)|\Big)\Big]u_i^2(t)\le 0.
\end{aligned} \tag{27}$$

According to Lemma 2 applied to the system in (25), with $t_0 = 0$, the inequality

$$\|u(t)\| \le \|u(0)\|e^{\frac{\rho-1}{2\rho}t}, \quad t \ge 0 \tag{28}$$

holds. This proves the claim of the Theorem, with $\lambda = 0.5$ and $m(s) = s$. □

From Corollary 2 we obtain the following (applied to (23) with $t_0 = 0$):

Corollary 3 (Boundedness). *Let $\alpha \in (0,1)$, $\rho \in (0,1]$, and conditions 2–5 of Theorem 1 are satisfied. Then, any solution $x(\cdot)$ of* (23) *satisfies $\|x(t) - x^*(t)\| \le \|x(0) - x^*(0)\|$ for all $t \ge 0$.*

Theorem 2 (Generalized Mittag–Leffler stability). *Let the following assumptions hold:*

1. *Conditions 1–4 of Theorem 1 are satisfied;*
2. *There exists a positive constant L, such that inequality*

$$2a_i(t) - \sum_{k=1}^n\Big(|b_{i,k}(t)| + M_i|b_{k,i}(t)|\Big) \ge L,\ t \ge 0,\ i = 1,2,\dots,n$$

holds.

Then, the equilibrium $x^*(\cdot)$ of (23) *is Mittag–Leffler stable.*

Proof. Let $x(\cdot)$ be a solution of (23) and consider the system in (25) with $u(t) = x(t) - x^*(t)$. Similar to the proof of Theorem 1, we prove the following inequality:

$$({}_0^C\mathscr{D}^{\alpha,\rho}(u^T(t)u(t)) \le 0.5\sum_{i=1}^n\Big[-2a_i(t)+\sum_{k=1}^n\Big(|b_{i,k}(t)|+M_i^2|b_{k,i}(t)|\Big)\Big]u_i^2(t) \le -0.5L\|u(t)\|^2. \tag{29}$$

Denote $m(t) = \|u(t)\|^2$, and from (29) and Condition 2 of Theorem 2, it follows that there exists a function $g(t) : [0,\infty) \to (-\infty, 0]$, such that

$$({}_0^C\mathscr{D}^{\alpha,\rho}m)(t) = -0.5Lm(t) + g(t), \quad t > 0. \tag{30}$$

According to Proposition 2, the solution of the linear Caputo proportional fractional initial value problem (30) is given by the following equation:

$$m(t) = m(0)e^{\frac{\rho-1}{\rho}t}E_\alpha\Big(-\frac{0.5L}{\rho^\alpha}t^\alpha\Big) + \rho^{-\alpha}\int_0^t e^{\frac{\rho-1}{\rho}(t-a)}s^{\alpha-1}E_{\alpha,\alpha}\Big(-\frac{0.5L}{\rho^\alpha}s^\alpha\Big)g(s)ds \le m(0)e^{\frac{\rho-1}{\rho}t}E_\alpha\Big(-\frac{0.5L}{\rho^\alpha}t^\alpha\Big). \tag{31}$$

From inequality (31), it follows that

$$\|x(t) - x^*(t)\| \le \|x(0) - x^*(0)\|e^{\frac{\rho-1}{2\rho}t}\Big(E_\alpha\Big(-\frac{0.5L}{\rho^\alpha}t^\alpha\Big)\Big)^{0.5}. \tag{32}$$

□

5. Applications

Example 1. *Consider the following neural networks of $n = 3$ neurons with a ring structure [6] with the following generalized proportional fractional derivatives:*

$$\begin{aligned}({}_0^C\mathscr{D}^{\alpha,\rho}x_1)(t) &= -6x_1(t) + 2\sin(x_1(t)) + 2\sin(x_2(t)) + \sin(x_3(t)) + I_1(t),\\ ({}_0^C\mathscr{D}^{\alpha,\rho}x_2)(t) &= -5x_2(t) - 2\sin(x_1(t)) - 0.4\sin(x_2(t)) + \sin(x_3(t)) + I_2(t),\\ ({}_0^C\mathscr{D}^{\alpha,\rho}x_3)(t) &= -8x_3(t) + \sin(x_1(t)) - 2.5\sin(x_2(t)) + 3.5\sin(x_3(t)) + I_3(t), \quad t > 0,\end{aligned} \tag{33}$$

where the activation functions are $f_k(x) = \sin(x)$, $k = 1,2,3$, i.e., condition 3 of Theorem 1 is satisfied by $M_i = 1$, $i = 1,2,3$.

Case 1. Let $I_i(t) \equiv K_i \neq 0$, $i = 1,2,3$ be constants. Then, for $\rho \in (0,1)$, the system in (33) *has no equilibrium because, for example, the following equality:*

$$-6C_1e^{\frac{\rho-1}{\rho}t} = 2\sin\left(C_1e^{\frac{\rho-1}{\rho}t}\right) + \sin\left(C_2e^{\frac{\rho-1}{\rho}t}\right) - 3\sin\left(C_3e^{\frac{\rho-1}{\rho}t}\right) + K_1,\ t \geq 0$$

is not satisfied by any constant C_i, $i = 1,2,3$ (compare with the case of the Caputo fractional derivative $\rho = 1$, [15]).

Case 2. Let $I_i(t) \equiv 0$, $i = 1,2,3$, $t \geq 0$. Then, for any $a_i(t) > 0$, the system in (33) *has zero equilibrium because* $\sin(0) = 0$ *(see Remark 6).*

Case 3. Consider the following neural network:

$$\begin{aligned}({}_0^C\mathscr{D}^{\alpha,\rho}x_1)(t) &= -\sin\left(e^{\frac{\rho-1}{\rho}t}\right)x_1(t) + \frac{6}{\sin\left(e^{\frac{\rho-1}{\rho}t}\right)}\sin(x_1(t)) + e^{\frac{\rho-1}{\rho}t}\sin(x_3(t)) - 6,\\ ({}_0^C\mathscr{D}^{\alpha,\rho}x_2)(t) &= -\sin\left(e^{\frac{\rho-1}{\rho}t}\right)x_2(t) + 0.5e^{\frac{\rho-1}{\rho}t}\sin(x_1(t)) + 0.5e^{\frac{\rho-1}{\rho}t}\sin(x_2(t)),\\ ({}_0^C\mathscr{D}^{\alpha,\rho}x_3)(t) &= -\sin^2\left(e^{\frac{\rho-1}{\rho}t}\right)x_3(t) + \sin\left(e^{\frac{\rho-1}{\rho}t}\right)e^{\frac{\rho-1}{\rho}t}\sin(x_1(t)) - 2\sin(x_3(t)) + 2\sin\left(e^{\frac{\rho-1}{\rho}t}\right).\end{aligned} \tag{34}$$

Thus, the coefficients are as follows:

$$a_1(t) = \sin\left(e^{\frac{\rho-1}{\rho}t}\right) > 0,\ a_2(t) = \sin\left(e^{\frac{\rho-1}{\rho}t}\right) > 0,\ a_3(t) = \sin^2\left(e^{\frac{\rho-1}{\rho}t}\right) > 0,$$

$$B = \{b_{i,k}(t)\} = \begin{bmatrix} \frac{6}{\sin\left(e^{\frac{\rho-1}{\rho}t}\right)} & 0 & e^{\frac{\rho-1}{\rho}t} \\ 0.5e^{\frac{\rho-1}{\rho}t} & 0.5e^{\frac{\rho-1}{\rho}t} & 0 \\ \sin\left(e^{\frac{\rho-1}{\rho}t}\right)e^{\frac{\rho-1}{\rho}t} & 0 & -2 \end{bmatrix},$$

and

$$I_1(t) = -6,\ I_2(t) = 0,\ I_3(t) = 2\sin\left(e^{\frac{\rho-1}{\rho}t}\right).$$

Then, for $\rho \in (0,1)$, the system in (33) *has the equilibrium*

$$\left(e^{\frac{\rho-1}{\rho}t}, e^{\frac{\rho-1}{\rho}t}, e^{\frac{\rho-1}{\rho}t}\right),$$

because

$$a_1x_1^*(t) = \sin\left(e^{\frac{\rho-1}{\rho}t}\right)e^{\frac{\rho-1}{\rho}t} = \frac{6}{\sin\left(e^{\frac{\rho-1}{\rho}t}\right)}\sin\left(e^{\frac{\rho-1}{\rho}t}\right) + 0 + e^{\frac{\rho-1}{\rho}t}\sin\left(e^{\frac{\rho-1}{\rho}t}\right) - 6$$

$$a_2(t)x_2^*(t) = \sin\left(e^{\frac{\rho-1}{\rho}t}\right)e^{\frac{\rho-1}{\rho}t} = 0.5e^{\frac{\rho-1}{\rho}t}\sin\left(e^{\frac{\rho-1}{\rho}t}\right) + 0.5e^{\frac{\rho-1}{\rho}t}\sin\left(e^{\frac{\rho-1}{\rho}t}\right) + 0 + 0$$

$$a_3(t)x_3^*(t) = \sin^2\left(e^{\frac{\varrho-1}{\rho}t}\right)e^{\frac{\varrho-1}{\rho}t} = \sin\left(e^{\frac{\varrho-1}{\rho}t}\right)e^{\frac{\varrho-1}{\rho}t}\sin\left(e^{\frac{\varrho-1}{\rho}t}\right) + 0 - 2\sin\left(e^{\frac{\varrho-1}{\rho}t}\right) + 2\sin\left(e^{\frac{\varrho-1}{\rho}t}\right)$$

hold.

Neither the conditions of Theorem 1 nor the conditions of Theorem 2 are satisfied. For example, the following inequality:

$$2\sin\left(e^{\frac{\varrho-1}{\rho}t}\right) \geq \gamma(\rho,t) := 2\frac{6}{\sin\left(e^{\frac{\varrho-1}{\rho}t}\right)} + 0.5e^{\frac{\varrho-1}{\rho}t} + e^{\frac{\varrho-1}{\rho}t}\left(1+\sin\left(e^{\frac{\varrho-1}{\rho}t}\right)\right), \ t \geq 0 \quad (35)$$

is not satisfied (see Figure 1, top left). Therefore, we are not able to conclude the stability properties of the equilibrium (see Figure 2).

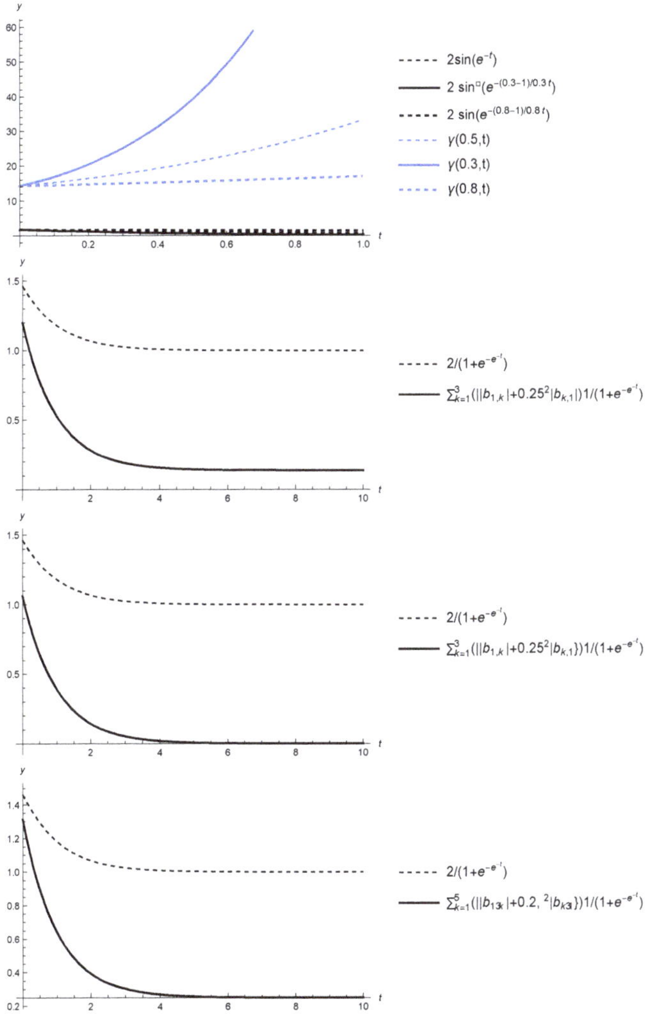

Figure 1. Graph of inequality (35) for various ρ (**1st plot**). Graph of inequality (37) for $\rho = 0.5$ (**2nd plot**), (38) for $\rho = 0.5$ (**3rd plot**), and (39) for $\rho = 0.5$ (**4th plot**).

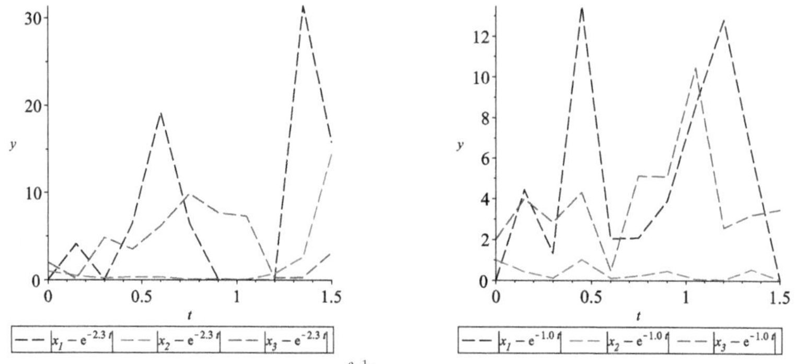

Figure 2. Graphs of functions $|x_i(t) - e^{\frac{\rho-1}{\rho}t}|$, with $i = 1,2,3$ and $\alpha = 0.6$. On the (**left**), $\rho = 0.3$, and on the (**right**), $\rho = 0.5$.

Example 2. *Consider the following neural networks of $n = 3$ neurons with the following generalized proportional fractional derivatives:*

$$\begin{aligned}
({}_0^C\mathscr{D}^{\alpha,\rho}x_1)(t) &= -\frac{1}{1+e^{-e^{\frac{\rho-1}{\rho}t}}}x_1(t) + \frac{0.1}{1+e^{-x_1(t)}} + e^{\frac{\rho-1}{\rho}t}\frac{1}{1+e^{-x_3(t)}} + \frac{-0.1}{1+e^{-e^{\frac{\rho-1}{\rho}t}}},\\
({}_0^C\mathscr{D}^{\alpha,\rho}x_2)(t) &= -\frac{1}{1+e^{-e^{\frac{\rho-1}{\rho}t}}}x_2(t) + e^{\frac{\rho-1}{\rho}t}\frac{1}{1+e^{-x_1(t)}},\\
({}_0^C\mathscr{D}^{\alpha,\rho}x_3)(t) &= -\frac{1}{1+e^{-e^{\frac{\rho-1}{\rho}t}}}x_3(t) + e^{\frac{\rho-1}{\rho}t}\frac{1}{1+e^{-x_1(t)}} + \frac{1}{1+e^{-x_3(t)}} + \frac{-1}{1+e^{-e^{\frac{\rho-1}{\rho}t}}},
\end{aligned} \tag{36}$$

with the coefficients

$$a_k(t) = \frac{1}{1+e^{-e^{\frac{\rho-1}{\rho}t}}} > 0, k = 1,2,3,$$

the activation functions $f_k(x) = 1/(1+e^{-x}) > 0,\ k = 1,2,3$ are equal to the sigmoid function, with $M_k = 0.25$, the perturbations are thus given by

$$I_1(t) = \frac{-0.1}{1+e^{-e^{\frac{\rho-1}{\rho}t}}},\ I_2(t) = 0,\ I_3(t) = \frac{-1}{1+e^{-e^{\frac{\rho-1}{\rho}t}}},$$

and

$$B = \{b_{i,k}(t)\} = \begin{bmatrix} 0.1 & 0 & e^{\frac{\rho-1}{\rho}t} \\ e^{\frac{\rho-1}{\rho}t} & 0 & 0 \\ e^{\frac{\rho-1}{\rho}t} & 0 & 1 \end{bmatrix}.$$

Then, for $\rho \in (0,1)$, the system in (36) has the following equilibrium:

$$x^*(t) = \left(e^{\frac{\rho-1}{\rho}t}, e^{\frac{\rho-1}{\rho}t}, e^{\frac{\rho-1}{\rho}t}\right)$$

because

$$a_1 x_1^*(t) = \frac{1}{1+e^{-e^{\frac{\rho-1}{\rho}t}}} e^{\frac{\rho-1}{\rho}t} = 0.1\frac{1}{1+e^{-e^{\frac{\rho-1}{\rho}t}}} + 0 + \frac{1}{1+e^{-e^{\frac{\rho-1}{\rho}t}}} e^{\frac{\rho-1}{\rho}t} + \frac{-0.1}{1+e^{-e^{\frac{\rho-1}{\rho}t}}},$$

$$a_2(t) x_2^*(t) = \frac{1}{1+e^{-e^{\frac{\rho-1}{\rho}t}}} e^{\frac{\rho-1}{\rho}t} = \frac{1}{1+e^{-e^{\frac{\rho-1}{\rho}t}}} e^{\frac{\rho-1}{\rho}t} + 0 + 0 + 0,$$

$$a_3(t) x_3^*(t) = \frac{1}{1+e^{-e^{\frac{\rho-1}{\rho}t}}} e^{\frac{\rho-1}{\rho}t} = e^{\frac{\rho-1}{\rho}t}\frac{1}{1+e^{-e^{\frac{\rho-1}{\rho}t}}} + 0 + \frac{1}{1+e^{-e^{\frac{\rho-1}{\rho}t}}} + \frac{-1}{1+e^{-e^{\frac{\rho-1}{\rho}t}}}.$$

Moreover, condition 5 of Theorem 1 is satisfied because of the following inequalities:

$$2\frac{1}{1+e^{-e^{\frac{\rho-1}{\rho}t}}} \geq 1 \geq (1+0.25^2)0.1 + (0+0.5*0.25^2) + (1+0.25^2)e^{\frac{\rho-1}{\rho}t}, \tag{37}$$

$$2\frac{1}{1+e^{-e^{\frac{\rho-1}{\rho}t}}} \geq (1+0*0.25^2) + (1+0.25^2)*0 + (1+0.25^2)*0, \tag{38}$$

$$2\frac{1}{1+e^{-e^{\frac{\rho-1}{\rho}t}}} \geq (1+0.25^2)e^{\frac{\rho-1}{\rho}t} + 0 + (1+0.25^2), \tag{39}$$

(see Figure 1, top right, bottom left, and bottom right, respectively).

From Theorem 1, the equilibrium is exponentially stable, i.e., (see Figure 3)

$$|x_i(t) - e^{\frac{\rho-1}{\rho}t}| \leq |x_i(0) - 1| e^{0.5\frac{\rho-1}{\rho}t},\ t \geq 0,\ i = 1,2,3.$$

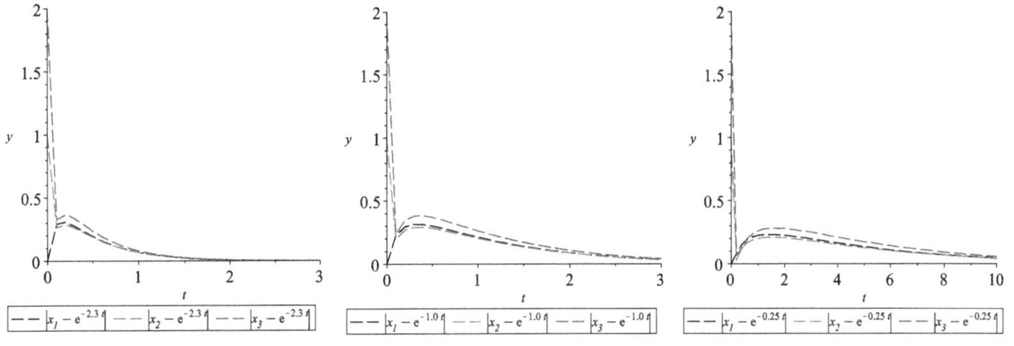

Figure 3. Graphs of the functions $|x_i(t) - e^{\frac{\rho-1}{\rho}t}|$, with $i = 1,2,3$, $\alpha = 0.6$, and $\rho = 0.3$ (**left**), $\rho = 0.5$ (**center**), and $\rho = 0.8$ (**right**).

6. Conclusions

Initially, we proved an important inequality concerning an estimate of the generalized proportional Caputo fractional derivative of quadratic functions. The result could be applied to the study of various types of stability for the solutions of various types of fractional differential equations with the generalized proportional Caputo fractional derivative. In our paper, we applied it to study the stability properties of the Hopfiel neural network with the generalized proportional Caputo type fractional derivative. An equilibrium of the studied model was then defined. This equilibrium is generally not a constant (different than the case of ordinary derivatives and the Caputo type fractional derivatives). We defined the exponential stability and the Mittag–Leffler stability of the equilibrium. Several sufficient conditions were presented to guarantee these types of stability. The theoretical results were illustrated, with two numerical examples.

Author Contributions: Conceptualization, R.A., R.P.A., S.H. and D.O.; methodology, R.A., R.P.A., S.H. and D.O.; formal analysis, R.A., R.P.A., S.H. and D.O.; investigation, R.A., R.P.A., S.H. and D.O.; writing—original draft preparation, R.A., R.P.A., S.H. and D.O.; writing—review and editing, R.A., R.P.A., S.H. and D.O. All authors have read and agreed to the published version of the manuscript.

Funding: R.A. is supported by Portuguese funds through the CIDMA—Center for Research and Development in Mathematics and Applications, and the Portuguese Foundation for Science and Technology (FCT-Fundação para a Ciência e a Tecnologia), within project UIDB/04106/2020. S.H. is partially supported by the Bulgarian National Science Fund under Project KP-06-N32/7.

Conflicts of Interest: The authors declare no conflict of interest.

References

1. Jarad, F.; Abdeljawad, T.; Alzabut, J. Generalized fractional derivatives generated by a class of local proportional derivatives. *Eur. Phys. J. Spec. Top.* **2017**, *226*, 3457–3471. [CrossRef]
2. Alzabut, J.; Abdeljawad, T.; Jarad, F.; Sudsutad, W. A Gronwall inequality via the generalized proportional fractional derivative with applications. *J. Ineq. Appl.* **2019**, *2019*, 1–12. [CrossRef]
3. Khaminsou, B.; Thaiprayoon, C.; Sudsutad, W.; Jose, S.A. Qualitative analysis of a proportional Caputo fractional differential pantograph differential equations with mixed nonlocal conditions. *Nonl. Funct. Anal. Appl.* **2021**, *26*, 197–223. [CrossRef]
4. Sudsutad, W.; Alzabut, J.; Nontasawatsri, S.; Thaiprayoon, C. Stability analysis for a generalized proportional fractional Langevin equation with variable coefficient and mixed integro-differential boundary conditions. *J. Nonlinear Funct. Anal.* **2020**, *2020*, 1–24.
5. Boroomand, A.; Menhaj, M.B. Fractional-Order Hopfield Neural Networks. In *Advances in Neuro-Information Processing*; 5506 of Lecture Notes in Computer Science; Springer: Berlin/Heidelberg, Germany, 2009; pp. 883–890.
6. Kaslik, E.; Sivasundaram, S. Nonlinear dynamics and chaos in fractional-order neural networks. *Neural Netw.* **2012**, *32*, 245–256. [CrossRef] [PubMed]
7. Wang, J.; Wen, Y.; Gou, Y.; Ye, Z.; Chen, H. Fractional-order gradient descent learning of BP neural networks with Caputo derivative. *Neural Netw.* **2017**, *89*, 19–30. [CrossRef] [PubMed]
8. Deng, J.; Ma, W.; Deng, K.; Li, Y. Tempered Mittag—Leffler stability of tempered fractional dynamical systems. *Math. Probl. Eng.* **2020**, *2020*, 7962542. [CrossRef]
9. Fernandez, A.; Ustaoglu, C. On some analytic properties of tempered fractional calculus. *J. Comput. Appl. Math.* **2020**, *366*, 112400. [CrossRef]
10. Meerschaert, M.M.; Sabzikar, F.; Phanikumar, M.S.; Zeleke, A. Tempered fractional time series model for turbulence in geophysical flows. *J. Stat. Mech. Theory Exper.* **2014**, *9*, 9023. [CrossRef]
11. Aguila-Camacho, N.; Duarte-Mermoud, M.A.; Gallegos, J.A. Lyapunov functions for fractional order systems. *Commun. Nonlinear Sci. Numer. Simul.* **2014**, *19*, 2951–2957. [CrossRef]
12. Li, Y.; Chen, Y.Q.; Podlubny, I. Stability of fractional-order nonlinear dynamic systems: Lyapunov direct method and generalized Mittag—Leffler stability. *Comput. Math. Appl.* **2010**, *59*, 1810–1821. [CrossRef]
13. Rajchakit, G.; Agarwal, P.; Ramalingam, S. *Stability Analysis of Neural Networks*; Springer: Singapore, 2021.
14. Tanaka, K. Stability analysis of neural networks via Lyapunov approach. In Proceedings of the ICNN'95—International Conference on Neural Networks, Perth, WA, Australia, 27 November–1 December 1995. [CrossRef]
15. Zhang, S.; Yu, Y.; Wang, H. Mittag–Leffler stability of fractional-order Hopfield neural networks. *Nonlinear Anal. Hybrid Syst.* **2015**, *16*, 104–121. [CrossRef]
16. Gu, C.-Y.; Zheng, F.-H.; Shiri, B. Mittag–Leffler stability analysis of tempered fractional neural networks with short memory and variable-order. *Fractals* **2021**, *8*, 2140029. [CrossRef]

axioms

Article

The Relationship between Fuzzy Reasoning Methods Based on Intuitionistic Fuzzy Sets and Interval-Valued Fuzzy Sets

Minxia Luo *, Wenling Li and Hongyan Shi

Department of Date Science, China Jiliang University, Hangzhou 310018, China
* Correspondence: mxluo@cjlu.edu.cn; Tel.: +86-571-8691-4480

Abstract: Two important basic inference models of fuzzy reasoning are Fuzzy Modus Ponens (FMP) and Fuzzy Modus Tollens (FMT). In order to solve FMP and FMT problems, the full implication triple I algorithm, the reverse triple I algorithm and the Subsethood Inference Subsethood (SIS for short) algorithm are proposed, respectively. Furthermore, the existing reasoning algorithms are extended to intuitionistic fuzzy sets and interval-valued fuzzy sets according to different needs. The purpose of this paper is to study the relationship between intuitionistic fuzzy reasoning algorithms and interval-valued fuzzy reasoning algorithms. It is proven that there is a bijection between the solutions of intuitionistic fuzzy triple I algorithm and the interval-valued fuzzy triple I algorithm. Then, there is a bijection between the solutions of intuitionistic fuzzy reverse triple I algorithm and the interval-valued fuzzy reverse triple I algorithm. At the same time, it is shown that there is also a bijection between the solutions of intuitionistic fuzzy SIS algorithm and interval-valued fuzzy SIS algorithm.

Keywords: Fuzzy Modus Ponens; Fuzzy Modus Tollens; reasoning algorithm; intuitionistic fuzzy sets; interval-valued fuzzy sets

MSC: 110.84

Citation: Luo, M.; Li, W.; Shi, H. The Relationship between Fuzzy Reasoning Methods Based on Intuitionistic Fuzzy Sets and Interval-Valued Fuzzy Sets. *Axioms* **2022**, *11*, 419. https://doi.org/10.3390/axioms11080419

Academic Editor: Yurii Kharkevych

Received: 24 July 2022
Accepted: 17 August 2022
Published: 20 August 2022

1. Introduction

In recent years, fuzzy control achieved great success in many aspects. Fuzzy reasoning is the core content of fuzzy control. As an important branch of approximate reasoning, fuzzy reasoning is close to human thinking mode. It has become the theoretical basis for fuzzy expert systems, fuzzy control systems and fuzzy intelligent decision systems, etc. In fuzzy reasoning, the most basic forms of fuzzy reasoning are Fuzzy Modus Ponens (FMP) and Fuzzy Modus Tollens (FMT) [1] as follows:

FMP: Given the input "x is A^*", and fuzzy rule "if x is A then y is B", try to infer a reasonable output "y is B^*";

FMT: Given the input "y is B^*", and fuzzy rule "if x is A then y is B", try to infer a reasonable output "x is A^*".

Zadeh [2] proposed the compositional rules of inference (CRI method for short) to deal with the above problem. Nevertheless, Wang [3] pointed out that the CRI method lacks strict logical basis and has no reducibility. Moreover, Wang [3] proposed full implication triple I method (triple I method for short), which improves the traditional CRI algorithm and brings fuzzy reasoning within the framework of logical semantic implication. Many researchers have done a lot of research on the triple I method and achieved a series of results. Wang and Fu [4] provided the unified forms of triple I method for FMP and FMT. Pei [5] comprehensively discussed the method based on residual fuzzy implication induced by left-continuous t-norms. Song and Wu [6] proposed a reverse triple I algorithm from the perspective of how to design a fuzzy system to minimize the number of elements in the fuzzy rule base under a given precision. Liu and Wang [7] proposed triple I method based on pointwise sustaining degrees. Luo and Yao [8] studied triple I algorithms based on

Schweizer–Sklar operators in fuzzy reasoning. In addition, the reducibility of the algorithm is one of the important criteria to evaluate the quality of fuzzy reasoning. Although the triple I algorithm and the reverse triple I algorithm have better properties in reducibility than CRI algorithm, their reducibility is not unconditional. Therefore, Zou and Pei [9] gave an SIS algorithm with the advantage of unconditional reducibility.

Although fuzzy sets have been successfully used in many fields, there are still some defects in describing the fuzziness and uncertainty of information. An interval-valued fuzzy set was introduced by Zadeh [10]. Many researchers extended approximate inference to the interval-valued fuzzy sets. An approximate reasoning method based on the interval-valued fuzzy sets was proposed [11]. Li et al. [12] discussed the robustness of interval-valued CRI method. Liu and Li [13] studied the interval-valued fuzzy reasoning with multi-antecedent rules. Luo and Zhang [14] extended the fuzzy inference triple I principle on interval-valued fuzzy sets, and gave the interval-valued fuzzy inference full-implication method based on the associated t-norms. Luo and Wang [15] further studied interval-valued fuzzy reasoning full implication algorithms based on the t-representable t-norm. Li and Xie [16] investigated universal interval-valued fuzzy inference systems based on interval-valued implications. Luo et al. [17] discussed the robustness of reverse triple I algorithms based on interval-valued fuzzy sets. Wang et al. [18] combined the SIS algorithm with interval-valued fuzzy sets to give a generalized SIS algorithm based on interval fuzzy reasoning and study its robustness.

Another extension of fuzzy sets, intuitionistic fuzzy sets, were proposed by Atanassov [19]. Many research results based on intuitionistic fuzzy sets have been obtained. Deschrijver et al. [20] proposed the intuitionistic fuzzy t-norm and t-conorm. Cornelis et al. [21] studied the intuitionistic fuzzy reasoning CRI method. Zheng et al. [22] studied the intuitionistic fuzzy reasoning triple I method and α-triple I method. Liu and Zheng [23] proposed the dual triple I method and the decomposition method for intuitionistic Fuzzy Modus Tollens, which improved the reductivity of triple I method for intuitionistic Fuzzy Modus Tollens. Peng [24] discussed the intuitionistic fuzzy reasoning reverse triple I algorithm and the reverse α-triple I algorithm. The literature [25] extended the SIS algorithm to intuitionistic fuzzy sets and then gave an SIS algorithm based on intuitionistic fuzzy reasoning and discussed its continuity.

Although scholars have made some research results based on intuitionistic fuzzy sets and interval-valued fuzzy sets, the relationship between the results has not been studied. This is the research goal of this paper. The structure of this paper is as follows: some concepts for intuitionistic fuzzy sets and interval-valued fuzzy sets are reviewed in Section 2. In Section 3, we study the relationship between the intuitionistic fuzzy reasoning triple I algorithm and interval-valued fuzzy reasoning triple I algorithm, the relationship between the intuitionistic fuzzy reasoning reverse triple I algorithm and interval-valued fuzzy reasoning reverse triple I algorithm, the relationship between the intuitionistic fuzzy reasoning SIS algorithm and interval-valued fuzzy reasoning SIS algorithm. The conclusions are given in Section 4.

2. Preliminary

In this section, we review some concepts for intuitionistic fuzzy sets and interval-valued fuzzy sets, which will be used in the paper.

Definition 1 ([26]). *An increasing, commutative, associative mapping $T : [0,1] \times [0,1] \to [0,1]$ is called a triangular norm (t-norm for short) if it satisfies $T(x,1) = x$ for any $x \in [0,1]$. An increasing, commutative, associative mapping $S : [0,1] \times [0,1] \to [0,1]$ is called a triangular conorm (t-conorm for short) if it satisfies $S(0,x) = x$ for any $x \in [0,1]$.*

Definition 2 ([27]). *The residuated implication R induced by left-continuous t-norm T is defined by $R(a,b) = \sup\{x \in [0,1] \mid T(a,x) \leq b\}, \forall a,b \in [0,1]$.*

Example 1 ([28]). (1) *The Godel implication (R_G for short) and the corresponding t-norm (T_G for short) have the following expression*

$$R_G(a,b) = \begin{cases} 1, & if \quad a \le b, \\ b, & if \quad a > b. \end{cases}$$

$T_G(a,b) = a \wedge b.$

(2) The Lukasiewicz implication (R_{Lu} for short) and the corresponding t-norm (T_{Lu} for short) have the following expression

$R_{Lu}(a,b) = (1 - a + b) \wedge 1.$

$T_{Lu}(a,b) = (a + b - 1) \vee 0.$

(3) The Gougen implication (R_{Go} for short) and the corresponding Product t-norm (T_{Go} for short) have the following expression

$$R_{Go}(a,b) = \begin{cases} 1, & if \quad a \le b, \\ \frac{b}{a}, & if \quad a > b. \end{cases}$$

$T_{Go}(a,b) = ab.$

Definition 3 ([19]). *An intuitionistic fuzzy set (IFS for Short) on nonempty universe X is given by*

$$A = \{(x, \mu_A(x), \vartheta_A(x)) \mid x \in X\}$$

where $\mu_A(x) \in [0,1]$ and $\vartheta_A(x) \in [0,1]$ with the condition $0 \le \mu_A(x) + \vartheta_A(x) \le 1 (\forall x \in X)$. $\mu_A(x)$ and $\vartheta_A(x)$ are called a membership function and a non-membership function, respectively.

The class of all intuitionistic fuzzy sets on nonempty universe X is denoted $IFS(X)$. For every $A, B \in IFS(X)$, some operations are defined as follows [29]:

(1) $A \subseteq_{L^*} B$ iff $\mu_A(x) \le \mu_B(x)$ and $\vartheta_A(x) \ge \vartheta_B(x), \forall x \in X$;
(2) $A \cup_{L^*} B = \{(x, \sup(\mu_A(x), \mu_B(x)), \inf(\vartheta_A(x), \vartheta_B(x)) \mid x \in X\}$;
(3) $A \cap_{L^*} B = \{(x, \inf(\mu_A(x), \mu_B(x)), \sup(\vartheta_A(x), \vartheta_B(x)) \mid x \in X\}$.

Let $L^* = \{(x_1, y_1) \mid (x_1, y_1) \subseteq [0,1]^2, x_1 + y_1 \le 1\}$. The order defined on L^* as $(x_1, y_1) \le_{L^*} (x_2, y_2)$ if $x_1 \le x_2$ and $y_1 \ge y_2$. $(x_1, y_1) \wedge_{L^*} (x_2, y_2) = (x_1 \wedge x_2, y_1 \vee y_2), (x_1, y_1) \vee_{L^*} (x_2, y_2) = (x_1 \vee x_2, y_1 \wedge y_2). \sup(x_i, y_i) = (\sup x_i, \inf y_i), \inf(x_i, y_i) = (\inf x_i, \sup y_i)$ for all $(x_i, y_i) \in L^*$. $0_* = (0,1)$ and $1_* = (1,0)$ are the smallest element and the greatest element in L^*, respectively. It is easy to verify that $(L^*, \wedge, \vee, 0_*, 1_*)$ is a complete lattice [30].

Definition 4 ([20]). *An increasing, commutative, associative mapping $\mathcal{T}_{L^*}$: $L^* \times L^* \to L^*$ is called an intuitionistic fuzzy t-norm if it satisfies $\mathcal{T}_{L^*}(x, 1_*) = x$ for any $x \in L^*$.*

Example 2 ([20]). *A binary mapping $\mathcal{T}_{L^*}$: $L^* \times L^* \to L^*$ is defined by $\mathcal{T}_{L^*}(\alpha, \beta) = (T(a_1, b_1), S(a_2, b_2))$, where $\alpha = (a_1, a_2), \beta = (b_1, b_2)$, S is the dual t-conorm of the t-norm T. Then, $\mathcal{T}_{L^*}$ is an intuitionistic t-norm, which is called the associated intuitionistic t-norm on L^*.*

The associated intuitionistic t-norm $\mathcal{T}_{L^*}$ is called left-continuous if T is a left-continuous t-norm and S is a right-continuous t-conorm.

Definition 5 ([20]). *The intuitionistic residuated implication $\mathcal{R}_{L^*}$ induced by left-continuous intuitionistic t-norm $\mathcal{T}_{L^*}$ is defined by $\mathcal{R}_{L^*}(\alpha, \beta) = \sup\{\eta \mid \mathcal{T}_{L^*}(\eta, \alpha) \le \beta\}$, where $\alpha, \beta, \eta \in L^*$, and $\mathcal{T}_{L^*}$ is a t-norm on L^*.*

Lemma 1 ([22]). *The intuitionistic residuated implication induced by left-continuous associated intuitionistic t-norm $\mathcal{T}_{L^*}$ is $\mathcal{R}_{L^*}(\alpha, \beta) = (R(a_1, b_1) \wedge R(1 - a_2, 1 - b_2), 1 - R(1 - a_2, 1 - b_2))$, where $\alpha = (a_1, a_2), \beta = (b_1, b_2) \in L^*$, and R is the residuated implication induced by the t-norm T.*

Definition 6 ([10]). *An interval-valued fuzzy set (IVFS for short) on nonempty universe X is given by*

$$B = \{(x, [B_l(x), B_r(x)]) \mid [B_l(x), B_r(x)] \subseteq [0,1], x \in X\}$$

The class of all interval-valued fuzzy sets on the nonempty universe X is denoted $IVFS(X)$.

For every $A, B \in IVFS(X)$, some operations are defined as follows [10]:

(1) $A \subseteq_{L^I} B$ iff $A_l(x) \leq B_l(x)$ and $A_r(x) \leq B_r(x), \forall x \in X$;
(2) $A \cup_{L^I} B = \{(x, [\sup(A_l(x), B_l(x)), \sup(A_r(x), B_r(x))]) \mid x \in X\}$;
(3) $A \cap_{L^I} B = \{(x, [\inf(A_l(x), B_l(x)), \inf(A_r(x), B_r(x))]) \mid x \in X\}$.

Let $L^I = \{[x_1, y_1] \mid [x_1, y_1] \subseteq [0,1], x_1 \leq y_1\}$. The order defined on L^I as $[x_1, y_1] \leq_{L^I} [x_2, y_2]$ if $x_1 \leq x_2$ and $y_1 \leq y_2$ is called component-wise order or Kulisch–Miranker order [31]. $[x_1, y_1] \wedge_{L^I} [x_2, y_2] = [x_1 \wedge x_2, y_1 \wedge y_2], [x_1, y_1] \vee_{L^I} [x_2, y_2] = [x_1 \vee x_2, y_1 \vee y_2]$. $\sup[x_i, y_i] = [\sup x_i, \sup y_i], \inf[x_i, y_i] = [\inf x_i, \inf y_i]$ for all $[x_i, y_i] \in L^I$. $0_I = [0,0]$ and $1_I = [1,1]$ are the smallest element and the greatest element in L^I, respectively. It is easy to verify that $(L^I, \wedge, \vee, 0_I, 1_I)$ is a complete lattice [31].

Definition 7 ([32]). *An increasing, commutative, associative mapping $\mathcal{T}_{L^I} : L^I \times L^I \to L^I$ is called an interval-valued t-norm if it satisfies $\mathcal{T}_{L^I}(1_I, x) = x$ for any $x \in L^I$.*

Example 3 ([33]). *A mapping $\mathcal{T}_{L^I} : L^I \times L^I \to L^I$ is defined by $\mathcal{T}_{L^I}(\alpha, \beta) = [T(a_1, b_1), T(a_2, b_2)]$, where $\alpha = [a_1, a_2], \beta = [b_1, b_2] \in L^I$, and T is a t-norm. Then, $\mathcal{T}_{L^I}$ is an interval-valued t-norm, which is called the associated interval-valued t-norm on L^I.*

The associated t-norm $\mathcal{T}_{L^I}$ is called left-continuous if T is a left-continuous t-norm on the interval $[0,1]$ [14].

Definition 8 ([20]). *The interval-valued residuated implication $\mathcal{R}_{L^I}$ induced by left-continuous interval-valued t-norm $\mathcal{T}_{L^I}$ is defined by $\mathcal{R}_{L^I}(\alpha, \beta) = \sup\left\{\mathrm{fl} \in \mathrm{L}^\mathrm{I} \mid \mathcal{T}_{\mathrm{L}^\mathrm{I}}(\mathrm{ff}, \mathrm{fl}) \leq \mathrm{fi}\right\}$.*

Lemma 2 ([34]). *The interval-valued residuated implication induced by left-continuous associated t-norm $\mathcal{T}_{L^I}$ is $\mathcal{R}_{L^I}(\alpha, \beta) = [R(a_1, b_1) \wedge R(a_2, b_2), R(a_2, b_2)]$, where $\alpha = [a_1, a_2], \beta = [b_1, b_2] \in L^I$, and R is the residuated implication induced by the t-norm T.*

Lemma 3 ([35]). *Mapping $\varphi : IFS(X) \to IVFS(X)$, $A \mapsto B$ is an isomorphism between the lattices $(IFS(X), \cup_{L^*}, \cap_{L^*})$ and $(IVFS(X), \cup_{L^I}, \cap_{L^I})$, where*

$$A = \{(x, \mu_A(x), \vartheta_A(x)) \mid x \in X\},$$

$$B = \{(x, [\mu_A(x), 1 - \vartheta_A(x)]) \mid x \in X\}.$$

3. The Relationship Based on Intuitionistic Fuzzy Sets and Interval-Valued Fuzzy Sets

3.1. The Relationship between the Triple I Methods Based on Intuitionistic Fuzzy Sets and Interval-Valued Fuzzy Sets

In this section, the relationship between the solutions of the triple I method based on the IFS and the IVFS will be studied.

Definition 9 ([22]). *The intuitionistic fuzzy reasoning triple I model is denoted as*

$$\mathcal{R}_{L^*}(\mathcal{R}_{L^*}(A_{L^*}(x), B_{L^*}(y)), \mathcal{R}_{L^*}(A^*_{L^*}(x), B^*_{L^*}(y))) \tag{1}$$

where $A_{L^*}, A^*_{L^*} \in IFS(X)$, $B_{L^*}, B^*_{L^*} \in IFS(Y)$, and $\mathcal{R}_{L^*}$ is the intuitionistic residuated implication on L^*. The smallest (greatest) intuitionistic fuzzy set $B^*_{L^*}(A^*_{L^*})$ of the universe $Y(X)$ such that Formula (1) attains the greatest value is called the intuitionistic fuzzy reasoning triple I solution for FMP(FMT) problem.

Theorem 1 ([22]). *Suppose that $\mathcal{R}_{L^*}$ is the intuitionistic residuated implication induced by left-continuous associated intuitionistic t-norm $\mathcal{T}_{L^*}$, then*

(1) *The intuitionistic fuzzy reasoning triple I solution for FMP (IFMP algorithm solution $B^*_{L^*}$ for short) is given by the following formula*

$$B^*_{L^*}(y) = \sup_{x \in X} \mathcal{T}_{L^*}(A^*_{L^*}(x), \mathcal{R}_{L^*}(A_{L^*}(x), B_{L^*}(y))) \quad (\forall y \in Y). \tag{2}$$

(2) *The intuitionistic fuzzy reasoning triple I solution for FMT (IFMT algorithm solution $A^*_{L^*}$ for short) is given by the following formula*

$$A^*_{L^*}(x) = \inf_{y \in Y} \mathcal{R}_{L^*}(\mathcal{R}_{L^*}(A_{L^*}(x), B_{L^*}(y)), B^*_{L^*}(y)) \quad (\forall x \in X). \tag{3}$$

Definition 10 ([14]). *The interval-valued fuzzy reasoning triple I model is denoted as*

$$\mathcal{R}_{L^I}(\mathcal{R}_{L^I}(A_{L^I}(x), B_{L^I}(y)), \mathcal{R}_{L^I}(A^*_{L^I}(x), B^*_{L^I}(y))) \tag{4}$$

where $A_{L^I}, A^*_{L^I} \in IVFS(X)$, $B_{L^I}, B^*_{L^I} \in IVFS(Y)$, and $\mathcal{R}_{L^I}$ is the interval-valued residuated implication on L^I. The smallest (greatest) interval-valued fuzzy set $B^*_{L^I}(A^*_{L^I})$ of the universe $Y(X)$ such that the Formula (4) attains the greatest value is called the interval-valued fuzzy reasoning triple I solution for FMP (FMT) problem.

Theorem 2 ([14]). *Suppose that $\mathcal{R}_{L^I}$ is the interval-valued residuated implication induced by left-continuous associated interval-valued t-norm $\mathcal{T}_{L^I}$, then*

(1) *The interval-valued fuzzy reasoning triple I solution for FMP (IVFMP algorithm solution $B^*_{L^I}$ for short) is given by the following formula*

$$B^*_{L^I}(y) = \sup_{x \in X} \mathcal{T}_{L^I}(\mathcal{R}_{L^I}(A_{L^I}(x), B_{L^I}(y)), A^*_{L^I}(x)) \quad (\forall y \in Y). \tag{5}$$

(2) *The interval-valued fuzzy reasoning triple I solution for FMT (IVFMT algorithm solution $A^*_{L^I}$ for short) is given by the following formula*

$$A^*_{L^I}(x) = \inf_{y \in Y} \mathcal{R}_{L^I}(\mathcal{R}_{L^I}(A_{L^I}(x), B_{L^I}(y)), B^*_{L^I}(y)) \quad (\forall x \in X). \tag{6}$$

Theorem 3. *The residuated lattice $(IFS(X), \cup_{L^*}, \cap_{L^*}, 0_*, 1_*, \mathcal{T}_{L^*}, \mathcal{R}_{L^*})$ and $(IVFS(X), \cup_{L^I}, \cap_{L^I}, 0_I, 1_I, \mathcal{T}_{L^I}, \mathcal{R}_{L^I})$ is isomorphic, where $\mathcal{R}_{L^*}$ is intuitionistic residuated implication induced by the left-continuous associated intuitionistic t-norm $\mathcal{T}_{L^*}$, $\mathcal{R}_{L^I}$ is interval-valued residuated implication induced by the left-continuous associated interval-valued t-norm $\mathcal{T}_{L^I}$.*

Proof. Let mapping $\varphi : IFS(X) \to IVFS(X)$, $(x_1, x_2) \mapsto [x_1, 1 - x_2]$, we prove that φ is an isomorphism between the residuated lattice $(IFS(X), \cup_{L^*}, \cap_{L^*}, 0_*, 1_*, \mathcal{T}_{L^*}, \mathcal{R}_{L^*})$ and $(IVFS(X), \cup_{L^I}, \cap_{L^I}, 0_I, 1_I, \mathcal{T}_{L^I}, \mathcal{R}_{L^I})$. According to Lemma 3, we have $(IFS(X), \cup_{L^*}, \cap_{L^*}, 0_*, 1_*) \cong (IVFS(X), \cup_{L^I}, \cap_{L^I}, 0_I, 1_I)$.

Let $\alpha = (x_1, x_2), \beta = (y_1, y_2) \in L^*$, then

$$\begin{aligned}
& \varphi(\mathcal{T}_{L^*}(\alpha, \beta)) \\
= \; & \varphi(\mathcal{T}_{L^*}((x_1, x_2), (y_1, y_2))) \\
= \; & \varphi(T((x_1, y_1), S(x_2, y_2))) \quad \text{(By Example 2)} \\
= \; & [T(x_1, y_1), 1 - S(x_2, y_2)] \\
= \; & [T(x_1, y_1), T(1 - x_2, 1 - y_2)] \\
= \; & \mathcal{T}_{L^I}([x_1, 1 - x_2], [y_1, 1 - y_2]) \quad \text{(By Example 3)} \\
= \; & \mathcal{T}_{L^I}(\varphi(x_1, x_2), \varphi(y_1, y_2)) \\
= \; & \mathcal{T}_{L^I}(\varphi(\alpha), \varphi(\beta))
\end{aligned}$$

$$
\begin{aligned}
& \varphi(\mathcal{R}_{L^*}(\alpha,\beta)) \\
= \ & \varphi(\mathcal{R}_{L^*}((x_1,x_2),(y_1,y_2))) \\
= \ & \varphi(R(x_1,y_1)\wedge R(1-x_2,1-y_2),1-R(1-x_2,1-y_2)) \quad \text{(By Lemma 1)} \\
= \ & [R(x_1,y_1)\wedge R(1-x_2,1-y_2),R(1-x_2,1-y_2)] \\
= \ & \mathcal{R}_{L^I}([x_1,1-x_2],[y_1,1-y_2]) \quad \text{(By Lemma 2)} \\
= \ & \mathcal{R}_{L^I}(\varphi(x_1,x_2),\varphi(y_1,y_2)) \\
= \ & \mathcal{R}_{L^I}(\varphi(\alpha),\varphi(\beta))
\end{aligned}
$$

□

Theorem 4. *There is a bijection between the IFMP algorithm solution $B^*_{L^*}$ (by Formula (2)) and the IVFMP algorithm solution $B^*_{L^I}$ (by Formula (5)).*

Proof. Let mapping $\varphi : IFS(Y) \to IVFS(Y)$, $(y_1,y_2) \mapsto [y_1,1-y_2]$.

$$
\begin{aligned}
& \varphi(B^*_{L^*}(y)) \\
= \ & \varphi \sup_{x\in X} \mathcal{T}_{L^*}(A^*_{L^*}(x),\mathcal{R}_{L^*}(A_{L^*}(x),B_{L^*}(y))) \\
= \ & \sup_{x\in X} \varphi(\mathcal{T}_{L^*}(A^*_{L^*}(x),\mathcal{R}_{L^*}(A_{L^*}(x),B_{L^*}(y)))) \\
= \ & \sup_{x\in X} \mathcal{T}_{L^I}(\varphi(A^*_{L^*}(x)),\varphi(\mathcal{R}_{L^*}(A_{L^*}(x),B_{L^*}(y)))) \quad \text{(By Theorem 3)} \\
= \ & \sup_{x\in X} \mathcal{T}_{L^I}(\varphi(A^*_{L^*}(x)),\mathcal{R}_{L^I}(\varphi(A_{L^*}(x)),\varphi(B_{L^*}(y)))) \quad \text{(By Theorem 3)} \\
= \ & \sup_{x\in X} \mathcal{T}_{L^I}(A^*_{L^I}(x),\mathcal{R}_{L^I}(A_{L^I}(x),B_{L^I}(y))) \\
= \ & B^*_{L^I}(y)
\end{aligned}
$$

It is shown that there is a bijection between the IFMP algorithm solution $B^*_{L^*}$ and the IVFMP algorithm solution $B^*_{L^I}$. □

Theorem 5. *There is a bijection between the IFMT algorithm solution $A^*_{L^*}$ (by Formula (3)) and the IVFMT algorithm solution $A^*_{L^I}$ (by Formula (6)).*

Proof. Let mapping $\varphi : IFS(X) \to IVFS(X)$, $(x_1,x_2) \mapsto [x_1,1-x_2]$.

$$
\begin{aligned}
& \varphi(A^*_{L^*}(x)) \\
= \ & \varphi \inf_{y\in Y} \mathcal{R}_{L^*}(\mathcal{R}_{L^*}(A_{L^*}(x),B_{L^*}(y)),B^*_{L^*}(y)) \\
= \ & \inf_{y\in Y} \varphi(\mathcal{R}_{L^*}(\mathcal{R}_{L^*}(A_{L^*}(x),B_{L^*}(y)),B^*_{L^*}(y))) \\
= \ & \inf_{y\in Y} \mathcal{R}_{L^I}(\varphi(\mathcal{R}_{L^*}(A_{L^*}(x),B_{L^*}(y))),\varphi(B^*_{L^*}(y))) \quad \text{(By Theorem 3)} \\
= \ & \inf_{y\in Y} \mathcal{R}_{L^I}(\varphi(\mathcal{R}_{L^*}(A_{L^*}(x),B_{L^*}(y))),B^*_{L^I}(y)) \quad \text{(By Theorem 3)} \\
= \ & \inf_{y\in Y} \mathcal{R}_{L^I}(\mathcal{R}_{L^I}(A_{L^I}(x),B_{L^I}(y)),B^*_{L^I}(y)) \\
= \ & A^*_{L^I}(x)
\end{aligned}
$$

It is shown that there is a bijection between the IFMT algorithm solution $A^*_{L^*}$ and the IVFMT algorithm solution $A^*_{L^I}$. □

Example 4. *The intuitionistic fuzzy numbers A_{L^*}, $A^*_{L^*}$,B_{L^*} are shown in Table 1, and the intuitionistic fuzzy numbers A, A^*,B is transformed into interval-valued fuzzy numbers A_{L^I}, $A^*_{L^I}$,B_{L^I} by mapping φ, as can be seen in Table 2. Take the triangular norm $T = T_G$, the intuitionistic fuzzy* *reasoning triple I solutions $B^*_{L^*}$ and the interval-valued fuzzy reasoning triple I solutions $B^*_{L^I}$ are shown in Table 3.*

Table 1. Data of $A_{L^*}, A^*_{L^*}$ and B_{L^*}.

	x_1	x_2	x_3
A_{L^*}	$(0.60, 0.30)$	$(0.90, 0.10)$	$(0.40, 0.50)$
$A^*_{L^*}$	$(0.20, 0.50)$	$(0.30, 0.60)$	$(0.10, 0.40)$
	y_1	y_2	y_3
B_{L^*}	$(0.50, 0.30)$	$(0.30, 0.60)$	$(0.10, 0.70)$

Table 2. Data of $A_{L^I}, A^*_{L^I}$ and B_{L^I}.

	x_1	x_2	x_3
A_{L^I}	$[0.60, 0.70]$	$[0.90, 0.90]$	$[0.40, 0.50]$
$A^*_{L^I}$	$[0.20, 0.50]$	$[0.30, 0.40]$	$[0.10, 0.60]$
	y_1	y_2	y_3
B_{L^I}	$[0.50, 0.70]$	$[0.30, 0.40]$	$[0.10, 0.30]$

Table 3. IFMP algorithm solutions $B^*_{L^*}$ and IVFMP algorithm solutions $B^*_{L^I}$.

	y_1	y_2	y_3
$B^*_{L^*}$	$(0.30, 0.40)$	$(0.30, 0.60)$	$(0.10, 0.70)$
$B^*_{L^I}$	$[0.30, 0.60]$	$[0.30, 0.40]$	$[0.10, 0.30]$

Use the mapping $\varphi(B^*_{L^*}) = D$, the calculation results are shown in Table 4. By comparing the data in Tables 3 and 4, the value of D is equal to the solution $B^*_{L^I}$ for solving the IVFMP problem. The results show that the solutions based on the two fuzzy sets are in one-to-one correspondence.

Table 4. The values of corresponding to under the mapping φ.

$B^*_{L^*}$	$(0.30, 0.40)$	$(0.30, 0.60)$	$(0.10, 0.70)$
D	$[0.30, 0.60]$	$[0.30, 0.40]$	$[0.10, 0.30]$

3.2. The Relationship between the Reverse Triple I Methods Based on Intuitionistic Fuzzy Sets and Interval-Valued Fuzzy Sets

In this section, the solutions of the reverse triple I method based on the IFS and the IVFS have been given, and the relationship between the two solutions will be studied.

Definition 11 ([24]). *The intuitionistic fuzzy reasoning reverse triple I model is denoted as*

$$\mathcal{R}_{L^*}(\mathcal{R}_{L^*}(A^*_{L^*}(x), B^*_{L^*}(y)), \mathcal{R}_{L^*}(A_{L^*}(x), B_{L^*}(y))) \tag{7}$$

where $A_{L^*}, A^*_{L^*} \in IFS(X)$, $B_{L^*}, B^*_{L^*} \in IFS(Y)$, and $\mathcal{R}_{L^*}$ is the intuitionistic residuated implication on L^*. The greatest (smallest) intuitionistic fuzzy set $B^*_{L^*}(A^*_{L^*})$ of the universe $Y(X)$ such that the Formula (7) attains the greatest value is called the intuitionistic fuzzy reasoning reverse triple I solution for FMP (FMT) problem, denoted by $B^*_{RL^*}(A^*_{RL^*})$.

Theorem 6 ([24]). *Let $\mathcal{R}_{L^*}$ be the intuitionistic residuated implication induced by left-continuous associated intuitionistic t-norm $\mathcal{T}_{L^*}$. Then*

(1) *The intuitionistic fuzzy reasoning reverse triple I solution for FMP is given by the following formula*

$$B^*_{RL^*}(y) = \inf_{x\in X} \mathcal{T}_{L^*}(A^*_{L^*}(x), \mathcal{R}_{L^*}(A_{L^*}(x), B_{L^*}(y))) \ (\forall y \in Y). \tag{8}$$

(2) *The intuitionistic fuzzy reasoning reverse triple I solution for FMT is given by the following formula*

$$A^*_{RL^*}(x) = \sup_{y\in Y} \mathcal{R}_{L^*}(\mathcal{R}_{L^*}(A_{L^*}(x), B_{L^*}(y)), B^*_{L^*}(y)) \ (\forall x \in X). \tag{9}$$

Definition 12 ([17])**.** *The interval-valued fuzzy reasoning reverse triple I model is denoted as*

$$\mathcal{R}_{L^I}(\mathcal{R}_{L^I}(A^*_{L^I}(x), B^*_{L^I}(y)), \mathcal{R}_{L^I}(A_{L^I}(x), B_{L^I}(y))) \tag{10}$$

where $A_{L^I}(x), A^*_{L^I}(x) \in IVFS(X)$, $B_{L^I}(y), B^*_{L^I}(y) \in IVFS(Y)$, and $\mathcal{R}_{L^I}$ is the interval-valued residuated implication on L^I. The greatest (smallest) interval-valued fuzzy set $B^*_{L^I}(A^*_{L^I})$ of the universe $Y(X)$ such that the Formula (10) attains the greatest value is called the interval-valued fuzzy reasoning reverse triple I solution for the FMP (FMT) problem, denoted by $B^*_{RL^I}(A^*_{RL^I})$.

Theorem 7 ([17])**.** *Let $\mathcal{R}_{L^I}$ be the interval-valued residuated implication induced by left-continuous associated interval-valued t-norm $\mathcal{T}_{L^I}$. Then*

(1) *The interval-valued fuzzy reasoning reverse triple I solution for FMP is given by the following formula*

$$B^*_{RL^I}(y) = \inf_{x\in X} \mathcal{T}_{L^I}(\mathcal{R}_{L^I}(A_{L^I}(x), B_{L^I}(y)), A^*_{L^I}(x)) \ (\forall y \in Y). \tag{11}$$

(2) *The interval-valued fuzzy reasoning reverse triple I solution for FMT is given by the following formula*

$$A^*_{RL^I}(x) = \sup_{y\in Y} \mathcal{R}_{L^I}(\mathcal{R}_{L^I}(A_{L^I}(x), B_{L^I}(y)), B^*_{L^I}(y)) \ (\forall x \in X). \tag{12}$$

Theorem 8. *There is a bijection between the intuitionistic fuzzy reasoning reverse triple I solution $B^*_{RL^*}$ for FMP (by Formula (8)) and the interval-valued fuzzy reasoning reverse triple I solution $B^*_{RL^I}$ for FMP (by Formula (11)).*

Proof. Let mapping $\varphi : IFS(Y) \to IVFS(Y), (y_1, y_2) \mapsto [y_1, 1 - y_2]$.

$$\begin{aligned}
& \varphi(B^*_{RL^*}(y)) \\
= \ & \varphi \inf_{x\in X} \mathcal{T}_{L^*}(A^*_{L^*}(x), \mathcal{R}_{L^*}(A_{L^*}(x), B_{L^*}(y))) \\
= \ & \inf_{x\in X} \varphi(\mathcal{T}_{L^*}(A^*_{L^*}(x), \mathcal{R}_{L^*}(A_{L^*}(x), B_{L^*}(y)))) \\
= \ & \inf_{x\in X} \mathcal{T}_{L^I}(\varphi(A^*_{L^*}(x)), \varphi(\mathcal{R}_{L^*}(A_{L^*}(x), B_{L^*}(y)))) \quad \text{(By Theorem 3)} \\
= \ & \inf_{x\in X} \mathcal{T}_{L^I}(\varphi(A^*_{L^*}(x)), \mathcal{R}_{L^I}(\varphi(A_{L^*}(x)), \varphi(B_{L^*}(y)))) \quad \text{(By Theorem 3)} \\
= \ & \inf_{x\in X} \mathcal{T}_{L^I}(A^*_{L^I}(x), \mathcal{R}_{L^I}(A_{L^I}(x), B_{L^I}(y))) \\
= \ & B^*_{RL^I}(y)
\end{aligned}$$

It is shown that there is a bijection between the intuitionistic fuzzy reasoning reverse triple I solution $B^*_{RL^*}$ and the interval-valued fuzzy reasoning reverse triple I solution $B^*_{RL^I}$. □

Theorem 9. *There is a bijection between the intuitionistic fuzzy reasoning reverse triple I solution* $A^*_{RL^*}$ *for FMT (by Formula (9)) and the interval-valued fuzzy reasoning reverse triple I solution* $A^*_{RL^I}$ *for FMT (by Formula (12)).*

Proof. Let mapping $\varphi : IFS(X) \to IVFS(X), (x_1, x_2) \mapsto [x_1, 1 - x_2]$.

$$\begin{aligned}
&\varphi(A^*_{RL^*}(x)) \\
= \;& \varphi \inf_{y\in Y}(\mathcal{R}_{L^*}(\mathcal{R}_{L^*}(A_{L^*}(x), B_{L^*}(y)), B^*_{L^*}(y))) \\
= \;& \inf_{y\in Y} \varphi(\mathcal{R}_{L^*}(\mathcal{R}_{L^*}(A_{L^*}(x), B_{L^*}(y)), B^*_{L^*}(y))) \quad \text{(By Lemma 3)} \\
= \;& \inf_{y\in Y} \mathcal{R}_{L^I}(\varphi(\mathcal{R}_{L^*}(A_{L^*}(x), B_{L^*}(y))), \varphi(B^*_{L^*}(y))) \quad \text{(By Theorem 3)} \\
= \;& \inf_{y\in Y} \mathcal{R}_{L^I}(\varphi(\mathcal{R}_{L^*}(A_{L^*}(x), B_{L^*}(y))), B^*_{L^I}(y)) \quad \text{(By Theorem 3)} \\
= \;& \inf_{y\in Y} \mathcal{R}_{L^I}(\mathcal{R}_{L^I}(A_{L^I}(x), B_{L^I}(y)), B^*_{L^I}(y)) \\
= \;& A^*_{RL^I}(x)
\end{aligned}$$

It is shown that there is a bijection between the intuitionistic fuzzy reasoning reverse triple I solution $A^*_{RL^*}$ and the interval-valued fuzzy reasoning reverse triple I solution $A^*_{RL^I}$. □

3.3. The Relationship between the SIS Methods Based on Intuitionistic Fuzzy Sets and Interval-Valued Fuzzy Sets

In this section, the solutions of the SIS method based on the IFS and the IVFS have been given, and the relationship between the two solutions will be studied.

Definition 13 ([25])**.** *Let* $A, B \in IFS(X)$, *and* $\mathcal{R}_{L^*}$ *be the intuitionistic residuated implication induced by left-continuous associated intuitionistic t-norm* $\mathcal{T}_{L^*}$. *Then, the intuitionistic fuzzy reasoning subsethood degree* S_{L^*} *is denoted as*

$$S_{L^*}(A, B) = \inf_{x\in X}(A(x), B(x))$$

Definition 14 ([25])**.** *The intuitionistic fuzzy reasoning SIS model is denoted as*

$$\mathcal{R}_{L^*}(S_{L^*}(A^*_{L^*}, A_{L^*}), S_{L^*}(B^*_{L^*}, B_{L^*})) \tag{13}$$

where $A_{L^*}, A^*_{L^*} \in IFS(X)$, $B_{L^*}, B^*_{L^*} \in IFS(Y)$, *and* $\mathcal{R}_{L^*}$ *is the intuitionistic residuated implication on* L^*. *The greatest intuitionistic fuzzy set* $B^*_{L^*}(A^*_{L^*})$ *of the universe* $Y(X)$ *such that the Formula (13) attains the greatest value is called the intuitionistic fuzzy reasoning SIS algorithm solution for FMP(FMT) problem, denoted by* $B^*_{SL^*}(A^*_{SL^*})$.

Theorem 10 ([25])**.** *Let* $\mathcal{R}_{L^*}$ *be the intuitionistic residuated implication induced by left-continuous associated intuitionistic t-norm* $\mathcal{T}_{L^*}$. *Then:*

(1) *The intuitionistic fuzzy reasoning SIS reasoning algorithm solution for FMP is given by the following formula*

$$B^*_{SL^*}(y) = \inf_{x\in X} \mathcal{R}_{L^*}(S_{L^*}(A^*_{L^*}, A_{L^*}), B_{L^*}(y)) \ \ (\forall y \in Y). \tag{14}$$

(2) *The intuitionistic fuzzy reasoning SIS reasoning algorithm solution for FMT is given by the following formula*

$$A^*_{SL^*}(x) = \inf_{y\in Y} \mathcal{R}_{L^*}(S_{L^*}(B^*_{L^*}, B_{L^*}), A_{L^*}(x)) \ \ (\forall x \in X). \tag{15}$$

Definition 15 ([18]). *Let $A, B \in IVFS(X)$, and $\mathcal{R}_{L^I}$ be the interval-valued residuated implication induced by left-continuous associated interval-valued t-norm $\mathcal{T}_{L^I}$. Then, the interval-valued fuzzy reasoning subsethood degree S_{L^I} is denoted as*

$$S_{L^I}(A, B) = \inf_{x \in X}(A(x), B(x))$$

Definition 16 ([18]). *The interval-valued fuzzy reasoning SIS algorithm model is denoted as*

$$\mathcal{R}_{L^I}(S_{L^I}(B^*_{L^I}, B_{L^I}), S_{L^I}(A^*_{L^I}, A_{L^I})) \tag{16}$$

where $A_{L^I}(x), A^*_{L^I}(x) \in IVFS(X)$, $B_{L^I}(y), B^*_{L^I}(y) \in IVFS(Y)$, and $\mathcal{R}_{L^I}$ is the interval-valued residuated implication on L^I. The greatest interval-valued fuzzy set $B^*_{L^I}(A^*_{L^I})$ of the universe $Y(X)$ such that the Formula (16) attains the greatest value is called the interval-valued fuzzy reasoning SIS algorithm solution for the FMP(FMT) problem, denoted by $B^*_{SL^I}(A^*_{SL^I})$.

Theorem 11 ([18]). *Let $\mathcal{R}_{L^I}$ be the interval-valued residuated implication induced by left-continuous associated interval-valued t-norm $\mathcal{T}_{L^I}$. Then:*

(1) *The interval-valued fuzzy reasoning SIS algorithm solution for FMP is given by the following formula*

$$B^*_{SL^I}(y) = \inf_{x \in X} \mathcal{R}_{L^I}(S_{L^I}(A^*_{L^I}, A_{L^I}), B_{L^I}(y)) \ \ (\forall y \in Y). \tag{17}$$

(2) *The interval-valued fuzzy reasoning SIS algorithm solution for FMT is given by the following formula*

$$A^*_{SL^I}(x) = \inf_{y \in Y} \mathcal{R}_{L^I}(S_{L^I}(B^*_{L^I}, B_{L^I}), A_{L^I}(x)) \ \ (\forall x \in X). \tag{18}$$

Theorem 12. *There is a bijection between the intuitionistic fuzzy reasoning SIS algorithm solution $B^*_{SL^*}$ for FMP (by Formula (14)) and the interval-valued fuzzy reasoning SIS algorithm solution $B^*_{SL^I}$ for FMP (by Formula (17)).*

Proof. Let mapping $\varphi : IFS(Y) \to IVFS(Y)$, $(y_1, y_2) \mapsto [y_1, 1 - y_2]$.

$$\begin{aligned}
& \varphi(B^*_{SL^*}(y)) \\
= \ & \varphi \inf_{x \in X}(\mathcal{R}_{L^*}(S_{L^*}(A^*_{L^*}, A_{L^*}), B_{L^*}(y))) \\
= \ & \inf_{x \in X} \varphi(\mathcal{R}_{L^*}(S_{L^*}(A^*_{L^*}, A_{L^*}), B_{L^*}(y))) \\
= \ & \inf_{x \in X} \mathcal{R}_{L^I}(\varphi(S_{L^*}(A^*_{L^*}, A_{L^*}), B_{L^*}(y))) \\
= \ & \inf_{x \in X} \mathcal{R}_{L^I}(S_{L^I}(\varphi((A^*_{L^*}, A_{L^*}), \varphi(B_{L^*}(y)))) \\
= \ & \inf_{x \in X}(\mathcal{R}_{L^I}(S_{L^I}(A^*_{L^I}, A_{L^I}), B_{L^I}(y))) \\
= \ & B^*_{SL^I}(y)
\end{aligned}$$

It is shown that there is a bijection between the intuitionistic fuzzy reasoning SIS algorithm solution $B^*_{SL^*}$ and the interval-valued fuzzy reasoning SIS algorithm solution $B^*_{SL^I}$. □

Theorem 13. *There is a bijection between the intuitionistic fuzzy reasoning SIS algorithm solution $A^*_{SL^*}$ for FMT (by Formula (15)) and the interval-valued fuzzy reasoning SIS algorithm solution $A^*_{SL^I}$ for FMT (by Formula (18)).*

Proof. Let mapping $\varphi : IFS(X) \to IVFS(X), (x_1, x_2) \mapsto [x_1, 1 - x_2]$.

$$\begin{aligned}
& \varphi(A^*_{SL^*}(x)) \\
= \; & \varphi \inf_{y \in Y} (\mathcal{R}_{L^*}(S_{L^*}(B^*_{L^*}, B_{L^*}) A_{L^*}(x)) \\
= \; & \inf_{y \in Y} \varphi(\mathcal{R}_{L^*}(S_{L^*}(B^*_{L^*}, B_{L^*}), A_{L^*}(x))) \\
= \; & \inf_{y \in Y} \mathcal{R}_{L^I}(\varphi(S_{L^*}(B^*_{L^*}, B_{L^*}), A_{L^*}(x))) \\
= \; & \inf_{y \in Y} \mathcal{R}_{L^I}(S_{L^I}(\varphi((B^*_{L^*}, B_{L^*}), \varphi(A_{L^*}(x)))) \\
= \; & \inf_{y \in Y} (\mathcal{R}_{L^I}(S_{L^I}(B^*_{L^I}, B_{L^I}), A_{L^I}(x))) \\
= \; & A^*_{SL^I}(x)
\end{aligned}$$

It is shown that there is a bijection between the intuitionistic fuzzy reasoning SIS algorithm solution $A^*_{SL^*}$ and the interval-valued fuzzy reasoning SIS algorithm solution $A^*_{SL^I}$. □

The flow diagram of results is shown in Figure 1.

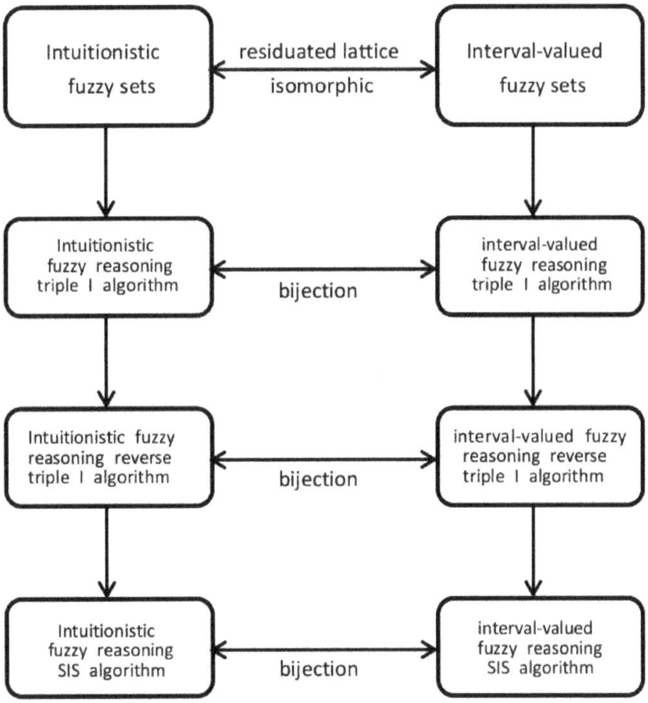

Figure 1. The flow diagram of results.

4. Conclusions

In this paper, we studied the relationship between intuitionistic fuzzy reasoning algorithm and interval-valued fuzzy reasoning algorithm. It is proved that there is a bijection between the intuitionistic fuzzy reasoning triple I solution and the interval-valued fuzzy reasoning triple I solution, and there is a bijection between the intuitionistic fuzzy reasoning reverse triple I solution and the interval-valued fuzzy reasoning reverse triple I solution. Moreover, it is proved that there is a bijection between the intuitionistic fuzzy reasoning

SIS solution and the interval-valued fuzzy reasoning SIS solution. Finally, a numerical example is given to show that there is a bijection between the intuitionistic fuzzy reasoning triple I method and the interval-valued fuzzy reasoning triple I method. We prove that the intuitionistic fuzzy reasoning method and interval-valued fuzzy reasoning method are equivalent in essence. In practical application, interval-valued fuzzy sets can effectively reduce the loss of fuzzy information, and intuitionistic fuzzy sets can characterize information from two aspects, intuitionistic fuzzy reasoning method and interval-valued fuzzy reasoning method can be used for one calculation and one test. Intuitionistic fuzzy reasoning method and interval-valued fuzzy reasoning method will be applied in many fields such as pattern recognition and medical diagnosis. In the future, how to apply the algorithm to practical applications is the next research direction. we will study how to apply intuitionistic fuzzy reasoning method and an interval-valued fuzzy reasoning method to practical problems such as pattern recognition and medical diagnosis.

Author Contributions: M.L. initiated the research and provided the framework of this paper. W.L. and H.S. wrote and completed this paper with M.L. who validated the findings and provided helpful suggestions. All authors have read and agreed to the published version of the manuscript.

Funding: This work is supported by the National Natural Science Foundation of China (No. 12171445).

Institutional Review Board Statement: Not applicable.

Informed Consent Statement: Informed consent was obtained from all subjects involved in the study.

Data Availability Statement: Not applicable.

Conflicts of Interest: The authors declare no conflict of interest.

References

1. Wang, G.J. *Non-Classical Mathematical Logic and Approximate Reasoning*; Science Press: Beijing, China, 2008.
2. Zadeh, L.A. Outline of a new approach to the analysis of complex systems and decision processes. *IEEE Trans. Syst. Man Cybern.* **1973**, *3*, 28–44. [CrossRef]
3. Wang, G.J. The full implication triple I method of fuzzy reasoning. *Sci. China* **1999**, *29*, 43–53.
4. Wang, G.J.; Fu, L. Unified forms of triple I method. *Comput. Math. Appl.* **2005**, *49*, 923–932. [CrossRef]
5. Pei, D.W. Unified full implication algorithms of fuzzy reasoning. *Inf. Sci.* **2008**, *178*, 520–530. [CrossRef]
6. Song, S.J.; Wu, C. Reverse triple I method of fuzzy reasoning. *Sci. China* **2002**, *45*, 344–364. [CrossRef]
7. Liu, H.W.; Wang, G.J. Triple I method based on point wise sustaining degrees. *Comput. Math. Appl.* **2008**, *55*, 2680–2688. [CrossRef]
8. Luo, M.X.; Yao, N. Triple I algorithms based on Schweizer-Sklar operators in fuzzy reasoninng. *Int. J. Approx. Reason.* **2013**, *54*, 640–652. [CrossRef]
9. Zou, X.F.; Pei, D.W. SIS Algorithms for Fuzzy Reasoning. *Fuzzy Syst. Math.* **2010**, *24*, 1–7. (In Chinese)
10. Zadeh, L.A. The concept of a linguistic variable and its application to approximate reasoning-I. *Inf. Sci.* **1975**, *8*, 199–249. [CrossRef]
11. Gorza lczany, M.B. A method of inference in approximate reasoning based on interval-valued fuzzy sets. *Fuzzy Sets Syst.* **1987**, *21*, 1–17. [CrossRef]
12. Li, D.C.; Li, Y.M.; Xie, Y.J. Robustness of interval-valued fuzzy inference. *Inf. Sci.* **2011**, *181*, 4754–4764. [CrossRef]
13. Liu, H.W.; Li, C. Fully implicational methods for interval-valued fuzzy reasoning with multi-antecedent rules. *Int. J. Comput. Intell. Syst.* **2011**, *4*, 929–945.
14. Luo, M.X.; Zhang, K. Robustness of full implication algorithms based on interval-valued fuzzy inference. *Int. J. Approx. Reason.* **2015**, *62*, 61–72. [CrossRef]
15. Luo, M.X.; Wang, Y.J. Interval-valued fuzzy reasoning full implication alogrithms based on the t-representable t-norm. *Int. J. Approx. Reason.* **2020**, *122*, 1–8. [CrossRef]
16. Li, D.C.; Xie, Y.J. Universal approximation of interval-valued fuzzy systems based on interval-valued implications. *Iran. J. Fuzzy Syst.* **2016**, *13*, 89–110.
17. Luo, M.X.; Zhou, X.L. Robustness of reverse triple I algorithms based on interval-valued fuzzy inference. *Int. J. Approx. Reason.* **2015**, *66*, 16–26. [CrossRef]
18. Wang, R.; Hui, J.X.; Jin, M. Robustness of SIS algorithm based on Interval-valued fuzzy reasoning. *Fuzzy Syst. Math.* **2018**, *32*, 1–6. (In Chinese)
19. Atanassov, K. Intuitionistic fuzzy sets. *Fuzzy Sets Syst.* **1986**, *20*, 87–96. [CrossRef]
20. Deschrijver, G.; Cornelis, C.; Kerre, E.E. On the representation of intuitionistic fuzzy t-norms and t-conorms. *IEEE Trans. Fuzzy Syst.* **2004**, *12*, 45–61. [CrossRef]

21. Cornelis, C.; Deschrijver, G.; Kerre, E.E. Implication in intuitionistic fuzzy and interval-valued fuzzy set theory: Construction, classification, application. *Int. J. Approx. Reason.* **2004**, *35*, 55–95. [CrossRef]
22. Zheng, M.C.; Shi, Z.K.; Liu, Y. Triple I method of approximate reasoning on Atanassov's intuitionistic fuzzy sets. *Int. J. Approx. Reason.* **2014**, *55*, 1369–1382. [CrossRef]
23. Liu, Y.; Zheng, M.C. The dual triple I methods of FMT and IFMT. *Math. Probl. Eng.* **2014**, *3*, 1–8.
24. Peng, J.Y. Reverse Triple I method for residual intuitionistic fuzzy reasoning. *Pattern Recognit. Artif. Intell.* **2018**, *31*, 525–536. (In Chinese)
25. Li, J.; Xu, P.X. SIS algorithms of Lukasiewicz-type intuitionistic fuzzy reasoning and its continuity. *J. Lanzhou Univ. Technol.* **2018**, *44*, 1–6. (In Chinese)
26. Klement, E.P.; Mesiar, R.; Pap, E. *Triangular Norms*; Springer: Dordrecht, The Netherlands, 2000.
27. Fodor, J.C.; Roubens, M. *Fuzzy Preference Modelling and Multicriteria Decision Support*; Springer: Dordrecht, The Netherlands, 1994.
28. Hajek, P. *Metamathematics of Fuzzy Logic*; Kluwer Academic Publishers: Dordrecht, The Netherlands, 1998.
29. Atanassov, K. *Intuitionistic Fuzzy Sets: Theory and Applications*; Physica-Verlag: Heidelberg, Germany, 1999.
30. Deschrijver,G.; Kerre, E.E. On the relationship between some extensions of fuzzy set theory. *Fuzzy Sets Syst.* **2003**, *133*, 227–235. [CrossRef]
31. Davey, B.A.; Priestley, H.A. *Introduction to Lattices and Order*; Cambridge University Press: Cambridge, UK, 1990.
32. Deschrijver, G. Triangular norms which are meet-morphisms in interval-valued fuzzy set theory. *Fuzzy Sets Syst.* **2011**, *181*, 88–101. [CrossRef]
33. Jenei, S. A more efficient method for defining fuzzy connectives. *Fuzzy Sets Syst.* **1997**, *90*, 25–35. [CrossRef]
34. Alcalde, C.; Burusco, A.; Fuentes-Gonzalez, R. A constructive method for the definition of interval-valued fuzzy implication operators. *Fuzzy Sets Syst.* **2005**, *153*, 211–227. [CrossRef]
35. Atanassov, K.; Gargov, G. Interval-valued intuitionistic fuzzy sets. *Fuzzy Sets Syst.* **1989**, *31*, 343–349. [CrossRef]

axioms

Communication

Selection of Appropriate Symbolic Regression Models Using Statistical and Dynamic System Criteria: Example of Waste Gasification

Pavel Praks [1,*], Marek Lampart [1,2], Renáta Praksová [1], Dejan Brkić [1,*], Tomáš Kozubek [1] and Jan Najser [3]

1 IT4Innovations, VSB—Technical University of Ostrava, 708 00 Ostrava, Czech Republic
2 Department of Applied Mathematics, VSB—Technical University of Ostrava, 708 00 Ostrava, Czech Republic
3 ENET Centre, VSB—Technical University of Ostrava, 708 00 Ostrava, Czech Republic
* Correspondence: pavel.praks@vsb.cz (P.P.); dejan.brkic@vsb.cz (D.B.)

Abstract: In this paper, we analyze the interpretable models from real gasification datasets of the project "Centre for Energy and Environmental Technologies" (CEET) discovered by symbolic regression. To evaluate CEET models based on input data, two different statistical metrics to quantify their accuracy are usually used: Mean Square Error (MSE) and the Pearson Correlation Coefficient (PCC). However, if the testing points and the points used to construct the models are not chosen randomly from the continuum of the input variable, but instead from the limited number of discrete input points, the behavior of the model between such points very possibly will not fit well the physical essence of the modelled phenomenon. For example, the developed model can have unexpected oscillatory tendencies between the used points, while the usually used statistical metrics cannot detect these anomalies. However, using dynamic system criteria in addition to statistical metrics, such suspicious models that do fit well-expected behavior can be automatically detected and abandoned. This communication will show the universal method based on dynamic system criteria which can detect suitable models among all those which have good properties following statistical metrics. The dynamic system criteria measure the complexity of the candidate models using approximate and sample entropy. The examples are given for waste gasification where the output data (percentage of each particular gas in the produced mixture) is given only for six values of the input data (temperature in the chamber in which the process takes place). In such cases instead, to produce expected simple spline-like curves, artificial intelligence tools can produce inappropriate oscillatory curves with sharp picks due to the known tendency of symbolic regression to produce overfitted and relatively more complex models if the nature of the physical model is simple.

Keywords: symbolic regression; Mean Square Error; Pearson Correlation Coefficient; oscillations in solutions; dynamic system criteria; waste gasification; Occam's Razor

MSC: 11Y16: 46N30; 65C60; 94A17

Citation: Praks, P.; Lampart, M.; Praksová, R.; Brkić, D.; Kozubek, T.; Najser, J. Selection of Appropriate Symbolic Regression Models Using Statistical and Dynamic System Criteria: Example of Waste Gasification. *Axioms* **2022**, *11*, 463. https://doi.org/10.3390/axioms11090463

Academic Editor: Yurii Kharkevych

Received: 26 July 2022
Accepted: 2 September 2022
Published: 8 September 2022

1. Introduction

We developed a set of curves for the gasification of municipal solid waste [1] using symbolic regression [2]. The curves were tested statistically, and among those with satisfactory results in terms of Mean Square Error (MSE) and Pearson Correlation Coefficient (PCC) some are not acceptable because they show unexpected oscillatory behavior. To eliminate them, we applied dynamic system criteria by measuring complexity using approximate and sample entropy where the inappropriate curves can be eliminated to persist Occam's Razor [3]. We prefer not to present more statistical metrics aside MSE and PCC because they cannot measure behavior between the testing points (on the other hand, dynamic system criteria can).

Gasification of municipal solid waste and biomass gives the different compositions of the synthetic gas (syngas) depending on the gasification temperature in the process [4]. Based on real measurements of a plasma gasifier, a symbolic model for an important component of the produced syngas is constructed where the percentage in the mixture is given depending on the gasification temperature. To construct these symbolic syngas composition models, the artificial intelligence provided outcomes using symbolic regression software tools AI Feynman [5] and PySR [6]. The candidate symbolic models were chosen among those with better statistical metrics; those with a lower Mean Square Error (MSE) and with the Pearson Correlation Coefficient (PCC) close to one. However, it was discovered that some of the obtained symbolic models, which fit very well the measured gasification datasets using statistical metrics, are of oscillatory nature, which was not expected and does not reflect the true physical properties of the modelled gasification process. However, using dynamic system criteria in addition to statistical metrics, such suspicious symbolic models that do fit well the measured gasification datasets were automatically detected and abandoned. This communication will show the universal method based on dynamic system criteria which can detect suitable models among all those which has good properties following statistical metrics. The dynamic system criteria measure the complexity of the candidate models using approximate and sample entropy. Our results indicate that candidate symbolic regression models with oscillations and other non-physical phenomena have higher complexity and can be automatically detected and excluded by approximate and sample entropy to persist Occam's Razor "science always prefers the simpler model or representation of two which give similar accuracy" [6]. Consequently, we propose that the dynamic system criteria based on approximate or sample entropy should be used for the automated evaluation of symbolic regression models, as it is not enough to evaluate the models by statistical metrics.

2. Gasification Models

Gasification models were developed for the production of hydrogen (H_2) and carbon dioxide (CO_2) from municipal solid waste for only six different temperatures, while the measurements were repeated four times.

These functions were introduced in symbolic regression software to provide numerically stable logarithm-based functions, which are defined for all real numbers. As logarithms are defined only for positive non-zero numbers, logarithms pose numerical problems in the symbolic regression procedure, when the argument is negative.

Mean Square Error (MSE) and with the Pearson Correlation Coefficient (PCC) were calculated using functions of Python 3.9 by:

```
MSE = np.square(np.subtract(data,y_pred)).mean()
```

```
coef = np.corrcoef(data,y_pred)[0][1]
```

where "data" means the measured data set and "y_pred" means the predicted values using the selected symbolic regression model.

MSE and corr.coef were calculated for all measured data.

The presented models in Matlab notifications are given in Appendix A to this Communication.

2.1. Hydrogen H_2

The train set for hydrogen H_2 is given in Table 1 while three test sets are given in Table 2.

Table 1. Train data for H_2.

t (°C)	750	800	900	1000	1050	1100
H_2 (%)	9.75	10.98	16.05	12.88	12.33	11.83

Table 2. Test data for H_2.

t (°C)	750	800	900	1000	1050	1100
H_2 (%)	9.69	11.54	15.91	12.77	12.48	11.56
H_2 (%) [1]	9.88	10.29	16.23	13.29	12.44	12.12
H_2 (%) [2]	9.68	11.12	16.01	12.58	12.08	11.82

[1] Second test measurement, [2] Third test measurement.

The expected shape of the modelled curves for hydrogen H_2 is given in Figure 1 where the trendline is based on data from Table 1 and was produced in MS Excel as a polynomial curve of order 4.

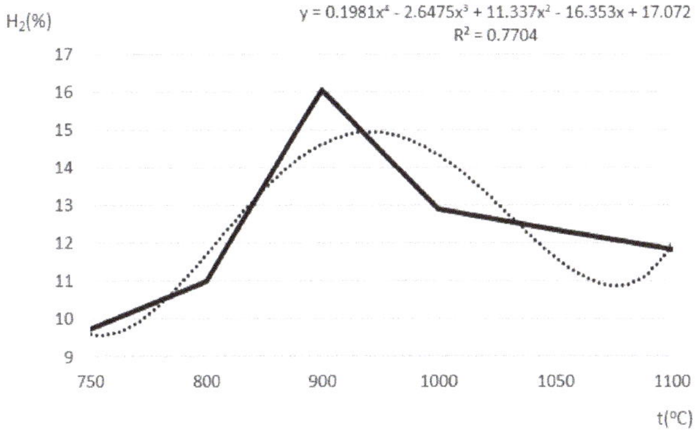

Figure 1. Expected shape for hydrogen H_2.

Using symbolic regression tools, three different models were produced as follows.

2.1.1. Model 1 of Hydrogen H_2

The first developed model is given in Equation (1)

$$H_2(\%) = \frac{8.9065269419}{\cos\left(\cos\left(e^{\sin(t+1)} - 2\right)\right)}. \quad (1)$$

This model performs good statistical metrics; MSE = 0.2897 and PCC = 0.9728 while anyway, it shows oscillatory tendencies as can be seen in Figure 2.

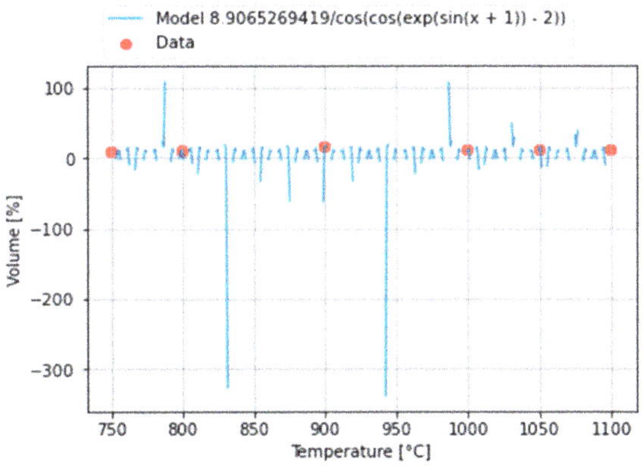

Figure 2. Model 1 of hydrogen H_2.

2.1.2. Model 2 of Hydrogen H_2

The second developed model is given in Equation (2)

$$\left.\begin{array}{c} H_2(\%) = \text{logm2}(7.744805\cdot(-9.837645 + \text{logm2}(t))^{-1.5165994}) + 0.0054770974\cdot t \\ \text{logm2}(t) = \log_2(|t| + 10^{-8}) \end{array}\right\}. \quad (2)$$

This model performs good, as indicated by statistical metrics, MSE = 0.08143851 and PCC = 0.989470395. Model 2 has improved shape compared with Model 1, despite the undesired tendency towards a sharp peak. It is given in Figure 3.

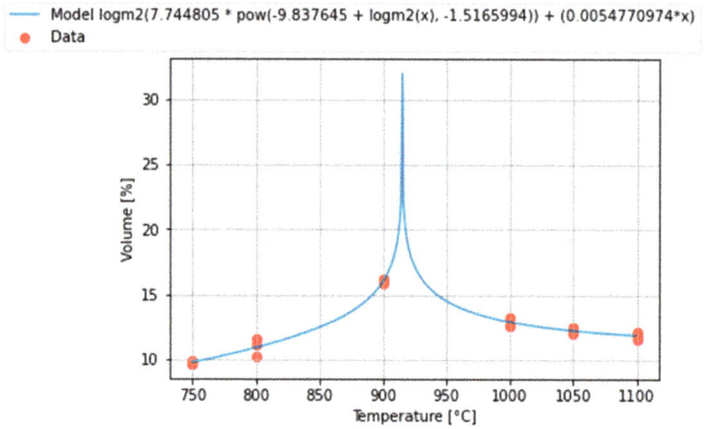

Figure 3. Model 2 of hydrogen H_2.

2.1.3. Model 3 of Hydrogen H_2

The second developed model is given in Equation (3)

$$\left.\begin{array}{c} H_2(\%) = 6.5368786 + \text{logm2}(|-9.864973 + \text{logm2}(t)|^{-2.1570945}) \\ \text{logm2}(t) = \log_2(|t| + 10^{-8}) \end{array}\right\}. \quad (3)$$

This model performs good statistical metrics, MSE = 0.362862372 and PCC = 0.952248777. It shows the same tendency as Model 2. Model 3 is given in Figure 4.

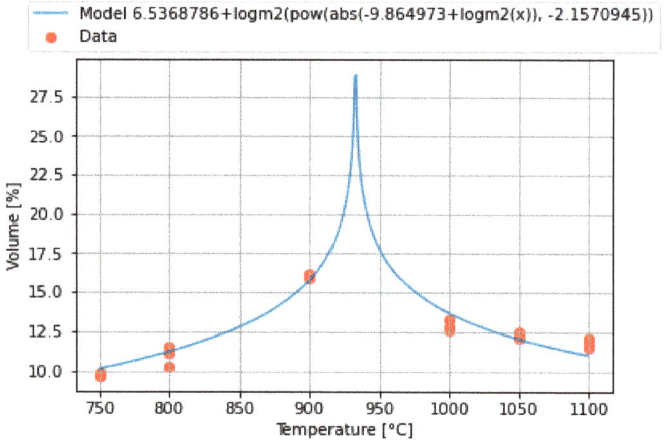

Figure 4. Model 3 of hydrogen H_2.

2.2. *Hydrogen* CO_2

The train set for hydrogen CO_2 is given in Table 3 while three test sets are given in Table 4.

Table 3. Train data for CO_2.

t (°C)	750	800	900	1000	1050	1100
CO_2 (%)	8.13	9.8	11.93	11.33	11.53	12.3

Table 4. Test data for CO_2.

t (°C)	750	800	900	1000	1050	1100
CO_2 (%)	8.05	9.52	11.63	11.5	11.56	12.27
CO_2 (%) [1]	8.09	9.83	12.31	11.23	11.5	12.21
CO_2 (%) [2]	8.24	10.05	11.84	11.27	11.54	12.43

[1] Second test measurement, [2] Third test measurement

The expected shape of the modelled curves for hydrogen CO_2 is given in Figure 5 where the trendline is based on data from Table 3 and was produced in MS Excel as a polynomial curve of order 4.

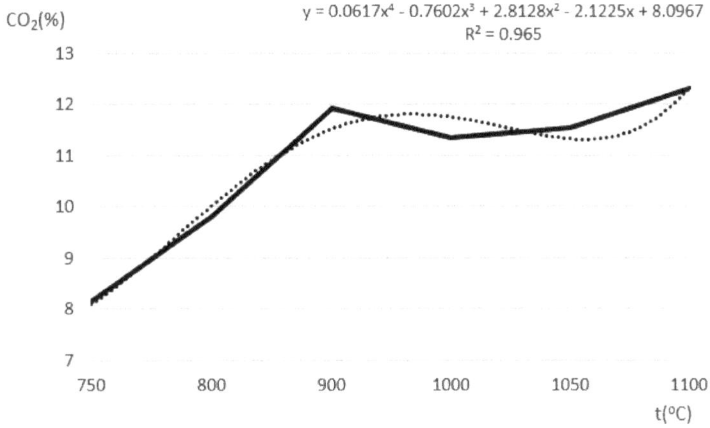

Figure 5. Expected shape for hydrogen CO_2.

Using the symbolic regression tools, three different models were produced as follows.

2.2.1. Model 1 of Carbon Dioxide CO_2

The first developed model is given in Equation (4)

$$\left.\begin{aligned} CO_2(\%) &= \text{logm10}\left(x \cdot e^{\sin(x+0.6718609)}\right)^2 \\ \text{logm10}(t) &= \ln(|t| + 10^{-8}) \end{aligned}\right\} \quad (4)$$

This model performs good statistical metrics, MSE = 0.3481 and PCC = 0.9171, while it shows oscillatory tendencies, as can be seen in Figure 6.

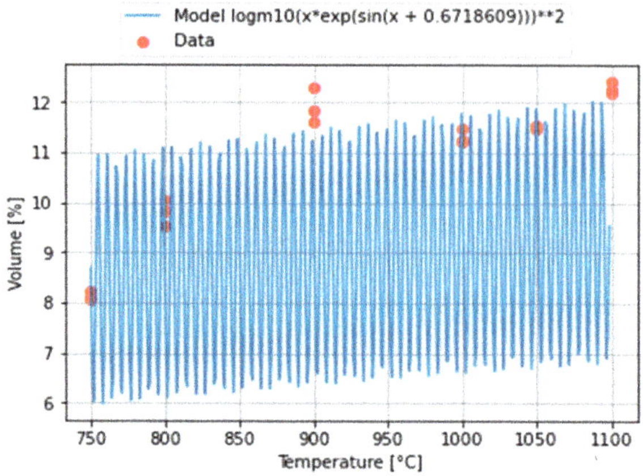

Figure 6. Model 1 of carbon dioxide CO_2.

2.2.2. Model 2 of Carbon Dioxide CO_2

The first developed model is given in Equation (5)

$$\left.\begin{array}{r} CO_2(\%) = \mathrm{logm}\left(-0.060511474 \cdot t^2\right) + 2.0503674 \\ \mathrm{logm}(t) = \ln\left(|t| + 10^{-8}\right) \end{array}\right\}. \quad (5)$$

This model performs good statistical metrics, MSE = 0.1985 and PCC = 0.9519, with a good shape of the developed curve, as can be seen in Figure 7.

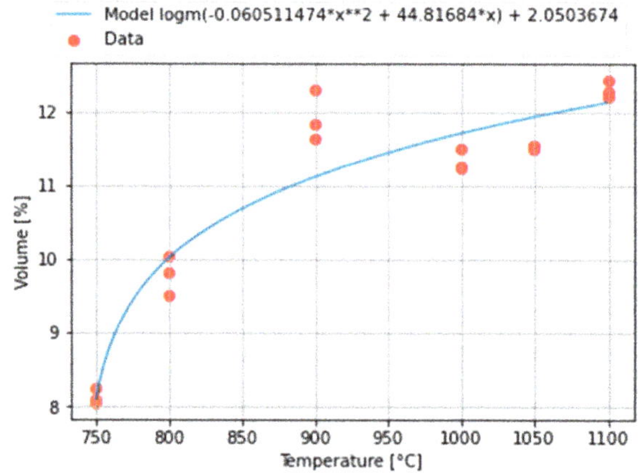

Figure 7. Model 2 of carbon dioxide CO_2.

3. Dynamic System Criteria for Selection of Appropriate Models

As observed, it is possible to construct many different models of the investigated phenomena having comparable precision. Now, the task is to select one of them that can be signed as the best choice under the assumption of Occam's Razor [3]. For this purpose, the qualification tools from the area of dynamical systems, like approximate E_{app} and sample E_{samp} entropy [7–11], can be applied.

Hence, the selection process, based on observation of the measure of complexity, works as follows. Firstly, construct models (e.g., as in the previous section). Secondly, measure the complexity of each model and order them with respect to this measure (in our case approximate and sample entropy). Finally, pick the model with the smallest complexity value (at this stage the assumption of Occam's Razor [3] is applied). Here, note that since the minimum need not be unique the output of this selection process will always exist, but should not be unique in general as we will show in the next section.

3.1. Entropy Notions

Approximate entropy E_{app} and sample entropy E_{samp} are tools of complexity measurement that were investigated by many authors and applied in numerous research fields (e.g., [12–14]) to measure and compare studied cases' complexity.

3.1.1. Approximate Entropy E_{app}

Recall these notions are defined for the input vector $X = x_1, x_2, \ldots, x_N$ of length N. Approximate entropy E_{app} is defined in Equation (6)

$$E_{app}(X, m, r) = \Phi^m(r) - \Phi^{m+1}(r), \tag{6}$$

where $\Phi^m(r) = (N - m + 1)\sum_{i=1}^{M-m+1} \log(C_i^m(r))$ and $C_i^m(r)$ is the number of $u_m(j)$ such that $d(u_m(i), u_m(j)) \leq r$, divided by $N - m + 1$. Here, $u_m(i) = [x(i), x(i+1), \ldots, x(i+m-1)]$ is an element of m-dimensional real space, m, r are test parameters and $d(p, q) = \max_a |p(a) - q(a)|$ is the maximum metric. For these parameters holds: m is the length of the window, r is the diameter of the region with a similar subsequence.

3.1.2. Sample Entropy E_{samp}

On the other hand, sample entropy E_{samp} is given in Equation (7)

$$E_{samp}(X, m, r) = -\ln \frac{A}{B}, \tag{7}$$

where A is the number of template vector pairs such that $d^c(u_{m+1}(i), u_{m+1}(i)) < r$, and B is the number of template vector pairs such $d^c(u_m(i), u_m(i)) < r$. Here, d^c is the Chebyshev distance and parameters m, r have the same meaning as in the case of E_{app}.

3.2. Benchmark Models Application

To depict previously mentioned complexity measurement tools, classical models from the theory of dynamical systems can be applied. The well-known logistic function can be used as example of normalized models (also can be thought as predictive one). Recall $L_1(x) = 4x(1-x)$ and $L_1 : [0,1] \to [0,1]$, this model is well understood from dynamical point of view [15]. The next model can be constructed as a second iteration of $L_1(x)$ that is $L_2 = L_1 \cdot L_1 = L_1^2$, and analogously $L_3 = L_1 \cdot L_1 \cdot L_1 = L_1^3$, $L_4 = L_1^4$, $L_5 = L_1^5$. The evolution of these models is shown in Figure 8a and their corresponding entropies are in Figure 8b, clearly showing increase of entropy while the complexity of the model increases.

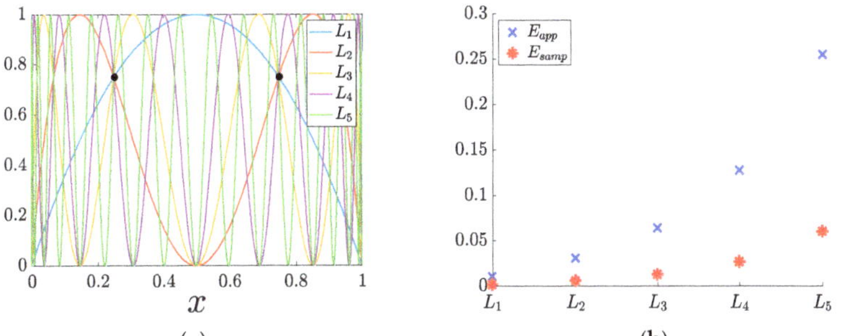

(a) (b)

Figure 8. Benchmark models' L_i evolution in (**a**) and corresponding entropies in (**b**).

3.3. Simulation Outputs

The numerical simulations of our models were performed in Matlab while the continuous models were discretized from 750 °C to 1100 °C by the step of 0.001 °C. Entropies tests were set classically, that is, r was picked as 20% of the standard deviation of the investigated vector and m was set to 1 as the minimum window length. Firstly, note that the test performed on all models coincides so, for simplicity, we can use the abbreviation of entropy for both tests. These outputs, rounded on four decimal places, are summarized in Table 5 for hydrogen H_2 and in Table 6 for carbon dioxide CO_2.

Table 5. Dynamic system criteria for hydrogen H_2.

	Model 1	Model 2	Model 3
Approximate entropy E_{app}	0.0442	0.0015	0.0015
Sample entropy E_{samp}	0.0197	0.0003	0.0003

Table 6. Dynamic system criteria for carbon dioxide CO_2.

	Model 1	Model 2
Approximate entropy E_{app}	0.0252	0
Sample entropy E_{samp}	0.0235	0

Model 1 of H_2 (which is periodic with a period of 6.283183 °C) has higher complexity than Model 2 of H_2 and Model 3 of H_2, so Model 1 of H_2 can be denied. It is also observable from Table 5 that entropies of Model 2 of H_2 and Model 3 of H_2 are comparable and much less than Model 1 of H_2.

It is observable from Table 6 that entropy of the Model 1 of CO_2 is much higher than that of Model 2 of CO_2, proving that Model 2 has lower complexity than Model 1 and is then a better choice.

4. Conclusions

We developed symbolic regression models for the gasification of municipal solid waste [16–21]. However, these models were developed using limited points of data and so, between these points, it shows unpredicted behavior (sharp picks or oscillatory motions) where all such models were acceptable using statistic metrics (Mean Square Error and the Pearson Correlation Coefficient) as criteria. In the end, the proposed application of approximate E_{app} and sample E_{samp} entropy automatically detected those models with higher complexity contradicting Occam's Razor assumption. Hence, the models with higher complexity can be excluded from further investigation. Moreover, it is possible to use these dynamic tools automatically in general for decision mechanisms. The example is about gasification of waste, but the shown method for rejection of inappropriate models is of general value and can be used in various scientific fields. It is based on dynamic system criteria and it is based on the measurement of entropy. In future, we would like to also test Symbolic Functional Evolutionary Search (SyFES), that automatically constructs accurate functionals in the symbolic form, which is more explainable to humans, cheaper to evaluate, and easier to integrate into existing software codes [22].

However, the proposed selection method is based on approximate and sample entropy, there are also other tools in the mathematical theory of dynamical systems that can be applied [23,24]. For example, metrics from recurrence quantification analysis (RQA) can be applied (or relevant alternatives mentioned in [25]). We propose these promising tools for further research.

In the end, since the proposed method is addressed in general to any set of models it can be also applied to prediction models. The application of the method to the prediction models is left for future research.

Author Contributions: Conceptualization, P.P., M.L., R.P. and D.B.; methodology, P.P., M.L. and R.P.; software, R.P., M.L. and P.P.; validation, P.P., M.L., J.N. and R.P.; formal analysis, P.P., T.K. and M.L.; investigation, P.P. and M.L.; resources, T.K.; data curation, J.N.; writing—original draft preparation, M.L. and D.B.; writing—review and editing, D.B., P.P. and T.K.; visualization, R.P., M.L. and D.B.; supervision, T.K. and P.P.; project administration, P.P. and J.N.; funding acquisition, P.P., T.K., J.N. and M.L. All authors have read and agreed to the published version of the manuscript.

Funding: This work was supported by the Ministry of Education, Youth and Sports of the Czech Republic through the e-INFRA CZ (ID:90140), by the Technology Agency of the Czech Republic through the project "Center of Energy and Environmental Technologies" TK03020027 and by VSB—Technical University of Ostrava, Czech Republic through the Grant of SGS No. SP2022/42.

Informed Consent Statement: Not applicable.

Data Availability Statement: All data to repeat computations are given in the text.

Conflicts of Interest: The authors declare no conflict of interest.

Appendix A

The models in Matlab notifications are:
H_2 models:
= 8.9065269419/cos(cos(exp(sin(x + 1)) − 2))
= logm2(7.744805 * pow(-9.837645 + logm2(x), −1.5165994)) + (0.0054770974*x)
= 6.5368786+logm2(pow(abs(−9.864973 + logm2(x)), −2.1570945))
CO_2 models:
= logm10(x.*exp(sin(x + 0.6718609))).^2
= logm(−0.060511474*x.^2+44.81684*x) + 2.0503674
pow = @(x,y) x.^y
logm = @(x) log(abs(x) + 1e-8);
logm2 =@(x) log2(abs(x) + 1e-8);
logm10 = @(x) log10(abs(x) + 1e-8)

References

1. Praks, P.; Brkić, D.; Najser, J.; Najser, T.; Praksová, R.; Stajić, Z. Methods of Artificial Intelligence for Simulation of Gasification of Biomass and Communal Waste. In Proceedings of the 22nd International Carpathian Control Conference (ICCC), Velké Karlovice, Czech Republic, 31 May–1 June 2021. [CrossRef]
2. Praks, P.; Brkić, D. Symbolic Regression-Based Genetic Approximations of the Colebrook Equation for Flow Friction. *Water* **2018**, *10*, 1175. [CrossRef]
3. Dresp-Langley, B.; Ekseth, O.K.; Fesl, J.; Gohshi, S.; Kurz, M.; Sehring, H.-W. Occam's Razor for Big Data? On Detecting Quality in Large Unstructured Datasets. *Appl. Sci.* **2019**, *9*, 3065. [CrossRef]
4. Baláš, M.; Lisý, M.; Štelcl, O. The Effect of Temperature on the Gasification Process. *Acta Polytech.* **2012**, *52*, 7–11. Available online: http://hdl.handle.net/10467/66949 (accessed on 10 July 2022). [CrossRef]
5. Udrescu, S.-M.; Tegmark, M. AI Feynman: A physics-inspired method for symbolic regression. *Sci. Adv.* **2020**, *6*, eaay2631. [CrossRef]
6. Cranmer, M.; Sanchez-Gonzalez, A.; Battaglia, P.; Xu, R.; Cranmer, K.; Spergel, D.; Ho, S. Discovering symbolic models from deep learning with inductive biases. *Adv. Neural Inf. Process. Syst.* **2020**, *33*, 17429–17442. Available online: https://proceedings.neurips.cc/paper/2020/file/c9f2f917078bd2db12f23c3b413d9cba-Paper.pdf (accessed on 8 July 2022).
7. Pincus, S.M. Approximate entropy as a measure of system complexity. *Proc. Natl. Acad. Sci. USA* **1991**, *88*, 2297–2301. [CrossRef]
8. Chon, K.H.; Scully, C.G.; Lu, S. Approximate entropy for all signals. *IEEE Eng. Med. Biol. Mag.* **2009**, *28*, 18–23. [CrossRef]
9. Delgado-Bonal, A.; Marshak, A. Approximate Entropy and Sample Entropy: A Comprehensive Tutorial. *Entropy* **2019**, *21*, 541. [CrossRef]
10. Richman, J.S.; Moorman, J.R. Physiological time-series analysis using approximate entropy and sample entropy. *Am. J. Physiol. Heart Circ. Physiol.* **2000**, *278*, H2039–H2049. [CrossRef]
11. Yentes, J.M.; Hunt, N.; Schmid, K.K.; Kaipust, J.P.; McGrath, D.; Stergiou, N. The appropriate use of approximate entropy and sample entropy with short data sets. *Ann. Biomed. Eng.* **2013**, *41*, 349–365. [CrossRef]
12. Buchlovská Nagyová, J.; Jansík, B.; Lampart, M. Detection of embedded dynamics in the Györgyi-Field model. *Sci. Rep.* **2000**, *10*, 21031. [CrossRef]
13. Lampart, M.; Vantuch, T.; Zelinka, I.; Mišák, S. Dynamical properties of partial-discharge patterns. *Int. J. Parallel Emergent Distrib. Syst.* **2018**, *33*, 474–489. [CrossRef]

14. Lampart, M.; Zapoměl, J. Motion of an Unbalanced Impact Body Colliding with a Moving Belt. *Mathematics* **2021**, *9*, 1071. [CrossRef]
15. Lampart, M.; Martinovič, T. A survey of tools detecting the dynamical properties of one-dimensional families. *Adv. Electr. Electron. Eng.* **2017**, *15*, 304–313. [CrossRef]
16. Akkaya, E.; Demir, A. Energy content estimation of municipal solid waste by multiple regression analysis. In Proceedings of the 5th International Advanced Technologies Symposium IATS'09, Karabuk, Turkey, 13–15 May 2009; pp. 13–15. Available online: https://www.academia.edu/download/54979427/IATS09_03-99_1292.pdf (accessed on 10 July 2022).
17. Liu, J.-I.; Paode, R.D.; Holsen, T.M. Modeling the energy content of municipal solid waste using multiple regression analysis. *J. Air Waste Manag. Assoc.* **1996**, *46*, 650–656. [CrossRef]
18. Chu, C.; Boré, A.; Liu, X.W.; Cui, J.C.; Wang, P.; Liu, X.; Chen, G.Y.; Liu, B.; Ma, W.C.; Lou, Z.Y.; et al. Modeling the impact of some independent parameters on the syngas characteristics during plasma gasification of municipal solid waste using artificial neural network and stepwise linear regression methods. *Renew. Sustain. Energy Rev.* **2022**, *157*, 112052. [CrossRef]
19. Malaťáková, J.; Jankovský, M.; Malaťák, J.; Velebil, J.; Tamelová, B.; Gendek, A.; Aniszewska, M. Evaluation of Small-Scale Gasification for CHP for Wood from Salvage Logging in the Czech Republic. *Forests* **2021**, *12*, 1448. [CrossRef]
20. Lapcik, V.; Lapcikova, M.; Hanslik, A.; Jez, J. Possibilities of gasification and pyrolysis technology in branch of energy recovery from waste. *Inżynieria Mineralna* **2014**, *15*, 149–154. Available online: http://potopk.com.pl/Full_text/2014_full/2014_1_19.pdf (accessed on 10 July 2022).
21. Kůdela, J.; Smejkalová, V.; Šomplák, R.; Nevrlý, V. Legislation-induced planning of waste processing infrastructure: A case study of the Czech Republic. *Renew. Sustain. Energy Rev.* **2020**, *132*, 110058. [CrossRef]
22. Ma, H.; Narayanaswamy, A.; Riley, P.; Li, L. Evolving symbolic density functionals. *Science Advances*. Available online: https://doi.org/10.1126/sciadv.abq0279 (accessed on 19 July 2022).
23. Kizielewicz, B.; Więckowski, J.; Shekhovtsov, A.; Wątróbski, J.; Depczyński, R.; Sałabun, W. Study towards the time-based MCDA ranking analysis—A supplier selection case study. *Facta Univ. Ser. Mech. Eng.* **2021**, *19*, 381–399. [CrossRef]
24. Bogach, N.; Boitsova, E.; Chernonog, S.; Lamtev, A.; Lesnichaya, M.; Lezhenin, I.; Novopashenny, A.; Svechnikov, R.; Tsikach, D.; Vasiliev, K.; et al. Speech Processing for Language Learning: A Practical Approach to Computer-Assisted Pronunciation Teaching. *Electronics* **2021**, *10*, 235. [CrossRef]
25. Kantz, H.; Schreiber, T. *Nonlinear Time Series Analysis*, 2nd ed.; Cambridge University Press: Cambridge, UK, 2003. [CrossRef]

axioms

MDPI

Article

Quasi-Density of Sets, Quasi-Statistical Convergence and the Matrix Summability Method

Renata Masarova [1], Tomas Visnyai [2] and Robert Vrabel [1,*]

1 Faculty of Materials Science and Technology in Trnava, Slovak University of Technology, Ulica Jána Bottu č. 2781/25, 917 01 Trnava, Slovakia; renata.masarova@stuba.sk
2 Faculty of Chemical and Food Technology in Bratislava, Slovak University of Technology, Radlinského 9, 812 37 Bratislava, Slovakia; tomas.visnyai@stuba.sk
* Correspondence: robert.vrabel@stuba.sk

Abstract: In this paper, we define the quasi-density of subsets of the set of natural numbers and show several of the properties of this density. The quasi-density $d_p(A)$ of the set $A \subseteq N$ is dependent on the sequence $p = (p_n)$. Different sequences (p_n), for the same set A, will yield new and distinct densities. If the sequence (p_n) does not differ from the sequence (n) in its order of magnitude, i.e., $\lim\limits_{n\to\infty} \frac{p_n}{n} = 1$, then the resulting quasi-density is very close to the asymptotic density. The results for sequences that do not satisfy this condition are more interesting. In the next part, we deal with the necessary and sufficient conditions so that the quasi-statistical convergence will be equivalent to the matrix summability method for a special class of triangular matrices with real coefficients.

Keywords: statistical convergence; quasi-statistical convergence; asymptotic density; quasi-density; the matrix summability method

Citation: Masarova, R.; Visnyai, T.; Vrabel, R. Quasi-Density of Sets, Quasi-Statistical Convergence and the Matrix Summability Method. *Axioms* **2022**, *11*, 88. https://doi.org/10.3390/axioms11030088

Academic Editors: Yurii Kharkevych and Shengda Zeng

Received: 4 January 2022
Accepted: 21 February 2022
Published: 23 February 2022

1. Introduction

The notion of asymptotic density for a subset of the set of natural numbers is known. It determines the size of the given subset compared to the set N.

Let $A \subseteq N$. We define $A(n) = |k \in A,\ k \leq n|$, i.e., as the number of elements of set A smaller than n.

Then

$$\underline{d}(A) = \liminf_{n\to\infty} \frac{A(n)}{n}$$

$$\overline{d}(A) = \limsup_{n\to\infty} \frac{A(n)}{n}$$

is the lower and upper asymptotic density of the set $A \subseteq N$, respectively.

If $\underline{d}(A) = \overline{d}(A)$, then there exists $\lim\limits_{n\to\infty} \frac{A(n)}{n} = d(A)$ that is called the asymptotic density of set A. It is evident that if for some set A there exists $d(A)$, then $0 \leq d(A) \leq 1$ (see [1]).

A different method for defining the density is based on the matrix method of limiting sequences of ones and zeros (see [2,3]).

Let

$$C = \begin{pmatrix} 1 & 0 & 0 & \cdots & 0 & 0 & \cdots \\ 1/2 & 1/2 & 0 & \cdots & 0 & 0 & \cdots \\ \vdots & \vdots & \vdots & \vdots & \vdots & \vdots & \vdots \\ 1/n & 1/n & 1/n & \cdots & 1/n & 0 & \cdots \\ \vdots & \vdots & \vdots & \vdots & \vdots & \vdots & \vdots \end{pmatrix}$$

be a regular (Cesáro) matrix (see [4]) defined as follows:

$$C = (c_{nk}),$$

where

$$\begin{array}{lll} c_{nk} = 1/n & \text{for } k \leq n & \\ c_{nk} = 0 & \text{for } k > n & n,k = 1,\ 2,\ \ldots \end{array}$$

Then, we define the asymptotic density of the set $A \subseteq N$ by the relation

$$d(A) = \lim_{n\to\infty} \sum_{k=1}^{\infty} c_{nk}\cdot\chi_A(k),$$

where $\chi_A(k)$ is the characteristic function of set $A \subseteq N$ (see [5,6]),

$$\chi_A(k) = \begin{cases} 1, & \text{if } k \in A \\ 0, & \text{if } k \notin A. \end{cases}$$

Agnew in [2] defined the sufficient condition for a matrix so that at least one sequence of ones and zeros to be limitable (summable) by the matrix.

Let $A = (a_{nk})$ be an infinite matrix with real elements. The requirements of summability are:

(a) $\sum_{k=1}^{\infty} |a_{nk}| \leq M < \infty,\ \forall n = 1,\ 2,\ \ldots$
(b) $\lim\limits_{n\to\infty} \max\limits_{1\leq k\leq n} |a_{nk}| = 0.$

Let $A = (a_{nk})$ be an infinite matrix with real elements. We say that the sequence $x = (x_k)$ is $A-$limitable to the number $s\epsilon R$ $(A - \lim x_k = s)$, if $\lim\limits_{n\to\infty} \sum_{k=1}^{\infty} a_{nk}x_k = s$.

If the implication $\lim x_k = s \implies A - \lim x_k = s$ holds true, we say that the matrix A is regular [2].

The necessary and sufficient condition for the matrix $A = (a_{nk})$ to be regular is

(a) $\exists K > 0\ \forall n = 1,2,\ldots\ \sum_{k=1}^{\infty} |a_{nk}| \leq K$
(b) $\forall k = 1,2,\ldots\ \lim\limits_{n\to\infty} a_{nk} = 0$
(c) $\lim\limits_{n\to\infty} \sum_{k=1}^{\infty} a_{nk} = 1$ (see [6]).

Example 1. *If $T = (t_{nk})$ is a regular matrix, then we can use it to define the density $d_T(A.)$ (see [5,6]). Let the matrix $T = (t_{nk})$, where*

$$\begin{array}{lll} t_{nk} = \frac{\frac{1}{k}}{s_n} & \text{for } k \leq n & \\ t_{nk} = 0 & \text{for } k > n & ,\ n,k = 1,\ 2,\ \ldots \end{array}$$

and $s_n = \sum_{j=1}^{n} \frac{1}{j}$, then

$$\delta(A) = \lim_{n\to\infty} \sum_{k=1}^{\infty} t_{nk}\cdot\chi_A(k)$$

is the logarithmic density of the set A.

Let the matrix $T = (t_{nk})$, where

$$\begin{array}{lll} t_{nk} = \frac{\phi(k)}{n} & \text{for } k \leq n,\ k \mid n & \\ t_{nk} = 0 & \text{for } k \leq n,\ k \nmid n & ,\ n,k = 1,2,\ldots \\ t_{nk} = 0 & \text{for } k > n & \end{array}$$

and ϕ is the Euler function, then

$$d_T(A) = \lim_{n\to\infty} \sum_{k=1}^{\infty} t_{nk}\cdot\chi_A(k)$$

is the Schoenberg density of the set A.

In this paper we define the quasi-density using a matrix, whose members satisfy special conditions.

In the next section, we will present the connection between statistical convergence and the matrix method of summability of the sequence of real numbers.

We say that $x = (x_n)$ converges statistically to the number $L \in R$, if

$$\forall \varepsilon > 0 : d(N_\varepsilon) = 0, \text{ where } d(N_\varepsilon) = \{k\epsilon N : |x_k - L| \geq \varepsilon\}.$$

Numerous writers extended this convergence by substituting a different density for the asymptotic density (or by a function with suitable properties, respectively) (see [7–11]).

We will endeavor to characterize the quasi-statistical convergence by using the matrix method.

In the paper [12] the authors defined the quasi-statistical convergence as:

Let $p = (p_n)$ be a sequence of positive real numbers with the properties:

(a) $\lim_{n\to\infty} p_n = +\infty$
(b) $\limsup_{n\to\infty} \frac{p_n}{n} < +\infty$.

The quasi-density of the set $A \subseteq N$ for the sequence $p = (p_n)$ is

$$d_p(A) = \lim_{n\to\infty} \frac{1}{p_n} |\{k\epsilon A,\ k \leq n\ \}|,$$

if such a limit exists.

If $p_n = n$, then $d_p(A)$ is the asymptotic density of set A.

We say that the sequence $x = (x_k)$ converges quasi-statistically (given the sequence $p = (p_n)$) to the number $L \in R$ ($\text{stq}_p - \lim x_k = L$), if $\forall \varepsilon > 0$ the set E_ε has a quasi-density equal to zero (t.j. $d_p(E_\varepsilon) = 0$), where $E_\varepsilon = \{k\epsilon N,\ |x_k - L| \geq \varepsilon\}$.

If we define $p_n = n,\ n = 1, 2, \ldots$, then the quasi-statistical convergence is identical to the statistical convergence.

If the sequence $x = (x_n)$ quasi-statistically converges to the number L, then it converges statistically as well. However, the reverse does not hold [12].

If $\liminf_{n\to\infty} \frac{p_n}{n} > 0$, then if the sequence $x = (x_n)$ statistically converges to the number L, then it converges quasi-statistically as well (see [12]).

2. The Quasi-Density

Let $p = (p_n)$ be a sequence of positive real numbers that satisfies the following properties:

(a) $\lim_{n\to\infty} p_n = +\infty$
(b) $\limsup_{n\to\infty} \frac{p_n}{n} < +\infty$.

We will call such a sequence permissible.

The lower quasi-density of the set $A \subseteq N$ for a permissible sequence $p = (p_n)$ is

$$\underline{d_p}(A) = \liminf_{n\to\infty} \frac{1}{p_n} |\{k\epsilon A,\ k \leq n\}|,$$

if such a limit exists.

The upper quasi-density of the set $A \subseteq N$ for a permissible sequence $p = (p_n)$ is

$$\overline{d_p}(A) = \limsup_{n\to\infty} \frac{1}{p_n} |\{k\epsilon A,\ k \leq n\}|,$$

if such a limit exists.

In case $\underline{d_p}(A) = \overline{d_p}(A)$, then there exists a quasi-density of set A and we denote it as $d_p(A) = \lim_{n\to\infty} \frac{1}{p_n} |\{k\epsilon A,\ k \leq n\}|$.

Example 2. *Sequences that satisfy these properties (a permissible sequences) are, for example,*

$$(p_n) = (\log n)_{n=1}^{\infty},\ (p_n) = (n{\cdot}\alpha + d)_{n=1}^{\infty},\ \alpha \in R^+,\ d \in R,\ (p_n) = (n^{\alpha})_{n=1}^{\infty},\ \alpha \in (0,1).$$

If the permissible sequence satisfies the following property, we can define the quasi-density of the set A using a matrix.

Let $p = (p_n)$ be a permissible sequence, let in addition $\liminf\limits_{n\to\infty} \frac{p_n}{n} = h,\ h \in R^+,\ h \neq 0$. We will create a matrix $B = (b_{nk})$ as follows:

$$b_{nk} = \begin{cases} 1/p_n, & k \le n \\ 0, & k > n \end{cases},\ \text{i.e.,}$$

$$B = \begin{pmatrix} 1/p_1 & 0 & 0 & \cdots & & 0 & 0 & \cdots \\ 1/p_2 & 1/p_2 & 0 & \cdots & & 0 & 0 & \cdots \\ \vdots & \vdots & \vdots & \vdots & & \vdots & \vdots & \vdots \\ 1/p_n & 1/p_n & 1/p_n & & \cdots & 1/p_n & 0 & \cdots \\ \vdots & \vdots & \vdots & \vdots & & \vdots & \vdots & \vdots \end{pmatrix}.$$

The matrix defined in this way does meet the Angew's conditions.

It is true that

$$\sum_{k=1}^{\infty} b_{nk} = 1/p_n + 1/p_n + \ldots + 1/p_n = n{\cdot}1/p_n = 1/{p_n/n} \le 1/h$$

and

$$\lim_{n\to\infty} \max_{1\le k\le n} |b_{nk}| = \lim_{n\to\infty} 1/p_n = 0,\ \text{because}\ \lim_{n\to\infty} p_n = \infty.$$

Then, we can define the quasi-density of the set $A \subseteq N$ as follows:

Let $\chi_A(k)$be the characteristic function of set A.

Then,

$$\underline{d_p}(A) = \liminf_{n\to\infty} \sum_{k=1}^{\infty} b_{nk}{\cdot}\chi_A(k)$$

and

$$\overline{d_p}(A) = \limsup_{n\to\infty} \sum_{k=1}^{\infty} b_{nk}{\cdot}\chi_A(k)$$

are the lower and upper quasi-density of set A, respectively.

In case $\underline{d_p}(A) = \overline{d_p}(A)$, then there exists a quasi-density of set A and we denote it as $d_p(A) = \underline{d_p}(A) = \overline{d_p}(A) = \lim\limits_{n\to\infty} \sum_{k=1}^{\infty} b_{nk}{\cdot}\chi_A(k)$.

We will now state several properties of a quasi-density.

Proposition 1. *Let$A \subseteq N$ be a finite set. Then, $d_p(A) = 0$ for every permissible sequence $p = (p_n)$.*

Proof of Proposition 1. If A is a finite set, then

$$d_p(A) = \lim_{n\to\infty} \frac{1}{p_n} |\{k\epsilon A,\ k \le n\}| \le \lim_{n\to\infty} \frac{|A|}{p_n} = 0.$$

The quasi-density of the set of all natural numbers N is dependent on the sequence (p_n). □

Proposition 2. *Let (p_n) be a permissible sequence.*

(a) *If $\limsup\limits_{n\to\infty} \frac{p_n}{n} = T \neq 0$, then $\overline{d_p}(N) = \frac{1}{T}$ (if $\limsup\limits_{n\to\infty} \frac{p_n}{n} = 1$, then $\overline{d_p}(N) = 1$).*

(b) *If* $\limsup\limits_{n\to\infty}\frac{p_n}{n}=0$, *then* $\overline{d_p}(N)=\infty$.

Proof of Proposition 2. (a) Suppose that $\limsup\limits_{n\to\infty}\frac{p_n}{n}=T\neq 0$. Then

$$\overline{d_p}(N)=\limsup_{n\to\infty}\sum_{k=1}^{\infty}b_{nk}\cdot\chi_k(N)=\limsup_{n\to\infty}\frac{n}{p_n}=\frac{1}{T}.$$

(b) Similarly

$$\overline{d_p}(N)=\limsup_{n\to\infty}\sum_{k=1}^{\infty}b_{nk}\cdot\chi_k(N)=\limsup_{n\to\infty}\frac{n}{p_n}=\limsup_{n\to\infty}\frac{1}{\frac{p_n}{n}}=\infty.$$

□

Note: Let exists a finite $\lim\limits_{n\to\infty}\frac{p_n}{n}$

(a) In the case of $\lim\limits_{n\to\infty}\frac{p_n}{n}=L\neq 0$, then $d_p(N)=\frac{1}{L}$.
(b) In the case of $\lim\limits_{n\to\infty}\frac{p_n}{n}=0$, then $d_p(N)=\infty$.
(c) In the case of $\lim\limits_{n\to\infty}\frac{p_n}{n}=1$, then $d_p(N)=1$.

We see that, generally, for any $A\subseteq N$: $0\leq \underline{d_p}(A)\leq\overline{d_p}(A)\leq+\infty$, i.e., quasi-density does not behave like any of the densities studied up to now.

If the sequence $p=(p_n)$ is such a permissible sequence, for which there exists a finite and non-zero limit $\lim\limits_{n\to\infty}\frac{p_n}{n}$, we can determine the relation between the asymptotic density and the quasi-density of a set.

Proposition 3. *Let $A\subseteq N$ be such a set, for which its asymptotic density is $d(A)=m$, $m\epsilon 0,1$. Let there exists a non-zero $\lim\limits_{n\to\infty}\frac{p_n}{n}=L$. Then, there also exists a quasi-density of set A and $d_p(A)=\frac{1}{L}\cdot m$ holds true.*

Proof of Proposition 3. When we use the definition of quasi-density we get the following.

$$d_p(A)=\lim_{n\to\infty}\frac{1}{p_n}|\{k\epsilon A,\ k\leq n\}|=\lim_{n\to\infty}\frac{n}{p_n}\cdot\frac{1}{n}|\{k\epsilon A,\ k\leq n\}|=\frac{1}{L}\cdot m.$$

□

Corollary 1. *Let $p=(p_n)$ be any arithmetic sequence of the type*

$$p_n=n\cdot\alpha+d,\ n=1,2,\ldots,\ \alpha\epsilon R^+,\ d\epsilon R.$$

Let $A\subseteq N$ be such a set that its asymptotic density $d(A)=m$, $m\epsilon R$.
Then, $d_p(A)=\frac{m}{\alpha}$.

Proof of Corollary 1. For an arithmetic sequence the following applies:

$$\lim_{n\to\infty}\frac{p_n}{n}=\lim_{n\to\infty}\frac{n\cdot\alpha+d}{n}=\alpha.$$

From the previous theorem we obtain $d_p(A)=\frac{1}{\alpha}\cdot m$. □

Example 3. *Let $A=\{1^2,\ 2^2,\ \ldots,n^2,\ldots\}$. It is evident that $d(A)=0$.*

We define the sequence $p = (p_n)$ by:

$$p_n = \begin{cases} 2n, & n = 2k \\ \frac{n}{2}, & n = 2k-1 \end{cases} \quad k = 1, 2, \ldots$$

This sequence satisfies the requirements of the definition. The quasi-density of set $A = \{1^2, 2^2, \ldots, n^2, \ldots\}$ given the sequence p is

$$d_p(A) = \lim_{n\to\infty} \frac{|A \cap \langle 1, n\rangle|}{p_n} = \lim_{n\to\infty} \frac{\sqrt{n}}{p_n} = 0.$$

Quasi-density of set $B = \{1, 2, \ldots, n, \ldots\} = N$ given the sequence p does not exist, because

$$\underline{d_p}(B) = \liminf_{n\to\infty} \frac{|N \cap \langle 1, n\rangle|}{p_n} = \liminf_{n\to\infty} \frac{n}{p_n} = 2,$$

$$\overline{d_p}(B) = \limsup_{n\to\infty} \frac{|N \cap \langle 1, n\rangle|}{p_n} = \limsup_{n\to\infty} \frac{n}{p_n} = \frac{1}{2}.$$

Example 4. *Let $p_n = \log n$, $n = 2, 3, \ldots$. It is evident that a sequence (p_n) defined as such is permisible, because $\lim_{n\to\infty} \log n = \infty$ and $\lim_{n\to\infty} \frac{\log n}{n} = 0$.*

Quasi-densities of the sets $A = \{1^2, 2^2, \ldots, n^2, \ldots\}$ and $B = \{1, 2, \ldots, n, \ldots\}$ given a sequence defined as preceding (p_n) exists and is identical: $d_p(A) = \infty$ a $d_p(B) = \infty$.

The asymptotic densities of these sets are not the same, because $d(A) = 0$ and $d(B) = 1$. We can say the following corollary:

Corollary 2. *If $\limsup_{n\to\infty} \frac{p_n}{n} = 0$, then there is a set $C \subseteq N$ such that it exists $d(C)$, but it does not exist $d_p(C)$.*

Proposition 4. *Let the following hold true for sequences $p = (p_n)$*

$$0 < \liminf_{n\to\infty} \frac{p_n}{n} \le \limsup_{n\to\infty} \frac{p_n}{n} = T < \infty$$

Then, for any sequence $A \subseteq N$, $0 \le \underline{d_p}(A) \le \overline{d_p}(A)$ and $\overline{d_p}(A) \le \frac{1}{T}$ is valid.

Proof of Proposition 4.

$$0 \le \underline{d_p}(A) = \liminf_{n\to\infty} \frac{|k \in A, k \le n|}{p_n} = \liminf_{n\to\infty} \frac{n}{p_n} \cdot \frac{|k \in A, k \le n|}{n} \le$$

$$\le \limsup_{n\to\infty} \frac{n}{p_n} \cdot \frac{|k \in A, k \le n|}{n} = \limsup_{n\to\infty} \frac{|k \in A, k \le n|}{p_n} = \overline{d_p}(A).$$

In addition to that $\overline{d_p}(A) = \limsup_{n\to\infty} \frac{n}{p_n} \cdot \frac{|k \in A, k \le n|}{n} \le \frac{1}{T} \cdot \overline{d}(A) \le \frac{1}{T}$. □

It is sufficient to realize that for every set $A \subseteq N$ there exists a $\underline{d}(A)$ and $\overline{d}(A)$ (an asymptotic density $d(A)$ does not have to exist).

Corollary 3. *If there exists an asymptotic density $d(A)$ of set $A \subseteq N$, the the quasi-density $d_p(A)$ of this set exists if and only if $\lim_{n\to\infty} \frac{p_n}{n} = L \neq 0$ and $d_p(A) \epsilon < 0, \frac{1}{L} >$ holds true.*

In the next example, we will assume that $\lim_{n\to\infty} \frac{p_n}{n} = L \neq 0$.

Proposition 5. *Let $A, B \subseteq N$ be a non-empty set for which their quasi-densities are $d_p(A)$ and $d_p(B)$. Let $d_p : \mathcal{P}_N \to \langle 0, \infty)$ be a function. Then*
(a) *If $A \subseteq B$ then $d_p(A) \leq d_p(B)$.*
(b) $\underline{d_p}(A \cap B) \leq d_p(A) + d_p(B), \overline{d_p}(A \cap B) \leq d_p(A) + d_p(B)$.
(c) *If $A \cap B = \varnothing$ then $d_p(A \cup B) = d_p(A) + d_p(B)$.*

Proof of Proposition 5. (a) Let $A \subseteq B$. Then, for every $n \in N$ the following holds true

$$|\{k\epsilon A,\ k \leq n\}| \leq |\{k\epsilon B,\ k \leq n\}|.$$

Then

$$\frac{1}{p_n}|\{k\epsilon A,\ k \leq n\}| \leq \frac{1}{p_n}|\{k\epsilon B,\ k \leq n\}|.$$

Transitioning to the limit, we obtain

$$\lim_{n\to\infty}\frac{1}{p_n}|\{k\epsilon A,\ k \leq n\}| \ \leq \lim_{n\to\infty}\frac{1}{p_n}|\{k\epsilon B,\ k \leq n\}|, \text{ i.e., } d_p(A) \leq d_p(B).$$

(b) It is evident that $|\{k\epsilon A \cup B,\ k \leq n\}| \leq |\{k\epsilon A,\ k \leq n\}| + |\{k\epsilon B,\ k \leq n\}|$.
From that we obtain the following:

$$\underline{d_p}(A \cup B) = \liminf_{n\to\infty}\frac{1}{p_n}|\{k\epsilon(A \cup B),\ k \leq n\}| \leq \limsup_{n\to\infty}\frac{1}{p_n}|\{k\epsilon(A \cup B),\ k \leq n\}| \leq$$

$$\leq \limsup_{n\to\infty}\frac{1}{p_n}(|\{k\epsilon A,\ k \leq n\}\ | + |\{k\epsilon B,\ k \leq n\}\ |) \leq$$

$$\leq \limsup_{n\to\infty}\frac{1}{p_n}|\{k\epsilon A,\ k \leq n\}| + \limsup_{n\to\infty}\frac{1}{p_n}|\{k\epsilon B,\ k \leq n\}| = \overline{d_p}(A) + \overline{d_p}(B) =$$

$$= d_p(A) + d_p(B).$$

(c) $A \cap B = \varnothing \Rightarrow |\{k\epsilon A \cup B, k \leq n\}| = |\{k\epsilon A,\ k \leq n\}| + |\{k\epsilon B,\ k \leq n\}|$

$$\overline{d_p}(A \cup B) \leq d_p(A) + d_p(B) = \liminf_{n\to\infty}\frac{1}{p_n}|\{k\epsilon A,\ k \leq n\}| + \liminf_{n\to\infty}\frac{1}{p_n}|\{k\epsilon B,\ k \leq n\}| \leq$$

$$\leq \liminf_{n\to\infty}\frac{1}{p_n}|\{k\epsilon(A \cup B),\ k \leq n\}| = \underline{d_p}(A \cup B).$$

□

Now, we will show that quasi-densities have the almost Darboux property.

Definition 1. *We say that the density $d(A)$ has the almost Darboux property, if for every real number $t \in <0, d(N))$ the exists such a set $A \subseteq N$, for which its density is $d(A) = t$.*

Theorem 1. *For every real number $t \in 0, \infty)$ there exists such a set $A \subseteq N$ and a permissible sequence $p = (p_n)$, that $d_p(A) = t$.*

Proof of Theorem 1. If $t = 0$, then we can choose A to be any finite set (Proposition 1).
Let $t \in (0, \infty)$, and let us choose any $m \in (0, 1]$.
For these chosen immutable numbers, we define a sequence $p = (p_n) = \left(\frac{m}{t}\cdot n\right)_{n=1}^{\infty}$.
This sequence is permissible, because

$$\lim_{n\to\infty} p_n = \lim_{n\to\infty}\frac{m}{t}\cdot n = +\infty \text{ a } \limsup_{n\to\infty}\frac{p_n}{n} = \lim_{n\to\infty}\frac{\frac{m}{t}\cdot n}{n} = \frac{m}{t} < +\infty.$$

An asymptotic density has the almost Darboux property:

For every $m \in \langle 0,1)$ exists such a set $A \subseteq N$ for which its asymptotic density is $d(A) = m$.

Let A be such a subset of natural numbers, such that its asymptotic density is m and the sequence $(p_n) = \left(\frac{m}{t}\cdot n\right)_{n=1}^{\infty}$. Then,

$$d_p(A) = \lim_{n\to\infty}\frac{1}{p_n}|\{k\epsilon A,\ k \le n\}| = \lim_{n\to\infty}\frac{t}{m\cdot n}|\{k\epsilon A,\ k \le n\}| = \frac{t}{m}\lim_{n\to\infty}\frac{|\{k\epsilon A,\ k \le n\ \}|}{n} = \frac{t}{m}\cdot m = t.$$

□

Theorem 2. *Let $A \subseteq N$ be such a subset of natural numbers, for which its asymptotic density $d(A) = 0$. Let $p = (p_n)$ be a permissible sequence that satisfies the condition $\limsup_{n\to\infty}\frac{p_n}{n} = T \neq 0$. Then, $\overline{d_p}(A) = 0$.*

Proof of Theorem 2. Let $d(A) = 0$ and $\limsup_{n\to\infty}\frac{p_n}{n} = T \neq 0$. The upper quasi-density of this set in regard to the sequence $p = (p_n)$ is

$$0 \le \overline{d_p}(A) = \limsup_{n\to\infty}\frac{|k\in A,\ k\le n|}{p_n} = \limsup_{n\to\infty}\frac{n}{p_n}\cdot\frac{|k\in A,\ k\le n|}{n} \le \limsup_{n\to\infty}\frac{n}{p_n}\cdot\limsup_{n\to\infty}\frac{|k\in A,\ k\le n|}{n} = \frac{1}{T}\cdot 0 = 0.$$

□

3. The Quasi-Statistical Convergence and the Matrix Transformation

In the final part of this paper, we will focus on the quasi-statistical convergence of sequences of real numbers.

We will show the equivalence between this convergence and a matrix transformation of the same sequence.

Let $p = (p_n)$ be a permissible sequence. By $\mathcal{T}_p$ we will denote the class of matrices with non-negative real members

$$B = (b_{nk})\quad n,k = 1,2,\ldots$$

for which the following conditions are true:

(a) $\sum_{k=1}^{n} b_{nk} = 1$

(b) If D is a subset of natural numbers for which $d_p(D) = 0$, then $\lim_{n\to\infty}\sum_{k\in D} b_{nk} = 0$.

It is evident that if a matrix belong to the class $\mathcal{T}_p$, then it is regular. However, the reverse does not hold.

Example 5. *Let $p = (p_n) = (2n+1)_{n=1}^{\infty}$. Let the set $D = \{1^2, 2^2, 3^2, \ldots\}$. According to Proposition 3, the quasi-density of this set in regard to sequence p is*

$$d_p(D) = \frac{1}{L}\cdot m = \frac{1}{2}\cdot 0 = 0,$$

where $L = \lim_{n\to\infty}\frac{p_n}{n} = \lim_{n\to\infty}\frac{2n+1}{n} = 2$ a $m = d(D) = 0$.

Let us define the matrix $C = (c_{nk})$ as follows:

$$\begin{aligned} c_{11} &= 1,\ c_{1k} = 0 \text{ for } k > 1 \\ c_{nk} &= \tfrac{1}{2k\log n} \text{ for } k \notin D,\ k \le n \\ c_{nk} &= \tfrac{1}{k\log n} \text{ for } k \in D,\ k \le n \\ c_{nk} &= 0 \text{ for } k > n. \end{aligned}$$

This matrix is the lower triangular regular, but do not belong to the class $\mathcal{T}_p$, because

$$\sum_{\substack{k < n^2 \\ k \in D}} b_{nk} = \frac{1}{\log n^2}\left(1 + \frac{1}{2} + \ldots + \frac{1}{n}\right) \geq \frac{\log n}{2 \log n} = \frac{1}{2} \nrightarrow 0 \text{ for } n \to \infty.$$

That is, if the matrix belongs to the class $\mathcal{T}_p$, so it is regular, the reverse is not true.

Lemma 1. *If the bounded sequence $x = (x_k)$ is not quasi-statistically convergent, then there exist real numbers $\lambda < \mu$ such that neither of the sets $\{n \in N,\ x_n < \lambda\}$ and $\{n \in N,\ x_n > \mu\}$ has quasi-density zero.*

Proof of Lemma 1. The proof is the same as the proof of the Lemma in [6].

We will now utter a theorem that connects quasi-statistically convergent the sequences of real number and a matrix transformation of the same sequence using matrices from the class $\mathcal{T}_p$. □

Theorem 3. *The bounded sequence $x = (x_k)$ of real numbers is quasi-statistically convergent to $L \in R$ $(\mathrm{st_q} - \lim x_k = L)$ if and only if it is summable to $L \in R$ for each matrix $B = (b_{nk}) \in \mathcal{T}_p$.*

Proof of Theorem 3. Let $\mathrm{st_q} - \lim x_k = L$, $L \in R$ and $B = (b_{nk}) \in \mathcal{T}_p$.

As B is regular there exist a $K \in R$ such that $\forall n = 1,2,\ldots\ \sum_{k=1}^{\infty} |b_{nk}| \leq K$.

It is sufficient to show that $\lim\limits_{n\to\infty} a_n = 0$ where $a_n = \sum_{k=1}^{\infty} b_{nk} \cdot (x_k - L)$.

For $\varepsilon > 0$ put $B(\varepsilon) = \{k \in N,\ |x_k - L| \geq \varepsilon\}$.

By the assumption we have $d_p(B(\varepsilon)) = 0$ we have $\lim\limits_{k \in B(\varepsilon)} \sum_{k \in B(\varepsilon)} |b_{nk}| = 0$.

As the sequence $x = (x_k)$ is bounded, there exist $M > 0$ such that $\forall k = 1,2,\ldots :$ $|x_k - L| \leq M$.

Let $\varepsilon > 0$. Then

$$|a_n| \leq \sum\nolimits_{k \in B(\frac{\varepsilon}{2K})} |b_{nk}| \cdot |x_k - L| + \sum\nolimits_{k \notin B(\frac{\varepsilon}{2K})} |b_{nk}| \cdot |x_k - L| \leq$$

$$\leq M \sum\nolimits_{k \in B(\frac{\varepsilon}{2K})} |b_{nk}| + \frac{\varepsilon}{2K} \sum\nolimits_{k \notin B(\frac{\varepsilon}{2K})} |b_{nk}| \leq M \sum\nolimits_{k \in B(\frac{\varepsilon}{2K})} |b_{nk}| + \frac{\varepsilon}{2}.$$

By the condition (b) there exists an integer n_0 such that for all $n > n_0$:

$$\sum_{k \in B(\frac{\varepsilon}{2K})} |b_{nk}| < \frac{\varepsilon}{2M}.$$

Together we obtain $\lim\limits_{n\to\infty} a_n = 0$.

Conversely, suppose that $\mathrm{st_q} - \lim x_k = L$ does not apply. We show that it exists a matrix $B^* = (b_{nk}{}^*) \in \mathcal{T}_p$ such that $B - \lim x_k = L$ does not apply too.

If $\mathrm{st_q} - \lim x_k = L' \neq L$ then from the first part of proof it follows that $B - \lim x_k = L'$ for any $B \in \mathcal{T}_p$. Thus we way assume that $x = (x_k)$ is not quasi-statistically convergent and by the above Lema there exist λ and μ $(\lambda < \mu)$ such that either the set $U = \{k \in N :\ x_k < \lambda\}$ nor $V = \{k \in N :\ x_k > \mu\}$ has quasi-density zero.

It is clear that $U \cap V = \varnothing$. Let $U_n = U \cap \{1,\ 2,\ \ldots,\ n\}$ and $V_n = V \cap \{1,\ 2,\ \ldots,\ n\}$. Therefore, there exists an $\varepsilon > 0$ and subsets $U' = \{u_k\}_{k=1}^{\infty} \subset U$ and $V' = \{v_k\}_{k=1}^{\infty} \subset V$ such for each $k \in N$: $\frac{1}{u_k} \cdot |\{n \in N : n \leq u_k\}| > \varepsilon$ and $\frac{1}{v_k} \cdot |\{n \in N : n \leq v_k\}| > \varepsilon$.

Now define the matrix $B^* = (b_{nk}{}^*)$ in the following way

$$b_{nk}{}^* = \begin{cases} 0 & k > n \\ \frac{1}{n} & k \leq n \ \wedge \ n \notin U' \cap V' \\ \frac{1}{|U_n|} & k \in U_n \ \wedge \ n \in U' \\ \frac{1}{|V_n|} & k \in V_n \ \wedge \ n \in V' \end{cases}$$

Check that $B^* = (b_{nk}{}^*) \in \mathcal{T}_p$. Obviously, B^* is a lower triangular nonnegative matrix. Condition (a) is clear from the definition of B^*, $\sum_{k=1}^{n} b_{nk}{}^* = 1$ for each n.

Condition (b) for this matrix:

Let for the set $C \subseteq N : \ d_p(C) = 0$.

Then,

$$\sum_{\substack{k \in C \\ n \notin U' \cup V'}} b_{nk}{}^* = \sum_{\substack{k \in C \\ n \notin U' \cup V'}} \frac{1}{n}\chi_k(C) = \sum_{\substack{k \in C \\ n \notin U' \cup V'}} \frac{p_n}{n} \cdot \frac{1}{p_n} \cdot \chi_k(C).$$

For $n \to \infty$ we have

$$\lim_{n \to \infty} \sum_{\substack{k \in C \\ n \notin U' \cup V'}} \frac{p_n}{n} \cdot \frac{\chi_k(C)}{p_n} \leq \limsup_{n \to \infty} \frac{p_n}{n} \cdot d_p(C) = 0$$

.

We proved that $B^* = (b_{nk}{}^*)$ belongs to $\mathcal{T}_p$.

Next, we will show $B^* - \lim x_k$ does not exist.

For $n \in U' : \ \sum_{k=1}^{\infty} b_{nk}{}^* \cdot x_k = \sum_{k \in U_n} \frac{1}{|U_n|} \cdot x_k < \lambda \cdot 1 = \lambda$ and for $n \in V' : \ \sum_{k=1}^{\infty} b_{nk}{}^* \cdot x_k = \sum_{k \in V_n} \frac{1}{|V_n|} \cdot x_k > \mu \cdot 1 = \mu$. □

4. Conclusions

In this paper we define the lower quasi-density $\underline{d_p}(A)$, the upper quasi-density $\overline{d_p}(A)$ and the quasi-density $d_p(A)$ of subsets of natural numbers, which we use to define the quasi-statistical convergence of sequences.

We proved some of the properties of quasi-densities (e.g., the quasi-density of a finite subset of natural numbers is zero and has the almost Darboux property). Given a permissible sequence, for which $\lim_{n \to \infty} \frac{p_n}{n} = L \neq 0$ there is a relation between the asymptotic and quasi-densities of set A, we have $d_p(A) = \frac{d(A)}{L}$.

The final section pertains to the quasi-statistical converge. We showed that the bounded sequence of real numbers is quasi-statistically convergent to $L \in R$ if and only if it is summable to $L \in R$ for each matrix $\mathrm{B} = (\mathrm{b_{nk}}) \in \mathcal{T}_\mathrm{p}$.

One of the most important applications of quasi-densities is connecting the quasi-statistical convergence with the summability method and by doing so generalize the term convergence.

Author Contributions: Conceptualization, R.M. and T.V.; formal analysis, R.M. and T.V.; methodology, R.M. and T.V.; validation, R.M. and T.V.; writing—original draft, R.M. and T.V.; writing—review and editing, R.M., T.V. and R.V. All authors have read and agreed to the published version of the manuscript.

Funding: This This article was written thanks to the generous support under the Operational Program Integrated Infrastructure for the project: "Strategic research in the field of SMART monitoring, treatment and preventive protection against coronavirus (SARS-CoV-2)", Project no. 313011ASS8, co-financed by the European Regional Development Fund.

Institutional Review Board Statement: Not applicable.

Informed Consent Statement: Not applicable.

Data Availability Statement: Not applicable.

Conflicts of Interest: The authors declare no conflict of interest.

References

1. Paštéka, M. *Density and Related Topics*; Academia, Veda: Bratislava, Slovakia, 2017.
2. Agnew, R.P. A simple sufficient condition that a method of summability be stronger than convergence. *Bull. Am. Math. Soc.* **1946**, *52*, 128–132. [CrossRef]
3. Petersen, G.M. *Regular Matrix Transformation*; Mc Graw-Hill: London, UK, 1966.
4. Freedman, A.R.; Sember, J.J. Densities and summability. *Pac. J. Math.* **1981**, *95*, 293–305. [CrossRef]
5. Fridy, J.A. On statistical matrix convergence. *Analysis* **1985**, *5*, 301–313. [CrossRef]
6. Fridy, J.A.; Miller, H.I. A matrix characterization of statistical convergence. *Analysis* **1991**, *11*, 59–66. [CrossRef]
7. Kostyrko, P.; Šalát, T.; Wilczynski, W. I-convergence. *Real Anal. Exch.* **2000**, *26*, 669–686. [CrossRef]
8. Mačaj, M.; Mišík, L.; Šalát, T.; Tomanová, J. On a class of densities of sets of positive integers. *Acta Math. Univ. Comen.* **2003**, *LXXII*, 213–221.
9. Baláž, V.; Šalát, T. Uniform density u and corresponding I_u-convergence. *Math. Commun.* **2006**, *11*, 125–130.
10. Gogola, M.; Mačaj, M.; Visnyai, T. On $I^c_{(q)}$-convergence. *Ann. Math. Inform.* **2011**, *38*, 27–36.
11. Baláž, V.; Visnyai, T. I-convergence of aritmetical functions. In *Number Theory and Its Applications*; Intech Open Limited: London, UK, 2020; pp. 399–421.
12. Ozguc, I.S.; Yurdakadim, T. On quasi-statistical convergence. *Commun. Fac. Sci. Univ. Ank. Ser. A1* **2012**, *61*, 11–17.